DUAL DESTINIES

DUAL DESTINIES

The Jewish Encounter with Protestant America

EGAL FELDMAN

UNIVERSITY OF ILLINOIS PRESS
Urbana and Chicago

© 1990 by the Board of Trustees of the University of Illinois
Manufactured in the United States of America
C 5 4 3 2 1

This book is printed on acid-free paper.

Library of Congress Cataloging-in-Publication Data

Feldman, Egal, 1925–
  Dual destinies : the Jewish encounter with Protestant America / Egal
Feldman.
      p.   cm.
  Includes bibliographical references.
  ISBN 0-252-01726-9 (alk. paper)
  1. Judaism—Relations—Christianity. 2. Christianity and other
religions—Judaism. 3. Protestant churches—United States—History.
4. Judaism—United States—History. 5. Jews—United States—
Politics and government. 6. Religion and state—United States—
History. 7. United States—Ethnic relations. 8. United States—
Religion. I. Title.
BM535.F44   1990
261.2'6'09—dc20   90-31392
                                                                CIP

To
My wife, Mary, and our daughters,
Tyla, Auora, and Naomi

"Destiny, not causality, governs Jewish history."
—Rabbi Joseph D. Soloveitchik

Contents

Preface

Until recently Protestant hegemony in America's religious culture has been a dominant characteristic of our national life. Even in this post-Protestant age, American society continues to bear the imprint of its Protestant past. Yet it was a divided hegemony that the legacy of the European Reformation had imposed upon Anglo-American civilization. American Protestantism was never a homogeneous system of belief. Its denominational and ideological diversity had implanted a religious outlook on American society unique in world Christendom.

How contrasting religious groups with incompatible theological perspectives interacted with each other is a question, therefore, of special significance for those seeking insight into the anatomy of American culture. *Dual Destinies* is an inquiry about such an interaction. Its theme, a history of the relationship of Protestants and Jews from the colonial beginnings of American history to the 1980s, is an examination of how two incompatible religious traditions, one dominant, the other subjugated, met and perceived one another.

My intention, I should clarify at the outset, is not to write a chronicle of American Protestantism. The works of Robert T. Handy, Martin E. Marty, Winthrop S. Hudson, and other scholars of American Christianity have no need for my duplication. Neither do I intend to add to the instructive narratives of Jacob R. Marcus, Leonard Dinnerstein, Moses Rischin, Jonathan Sarna, and others, who have unfolded historical vistas of the American Jewish experience for which we are all indebted. Rather, my focus is upon that point at which Jews and Protestants have met, the thoughts and activities that this confrontation engendered, and its meaning for the destinies of both.

Surprisingly, the mounting interest in interreligious affairs that all of us have witnessed during the past few decades has not inspired a comprehensive examination of the history of Jewish-Christian relations in the United States. Even the history of American antisemitism, a subject that this book skirts but does not fully develop, continues to wait for a historian. It is my hope, therefore, that this work will motivate additional efforts in this neglected but important area.

Although I frequently employ throughout this study the term *Protestant,* I recognize its limitations and lack of usefulness. Its usage does not intend to imply that there exists in Christianity a homogeneous division of believers, whose adherents have rebelled against Roman Catholicism and who eventually came to share a common religious allegiance. This may be true to some degree; but it should also be recognized that denominational and ideological rifts appeared on the surface of American Christianity from the very beginning of American history. Jews, too, despite their small numbers, isolation, and vulnerability, did not remain unified in their ecclesiastical and theological outlook. Protestants and Jews rarely confronted each other, therefore, with a single voice. Orthodox and liberal Protestants and various shades of each, then as now, agreed on very little; yet both played significant religious roles. Each enjoyed a period of prominence and each has molded a peculiar theological and social outlook toward Jews. How each of these wings of Protestantism perceived and behaved toward Jews and Judaism is a subject that preoccupies this study.

This book is an outgrowth of years of reading in both American Protestant and Jewish history. To the numerous scholars, most of whom I have met only through their writings, I owe my deepest gratitude. They have offered me insight and direction, without which, as is evident by my bibliographical acknowledgments, this book could not have been written.

Librarians have played a special role in my life during the past few years. I offer a special tribute to David H. Lull of the Superior Public Library (who helped to compile the index), Laura Kremer of the Interlibrary Loan Division of the University of Wisconsin–Superior, the helpful and efficient staffs of the Library of Congress, the Memorial Library of the University of Wisconsin–Madison, the Wisconsin State Historical Society, and the Wilson Library of the University of Minnesota, all of whom were available to untangle bibliographical knots or sooth my transition from card catalog to the computerized index.

Grants from the National Endowment for the Humanities and the University of Wisconsin Institute on Race and Ethnicity enabled me to travel to collections and examine material not readily available. For a release from teaching duties and a grant for research assistance, I am grateful to Prof. Nancy Minahan, Division Chair, Vice Chancellor John C. Haugland, and Chancellor Terrence J. MacTaggart, of the University of Wisconsin–Superior.

Encouragement from Prof. A. Roy Eckardt of Lehigh University came at a most appropriate time. Lengthy phone conversations with Dr. Carl Hermann Voss have enlarged my understanding of the recent record of American Protestantism. My gratitude is also extended to Prof. Alan L. Mittleman of Muhlenberg College, who introduced me to a number of contemporary sources that I had overlooked; and to Prof. Joan Bischoff of the University of Wisconsin–Superior for her perceptive comments. Needless to say, I hold none of the above individuals responsible for any errors or misrepresentations that might be found in the following pages. For skillful secretarial assistance I thank Grace Forseth and Kristina Johnson. My sincerest appreciation, however, I reserve for my wife, Mary, who has endured the many months of my preoccupation with this book with patience and good humor.

1

From the Old World to the New

1

The origins of American-Jewish Protestant relations are found in Europe's sixteenth and seventeenth centuries' religious upheavals. One could characterize the handful of Jews who arrived in British colonial America as refugees fleeing the discomforts of Catholic Europe. By the time of the Protestant Reformation most Jews had been expelled from western European societies. Almost none lived in England and France. Spain, which for centuries had provided a haven for the largest Jewish community, expelled all who resisted conversion in 1492. Portugal followed Spain's example a few years later, while the ecclesiastical courts of both Iberian states kept careful watch on those who had reluctantly elected baptism. The Iberian Inquisition was brutal in its suppression of even a hint of religious slippage. While pockets of Jews remained in the Holy Roman Empire, most of the western European Jews escaped either to the Netherlands or eastward. One-half million inhabited the Kingdom of Poland in the early seventeenth century. Yet even in the hospitable climate of Catholic Poland thousands were massacred by the tyrant Bogdan Chmielniski and his gangs of Cossacks, Ukrainian serfs, and Tartars during the anti-Jewish uprising of 1648.[1]

The brutality suffered by Europe's Jews during the sixteenth century coincided with and, in some respects, was an outgrowth of the frustrations suffered by the Roman Catholic church. In its efforts to stem the tide of heresy that swept across the continent following the intellectual awakening of the previous century, church administrators placed part of the blame upon Jewish teachings. Jews were not responsible for the beginnings of the Christian rebellion, but ecclesiastical authorities found it convenient to suspect their influence. As the Middle Ages waned Jews became a convenient target upon which the Church of Rome could vent its frustrations.[2]

Catholic anxieties were understandable, for early in the sixteenth century

Christian Europe suffered a religious upheaval from which it never recovered. The cataclysm, known as the Protestant Reformation, splintered the Roman Catholic church, the institution that had supplied a spiritual unity for western Christendom for fifteen hundred years. The causes that brought about such a religious upheaval were varied and had been festering for years. Papal political power was challenged as the authority of the secular prince increased, and the idea of the national sovereign state flowered. The Roman Catholic church's economic authority, its power to exact religious tribute upon which its pomp and religious ostentation rested, generated popular disillusionment, cynicism, and resentment. By 1517, when Martin Luther, a Catholic monk and priest, made public his Ninety-five Theses that challenged the church's traffic in indulgences, the Catholic church was about to lose its Catholicity.[3]

Other rebels, traveling different paths, arrived at a similar destination. While Christian mystics argued that each individual could experience God's presence directly, Rome insisted that divine knowledge could be achieved only through its own mediation. Christian humanists, infected by the intellectual currents of the Renaissance, gave support to the religious rebellion by elevating, on the one hand, the individual's right to think freely and on the other, his or her obligation to seek the will of God in the sacred biblical texts. In either case the religious quest had separated itself from the jurisdiction of Rome.

This was the intended result of Martin Luther's search for salvation and his conviction that its attainment hinged solely upon one's faith in God through Christ. Luther's justification by faith eliminated the need for papal intrusion and increased the burden of the individual's search for heavenly favor. Through study and reflection Luther concluded that God's mercy was freely granted to individuals, not as a result of merit, but through faith. The immediate result of this revelation was Luther's excommunication in 1521. More important, it marked the beginning of a widespread religious rebellion that would destroy forever the unity of Catholic Christendom.[4]

Following Luther's death, John Calvin emerged as the most important Protestant reformer of the sixteenth century. Like Luther, Calvin preached that the sinful individual could find salvation only through faith in Christ. Unlike Luther, however, Calvin imposed a greater stress on the innate sinful nature, the total depravity, of the individual. Faith, he taught, was a gift presented by God only to those who were elected by him for salvation. He underscored more strongly than did Luther the perpetual validity of the moral (as distinct from the ceremonial) commandments of the Old Testament.[5] The idea of predestination, the belief that one's fate was predetermined by God, also assumed a striking importance in Calvinist theology. To Protestant reformers, predestination was a liberating doctrine, for it underscored the futility of human effort to achieve salvation through good works, acts which were themselves infected with sin. Yet, at the same time, only through the performance of good works could the faithful detect a hint of their possible election. Although they could never be certain of their ultimate destiny, professing Christians were required to live a life of pious dedication, penance, and struggle against evil temptations.[6]

Calvin first imposed his religious ideas upon the city of Geneva, where he settled in 1536 and where he had gained considerable influence. According to George L. Mosse,

> A pleasure-loving, wealthy city was transformed into a theater for the glory of God. Profane theatrical plays were forbidden. . . . Inns were closed and hostels substituted. . . . [T]he only distraction allowed was the reading of the Bible. . . . Dancing, card playing, and playing bowls at Easter led to prison. One young woman who sang profane songs was banished, and another, who sang them in Psalm tunes, was scourged.[7]

Clearly, as Owen Chadwick observes, "The Reformation had set out to remedy the corruption, superstition, and immorality of the Church and of society. The pendulum had swung. The remedy was beginning to work with effectiveness beyond expectation."[8]

The Church of Geneva became the model for continental Calvinists. As Protestant refugees flocked to Geneva to avoid religious persecution in their own countries, they absorbed the theological idea of Calvin as they saw it put into practice. Geneva supplied the impulse that transported Calvin's beliefs and practices to France, Holland, England, and Scotland. Calvin's form of Protestantism became particularly influential in shaping religious thought in the American colonies.[9]

Jewish life was also affected by the Christian rebellion. The prominent Jewish historian Salo Wittmayer Baron has argued that with the spread of humanistic learning Judaism came to be viewed more tolerantly in selected Christian circles. Humanism produced an interest in Hebrew scholarship and in Hebrew manuscripts, and for the first time encouraged the employment of Jewish tutors. At least "in the long run," writes Baron, "humanism operated largely in the direction of greater religious toleration."[10] More significantly, the religious diversification produced by the Protestant Reformation added a margin of safety that the Jewish community lacked in a monolithic Catholic world. Nevertheless, one should not ignore Ernst Troeltsh's remark that in respect to Jews the Reformation was "in the first place simply a modification of Catholicism, in which the Catholic formulation of the problems was retained, while a different answer was given to them."[11]

Martin Luther's relationship with Jews exemplified the ambivalent strain spawned by the Reformation. At first, hopeful that because of his reforms Jews would recognize the truth of Christianity, Luther befriended Jews and posed as a champion of their rights as human beings. But he soon became disappointed at their stubborn insistence to remain Jews. With a viciousness inflamed by a religious zeal, Luther turned against the Jews, encouraging violent acts against them and urging their expulsion from Saxony in 1536. Luther published hateful polemical pamphlets against the Jews. One, printed in 1542, was entitled *On the Jews and their Lies*. "Know my dear Christians," declared the German reformer on this occasion, "and do not doubt that next to the devil you have no enemy more cruel, more venomous and virulent, than a true Jew." He was not averse to comparing Jews "to pigs, asses, animal excrements, and particularly the devil." Luther's anti-Jewish views were embraced by many of his close disciples.[12]

John Calvin had fewer contacts with contemporary Jews. Hardly any resided in France, where Calvin spent the early years of his life, or in Geneva, from where they had been expelled in 1491. Judaism, however, interested Calvin deeply, although he considered it a system of belief riddled with errors, a religion whose purpose was to prepare the world for Christianity. He too attacked Jews for their refusal to accept the Christian biblical prophecies. He lumped Jews and papists in the same hateful package, attributing Jewish dispersion and suffering to their repudiation of the Christian Savior.

Yet Calvin's hostility toward Jews did not attain the polemical harshness of Luther.[13] What is more, notwithstanding the discordant views of Judaism in the eyes of Protestantism's founders, the new Christian outlook altered traditional Christian perceptions of Jews. With the new stress on individual conscience, the supremacy of biblical rather than ecclesiastical authority, a more meaningful relationship between Jews and Christians could now be forged.

2

In its tolerance of Jews, Holland, a country in which Calvinist doctrine struck deep roots, had no match on the continent of Europe. From the very outset of the Spanish Inquisition it welcomed marranos, or Crypto-Jews, fleeing the Spanish authorities. Catholic Spain was not at all popular with its Dutch subjects. As a possession of Spain, Holland, which viewed Protestant reformers with favor, became a political and religious thorn in the side of the Iberian monarchy. A Spanish attempt to suppress Calvinist heresy and enforce religious obedience in 1566 met with determined resistance. Holland fought and gained its independence from Spain in 1579, a fact that Spain did not acknowledge until 1609.[14]

Not only Christian heretics, but also Jews from Spain, Germany, Poland, and Russia found a welcome haven in seventeenth-century Holland. A model of liberality, Holland became a country in which all shades of religious opinion were tolerated. For humanitarian as well as religious reasons Dutch scholars and theologians took an interest in their Jewish subjects. Jewish antiquities and

Hebrew sacred texts were studied in the nation's universities. A Calvinistic orientation toward Old Testament literature motivated a broad interest in Judaism. By the late seventeenth century Dutch leaders of the Reformed church urged their national congregations to divest themselves of anti-Jewish polemics. Ministers were advised to study the Hebrew language and to invite rabbis and other learned Jews for friendly conversations. All this led to an increased understanding and some friendship between representatives of the two faiths, although much of it, to be sure, was designed by the pious Dutch to prepare a path for the ultimate conversion of the Jewish people.[15]

The English Reformation moved more slowly than did its continental counterpart. Here it was led, not by rebellious clerics, but by the state. It was a political as well as a religious upheaval in which the king and Parliament worked together to achieve religious change. Parliament legislated religious statutes to regulate religious behavior and practice for the entire realm, while the king replaced the pope as the head of his church. By the time of its consummation the Church of England had retained much more of the flavor of Roman Catholicism than was evident in other parts of Protestant Europe. But the conservative character of the English Reformation planted the seeds for further unrest among those who hoped to duplicate at home the model they enjoyed briefly in Geneva.[16]

Significant also was the altered image of the Jewish people that developed among English Protestant radicals. The break with Rome, which occurred during the reign of King Henry VIII, eventually led to the elevation of the Bible to the pinnacle of English religious life. The voice of the pope was displaced by the Word of God. By 1600 Jewish law and history had earned a central place in British culture.[17]

The English Reformation paralleled the Jewish expulsion from the Iberian Peninsula, the flight and scattering of the marranos, and the convulsions that befell the Jews of eastern Europe. Religious minds in Elizabethan England, especially Puritan, reflected on their rediscovery of readings in the books of *Isaiah, Ezekiel,* and *Daniel.* They compared contemporary events to biblical prophetic utterances and detected heavenly signs of the approaching millennium. A few postulated that the gathering, conversion, and restoration of the Jewish people to their Promised Land was imminent. Some sought to identify the location of the Lost Ten Tribes of Israel; for English millenarians believed that an essential precondition for world redemption was the universal dispersion of the Jews.[18]

For the first time English officials gave serious thought to readmitting Jews to England, from where they had been expelled in 1290. Some Jews also began seriously contemplating their own return to the British Isles. Mennaseh ben Israel, a highly regarded rabbinical figure residing in Holland, was acquainted with English millennial aspirations. One of the few Jewish exponents of eschatology in his own right, ben Israel initiated a dialogue with English Puritan leaders for the readmission of Jews to their country.[19] His efforts, motivated primarily by a desperate need to find an additional haven for Europe's Jews, bore fruit. In 1648 a formal petition to Parliament for the repeal of the banishment decree was presented by two Baptists, Johanna Cartwright and her son Ebenezer, residents of Amsterdam. At the same time, Edward Nicholas, an Englishman, published his *Apology for the Honourable Nation of the Jews, and All the Sons of Israel,* in which he implored his countrymen to act benevolently toward the Jews.[20] Mennaseh ben Israel died in 1657, before he could witness the triumph of his efforts. Yet his eschatological writings helped to quicken English Protestant speculation about the Jewish role at the End of Days.[21]

3

The commercial advantages that would accrue to a rising empire by an influx of economically sophisticated people did not go unnoticed in England and Holland. It was in part for commercial reasons that both countries opened their overseas possessions to a Jewish presence during the sixteenth century. Amsterdam's Sephardic community, for example, worked closely with the Dutch West India Company in its efforts to gain a foothold in the Portuguese colony of Brazil. When in 1630 the Dutch captured the port city of Recife in the province of Pemambuco, the world's richest sugar-producing area, which it held until 1654, a haven for marranos and other Old World Jews was quickly established. Despite the rigid Calvinist standards transplanted from the Netherlands and imposed upon the spiritual life of the Dutch possession, largely due to the lobbying efforts of Amsterdam's influential Jewish community, Jews enjoyed a measure of religious tolerance.[22]

Other Jewish settlements took root in the British Caribbean colonies of the seventeenth century. Jamaica and Barbados harbored the largest concentrations of Jews in the West Indies. By 1715, 275 Jews resided in Barbados alone. For commercial and imperial reasons the English government encouraged Jews to settle in the Caribbean. Here Jews found, despite the absence of political equality and considerable popular hostility, economic opportunity and the freedom to live as Jews.[23]

There were good reasons why Jews moved to the mainland colonies with greater hesitancy and in smaller numbers. The early Dutch and British settlements of the seventeenth century did not provide a hospitable climate for Jews and other non-Protestants. The intolerance that the director general of New Netherlands, Petrus Stuyvesant, displayed toward the handful of Jewish refugees fleeing the fall of the Dutch Brazilian colony in 1654 did not conform to traditional Dutch behavior. Stuyvesant, who had assumed his office in New Netherlands in 1647, was determined to reverse what he envisioned was a growing religious indifference in the Dutch possession. As the son of a Dutch Reformed minister and son-in-law of another, he was admirably trained to enforce the religious discipline demanded by the West India Company, whose charter stipulated that "no other religion shall be publicly admitted in New Netherlands, except the Reformed."[24]

Even so, Stuyvesant's rigor contradicted the spirit and practice of his motherland, whose liberality for attracting the persecuted to its possessions was well documented. But the ethnic and religious diversity that appeared acceptable in Europe seemed intolerable to a governor of an isolated transatlantic settlement. Not only Jews, but German Lutherans fleeing the Thirty Years War, Huguenot refugees from Catholic France, Presbyterians from Scotland and Massachusetts, not to mention Quakers and Anabaptists, were also drawn to the Dutch colony of New Netherlands. They all added immeasurably to the governor's frustrations.[25]

The first Jews to arrive in New Netherlands came from Holland, but they were too few to be viewed as a problem. When twenty-three followed from Brazil, penniless and lacking the appropriate papers, they were immediately seen as an economic and religious threat to the stability of the Dutch community. Stuyvesant petitioned his company for the right to deport them. His letter did little to conceal his animosity toward Jews. He requested "that the deceitful race, —such hateful enemies and blasphemers of the name of Christ, —be not allowed further to infect and trouble this new colony."[26] Recognizing Stuyvesant's deeply ingrained bias, and reminded of the cordial relations they had traditionally maintained with Amsterdam's Jews, the members of the Chamber of the West India Company rejected the governor's request. "We should have liked to effectuate and fulfill your wishes," they wrote to Stuyvesant, "but after having further weighed and considered the matter, we observe that this would be somewhat unreasonable and unfair."[27]

Compelled to allow Jews to reside in New Amsterdam, Stuyvesant was never fully reconciled to their presence and took every opportunity to make their existence uncomfortable. Jews, for example, were unfairly taxed and were prohibited from erecting synagogues, buying real estate, participating in retail trade, or serving in the militia. Not surprisingly, by the time the British had conquered the Dutch possession in 1664 and renamed it New York, most of the Jewish inhabitants had temporarily disappeared.[28]

Economic prosperity and growth that came to New York as a result of British occupation was not always matched, however, with a corresponding cordiality toward the colony's Jewish inhabitants. The degree of religious liberty that Jews enjoyed depended frequently upon the whim of each of the colony's governors. While Edmund Andros, who became governor in 1674, permitted the free exercise of religion to all groups, including Jews, his successor, Thomas Dongan, accorded the right only to those who "professed faith in God by Jesus

Christ." But when James, the duke of York, an avowed Roman Catholic, became king of England in 1685, Dongan was instructed to grant equal protection to all religions. His magnanimity, no doubt, was motivated by a desire to guarantee equal rights to Roman Catholics, but in the process Jews also gained a measure of toleration.[29]

4

Protestant exclusiveness was incorporated in the statutes of many of Britain's colonial settlements. Virginia's code of laws formulated in 1610, later known as the Duke's Laws, required settlers to accept the Trinity, imposed severe punishment for religious blasphemy, and demanded that all attend two religious services daily, "upon pain of losing his or her dames allowance for the first omission, for the second to be whipped, and for the third to be condemned to the Gallies for six months." Failure to observe the Christian Sabbath was also subject to a hierarchy of penalties, culminating in death. Not surprisingly, seventeenth-century Virginia did not hold a strong attraction for Jewish settlers. Individual Jews might have passed through periodically, but no permanent Jewish settlement took root in England's first mainland colony before the American Revolution.[30]

Maryland's early history also serves as an example of frustrated aspirations in early Jewish-Protestant relations. Its Roman Catholic beginnings mark it as unique in British colonial history. George Calvert, the first Lord Baltimore, a personal friend of James I, was responsible for its founding. Upon his conversion to Catholicism in 1624, he persuaded James's successor, Charles I, to support him in a colonization scheme in the New World, where he hoped to plant a secure settlement for his Catholic coreligionists. The actual settlement, named Maryland, in honor of Queen Henrietta Maria, the wife of King Charles I, was undertaken upon his death by his son, Cecelius Calvert, the second Lord Baltimore.

The new proprietor soon realized that because few Roman Catholics were interested in migrating to Maryland, a greater effort would have to be exerted to attract Protestant settlers. Consequently, the few Catholic settlers already there soon found themselves outnumbered and threatened by a Protestant majority. To mollify Catholic fears, Maryland's legislature passed in 1649 an Act Concerning Religion, generally known as the Toleration Act.[31]

Without considering the possibility that Jews might someday desire to settle in Maryland, the colonial lawmakers couched their magnanimity in language that offered equality only to the two branches of Christendom, warning that if anyone would dare to deny the divinity of Christ or the holy Trinity he or she would be subject to the death penalty. With minor modifications the act remained incorporated in Maryland's statutes for almost a century and a half. To be sure, such legislation, not designed with Jews in mind, was difficult to enforce in a frontier society. Yet, strangely, the only recorded trial that grew out of its ominous wording involved a Jewish settler, James Lumbrozo.[32]

A physician, farmer, and merchant who came to Maryland in 1656, Lumbrozo was accused two years later of blasphemy. At his trial two witnesses testified that the accused had denied the divinity of Jesus Christ. In his own defense, Lumbrozo stated that as a Jew he had merely expressed an opinion in response to a question posed to him by the two witnesses, that as a Jew he could not have answered otherwise, and that his denial of the divinity of Jesus was not intended to denigrate Christianity. The court had no intention of offering Lumbrozo leniency. Fortunately, ten days after his arrest, while awaiting the continuation of his trial, Lumbrozo was suddenly released because of an amnesty proclamation issued in honor of Richard Cromwell's accession as Lord Protector of England. The event also accounts, in part, as did the lack of economic opportunities, for the small number of Jews who settled in the colony of Maryland before the Revolution.[33]

Consistency, however, was not a virtue in colonial Protestant-Jewish relations. A different climate prevailed in the colony of South Carolina, a grant that King Charles II gave to eight English noblemen, one of whom was John Locke. The *Fundamental Constitutions*, a series of laws agreed upon by Carolina's proprietors, established the Anglican church as an official institution of the colony. But they also offered non-Anglicans freedom of conscience. In an unprecedented fashion Carolina's colonial laws singled out "Jews and Heathens" among those who were to be allowed to settle in the new colony, with the hope that after a while the good example set by their Christian neighbors would induce them to adopt the majority faith. It also expressed the desire that "civil peace may be maintained amidst diversity of opinions," and demanded that "No person whatsoever shall disturb, molest, or persecute another for his speculative opinions in religion, or his way of worship."[34]

Although never officially adopted as the law of the colony the *Fundamental Constitutions* inspired an air of tolerance toward Jews in South Carolina that was absent in other southern settlements during these early years. Even after the colony fell under royal control in 1729, at which time the Church of England became even more firmly implanted, Jews were left relatively free to worship as they pleased. Here, too, business opportunities abounded. For good reason, by the time Americans declared their independence, the city of Charleston had emerged as the leading Jewish community in the new nation.[35]

The ambivalence toward Jews prevalent in many of the British colonies was evident even in the more progressively designed settlements of Pennsylvania and Georgia. One would have expected a more wholesome environment for Jews in Pennsylvania. William Penn, who assumed the proprietorship of the colony in 1681, was strongly influenced by the radical Protestant ideas of his generation. Greeted by a group of Indians during his first visit to the New

World, Penn remarked to an acquaintance how strongly the natives resembled Jews. Like many Englishmen he believed the American natives to be descendants from Israel's Lost Ten Tribes. Penn shared with other English missionaries messianic notions about a Jewish regathering in England and their eventual conversion.[36]

As a Quaker who had suffered imprisonment and humiliation in England for his religious beliefs, Penn, one might assume, would have extended a measure of hospitality to Jews as he did to other religious nonconformists. "I abhor two principles in religion," he wrote to a friend, "and pity them that own them; the first is obedience to authority without conviction; and the other is destroying them that differ from me for God's sake." Yet in respect to Jews, Penn's proprietorship did not measure up to its expectations. Although his *Frame of Government* required no compulsory support of an established church, offered freedom of conscience to those who acknowledged "the one Almighty and Eternal God," and assured prospective settlers that they "shall in no ways be molested or prejudiced in their religious profession," it also included a number of restrictions particularly annoying to the Jewish inhabitants of Pennsylvania. Of these, the most onerous was the stipulation that all public servants and all those who voted in their election profess their faith in Jesus Christ.[37]

All this should not be surprising. Quakers, after all, as did other radical Protestant groups, viewed Jews from the christological perspective of the seventeenth century. While professing "tender compassion" for the Jewish people, and while recognizing their long years of suffering, William Penn was convinced also that their misfortune was caused by their rejection of Jesus Christ.

Penn inherited these axioms from his mentor and friend, George Fox, the founder of the Society of Friends.[38] Fox's perception of Judaism as a short step beyond heathenism would not have escaped William Penn. Fox was sharply critical of the Jewish rejection of the Christian message and, like Penn, accused collective Judaism of the crucifixion of the Christian Savior. Fox portrayed Jews as a cruel people, always ready to instigate violence against the saintly. Yet he was eager to achieve their conversion and for that purpose composed two tracts, *A Visitation to the Jews* and *A Looking Glass for the Jews*, in which he urged the Jewish people to accept the error of their teachings and accept the Christian message. Penn must have been familiar with these writings, since they were distributed widely throughout the British possessions of North America.[39]

Like Penn, other prominent colonial Quakers harbored a mixture of suspicion and curiosity about Jews. Elias Hicks, a contemporary of Penn, displayed an unusual inquisitiveness about what he viewed as a defunct and superseded system of belief. James Logan, who arrived in Philadelphia as William Penn's secretary in 1699 and who, according to his biographer, "was the region's most influential statesman, its most distinguished scholar," also possessed a collection of Hebrew books and manuscripts. [40]

Clearly the mixed signals that Jews received from the Quaker colony made them hesitant about residing there. It was not until the middle of the eighteenth century that Philadelphia joined New York as a major center of Jewish colonial life. [41]

The colony of Georgia, founded in 1732, differed from the twelve that preceded it by the Christian humanitarianism that motivated its founders. Placed by the Crown under the charge of a group of trustees headed by James Oglethorpe, a philanthropist and a member of Parliament, the colony of Georgia was designed as a home for the underprivileged. From the very first the Georgia venture received the endorsement of the Church of England and other Protestant religious societies. The colony's charter provided "liberty of conscience" to all persons, except Roman Catholics. Its trustees' intention was to assist needy but respectable Protestants with passage and initial expenses for settlement in Georgia. While the king hoped that the experiment would bring economic and imperial advantages, the trustees expected that their charitable work would enhance the Christian spirit in the New World.

Sephardic-Jewish residents of London were included among the contributors to the Georgia experiment. The small Jewish community of London was also burdened with a need to provide for its brethren—primarily impoverished German Jews who had found refuge in England, adding to the numbers of erstwhile Spanish Jews under their care. Without waiting for official approval from the trustees, the Sephardic London congregation dispatched a group of forty-three Jews to Georgia. Their hasty action was prompted by the realization that while the framers of Georgia's charter guaranteed liberty of conscience "to all settlers except Papists," the authors of the document did not realistically anticipate a migration of Jews, to which they would have undoubtedly objected. Indeed, when the trustees learned of the Jewish arrival in Savannah in July 1733, they were deeply perturbed, since they regarded Georgia as a purely Christian philanthropy. They feared that a Jewish presence would discourage Protestants from going to the colony. [42]

The trustees urged Oglethorpe to dissuade the Jews from settling there. "You will use your best endeavors that the said Jews may be allowed no kind of settlement," they wrote Oglethorpe. "The Trustees being apprehensive they will be of prejudice to the Trade and Welfare of the Colony." [43] Oglethorpe, however, took the wording of the charter more seriously than did the trustees. Expelling the Jews, he believed, might result in legal complications. He also detected talent among the Jewish newcomers, which the colony could not afford to lose. On his own initiative, therefore, he permitted the Jews to remain in Georgia. [44]

As it turned out, Protestant-Jewish relations followed a relatively harmonious course during the early years of the colony's history. A clergyman conducting a group of refugees from Salzburg in 1734 described in his journal "the kindly reception given to his flock by the Jews of Georgia." The evangelist and founder of Methodism John Wesley, who resided in Georgia two years, recorded in his journal on April 4, 1737, that he "began learning Spanish, in order to converse with my Jewish parishioners, some of whom seem nearer the mind that was in Christ than many of those who call him Lord." Unfortunately, such cordiality was interpreted on the part of some of the Christian inhabitants as a signal to witness to Jews. As one minister put it: "Because these Jews show a great love for us . . . we will hope we will preach the Gospel of Jesus Christ to them with good success."[45] Actually, as an early historian of Georgian Jewry explains, Georgia's tolerance of its small Jewish population stemmed less from its Christian humanitarianism than from the general religious apathy and indifference that pervaded this frontier community.[46]

5

What this glimpse of the Protestant character of colonial society suggests is that the few Jewish inhabitants of colonial America found themselves surrounded by a Christian diversity which they found difficult to comprehend. If in some cases it proved threatening to their survival, as in the case of Virginia, Maryland, New York, and elsewhere, denominational heterogeneity also constituted a safety valve for Jews as it did for other Christian minorities. If they had their way, seventeenth- and eighteenth-century Protestant sects would have liked to impose a religious rigidity upon the American social landscape. And, as the American church historian Sidney E. Mead tells us, the colonial churches made every effort to do so.[47]

American Protestants were intolerant of religious ideas and practices that differed from their own. At least before the eighteenth century, Enlightenment Protestant liberalism was an alien concept to early colonial Americans. But reality preceded philosophy as colonial Protestants, with reluctance, to be sure, learned to accept each other. It was a tolerance that grew out of pragmatic necessity. It was dictated by American conditions—remoteness from Europe's ecclesiastical authority, the lack of ordained ministers, and as in the case of Georgia, religious apathy. Such conditions militated against any attempt to enforce religious orthodoxy or uniformity. What is more, as Mead reminds us, a deep and common disdain and fear of Roman Catholicism blurred the significance of denominational differences. In the colonial world to be a non-Catholic, or any kind of Protestant for that matter, was virtue enough.[48]

Religious diversity pointed inevitably in the direction of religious toleration. With so many denominations competing for preeminence, each claiming a total grasp of God's truth, Protestants had little choice but to accept with reluctance the reality of each other's existence. Although Jews were neither a dissenting sect nor a denomination, they too found in a religiously fragmented environment a measure of security generally unknown in the world that they had left behind.[49]

2

New England Puritans and the Biblical Jews

1

New England Puritans helped fashion the character of American Protestantism and in the process shaped its perspective of Jews and Judaism. An unusual group, English Puritans risked the dangers of an Atlantic crossing early in the seventeenth century to practice and preach a style of Christianity forbidden to them at home. They came to New England to escape a sinful world and to build a Christian commonwealth in accordance with their version of God's will.

They would have preferred to stay in England, but conditions dictated otherwise. When the Act of Supremacy determined that England's monarch would lead his nation's church independently of Rome, Puritans anticipated the beginning of religious progress. But the Elizabethan and Stuart leadership showed less interest in continuing Protestant reforms than in gathering religious control in their own hands. To Puritans, centralized spiritual authority was bad enough, but when imbedded in a corrupt hierarchy of sinful mortals it became intolerable. In accordance with Calvin's teachings, ecclesiastical truth was lodged only in the Word of God, in the infallible Scriptures. Such talk angered and shocked England's monarchs, for it bored threateningly into the very core of the British state.[1]

This is not to suggest that Puritans were in complete accord with one another on all matters of religion. Some, more moderate in their demands, asserted that a presbyterian polity would be an adequate substitute for England's episcopal hierarchy. Presbyterianism offered England's pious a more democratic model than did the official Church of England, but one which allowed a degree of centralization of ecclesiastical government. Presbyterians were willing to accept a national church, open to all believers, and governed by a series of ministerial conferences, each possessing a degree of local jurisdiction. It was a structural concept in accord with the teachings of John Calvin.[2] The more radical Puritans demanded a more restrictive church membership, open only to the truly faithful, one which separated the holy from the rest of the population. They rejected the Presbyterian recommendation for a national church open to all believers without distinction. The more radical Protestants, called congregationalists or Separatists, aspired toward a separation of church and state. Although Calvinists, they were not attracted by the model of Geneva, aspiring rather toward congregational independence.

Both groups settled in New England during the seventeenth century, the Separatists in New Plymouth, the Presbyterian Puritans in Massachusetts Bay. Within a few years New Plymouth merged with Massachusetts and disappeared as a separate colony. By that time the line that divided their different religious postures became so blurred that it was indistinguishable.[3] Together, convinced of the righteousness of their holy mission, they became even more rigorous and intent upon uniformity in all matters of faith than was the archbishop of Canterbury, William Laud, from whom they fled to the New World.

2

The centrality of the Bible in the life of early Puritanism bequeathed upon the historical Jew a special place in the mind of Protestant America. New England Puritans patterned their laws upon the Mosaic codes of the Old Testament, and they adopted the experiences of the early Hebrews as a model upon which to shape their own lives. Like the Jews of old they conceived themselves to be chosen by God to perform a special mission in the wilderness of the New World.[4] This does not mean that the Puritans preferred the Old Testament to the New; they were Christians first and foremost. But their rediscovery of the Jewish biblical past strengthened a link with it that had grown tenuous before Calvin.[5]

One manifestation of this link was the interest and affection for the Hebrew language that the early settlers of New England shared with the Jews. Puritans gave their children Hebrew names and encouraged them to master the holy tongue. They included the Hebrew language as an integral part of their college curricula.[6] They recognized, as did William Bradford, New Plymouth's second governor, that it was the "holy tongue, in which the law and oracles of God were writ, and in which God and angels spoke to the holy patriarchs of old time." Bradford was driven to study Hebrew in order to catch a glimpse of Israel's past, a past he wished to re-create in New Plymouth.[7]

Separatists had inherited their dedication to Hebrew studies from Holland, where they had taken refuge from the Church of England early in the seventeenth century. There they were inspired by such masters as Henry Answorth and John Robinson, leading Hebraists at the University of Leyden. Answorth was an English Separatist whose Old Testament commentaries were widely read by Anglicans and Puritans and were included in the library of William Bradford.[8]

In Massachusetts Bay the Puritan founders of Harvard College insisted that all graduates master the Hebrew language, primarily for religious reasons, but not exclusively so. Even in England the better-established Puritans considered the language of Hebrew an important element of classical learning, one which every cultivated citizen should know. A number of Harvard's early presidents were noted for their Hebraic scholarship. Henry Dunster, Harvard's first president, insisted that Hebrew be included in Harvard's curriculum. Dunster corresponded with European Hebraists of grammatical matters and was considered a leading authority of the language in early Massachusetts. Harvard's second president, Charles Chauncy, continued the stress by reciting each day in the college hall a chapter from the Old Testament in Hebrew. Increase Mather, another of Harvard's early leaders, dedicated an oration in Hebrew to the graduates during the commencement exercises of 1685.[9]

A number of New England's ministers, some of whom had graduated from Harvard or Yale, were recognized by their contemporaries as learned in Hebrew letters. Michael Wigglesworth, a Congregationalist pastor and poet, was convinced that reading Hebrew in the original was a more fulfilling exercise than indulging in other humanistic studies. Every Hebrew word, every vowel, excited him. Richard Mather, Increase's father, a Congregationalist minister who had fled England because of his religious nonconformity, made important contributions to New England's store of Hebrew knowledge. He was the chief editor of the *Bay Psalm Book,* issued in 1640 by the Cambridge Press of Massachusetts and considered the first important English book printed in America. It was a task that required a command of the intricacies of Hebrew grammar. John Cotton, who was also forced to flee England, was reputed to be able to converse in Hebrew.[10] No doubt, perhaps with the exception of the Mathers, Puritan mastery of Hebrew literature did not measure up to the exacting standards of Jewish scholarship. After all, a multitude of original rabbinic works were unavailable in the libraries of colonial America. What is surprising, given the remoteness of the colonies from Old World expertise, the lack of Hebrew teachers, the unavailability of original Hebrew texts, and a very occasional visit of a traveling rabbi, is that Hebrew erudition existed at all in colonial New England.[11]

The study of Hebrew did not necessarily generate affection for the living Jews. It was a Christian endeavor and those who taught it in the colonial colleges were steeped in Calvinist doctrine. In this connection the case of Judah Monis, a Jewish convert to Christianity and Harvard's first instructor in Hebrew, is illuminating. Born in 1683, possibly to an Italian marrano family, Monis received a Jewish education in Leghorn and Amsterdam, before serving as a Hebrew teacher in Jamaica and New York. After moving to Boston he became acquainted with several ministers, including Increase Mather, who viewed him as an Hebraic scholar. One minister described Monis at this time as "truly read and learned in the Jewish Cabala and Rabbinics, a Master and Critic in the Hebrew. He reads, speaks, writes and interprets it with great readiness and accuracy."[12]

In 1720, with the support of Increase Mather, Harvard College awarded Monis an M.A., at which time Monis prepared a manuscript entitled "Facilitating the Instruction of Youth in the Hebrew Language." These events were coupled with, indeed dependent upon, Monis's conversion to Christianity. Monis's baptism ceremony was performed publicly, under the direction of Increase Mather. As part of the ceremony Monis preached a sermon entitled "Truth," in which he elaborated upon the modern rabbinic view of the Messiah, and expounded his newly adopted conviction that the Messiah had already appeared. The discourse, which included a preface by Increase Mather, was widely circulated and discussed in Boston. Following Monis's baptism the Harvard corporation agreed to appoint the new convert as an instructor of the Hebrew language.[13]

John Cotton thought highly of Monis, remarking at this time that he had contributed new religious insights to the Christian community of Boston. "Rarely does a Jew of any Erudition come over to Christianity," declared Cotton. "He brings with him some Treasures of illustration upon the Sacred Scriptures," and he "is a great Master of the Hebrew Language."[14] Despite Monis's conversion and his dedication to his adopted faith, he was always looked upon by his colleagues and New England neighbors as a converted Jew. Buried in Westboro in 1764, his epitaph read:

> Here lie buried the remains of
> Rabbi Judah Monis, M.A.
> Late Hebrew instructor,
> at Harvard College in Cambridge,
> In which office he continued forty years
> He was by birth and religion a Jew
> But embraced the Christian faith,
> And was publicly baptized.[15]

3

Hebrew was not the only ingredient that Puritans shared with the biblical Jews; a sense of destiny and providential mission also pervaded Puritan thinking as it did the life of early Israel. It was an infectious conviction, which was eventually inherited by colonial Americans in general. During the early years of Puritanism it was most clearly articulated by the Puritans of New England, whose lives were shaped and directed by a sense of religious purpose. They envisioned America as a place where the Protestant Reformation would be consummated; that, as Conrad Cherry writes, "like Israel of old, they had been singled out by God to be an example for the nations."[16]

Puritan religious expectations engendered not only a sense of hope and optimism, but also a sense of frustration, sin, and failure. To be singled out as God's chosen people imposed upon those who were called a burden of responsibility. Mid-seventeenth-century Puritan sermons are replete with lamentations over New England's failure to measure up to its divine calling. In these jeremiads the Puritans imagined themselves to be the ancient Israelites, who had neglected their covenant with God and the warnings of his Prophets.[17]

Like the ancient Israelites the Puritans viewed themselves as a covenant people, reenacting Israel's early history. It was a comforting thought that provided the early American settlers not only with a religious assurance but also with political unity and a common vision of things to come.[18] They were proud of their common conviction and were eager for all to recognize their unique relationship with God. Peter Bulkley, a founder of the town of Concord, put it this way:

> We are a city set upon a hill, in the open view of all the earth; the eyes of the world are upon us because we profess ourselves to be a people in covenant with God. . . . Let us study to walk, that this may be our excellency and dignity among the nations of the world, among whom we live: That they may be constrained to say of us, "Only this people is wise, an holy and blessed people," that all that see us and know that the name of the Lord is called upon us, and that we are the seed which the Lord hath blessed.[19]

On what basis did the New England Puritans presume to have inherited the covenant of Israel? Perry Miller points to *Genesis* 17 as legitimizing the Puritan claim. In this passage of the opening book of the Scriptures, God states to the Israelites that a covenant had been established "between me and thee and thy seed after thee in their generations for an everlasting covenant, to be a God unto thee, and to thy seed after thee." Puritans considered themselves the "seed" that had inherited the awesome responsibility assumed by the first covenant people.[20]

The evolutionary process was hardly a flattering one for Jews. As the covenant passed to New England Puritanism it was lost to the Jews, who because of their sinful transgressions were deprived of their special relationship with God. Such a theology of supersessionism was not uncommon in Puritan writings. The refrain that the Jewish covenant had been displaced by the Christian had been heard before. In this instance the Puritan attitude toward Jews did not differ markedly from that found throughout Christendom.[21]

As the New England Puritans read their Bibles, they also visualized the leading characters not always as historical figures, but as "types" who foreshadowed Christ and the various events surrounding his ministry. This tendency, called typology, which the Puritans found convenient to employ in their interpretation of Scripture, was first exercised by Saint Paul and the church fathers in their attempt to bridge the Jewish and Christian testaments. Moses at Mount Sinai was said to have foreshadowed Christ on the Mount, or the Jewish enslavement in Egypt typified Christ's agony. It was a convenient technique that reconciled for the New Israel the Jewish and Christian Bibles.[22]

It also draped mid-seventeenth-century events with spiritual meaning. As John Berens remarks, "the Flood, the Exodus, and the Exile were interpreted as types of the present tribulations and future triumphs of Christ's chosen remnant," the Puritans. The Separatist William Bradford compared the flight of his own flock from England's oppressions to the New World with the Exodus of the Israelites from Egypt to the Promised Land; he believed that God's hand guided the affairs of New Plymouth as it had the lives of the Hebrew people of Canaan. For Bradford the Plymouth plantation was a replication, the antitype of that ancient biblical land.[23]

Shadowy as it was, typology engendered among some Puritan thinkers a deeper awareness of the Jewish past. In this sense Jews were accorded a unique place in the Puritan imagination. Since early Puritan lives, tribulations, and aspirations were intertwined with the events of the ancient Israelites, a peculiar Judaic spirit hovered about New England and other Christian centers of colonial America. Like other elements in Puritan thought, however, typology did not generate interest in more recent Jewish history. Nor did it contribute to the improvement of understanding between Jews and Christians. On the contrary, by relegating the Jewish people to a mythical past, one which served no other purpose but to direct attention to a Christian future, the typological mind robbed the living Jews of their ancient roots, their unique history, and their meaningful existence. To some New England Puritans the Jewish past did not exist except insofar as it provided Christendom with a mirror for its own time.

With respect to Jews, however, Puritan thinking was never consistent. Whereas some saw Jews as biblical types, others believed that the living Jews were destined to perform an important role at the End of Days. Many Puritans adhered to what would later be described as a postmillennial outlook, that is, an idyllic vision of a future age prophesied in biblical literature. Important world events, they believed, would precede the culmination of that momentous time. These would include the downfall of the papacy, the destruction of the Roman church, the demise of the Turkish empire, and the ultimate triumph of Protestant Christianity.[24]

Millennial thinking, as Ruth H. Bloch observes, "is one of the oldest and most enduring patterns of thought in Western civilization." From its Judaic roots the idea surfaced "that human history is divinely ordained and will inevitably lead to a period of heavenly perfection on earth." Significantly,

Puritan postmillennialists took a particular interest in the conversion and restoration of the Jews, a group whose fate, they believed, was inextricably tied to their own.[25] Such thoughts were transported to New England during the seventeenth century and, given the religious fluidity of colonial American Protestantism, modified. Like their English counterparts, New England Calvinists included in their eschatological scenario the belief that as the end of the present age approached large numbers of Jews would be converted to Christianity and returned to their ancestral homeland. These events, they believed, would be accomplished by a great spiritual revival that would begin in New England.[26]

Increase Mather and his son Cotton waited impatiently for the conversion of the Jews, an event which they interpreted as the prelude to the Second Advent. Increase's tract, "The Mystery of Israel's Salvation," published in 1667, reveals his preoccupation with this theme. He assures his readers that "New Jerusalem shall come down from God out of Heaven," and that the Jews, despite "the gross and carnal concepts about the temporal glory of Messiah and his Kingdom" contained in their Talmud and their heresies, will shortly see the light. "The salvation of all Israel," Increase Mather predicted, "is now near to be revealed." He urged his fellow Puritans to pray for Israel's conversion. "Prayer may be a means to hasten the coming of this glorious day of Israel's salvation," he urged his readers. "Pour forth earnest and continual prayer, and it will hasten the birth of Sion."[27]

The close attentiveness that Puritans paid to Jewish salvation encouraged them to study Hebrew. New England scholars, Rabbi de Sola Pool informs us, "were daily expectant of hearing of the discovery of some Indians whose vernacular should contain elements recognizable as Hebrew." Since American Indians were believed to be Jews, the anticipation spurred the Puritan divine, John Eliot, to translate the Bible into a native American language. Samuel Sewall, born in 1675, who became a wealthy landowner and served as a chief justice of the Massachusetts court, was also convinced that the Indians were members of the Lost Ten Tribes. Given to eschatological speculation and "nursing a hope that the millennium would begin in New England," Sewall focused his attention on these indigenous Americans, insisting that their conversion would mark a major step toward the coming of the millennium. Like other Puritans Sewall was a careful student of the Hebrew language and Jewish religious customs. He was particularly curious about Jewish converts to Christianity, always seeking information about them. A mere hint of a Jewish baptism would earn an entry in his diary.[28] Clearly, Puritan eschatological preoccupations placed Jews at the center of their theology, but at what cost to the living Jews? To the New England orthodox mind Jews were mere instruments to be employed for the salvation of the Christian soul, not autonomous human beings.

One of the most representative voices of American Puritanism and its perspective of the Jew was that of Cotton Mather. His biographer, Kenneth Silverman, writes that "Many of the beliefs attached to his name and scorned were after all shared by thousands of other settlers whose names few remember." Born in 1663 to a devout family of distinguished ministers who led the migration from England to the New World, Cotton Mather revealed an early tendency toward religious mystical speculation. By the time he was forty he had replaced his father as the most prominent and learned of the New England clerics.[29]

Mather's study of ancient Palestine inspired him to reproduce the Jewish system of education at Harvard. "The reader knows," he wrote admiringly, "that in every town among the Jews, there was a school, whereat children were taught the reading of the law, and if there were any town destitute of a school, the men of the place did stand excommunication until one were erected."[30] Mather was the first American to compose a post-biblical Jewish history, a task which he began in 1693 and labored at for the next thirteen years. "Tho my extraordinary Application to that Work . . . was doubtless a Disadvantage to my Health," he recorded in 1706, "Yet the Lord favoured me with a singular Success in it . . . And on this Day I finished my BIBLICA AMERICAN." Mather's inability to find a publisher for the work remained one of his chief regrets.[31]

He was enamored with the Hebrew language; he studied it diligently and collected and translated a number of religious works. At a time when interest in Hebrew at Harvard was declining, he urged his students to spend as much time in the study of Hebrew "as is given up to smoking tobacco."[32] Mather's Hebraic studies stemmed from his keen interest in eschatology. He was gripped throughout his adult life by "millennial expectations." These quickened his interest in the history of ancient Israel and its biblical geography. Mather searched the Jewish scriptures for signs and prophecies of the coming of Christ. Contemporary political and military upheavals abroad aroused his hopes for a sign of the Second Coming. As he indicated in his diary in October 1696:

> I have this Day . . . wrestled with the Lord, until I have obtained it, that a mighty Convulsion shall be given to the *French* empire; and that *England, Scotland,* and *Ireland,* shall be speedily illuminated, with glorious Anticipations of the *Kingdom of God.* Moreover, a Revolution upon the *Turkish* Which is now attempted by troubles in *Asia* . . . that so we may have another good symptom of the Approach of the Time, when the *Kingdom of this world shall become the Kingdom of our Lord of His Christ.*[33]

To hasten the coming of the Kingdom, Mather remained attentive to any signs of Jewish conversion. It was a concern with which he was preoccupied until a few years before his death. It accounts for his involvement with the establishment of missions among the Indians. Since there were hardly any

European Jews in his vicinity, he prayed for an opportunity to convert even a single Hebrew. His tract, "The Faith of the Fathers," was prefaced with a special plea to Jews to "return to the faith of the Old Testament," a work which he considered a Christian document. He dedicated the work to the "Jewish Nation," exhorting its people to see the error of their ways. "O ye Rebellious and rejected People of our Great Messiah. . . . Return O backsliding Israel!"[34]

The mere mention of a successful conversion in any part of the world threw Mather into a state of exaltation. Early in 1700 he recorded in his diary the most unlikely story about a handful of Jewish children "from eight to twelve years of age," who, against the wishes of their mortified parents, fled to a nearby Protestant church demanding to "be initiated into Christianity. They embraced it with such rapture that when they saw the name of Jesus, in a book, they kissed it a hundred times, and shed floods of tears upon it. No methods used by their parents to reduce them are effectual; but they say to their parents 'we shall not return to you; it is time for you to come over to us!'"[35] Jews served as an indispensable link in the chain that would lead Mather and other Puritans toward the Kingdom of Heaven. Although Mather's interest in Jewish matters was deep, he was unable to see Judaism as a living faith among the nations of his own time, seeing it only as an instrument for his own spiritual fulfillment.

4

It is ironic that Roger Williams, the most radical of the Puritan Separatists, would be remembered for his sympathetic relationship with seventeenth-century Jewry. Growing up near London during the reign of Queen Mary, Williams was moved by the martyrdom of Puritan dissenters within whose ranks he soon felt most at home. He sailed for Boston in 1631, two years after graduating from Cambridge where he had studied law and theology. Upon his arrival in Massachusetts he accepted an invitation to become the minister of the First Church.

His restless spirit, however, was unable to find religious resolution in the Bay Colony. The Puritan leadership that he had first admired soon became a butt for his criticism. He challenged the colony's land policies and the legitimacy of its charter. The English monarch, he insisted, possessed no valid claim to land that belonged to the Indian inhabitants and consequently had no right to permit the establishment of a colony upon territory that belonged to others. Neither did the Puritan government, he said, possess the right to dictate religious standards. In short, Williams challenged the very basis upon which the colony was founded.[36]

Williams's dissatisfaction with the theocratic character of Massachusetts earned him the greatest resentment of the clerical authorities. Williams's arguments that the nonreligious nature of government disqualified it from the right to dictate religious beliefs, and that all citizens possessed equal rights and privileges irrespective of their theological views, threatened the authority of the Puritan leadership. Williams was a radical Protestant and his concern, however, was less for the protection of individual freedom in matters of religion than it was for the defense of the church against civil contamination. "The civil magistrate [be] armed by God with a civil sword," he wrote, "to execute vengeance against robbers, murderers, tyrants, etc.," but not in matters "where it concerns Christ."[37]

Accused of subversion, Williams was banished from Massachusetts in 1635. His new home, which he called Providence, soon became the nucleus of the colony of Rhode Island and a center for religious diversity and unorthodoxy. The new colony's charter, which declared "that no person within the said colony shall hereafter be any wise molested or called in question for any difference in opinion in matters of religion," was a clear invitation for Jews and dissenting Protestants to make Rhode Island their home. During Williams's tenure as governor from 1654 to 1657, Quakers and Jews were invited to settle in Rhode Island. Not precise about his own Christian direction, Williams enjoyed the religious multiplicity about him. He needed to think freely about religious matters and wished that others might do the same.[38]

Williams's interest in the Jewish people and his sharp censure of their persecutors set him apart from other New England religious thinkers of his time. His polemical exchanges with John Cotton include frequent reminders that Jews, whom Williams frequently grouped with other nonbelievers (pagans, Turks, and anti-Christians), be granted freedom of conscience. "God requireth not any uniformity of Religion," he reminded his correspondent. He instructed the Puritan leadership that "we hold it not lawful for a Christian Magistrate . . . to compel by civil sword, whether Pharisee, or pagan, or Jew, to profess his religion."[39]

His deep commitment to Christian revelation did not blind him to the intolerable treatment that Europe's Jews had sustained at the hands of his fellow Christians. "I judge here only reasonable to say, that no opinion in the world is comparatively so bloody," he wrote in his journal. He reminded his fellow Englishmen of the burden of responsibility that they must sustain for the plight of the Jews. "What horrible oppressions and horrible slaughters have the Jews suffered from the Kings and peoples of this Nation, in the Reigns of Henry 2. K. John, Richard 1. and Edward 1. Concerning which not only we, but the Jews themselves keep Chronicles."[40]

Roger Williams's reputation of friendliness toward the Jews of his day did not conceal a baggage of christological notions about Jews that he transported from England. There were occasions when he struck out at Jews for their stubborn adherence to the laws of Moses. As he once put it: "bondage to Moses would separate from Christ." Like other Puritans he succumbed occasionally to typological reflection, admitting that Israel of the Bible was merely a "type of all the children of God in all ages under the profession of the Gospel." He concluded that the real Jews have disappeared from history; that "Christians are now figuratively in this respect called Jews."[41] One historian recently suggested that Williams's reading of scripture convinced him that "Jews are no longer the 'chosen people,' and their book, the Old Testament, is now a book of interest only as it types the anti-types fulfilled in Christ's life, death and resurrection."[42] In short, there were significant moments when Williams's thought about the Jewish people did not contain the elements for a healthy relationship between the two systems of belief.

Following Roger Williams's death in 1683, Rhode Island became less receptive of diversity. Religious qualifications for voting and holding public office were imposed upon Jews as they were in the other British colonies. When in 1761 two of Newport's leading Jewish citizens, Aaron Lopez and Isaac Elizer, applied for naturalization, a request in accord with the Act of Naturalization passed by Parliament in 1740, which offered naturalization to all colonial settlers except Roman Catholics, their petition was denied. Received by the General Assembly of Rhode Island, Lopez was informed that "inasmuch as the said Aaron Lopez declared himself by religion a Jew this Assembly doth not admit himself nor any other of that religion to the full freedom of this colony." Hearing about this rebuff, Ezra Stiles, a Congregationalist minister and friend of Lopez, mused in his diary that "Providence seems to make every Thing to work for Mortification to the Jews."[43] The Lopez naturalization case reminds us, as Abram Goodman notes, of the inferior status of the Jews of Rhode Island, a colony reputed to be the most liberal in colonial America. Here Jews might enjoy equal economic opportunity and freedom of worship without the necessity of supporting a state church with their taxes; but they were, nevertheless, second-class citizens who could not vote or hold public office and whose rights could at any time be curtailed by the colonial court or assembly.[44]

3

Revivalism and Rationalism

1

About a century after the founding of the first English colonies in America, from about 1720 to 1750, a series of disconnected religious upheavals, outbursts of religious enthusiasm, enveloped a number of Protestant communities. Later generations would call these Christian experiences the Great Awakening; they comprised the first example of Christian revivalism on a massive scale in American life. The movement was designed in part to rekindle the cooling religious embers of the early settlers, especially in New England, a task which the established churches seemed unable to do.

The decline of religious enthusiasm by the early eighteenth century was hardly surprising. In the process of transplantation to America and during the passage of time, Protestantism had lost a measure of its vitality. Religious attentiveness was further weakened because of its remoteness from the centers of ecclesiastical authorities of the Old World, and the theological pluralism of the New. By 1720 it was apparent that church membership had declined to an unprecedented low.[1]

The Great Awakening grew chiefly out of the work of a selected group of talented Calvinist preachers of various denominations—Theodore J. Frelinghuysen, Dutch Reformed; Gilbert Tennent, Presbyterian; George Whitfield, Anglican; Jonathan Edwards, Congregationalist; and others—who by 1740 had succeeded in extending their crusade along the entire seaboard of the British colonies.[2] In the process they introduced a new style of preaching to America, unwittingly unified Protestantism's diverse elements under a broad umbrella of shared religious renewal, and at the same time, strengthened its denominational structure.[3]

A more immediate result of the Great Awakening, according to some American historians, was the democratization of the Christian experience. The Awakening universalized the opportunity for Christians to earn salvation; it made the Christian message more intelligible and rendered its theological underpinnings less abstract, more personally meaningful. In the process the movement also spread the mantle of the New Israel from New England south-ward. All Americans, imbued with millenarian ideas, could now claim to be participants in the Covenant of Israel. Likewise, the notion of separation of church and state and the individual's right to dissent from popular religious norms, ingredients of particular significance to religious minorities, became important by-products of this religious movement.[4]

It would be wrong, however, to be carried away with the purported demo-cratic results of the Great Awakening. Revivalists, conservative in their theo-logical views, were not champions of democracy. Their emphasis on toleration was a pragmatic gesture that stemmed from a desire to free themselves from the restraints of established churches. Dissenters, as Professor Mead notes, "were thrown willy-nilly—but somewhat incidentally—on the side of greater tolera-tion and freedom." Liberty to Awakeners meant the liberation from corrupt religious views, the freedom to preach the scriptural message, not freedom from Christianity.[5]

From a Jewish standpoint the immediate consequences of the Great Awak-ening were far from positive. A multitude of new converts brought into the Protestant fold might only spawn suspicion of those who remained uncon-verted. Salvation and magnanimity were not necessarily synonymous in this age of religious zealotry. As one student of that era notes: "Where religion is widespread, tolerance is no problem; but when religion becomes intensely vital, bigotry becomes more pervasive."[6] Moreover, the religious spirit of revi-valism, a Protestant phenomenon, was alien, if not incomprehensible, to Jewish sensibilities. As Prof. Jacob Marcus notes: "Such religious frenzy of revivalism as revolutionized Christian religious thinking and feeling on this continent during the eighteenth century had no analogues in the Jewish community."[7]

Yet Jews could hardly be impervious to the impassioned rhetoric that sur-rounded them, especially when it was riddled with Christian misrepresenta-tions of their sacred doctrines. Gilbert Tennent, who became pastor of the Presbyterian church in New Brunswick, New Jersey, in 1726, and one of the leading voices of the great revival that swept the middle colonies, was not averse to depicting the ancient Jews as the villains of biblical history. In an emotional sermon delivered on March 8, 1740, in Nottingham, Pennsylvania, Tennent repeatedly denounced the Pharisees of Jesus' day. On that occasion Tennent compared his own conflict with uncooperative Presbyterian leaders to "the old Pharisees," who, as he put it,

> were very proud and conceited; they loved the upper-most Seats in the Syna-gogue, and to be called Rabbi, Rabbi . . . they looked upon others that differed from them, and the common People with an Air of Disdain; and especially any who had a Respect for Jesus and his Doctrine. . . . The old Pharisee-Shepherds were as crafty as Foxes. . . . But while they exerted the craft of Foxes, they did

not forget to breathe the Cruelty of Wolves, in a malicious Aspersing the Person of Christ.[8]

Examples of christological anti-Judaism during the Great Awakening could be multiplied. In Pennsylvania, Henry Melchior Muhlenberg, one of the founders of the American Lutheran church, was disturbed by the few Jews he noticed around him. He called them "practicing atheists" and, as an evangelist, believed it was his duty to preach the gospel to them. From Europe he imported a supply of Yiddish-language missionary tracts that he distributed to the Jews of Pennsylvania, much to their annoyance. One Jewish recipient returned the tracts to Pastor Muhlenberg, responding with unusual boldness that, "The most representative men in the city, with whom I associate, admit that their Messiah . . . was an impostor. Give your writings to these gentlemen. I have no intention or time to read them." Muhlenberg informed his own congregation that unless the Jews accepted Jesus, they would be damned for eternity.[9]

2

Yet the presence of Jews was not necessarily required for serious thinking about them to take place in colonial America. This was seen, for example, in the case of Jonathan Edwards, the most important American theologian of the Great Awakening. Jonathan Edwards's sermons and writings, many of which were not published until years after his death, mark him as the most creative American Calvinist thinker of the eighteenth century. He was, in a sense, the religious theoretician of the Great Awakening.

Born in East Windsor, Connecticut, in 1703, Edwards graduated from Yale, where he mastered both the old theology and the new philosophy of the eighteenth century; but from the very first, Edwards felt more at peace with orthodox Calvinism. Assuming charge of Northampton, Massachusetts' Congregationalist pulpit in 1729, he soon acquired a widespread reputation for his thoughtful and effective preaching. Fascinated by millennial prophecy, Edwards was a writer who reflected a lifetime of eschatological speculation. Edwards anticipated that the consummation of history would occur in New England. His militant preaching grew out of his restless desire to hasten mankind's redemption as a prelude to the Second Coming.[10]

From a theological perspective, as C. C. Goen observes, Edwards may be classed as a postmillennialist, that is, he expected the imminent return of the Savior "within ordinary history." His was an optimistic theology, for he expected mankind's salvation to materialize in this world and in his own time; and what better way to achieve this glory, he believed, than to preach the gospel. As Edwards saw it, the chief obstacle that stood in the way of this imminent golden age was Christianity's greatest foe, the Roman Catholic church. The millennium would not come, Edwards was convinced, as long the pope ruled in Rome.[11]

For Edwards the unconverted state of the Jews constituted a second important barrier to the arrival of the Kingdom. He could not rid his mind of the Jews and their biblical past. Like his Puritan forebears he read the Old Testament with the mind and eye of a typologist. "The return of the ark of God to dwell in Zion, in the midst of the land of Israel, after it had been long absent . . . the exceeding rejoicing of Israel on that occasion represented the joy of the church of Christ on his returning to it."[12] It was a typical passage found in his writings. At the same time and in a somewhat contradictory vein, Edwards did not overlook the Jewish rejection of Christ. "They crucified the Lord of Glory, with the utmost malice and cruelty, and persecuted his followers." For this terrible act the Jews were and will continue to be severely punished, predicted Edwards.[13]

To Edwards the destruction of Jerusalem and its Temple by the Roman armies stood as a singular example of God's anger with the Jewish people. "Jerusalem was like Sodom, in that it was devoted to destruction, by special divine wrath." Sensing the impending calamity, Christ urged his followers to flee Jerusalem, because, explains Edwards, "fleeing out of Jerusalem was a type of fleeing out of a state of sin." Edwards found little difficulty in transforming the most tragic and hallowed event of the Jewish past into a stepping stone for Christian ascendancy. It underscored the wide chasm that separated Jew from Gentile in the eighteenth century.[14]

Like other Christian thinkers through the centuries, Edwards succumbed to the view that it was the Jewish slavish adherence to the Law that made them sinful and corrupt. "One reason why the Jews looked upon themselves as better than the Gentiles, and called themselves holy and the Gentiles sinners, was that they had the law of Moses," sermonized Edwards. The Jews, he declared on another occasion, had "a very superstitious and extravagant notion of their law . . . as if it were the prime, grand, and indeed only rule of God's proceeding with mankind."[15]

It was important to Edwards that pious Christians separate themselves and their practices from those of the Jews. Despite his attachment to the Old Testament, he was concerned that some of his coreligionists might follow too closely the strictures of the Jewish Bible. In this connection he singled out the prevailing confusion that he detected in some New England circles over the true Sabbath. In a series of sermons entitled "The Perpetuity and Change of the Sabbath," Edwards instructed his listeners that in Christianity "the first day of the week was preferred before any other day." He regretted "that some deny it"; even worse, "others religiously observe the Jewish Sabbath," even though it had been "abrogated, and another day of the week is appointed in the room of the seventh."[16]

Edwards's chief concern was that New Englanders had lost sight of the Christian meaning of Sunday; that it symbolized for them a new creation, one represented by the resurrection of Jesus, one which was distinct from and which had displaced the old creation celebrated by the Jews. Edwards opposed the Jewish contention that the Sabbath was to remain a perpetual reminder of the Jewish deliverance from Egypt. "The Holy Ghost hath implicitly told us, that instituted memorials of the Jews' deliverance from Egypt should be no longer upheld as in Gospel-times." The Christian Sabbath was designed to commemorate "Christ's redemption," not Israel's. What is more, from Edwards's typological perspective, one which he was so fond of employing, Israel's old Sabbath was in reality the new. Israel's redemption from Egypt "was only a *type* of the resurrection of Christ . . . and Moses was a great type of Christ himself."[17]

As a postmillennialist who looked forward to the return of Christ, Edwards yearned for the conversion of the Jews, so that the glory of "latter days" would be hastened. Like Mather and other Puritans before him, he watched contemporary events for signs of a Jewish repentance and conversion to the true faith. He made careful note of any news that reached his way regarding a Jewish conversion. He wrote admiringly, almost effusively, of those London missionaries (since they lived with Jews and he did not) who labored to bring Christ to the Jews of their city. He clipped from Boston's newspapers any items pertaining to reports of baptized Jews in any part of the world.[18]

Edwards's theological speculation contains a modern, dispensationalist ring when he contends that the inevitable result of a Jewish conversion would be their collective return to their ancestral land, because, as he put it, "they have never yet possessed one quarter of that land, which was so often promised to them, from the Red Sea to the river Euphrates." Once brought to Christ, the Jews were assured by Edwards that "their dispersion, that dreadful and signal punishment of their unbelief, will cease too." At that time, although transformed to Christianity, they will continue to remain a distinct nation, "that they may be a visible monument of God's wonderful grace and power in their calling and conversion." These momentous events, Edwards calculated, were destined to take place in the year 2000.[19] Clearly, as Edwards saw it, the purpose of Jewish existence was to provide the indispensable conditions for the drama of Christian fulfillment.

3

Awakeners who lacked the systematic theological mind of Edwards also shared his ambivalence about Jews. John Wesley, for example, unlike Edwards an Englishman by birth who only briefly visited the colonies on a missionary venture, was first attracted to the colony of Georgia. The trusteeship's philanthropic program seemed to provide an appropriate environment for the spread of his religious ideas. After returning to England he launched a revival, which at first he conducted within the Church of England, but one which would shortly break away from its parent and flower into the Methodist church, one of the most successful by-products of the Great Awakening.

Unlike Edwards, Wesley was interested, as he once admitted, in "plain truth for plain people," and in directing his Christian message to the heart rather than to the mind. "I abstain from all nice and philosophical speculations," he declared, "from all perplexed and intricate reasonings, and, as far as possible, from even the show of learning. . . . My design is, in some sense, to forget all that ever I have read in my life. . . . I want to know one thing—the way to heaven; how to land safe on that happy shore."[20]

His intellectual self-effacement notwithstanding, Wesley maintained a keen interest in the customs and beliefs of the Jewish people. Like many of the pious of his day, Wesley studied the Hebrew language and even published "A Short Hebrew Grammar," and he displayed annoyance at the secular assaults directed at the Jewish system of belief by the rational thinkers of his day.[21]

At the same time, however, Wesley's sermons and writings suggest that he had inherited many of the negative myths about Jews common to most inhabitants of western Christendom. He turned to Christian theology to seek an explanation for Jewish suffering and concluded that Jews, because of their delinquent behavior, had brought their misfortunes upon themselves.

> Outcasts from thee, and scattered wide
> Blaspheming whom they crucified,
> Unsaved, unpitied, unforgiven,
> Branded like Cain, they bear their load,
> Abhorred of men, and cursed of God.[22]

Jewish religious services, which he occasionally visited during his travels on the continent of Europe, irritated him. "I do not wonder that so many Jews (especially those who have any reflection) utterly abjure all religion," he wrote after leaving a synagogue in the fall of 1738. "My spirit was moved within me, at that horrid, senseless pageantry, that mockery of God, which they called public worship." A few years later Wesley exclaimed: "I cannot possibly, I cannot respect, either the Jewish (as it is now) or the Romish religion."[23]

Wesley's remarks about the Pharisees differed little from those made by other Awakeners. He saw them as "the Jewish teachers of that age," who "had perverted the word of God." A few, he acknowledged, might have been people of genuine piety who were "zealous of the law in the minutest points" and "generally esteemed the holiest of men." But, in general, Wesley had little use for their teachings and character. Pharisees had too much trust in their own righteousness; and they despised those who they believed were not able to measure up to their inflated standards. Always ready to display their virtuous behavior, "it was a common thing among the Jews," wrote Wesley, "who were men of large fortunes, particularly among the Pharisees, to cause a trumpet to be sounded before them in the most public parts of the city, when they were about to give any considerable alms."[24]

Like other Calvinists Wesley condemned what he believed was the Jewish dependence upon the Law for their salvation, which he conceived as a yoke from which Christ had freed all those who believed in him. "What stupidity," exclaimed Wesley, "what senselessness must it be for such an unclean, guilty, helpless worm as this, to dream of seeking acceptance by his own righteousness, of living by 'the righteousness which is of the law!'" But there were times when Wesley drew a distinction between the moral and ceremonial law, agreeing that the former "must remain in force upon all mankind, and in all ages."[25]

Wesley's deep regard for the moral law exposed a vein of ambivalence in his outlook upon Judaism. It is reflected in his annoyance with the writings of Charles Louis Montesquieu, who, on one occasion, belittled the contributions of Moses the lawgiver. In reviewing Montesquieu's *Spirit of the Laws* in 1781 for a British audience, Wesley disagreed with the universally warm reception accorded the Frenchman's work. Wesley disapproved of Montesquieu's "laying hold on every opportunity to deprecate the inspired writers; Moses in particular. Indeed, here his prudence and decency seem to fail him; and he speaks of the Jewish lawgiver with as little respect or reserve as would have . . . Romulus, or Numa Pompilius. . . . Upon the whole, I think Baron Montesquieu was wholly unworthy of the violent encomiums which have been bestowed upon him."[26]

Yet Wesley's support of the "moral law" did not inhibit him from rejecting all other Jewish religious practices, most of which he considered wasteful and sinful. For personal reasons he hoped that the Jews would hasten to see the light of Christianity. That Jewish hesitancy in this matter was delaying the Second Coming added to his consternation. "If therefore the coming of the Messiah was hindered by the sins of your forefathers, then, by the same rule," complained Wesley, "your continuance therein will hinder His coming to the end of the world."[27] He prayed that Jews would enter the fold of Christianity.

> Send then thy servant forth,
> To call the Hebrews home,
> From East, and West, and South, and North,
> Let all the wanderers come. . . .
> Bid every creature help them on. . . .
> Let all the nations meet,
> And show the mystery fulfilled,
> Thy family complete.[28]

4

The Great Awakening represented only one side of the mid-eighteenth-century American religious mood. Corresponding to it, and in conflict with it, was a liberalizing tendency, designated by historians of religion as Arminianism (a reference to Jacobus Arminius, a Dutch theologian who revised Calvinist doctrine). Arminianism reflected the influence of the eighteenth-century Enlightenment on Protestant religious doctrine. Unlike the gloomy view of humans associated with orthodox Calvinists, Arminians imagined a benign Providence. They resented the traditional Calvinists whose preaching had captured the spirit of Protestant America. Persuaded by the rational currents of their age, Arminians were more inclined to view Christianity in rational and benevolent terms. They were appalled at the emotional excesses and the unbridled "enthusiasm" generated by the revivals of the Great Awakening, and they were less inclined than Awakeners to recoil from the new scientific knowledge that was spreading across the Western world. Two of the most influential liberal clergymen of the Arminian school were Charles Chauncy and Jonathan Mayhew. Both were graduates of Harvard, where they were first infected by the philosophical virus of the Age of Reason. Shunned by the orthodox clergymen around them, they labored stubbornly to strip New England Protestantism of its trinitarianism, its doctrine of unconditional election, and to open a pathway for a more liberal Protestant sentiment in New England, one which eventually became Unitarianism.[29]

To what extent the relationship of Jews and Christians would be altered as a result of the new liberalism was not immediately evident. However, the lives of few Protestant ministers show better the limitations inherent in the rational currents of the eighteenth century in bringing about acute alteration in traditional Christian attitudes toward Jews than does the life of Ezra Stiles. Born in New Haven, Connecticut, in 1727 and raised in a religious but liberal Congregationalist household, Stiles graduated from Yale College in 1746. After trying his hand at the practice of law, in 1755 Stiles accepted an appointment as minister of the Second Congregational Church in Newport, Rhode Island, a post he held for the next twenty years. During that time Stiles's reputation as a religious thinker spread throughout the American colonies. In 1765, upon the recommendation of Benjamin Franklin, Stiles was awarded a degree of Doctor of Divinity from the University of Edinburgh. In 1777 he was appointed president of Yale, where he also held a professorship in ecclesiastical history.[30]

Caught between the Great Awakening, which swept across New England during his youth, and the rational Christianity of his father, who was also a Congregationalist minister, Stiles, at least at first, leaned toward the latter. Edmund S. Morgan tells us that in the 1740s, as New Englanders divided into New Lights (supporters of the Awakening) and Old Lights (opposers), Stiles contended against the popular tide and became an opposer. Actually, according to his biographer, Stiles, although he might have appeared to be an Arminian to his neighbors, would have personally rejected that designation. A deeply religious man, Stiles possessed also a questioning mind, a product of the Enlightenment. He accepted his pastorship in Newport, by his own admission, in part because he enjoyed living in Newport, near its Redwood Library where he could enjoy his pastime of extensive reading.[31]

When he entered upon his duties at Newport's Second Congregational Church, although firmly convinced of the essential doctrines of Christianity, Stiles was nevertheless uncertain about many of the Calvinist standards of his Puritan forebears. Although in his later years Stiles's attachment to Arminianism waned, it never completely disappeared. Stiles reserved the right to blend a measure of reason with his New England religious beliefs.[32] While he never veered as far left as did the Unitarians, Stiles was always ready to grant a hearing to those whose views differed from his. His was a benevolence that stemmed in part from the strain of skepticism that dominated his religious thought.[33]

The Newport in which Stiles spent twenty productive years was the largest town in the colony of Rhode Island. Its inhabitants represented an unusual diversity of religious opinions, including Judaism. It was a cosmopolitanism that Stiles found exhilarating and challenging. Before long he became acquainted with the town's small but enterprising Jewish population, the majority of whom were of Spanish-Portuguese, that is, of Sephardic heritage. He befriended Isaac Touro, the cantor and spiritual leader of Newport's synagogue. (There were no ordained rabbis in colonial America.) Both spent hours promenading the streets of the colonial city; they visited each other's homes and conversed about biblical and theological topics.[34]

Jews figured prominently in the life of Ezra Stiles. Their history, religious practices, beliefs, and messianic aspirations (which, from his Christian perspective, Stiles had a tendency to inflate) were of paramount concern to this Congregationalist minister. Newport's Jews were flattered by his attentions, for no Protestant minister during the colonial era had established as close a friendship with Jews as did Ezra Stiles.

His diary, into which he made daily entries, is replete with references to the Jewish people. He knew by name every one of the fifty-six Jewish residents of the city of Newport. He attended frequently the Jewish Sabbath and holiday services at Newport's synagogue over which his friend Touro presided. He was present at the synagogue's dedication on December 2, 1763, noting on that occasion that

> It began by a handsome procession in which were carried the Books of the Law, to be deposited in the Ark. . . . The Order and Decorum, the Harmony & Solemnity of the Musick, together with a handsome Assembly of People, in an

Edifice the most perfect of the Temple kind perhaps in America . . . could not but raise in the Mind a faint idea of the Majesty & Grandeur of the Ancient Jewish Worship mentioned in Scripture.[35]

Stiles displayed an insatiable curiosity about Jewish customs and religious ceremonies. While attending a synagogue service in the summer of 1770, for example, he asked "a little Jew Boy" about "the use of the strings at the Corner of the White Surplice worn by all Jews in their Worship." During a Passover service in 1771, Stiles noticed the special reading that took place on that festive occasion. He recorded that the congregants "began by reading a Portion out of *Solomon's Song*. This was new to me. I knew not before that the Canticles were ever publicly read in the Synagogue." He was curious about the procedure of naming a child in the synagogue and he noticed on one occasion that "it was customary with the Jews to lay their hands on the Heads of their children and give them their Blessing."[36] He was fascinated by the apparel worn by a rabbi who visited Newport—"Common English Shoes, black leather, Silver flowered Buckles, White Stockings. His general habit was Turkish. A green Silk vest or long under Garment reaching down more than half way the legs or within 3 inches of the Ankles. . . . A Girdle or Sash of different Colors red and green girt the Vest around his Body. . . . Under this was an inner vest of Calico, besides other Jewish Talismans."[37] In the course of his observations and in-quiries Stiles became acquainted with the fine points of Jewish law. When in 1780 a Newport Christian clergyman requested the use of the Newport synagogue for a religious exercise, Ezra Stiles intervened and explained to the clergyman quite accurately that in accordance with Jewish law Christian services were not permitted to be held in a Jewish house of worship.[38]

Ezra Stiles's knowledge of Judaism was enhanced by a series of friendships that he made with rabbis visiting Newport. In a presidential address to the Yale faculty and students, Ezra Stiles acknowledged his debt to his rabbinical acquaintances.

I have been taught personally at the mouth of the Masters of Wisdom, at mouths of five rabbis, Hochams of name & Eminence viz, R. Moses Malachi of Saphat in the holy land, a Tzadik, and learned in the Cabala; R. Moses Askanazi; R. Raphael Haim Isaac Karigal of Hebron & Jerusalem, like Joseph of a comely aspect & beautiful Countenance; R. Tobiah Bar Jehudah of the blood & sixth Generation from Selomoh Ishaaki—an eloquent man, a great Cabalist, a Philosopher, and profoundly versed in the lights of the celestial Wisdom. Besides these and R. Bosquilla I have been acquainted with R. Samuel Cohen of Jerusalem . . . in all of them I took great Delight, for I know them to be Men of Light as well to be Men of Name.[39]

Stiles was proud of his rabbinical friends. He spent hours discussing a wide variety of religious subjects with each of them, but he was most impressed with

Rabbi Karigal, who arrived in Newport from Palestine in March 1773. A close friendship developed between the two, one which continued for years via a Hebrew correspondence. While in Newport, Rabbi Karigal attended one of Stiles's church services and listened to his sermon. The visit was a measure of the depth of Karigal's friendship with Stiles, for it was the first time the rabbi had ever attended a Protestant church service. When Stiles became president of Yale, he hung a portrait of Rabbi Karigal in the college library.[40]

Stiles's interest in Judaism also manifested itself in an attachment to the Hebrew language, especially in rabbinical Hebrew. It was an interest he developed in his fortieth year, while a pastor in Newport, and it remained with him the rest of his life. From the start, when his friend Isaac Touro offered him instruction in the basics of Hebrew grammar in 1767, Stiles was a diligent student. Within a few months the Congregationalist pastor was boasting of his ability to read the Bible in Hebrew. In a few years he was reading rabbinical treatises. His ultimate objective, which he also attained, was to master the mystic works of the *Cabala*, especially the *Zohar*.[41] He recorded his progress periodically in his diary, noting for example in January 1771 that "It has been my manner for some years daily to read a chapter more or less in the Hebrew Bible. With this I have lately joined the reading or Examination of the Rabbinical Commentaries." Two years later he recorded again that "It is my manner every day . . . to examine some texts in the Hebrew Bible; and besides this to read a portion in some Rabbinical Author. I am now reading the Zohar."[42] As president of Yale, Stiles insisted that all freshmen be required to study the Hebrew language, and he personally offered instruction to the more advanced students. He wanted all Yale graduates to know Hebrew because, as he once explained, "it was the language [in which] they would hear psalms sung in heaven."[43]

Stiles's preoccupation with the Hebrew language was religiously motivated. Through the study of the language of the ancient Hebrews Stiles hoped to gain insight into the mystery of Christianity, the life and death of the Savior, and the time of his second arrival. Jewish indifference to his messianic speculations puzzled him. He frequently sought some confirmation that the Jews, too, were awaiting anxiously for the redeemer. "The Jews are wont in thunder storms to set open all their Doors & windows for the coming of Messiah," he remarked, somewhat pleased, in the summer of 1769. He often quizzed his Jewish acquaintances and visiting rabbis about their messianic opinions and the possibility of a messianic arrival in the near future. He computed the number of Jews in the world and their locations, and he speculated about the possible date for the coming of the Messiah.[44]

Jewish alienation from Christianity gnawed at him. Even when attending a synagogue service he found it difficult to conceal his disappointment. "How melancholy to behold an Assembly of Worshipers of Jehovah, Open & professed Enemies to a crucified Jesus!" he noted on one occasion. And when his friend Aaron Lopez accidentally drowned in 1782, Stiles lamented: "Oh! how often I wished that sincere pious & candid mind could have perceived the Evidences of XTY, perceived the Truth as it is in Jesus Christ, knowing that JESUS was the MESSIAH predicted by Moses & the Prophets!"[45]

Like his contemporaries, Stiles prayed for the conversion of the Jews, because unlike Benjamin Franklin, Thomas Jefferson, or Thomas Paine, he was by no means a complete child of the Enlightenment. Like many colonial subjects, Stiles straddled the two worlds of the past and the present; he was only partially liberated from his ancestral traditions. Yet unlike the more rigid adherents to New England's orthodoxy, as an early student of Stiles observed, "his humanitarian instincts were not choked by his theological zeal."[46] Stiles's unprecedented friendship with the Jews of his day, despite some ambivalent moments, was conditioned by and reflected the intrusion of eighteenth-century liberal thought upon Protestant orthodoxy.

4

Revolutionaries and
the Jewish Past

1

The rebellious mood that enveloped the British-American colonies at the close of the French and Indian War in 1763, one which would shortly result in the Declaration of Independence, contained a religious dimension sometimes undervalued. Historians have only recently begun to recognize that the mid-eighteenth-century Protestant revivals did not challenge but complemented the liberal constitutional ideas of the Age of Reason.

American revolutionary leaders, although rationalists in many respects, when addressing the subject of their nation's destiny vied with their clerical contemporaries in invocations of religious and biblical images. Like their Puritan forebears, whose ideas had been spread by the recent revivals across the colonial landscape, leaders of the American rebellion frequently compared their own struggle with Great Britain to that of Israel's contest against Egypt.[1] The revolutionary atmosphere activated millennial expectations inherited and shared by Calvinists who differed sharply from each other in the degree of their orthodoxy. Many of the rebellious generation supported the patriotic cause not only because of ideological reasons, but because of the expectation that historical time was approaching its culmination, in which, as Ruth Bloch notes, the world was about to be transformed into "a paradise for the righteous."[2]

Contemporary sermons reveal that Old Testament analogues were frequently drawn by preachers in their efforts to justify or explain the common desire to break away from British rule. Colonists detected elements in their own clashes with England over the Stamp Act, the Townshend duties, the Coercive Acts, and other English measures that were similar to the quarrels which the ancient Hebrews sustained against Pharaoh. And they anticipated that God would deliver them from the clutches of England as he once had the ancient Jews from their bondage. They urged their congregants to resist the British just as the biblical Hebrews, led by Moses, had resisted the Egyptians.

And as Americans prepared to found a new nation, they looked to the polity of ancient Israel for an inspiring model upon which to pattern their own.[3]

When independence was declared in 1776 and the colonial Congress requested Benjamin Franklin, John Adams, and Thomas Jefferson to recommend a design for a seal appropriate for the new nation, the proposals that the revolutionary leaders submitted to the legislatures reflected the degree of intensity with which biblical symbolism had been impressed upon their consciences. Franklin, for example, described his design as follows: "Moses standing on the shore, and extending his Hand over the Sea, thereby causing the same to overwhelm Pharaoh who is sitting in an open Chariot, a Crown on his Head and a Sword in his Hand. Rays from a pillar of fire in the Clouds, reaching to Moses, to express that he acts by Command of the Deity, Motto. *Rebellion to Tyrants is Obedience to God.*"[4]

Indeed, while King George was viewed as Pharaoh, George Washington symbolized to the colonists Moses, who was called up by God to bring freedom to his nation. Robert Hay's study of the first president underscores the American public's repeated efforts to compare Washington to the biblical Moses, especially during the first few weeks following the president's death in 1799. Contemporary eulogies suggest that both men had been summoned by God to fulfill a great task in accordance with a divine plan. Both individuals, against overwhelming odds, liberated their people from oppressive tyranny and both, once their struggles had been resolved, offered their followers civil and moral guidance. Both deliverers faced not only external foes but sustained and overcame domestic grumbling. Hay concludes that "George Washington's life and death were meticulously fitted into the religious motif which enabled these New England patriots with a Puritan heritage to understand man and history."[5]

No sooner was the Constitution of the United States drafted in 1787 than a number of clergymen turned to the Pentateuch to seek arguments for its endorsement. Samuel Langdon, for example, a clergyman and president of Harvard College during the Revolution, remarked in a 1789 sermon that

> When first the Israelites came out from the bondage of Egypt . . . the great thing wanting was a permanent constitution, which might keep the people peaceable and obedient while in the desert. Therefore, upon the complaint of Moses that the government was too heavy for him, God commanded him to bring seventy men, chosen from among the elders and officers . . . that they might bear the burden with him. Thus a Senate was evidently constituted. . . . And as to the choice of this Senate, doubtless the people were consulted . . . the government therefore was a proper republic.[6]

Another clergyman declared that the Republic of Israel, like the present Confederation, was a collection of "Thirteen United States or tribes," destined to be united into one United States. The revolutionary generation found it important to make such associations for it added confirmation to the prevailing conviction that America was divinely elected.[7]

Such biblical analogues, however, did not always conceal a triumphal note in respect to the Judaic past. Americans were reminded that as exemplary as Moses was, George Washington was superior. Unlike the Hebrew leader, who was left to die in an unknown grave and not even allowed to enter the Promised Land, Washington was buried with his own people, in the New Israel. Americans were informed that as Christians, they were more worthy than the ancient Israelites who lived in the midst of idolatry and practiced pointless rituals.[8] Christian triumphalism was not one of the casualties of the War for Independence.

2

Even so, Jews welcomed a new society that held out assurances for liberty of conscience and religious equality. Unfortunately, such ideals materialized, especially on the state level, more rapidly in theory than in actual practice. For a while Americans preferred to view religious equality primarily in Protestant and ecumenical terms. At its best the ideal of religious equality pertained to all Christians, more frequently it was limited to all Protestants; rarely did it include all believers. As new state constitutions were being molded, the challenge that Jews, enlightened liberals, and minority Protestant sects faced was how to prevent a narrow interpretation of equality from being translated into law; if possible, to convince a Protestant majority to separate state governments from any ecclesiastical involvement. That Jews eventually prevailed in this contest was due less to their own efforts than to the sectarian rifts which had developed in American Protestantism.

One of the earliest and most significant struggles took place in the state of Virginia, where in support of those who spoke for religious liberty—Thomas Jefferson, James Madison, and George Mason—stood Baptists, Presbyterians, and Lutherans. Together they formed a formidable combination, one which enabled the Virginia legislature to push through by 1785 a series of laws that in respect to religious freedom were the most advanced in the world.[9] Since few Jews resided in Virginia, such measures did not affect them directly. In New York, the principal Jewish community in the new nation, the situation was more meaningful. Here the new Constitution of 1777 was the first to allow Jews to hold public office. It also excluded all ministers of the gospel from so doing, thereby touching upon the idea of separation of church and state, a concept that was of great importance to a Jewish minority. Roman Catholics, however, were prohibited from holding public office in New York.

New England states, such as Connecticut and Massachusetts, moved more slowly. Here, the established Congregationalist church, not having been associated with English tyranny as was the Anglican church of Virginia and New

York, was more difficult to dislodge. In Massachusetts, notwithstanding the liberal rhetoric of the state's first constitution—"no subject shall be hurt, molested, or restrained, in his person, liberty, or estate, for worshipping GOD in the manner and season most agreeable to the dictates of his own conscience"—the Congregationalist church continued to be supported with public funds for a half a century following the Revolution, during which time non-Protestants were prohibited from holding public office.[10]

Such a prohibition was common in revolutionary America. South Carolina's constitution, adopted in 1778 and not revised until 1790, was blunt in its ecclesiastical intention that "The Christian Protestant religion shall be deemed, and is hereby constituted and declared to be, the established religion of this state."[11] Neither did conditions differ drastically in Pennsylvania, a state which had acquired a reputation for liberalism and where Protestant Christianity was not deemed the state's official religion. The Jewish community of Philadelphia increased in size and importance during the Revolution, when many Jews arrived there after New York's capitulation to the British. The religious clauses of Pennsylvania's first constitution, drafted in 1776, were, therefore, of importance to them. Their disappointment was intense when early attempts to include broad guarantees of religious liberty and equality were condemned by a number of conservative Protestant clergymen. The state's leading Lutheran pastor led a movement to prevent the framers of the new constitution from offering religious equality to Pennsylvania's Jewish population.[12] In the state's legislative council only one voice, that of Benjamin Franklin, was raised in protest against these religious limitations. As one of Philadelphia's historians notes, in Pennsylvania's first constitution, "Protestantism, as the unofficial religion of the new state, was successful in reserving political rights for those who adhered to its doctrines." It was not until 1790 that Pennsylvania removed its religious restrictions against Jews. Pennsylvania's experience was not unusual. Its political disabilities against Jews were duplicated throughout revolutionary America.[13]

It was not in the state constitutions, however, that the framers of the federal Constitution of 1787 sought a model for the role that religion would play in the new nation. For a precedent they focused rather on what they sensed was the common aversion for established churches as was evidenced, for example, by the public's outcry against the Quebec Act of 1774, which endorsed the establishment of Roman Catholicism in Quebec. Similarly, the Northwest Ordinance of 1787, adopted by the Continental Congress, which in its first article stated that "No person demeaning himself in a peaceable and orderly manner, shall ever be molested on account of his mode of worship or religious sentiments in the said territory," served as a constitutional model, as did the Virginia Act for Religious Freedom, authored by Thomas Jefferson.[14]

Actually, every effort was made by the framers of the federal Constitution to exclude from the finished document references to religious matters. The attitude was quite unlike that of the authors of the Declaration of Independence who made frequent reference to "Nature's God," the "Creator," and "Divine Providence." Neither were the composers of state documents, as we have seen, reticent about legislating religious requirements. The religiously antiseptic approach of the authors of the federal document worried some pious Americans, who in a number of states worked to delay the Constitution's ratification. Yale's president Timothy Dwight, who may be considered representative of the conservative Christian element, thought it "highly discreditable to us that we do not acknowledge God in our constitution." *The Federalist Papers* were also silent on religious matters. "Nowhere in its eighty-five essays," writes William Lee Miller, "is there any discussion of religion as an element in the social order."[15]

Jews were not oblivious toward these matters; on the contrary, they were very conscious of what was at stake. While the Constitutional Convention was meeting in Philadelphia in 1787, Jonas Phillips, a Jewish resident of the city, petitioned the delegates not to include a religious test for office holding in their final document, as was the case in the constitution of his own state of Pennsylvania. "It is well known among all the citizens of the 13 United States," wrote Phillips, not knowing that the Convention, in formulating Article IV, section 3 of the Constitution, had already fulfilled his request,

> that the Jews have been true and faithful whigs, therefore, if the honourable convention shall in their wisdom think fit and alter the said oath & leave out the words . . . and I do acknowledge the scripture of the New Testament to be given by divine inspiration, then the Israelites will think themselves happy to live under a government where all Religious societys are on an Equal footing—I solicit this favour for myself my children & posterity, & for the benefit of all the Israelites throughout the 13 united states of America.[16]

To be sure, the culminating constitutional achievement of the proponents of religious equality and freedom of conscience was not achieved until the passage of the First Amendment to the Constitution, adopted by Congress in 1789 and ratified by the required number of states in 1791. Its wording, "Congress shall make no law respecting the establishment of religion, or prohibiting the free exercise thereof," although its true meaning would perplex future generations, nevertheless offered additional protection to the small Jewish community and other religious minorities of the revolutionary era.

3

Such constitutional protection could not have been attained without the persistent effort and dedication of a select group of American revolutionary leaders. Their names are not unfamiliar, but high on this list of remarkable individuals stands Thomas Jefferson, author of the Virginia Statute for Religious Freedom, an achievement he considered second in importance only to his authorship of the Declaration of Independence. Because of his assault upon religious privilege, Jefferson acquired the reputation of being the most outspoken critic of Protestant orthodoxy. What precisely were Jefferson's views about religion, Christianity, or for that matter, Jews and Judaism?

Born in 1743, Jefferson was raised in an Anglican home, where he received a thorough grounding in his faith. He was married in an Anglican church, raised his children as Anglicans, and at least in his early life, attended the Anglican church with regularity. Jefferson earned a law degree from the College of William and Mary and entered Virginia's political life at the time when the rebellion against England was beginning to take root in the colonies. Widely read and politically perceptive, he soon achieved a commanding role in the budding Revolution.[17]

A product of the eighteenth-century Enlightenment, Jefferson considered himself a "rational Christian," but on separate occasions characterized himself as a "Deist," a "Theist," and a Unitarian. He believed in a God who was benevolent and just, and that man, created in the image of God, was potentially good and capable of great intellectual and moral progress. He rejected all biblical accounts of miracles and ruled out the need to rely upon revelation as a source of religious knowledge. The discovery of religious truth, even a knowledge of God, Jefferson believed, could be attained through reason.[18]

In keeping with his rational outlook, Jefferson was disdainful of Presbyterians and unsympathetic toward the Roman Catholic or Anglican priesthood, whom he considered to be the corruptors of the moral message of Jesus. The doctrine of the Trinity, he argued, served no purpose but to confuse mankind and keep it subservient to the clergy. In this connection he wrote to Timothy Pickering: "When we shall have done away with the incomprehensible jargon of the Trinitarian arithmetic, that three are one, and one is three; when we shall have knocked down the artificial scaffolding, reared to mask from view the simple structure of Jesus. . . . we shall then truly and worthily be his disciples."[19]

Jefferson's emphasis, unlike that of the majority of American Protestants, was upon moral behavior rather than on religious doctrine. For him the ultimate test of religion was how it affected individual behavior. In this sense he detected little difference between one system of belief and another. He viewed himself as neutral rather than as an advocate of any particular religious point of view. Neither did Jefferson accept the Bible as a sacred work, but rather as an important literary endeavor that should be read critically, without preconceptions.[20]

Jefferson's studies convinced him that Christ was not divine, nor that he claimed to be divine. He classed the story of the virgin birth and the Resurrection with other popular fables of religious history. Like the Deists of his day Jefferson viewed the Christian Savior as a great moral teacher, but not one without faults; and he regarded his apostles as fallible and ignorant men who had mutilated the lessons of their teacher.[21]

For Jefferson, the only basis upon which religion could thrive was freedom of conscience; it was a concept for which he contended throughout his adult life. He considered as threatening any group that claimed to possess a monopoly of religious truth. The heart of Jefferson's Act for Establishing Religious Freedom, passed by the Virginia Assembly in 1785, was designed to guard against attempts to impose such a claim on the citizens of Virginia. Its wording, which inspired the framers of the federal Constitution, declared that

> We the General Assembly of Virginia do enact that no man shall be compelled to frequent or support any religious worship, place, or ministry whatsoever, nor shall be enforced, restrained, molested, or burdened in his body or goods, or shall otherwise suffer, on account of his religious opinions or beliefs, but that all men shall be free to profess, and by argument to maintain, their opinions in matters of religion, and that the same shall in no wise diminish, enlarge, or affect their civil capacities.[22]

Consistent with his philosophical position, when Jefferson became president in 1800, he broke with the custom established by Washington and Adams of proclaiming days of national prayer and thanksgiving. In reply to a Presbyterian clergyman in 1798 who asked Jefferson to resume the practice of his predecessors, he replied that "I consider the government of the United States as interdicted by the Constitution from intermeddling with religious institutions," and that he did "not believe that it is for the interest of religion to invite the civil magistrates to direct its exercises."[23] One of Jefferson's greatest disappointments during his later years was the reluctance of state legislative bodies to grant religious equality to their citizens and their hesitancy to separate church and state within their domains.[24]

Jefferson did not think about Jews specifically when he wrestled with these constitutional and religious issues, although he was aware of their plight and presence. He was interested in the progress of European Jewish emancipation.[25] He maintained a cordial relationship with a few Jews in the United States, although there is no indication that Jefferson developed a strong friendship with any of them. Jews were not unmindful of his cordiality and religious leaders periodically sent him copies of their sermons that they preached on special occasions, which he appeared pleased to receive. In July 1820 he corresponded with Joseph Marx, a Jewish resident of Richmond, about "the proceedings of the Sanhedrin, convened by order of the Emperor Buonaparte." He assured Marx of his regret at "seeing a sect, the parent and basis of all those of Christendom, singled out by all of them for a persecution and oppression."

He believed that Christians had gained "nothing from the benevolent doctrines of him whom they profess to make the model of their principles and
practice."[26] Informed on September 1, 1820, by Jacob De La Motta of the
consecration of a new synagogue in Savannah, Jefferson wrote that he was
pleased to see Jews living in a society which granted them an equal status with
other religious groups. He voiced the hope that soon "they will be seen taking
their seats on the benches of science as preparatory to their doing the same at
the board of government."[27] Jefferson hoped for a more rapid Jewish assimilation into American society. To bring about this acceleration Jefferson recommended that American colleges secularize their programs of study so that Jews
would also benefit from their academic programs. Shortly before his death, he
wrote: "I have thought it a cruel addition to the wrongs which that injured sect
have suffered that their youths should be excluded from the instructions in
science afforded to all others in our public seminaries by imposing on them a
course of theological reading in our public seminaries which their consciences
do not permit them to pursue."[28]

Jefferson's sympathetic attitude toward the plight of the Jewish people and
his opposition to religious bigotry did not necessarily imply that he approved of
Judaism as a religious experience. Jefferson shared with other rationalists, both
American and European, many of the negative attitudes of his generation
toward religion in general and Judaism in particular.[29] Actually Jefferson's
knowledge of Judaism, derived mostly from his early Christian education, was
skimpy. Critical of Judaism's claim to a divine revelation, he considered its
biblical history distorted, its God and law cruel, its form of worship meaningless, and its morality ethnocentric.[30] He attributed to his own Unitarian faith a
moral superiority to that of Judaism. He explained to Ezra Stiles that "I am not
a Jew, and therefore do not adopt their theology, which supposes that God of
infinite justice to punish the sins of the fathers upon their children, unto the
third and fourth generations." And to John Adams he declared: "Ethics was so
little understood among the Jews, that in their whole compilation called the
Talmud, there is only one treatise on moral subjects."[31]

Since Jefferson did not consider Jesus divine, he did not accuse the Jewish
people of deicide. Yet he did believe that Jesus' historical vocation was to
cleanse Judaism of its corrupt practices. He considered Jesus "the greatest of all
reformers of the depraved religion of his own country." Jesus' moral doctrines,
according to Jefferson, "were more pure & perfect than those of the most
correct of the philosophers, and greatly more so than those of the Jews."[32]
What is more, as Robert Healey observes, Jefferson agreed with the traditional
Christian view that Jews were a threat to Jesus' ministry. "A step to the right or
left might place him within the grasp of the priests of the superstition, a blood-
thirsty race, as cruel and remorseless as the being whom they represented as the
family of God of Abraham, of Isaac and of Jacob, and the local God of Israel.

They were constantly laying snares, too, to entangle him in the web of the law."[33]

Like other rationalists Jefferson was capable of linking his own liberal sentiments about Jewish emancipation to a sharp critique of historical Judaism. He classed Judaism together with traditional Christian orthodoxy as outmoded superstitions, but to the former he added the stigmatic doctrines and beliefs that grew from two thousand years of Christian teachings.

4

Also a product of the Age of Reason, John Adams's New England Calvinist roots shielded him from developing a Jeffersonian disdain toward historical Judaism. A contemporary of Jefferson, Adams was born in Massachusetts in 1735 and like other New Englanders was steeped in Protestant orthodoxy, modified by the currents of the Age of Reason. Like Jefferson, Adams found little value in Protestant's denominational divisions, which he considered a product of human stupidity. His original intention was to respond to his father's wishes and pursue a clerical career, but he was soon repelled by the spirit of dogmatism that he detected among the clergy. He concluded "that the study of theology, and the pursuit of it as a profession, would involve me in endless altercations, and make my life miserable, without any prospect of doing any good to my fellow-men."[34]

The study and practice of law and politics, pastimes for which he showed a talent and preference, did not diminish in Adams an interest in theological questions. When with friends it was not unusual for the conversation to turn upon the subjects of biblical prophecies and the Jews. He was never reticent about expressing his religious opinions. To a Dutch friend he admitted in 1815: "My religion is founded on the love of God and my neighbor . . . in the duty of doing no wrong, but all the good I can."[35] The statement was clearly out of step with the New England orthodoxy in which he was raised. Rather it was more in harmony with the deistic tendencies of his generation.

Like other revolutionaries Adams believed that there was only one God, whom he occasionally referred to as the "Author of the universe," or an "intelligent and benevolent mind," who "governs his universe by general laws." Yet Adams stopped short of offering Deism a complete endorsement. Although he rejected a theology of man's total depravity and original sin, he could never divest himself fully of his Calvinist roots.[36] Adams's political and religious comments suggest that he considered humans, if not innately wicked, weak and easily susceptible to ignorance and bigotry, failings which required appropriate guidance and leadership. Adams, for example, detected no contradiction between America's lofty constitutional and democratic principles and the establishment of the Congregationalist church in Massachusetts and its support by public taxation.[37] A regular attender of church services, Adams did not preclude the recognition of the importance of religious observance and the granting of a prominent role to clergymen. In this sense he differed somewhat from Jefferson and other American radicals. Actually, as Prof. Paul Conkin notes, "Religion, or more specifically the authority of God, was the backbone not only of Adams' personal creed but of the whole American Enlightenment." Adams was simply more conscious of this obligation than were some of his contemporaries. Although he recognized the intolerance that organized religion could foster, like his Puritan ancestors he also respected the Bible and its teachings. [38]

In accordance with his Puritan heritage, Adams's personal library contained a number of books that dealt with biblical and modern Jewish issues that he read and remembered. His interest in Jews stemmed also from his association with George Duffield, a Presbyterian minister and patriot. Adams was impressed with Duffield's sermons, which often compared the plight of the American people to the tribulations of the ancient Israelites. On May 17, 1776, Adams wrote to his wife, Abigail: "I have this morning heard Mr. Duffield, upon the signs of the times. He ran a parallel between the case of Israel, and that of America; and between the conduct of Pharaoh, and that of George. . . . He concluded, that the course of events indicated strongly the design of Providence, that we should be separated from Great Britain."[39]

His interest in the progress of Jewish emancipation, although not as strong as Jefferson's, was evident in the years following independence. "I wish your nation may be admitted to all privileges of citizens in every country in the world," he wrote to the prominent American-Jewish leader Mordecai Manuel Noah in 1818. "This country has done much, I wish it may do more; and annul every narrow idea in religion, government, and commerce." He was conscious of the religious role Jews had played in the past. "Let the wits joke," Adams wrote early in the nineteenth century, "the philosophers sneer! What then? It has pleased the Providence of the 'first cause,' the universal cause, that Abraham should give religion, not only to Hebrews, but to Christians and Mahometans, the greatest part of the modern civilized world."[40]

Neither did Adams laugh, as did others, when he heard of Noah's attempt to collect the oppressed Jews of Europe into a temporary American Zion near Buffalo, New York. On another occasion he told the imaginative New Yorker that he hoped to see him shortly "at the head of a hundred thousand Israelites . . . marching with them into Judea & making a conquest of that country & restoring your nation to the dominion of it. For I really wish the Jews again in Judea an independent nation."[41] Once, when confronted while reading Machiavelli with a disparaging statement about the contributions of Jews to history, Adams was quick to remark: "How is it possible this old fellow should represent the Hebrews in such a contemptible light? They are the most glorious Nation that ever inhabited this Earth. . . . they have given religion to three quarters of the Globe and have influenced the affairs of Mankind more, and more happily than any other Nation ancient or modern." John Adams's interest in the Jewish people grew out of his knowledge of their biblical past, somewhat tempered by democratic ideas of the revolutionary age. To Adams, Jews were chiefly "Hebrews," Old Testament personalities, destined to play a unique role in future history as they had in the past. Yet he viewed them with considerable ambivalence; and he hoped that they would someday become "liberal Unitarian Christians."[42]

5

In some respects this type of thinking about Jews was also a characteristic of the most venerable leader of the revolutionary generation. Benjamin Franklin, whose life spanned almost the entire eighteenth century, achieved national fame as a newspaper publisher, scientist, inventor, and political statesman. Transplanted early in life from Boston and its Calvinist tradition in which he was raised to the more liberal religious environment of Philadelphia, Franklin remained both tolerant of and aloof from organized religion. Like other revolutionary leaders, he straddled two religious ages. He was, according to Martin E. Marty, "friendly to evangelists but was unmoved by their calls for his conversion. . . . He belonged to the Age of Reason," yet he carried with him "some leftovers of Puritanism."

Like Jefferson, Franklin believed in a benevolent deity, rejected revelation as a source of religious knowledge, and denied the divinity of Jesus, yet acknowledged that his system of morals was the best the world had ever seen. In his youth he flirted with the idea of becoming a Deist, but concluded that religious institutions served, after all, a useful moral and social purpose. "Though I seldom attend any public worship," he admitted in his autobiography, "I had still an opinion of its propriety, and of its utility when rightly conducted, and I regularly paid my annual subscription for the support of the only Presbyterian minister or meeting we had in Philadelphia."[43]

Although not a crusader for religious liberty, Franklin was recognized by his contemporaries as a defender of freedom of conscience. Protestant dissenters who found themselves in legal or social difficulties felt free to enlist his aid, knowing that Franklin would always be attentive to what they had to say.[44] Franklin sympathized with the plight of religious dissenters because he shared with the enlightened minds of his day a suspicion of religious orthodoxy. All Christian sects, he was convinced, even those who were themselves victims of persecution, were potentially capable of inflicting abuse upon those who disagreed with their sacred principles. In 1772 he wrote:

The primitive Christians thought persecution extremely wrong in the pagans, but practiced it on one another. The first Protestants of the Church of England, blamed persecution on the Roman Church, but practiced it against the Puritans. . . . Thus every sect believing itself possessed of *all truth*, and that every tenet differing from theirs was *error*, conceived that when the power was in their hands, persecution was a duty required of them by that God whom they supposed to be offended with heresy."[45]

Notwithstanding his attitude toward those who drew their inspiration from biblical revelation, Franklin was a careful student of the holy scripture, especially the Old Testament. He referred to it frequently and often drew from its accounts analogues to illuminate the events of his own life. He wrote a number of literary pieces, such as the "Parable Against Persecution" and the "Parable on Brotherly Love," in biblical language. Both pieces were grounded in Old Testament accounts and in rabbinic sources that Franklin had come to understand by reading them in English translation.[46] He wrote admiringly about the heroic role Jews played in biblical history. Not unlike Adams, he observed in the *Pennsylvania Gazette* that

> "the Jews were acquainted with several Arts and Sciences long e'er the Romans became a People, or the Greeks were known among the Nations." Indeed, "If the Greeks had been acquainted with the songs of Moses . . . or the Romans had ever known the odes of David . . . they would never have spoke of the Jews with so much Contempt. . . . I believe I might fairly challenge all the Antiquity of the Heathens, to present us with an Ode of more beautiful sentiments, and greater Elegancy than the Lamentations over Saul and Jonathan."[47]

Like Adams, Franklin, either because of lack of knowledge or an inherited sentiment, found it difficult to focus on the living Jews of his own time, about whom he had little to say, preferring rather to reduce his memory to the heroic, biblical, pre-Christian era.

5

Liberating American Christianity

1

Jewish population increased a hundredfold, from 2,500 to 250,000, between 1790 and the mid-1870s, with the largest increase coming after 1855. Growth before that date was slow. Less than 4,000 Jews lived in the United States in 1826, at which time a substantial immigration began to arrive from central Europe. Figures climbed during the 1830s, reaching 50,000 in 1840 and 150,000 in 1860; but even these comprised only a fraction of the total American population, one-half of one percent by 1877. Had Jews been dispersed throughout the new Republic their numbers would have been even less imposing; but they were concentrated in a few urban enclaves. By 1830 three cities—New York, Philadelphia, and Charleston—claimed two-thirds of the entire Jewish population, with New York City alone providing a home for 1,150. The rest lived in Baltimore, New Orleans, Cincinnati, Richmond, and Savannah, with a handful scattered throughout smaller towns.[1]

Jews resided in a nation of unprecedented religious division. By the early nineteenth century a divided Protestantism had become a fixed tradition of American culture. It was a multiplicity that, as Will Herberg remarks, did not result from the breakdown of a single established national church, but "was almost the original condition and coeval with the emergence of the new society . . . an essential aspect of the American way of life."[2]

Although numerical precision is elusive, the American Education Society estimated in 1830 that of the nation's leading denominations, there were 2,743,453 Calvinist Baptists, 2,600,000 Methodists, 1,800,000 Presbyterians, 1,260,000 Congregationalists, and 1,260,000 Episcopalians. These larger groups were trailed by a number of smaller ones, a few of which were also growing rapidly. The Lutherans, for example, who were about to profit by a surge of German immigration, counted 163,000 members by 1850. That year, the Disciples of Christ, also a relatively new group, counted 118,000 adherents.[3] Charles Cole, a student of American Christian history, tells us that during the first half of the nineteenth century Protestant churches experienced a tenfold increase in their membership; that while in 1800 one out of every fifteen Americans belonged to a Protestant church, by 1835 "the ratio was one out of eight." Although most American church attenders could be classed as evangelical Christians, a small section of Protestant opinion, smitten by the rationalism of the previous century, was liberal. Together they exerted a commanding influence on American religious and popular thought.[4]

Americans, observed the famous French traveler Alexis de Tocqueville in 1828, took their religion seriously. "There is no country in the World," he remarked, "where the Christian religion retains a greater influence over the souls of men than in America."[5] De Tocqueville acknowledged that while America's religious institutions were lodged comfortably in a tolerant, democratic society, nonbelievers did not at all share in its hospitality. Social pressure forced doubters to fall in line with the believing multitude. What is more, Americans equated Christianity—more precisely, Protestantism—with liberty; they could not imagine that one could exist without the other.[6]

Also implied in de Tocqueville's observations was that an element of voluntarism guided America's religious fortunes. Since no single denomination or church was publicly supported or was dominant over the rest, to survive and grow each was compelled to rely upon its own resources; each denomination was responsible for its own destiny.[7] To European observers accustomed to the monolithic ecclesiasticism of the Old World, American Protestantism appeared chaotic, even threatening to the survival of sacred values. The concern, for example, prompted German Lutherans to send the twenty-four-year-old, Swiss-born Philip Schaff, who had recently earned a doctorate at the University of Berlin, to minister to the Pennsylvania Lutherans. From their European perspective, their American coreligionists appeared to be in imminent danger of succumbing to America's sectarian chaos. It did not take Schaff long, however, to learn to appreciate the advantages of America's religious independence from any central authority. He concluded that the voluntary nature of America's churches not only relieved the state "From the terrible burden of suppressing dissent, but the churches so prospered that there was virtually no real heresy."[8]

2

Protestant inhabitants of the early Republic knew little about the Jewish population concentrated in the small urban areas along the Atlantic seaboard. Most lived away from such enclaves, on farms and small country towns where Jews were seldom seen. The few non-Jews who did inhabit the small eastern cities were hardly aware of their Jewish neighbors, or if they were, viewed them more with curiosity than with suspicion; they were not disturbed by the presence of Jews, who because of their small numbers did not appear particularly threatening. Historians who have examined America's early Jewish life suggest that a climate of cordiality prevailed between Jew and Gentile in such places as Philadelphia, New York, and Charleston. When shortly after the Revolution Congregation Mikveh Israel of Philadelphia found itself in financial difficulties, its directors did not hesitate to appeal for help to the Gentile community. Among those who responded with generous contributions were Benjamin Franklin, David Rittenhouse, Charles Biddle, and other prominent Philadelphians.[9]

The Revolution left in its wake, especially in enlightened American circles, a sentiment of tolerance between Jews and Gentiles. Benjamin Rush, a revolutionary leader and prominent physician, mingled socially with the Jews of Philadelphia. In June 1787 he accepted an invitation to attend the wedding of the daughter of Jonas Phillips, a prominent Philadelphia Jew. "I accepted the invitation with great pleasure," Rush wrote to his wife, "for you know I love to be in the way of adding to my stock of ideas upon all subjects."[10] In New York, Gershom Mendes Seixas, *hazzan* (cantor) and spiritual head of the Hebrew Congregation Shearith Israel, although not ordained according to rabbinical standards, was accepted as their equal by the local Christian clergy. In 1784 Seixas was appointed to the Board of Regents of Columbia University, an Episcopalian institution, an assignment he held until his resignation in 1815. As a regent he served together with some of the most distinguished New Yorkers—Alexander Hamilton, Gouvernor Morris, John Jay, Robert Livingston, and others. Seixas, according to Jacob Marcus, "lived in no spiritual or physical ghetto. He moved easily and comfortably in Christian circles."[11] Such intermingling was not uncommon in an age when Jews were few, assimilated, and their Gentile counterparts still basking under the influence of the values of the American Revolution and the Age of Reason. Yet such social attitudes did not always impress themselves upon the liberal Protestant thought of the early American Republic.

3

New England was the recognized home of liberal Protestantism during the early nineteenth century. Its adherents, known as Unitarians, would differ strikingly in their theological outlook from the majority of American Protestants, more appropriately characterized as evangelical Calvinists. Unlike the latter group, Unitarians wanted to perpetuate the optimistic mood of the Enlightenment, to make Calvinist doctrine less rigid, more benevolent, so that it would conform better to the spirit of science and modernity. They sought to liberate themselves from the theology of total depravity and predestination. Centered in Harvard University and Boston's intellectual circles, Unitarian ideas appealed primarily to the few, the well-to-do, the learned, and all those who found Protestant orthodoxy distasteful. Included in this group were some of the most distinguished minds of New England.

The Unitarian movement had its roots in eighteenth-century Arminianism. Its popularity grew and intensified during the revolutionary era and by 1825, following a rupture of the Congregationalist church, its followers organized themselves into the American Unitarian Association. For leadership the Unitarians turned to an articulate and learned clergyman, William Ellery Channing. Born in Newport, Rhode Island, in 1780, Channing was educated at Harvard, where his suspicions of orthodoxy were aroused. In 1803 he accepted the pastorate of Boston's Federal Street Church, where he remained until his death in 1842.[12]

Little has been recorded about Channing's relationship with the Jews of Newport, where he spent his early years. His family, liberal in their religious outlook, maintained a cordial relationship with the local Jewish community. Aaron Lopez had business dealings with Channing's father, who, like his Jewish counterpart, was involved in Newport's international commerce. What impact such early experiences had upon Channing's thinking is unclear, although as he grew in intellectual stature he gained the respect of a number of Jews. Toward the end of his life Channing's reputation as a prominent preacher was such that even some Jews went to hear his sermons. Channing's liberal interpretation of Christ's place in Christian history, emphasizing his humanity rather than divinity, even tempted an occasional Jew to join the Unitarian movement.[13]

Even so, a closer examination of Channing's utterances about Jews and Judaism exposes a strain of negativism difficult to ignore. Unlike orthodox Calvinists, Channing was interested less in the conversion of Jews to Christianity than in preventing their ideas from obstructing spiritual progress. Commenting on Channing's theological views, his biographer, Andrew Delbanco, observes that from Channing's point of view "the last straw man to be knocked down" before mankind will attain its ultimate fulfillment "is invariably the kind of man who scorns the claims of Christian history, the Jew." The existence of the Jew represented to this Unitarian minister the stubborn persistence of "national distinctions." He saw the Jewish mind as "closed, circumscribed by the arrogance of self-interest and the idiocy of 'chosenness.'"[14]

The ordination ceremony of the Reverend Jared Sparks in 1819 furnished Channing with the occasion to deliver the most important sermon of his ministry. The discourse provided religious liberals with a comprehensive statement for their theological beliefs, one which American Unitarianism heretofore lacked. Much to the delight of his listeners, and in a deliberate defiance of his orthodox neighbors, Channing affirmed the unity of God, stressed his benevolent and forgiving nature, and rejected the doctrine of the Trinity.[15] At the same time Channing also took the opportunity to reveal Unitarianism's triumphant views. "Our religion," declared Channing, "lies chiefly in the New Testament. The dispensation of Moses, compared with that of Jesus, we consider as adopted to the childhood of the human race, a preparation for a nobler system."[16]

The mood of a victorious Unitarianism set by Channing was reflected in the thinking of other leading Unitarians, in the comments of James Walker, for example. A liberal Protestant whose life spanned the first three quarters of the nineteenth century and whose reputation vied with that of Channing, Walker graduated from Harvard College in 1814 and its Divinity School three years later. He went on to distinguish himself as a preacher and scholar. In 1839 he was appointed to the Alford Professorship of Natural Religion, Moral Philosophy, and Civil Polity at Harvard and in 1853 he assumed the presidency of his alma mater.[17] Walker's views of Judaism became evident in one of his discourses on Unitarian eschatology, entitled, "The Day of Judgment."

> And what shall I say of Judaism? Every thoughtful reader must be struck with the lofty tone of monotheistic morality pervading the Old Testament; but it was never understood to come up with the Christian standard. . . . Judaism is marred throughout—sometimes in principle, and still oftener in spirit—by the narrowness and arrogance of a people educated in the belief that God was *their* God . . . not the God of all mankind.[18]

4

Neither were the New England Transcendentalists, members of a radical offshoot of Unitarianism, sympathetic to the Judaism of the past or, for that matter, to the Jews of their own time. Many of Transcendentalism's leading lights were disillusioned Unitarian ministers and, unlike Unitarians, sought to break their bonds with the rational tendencies of the Enlightenment. Instead of reason, they found their religious answers in human intuition. Like Unitarians, however, Transcendentalists turned their backs on the creeds and rites of historic Christianity. Transcendentalism was a fiercely democratic movement, for it exalted the individual and viewed nature, rather than social and political bureaucracy, as the true source of wisdom and power. Yet its mystic flirtations and reliance upon instinct and intuition, rather than upon science and learning, for guidance exposed a streak of anti-intellectualism in this New England movement.[19]

Transcendentalism's leading interpreter was Ralph Waldo Emerson, who was born in Boston in 1803. He, like many of the Unitarians of his day, was a graduate of Harvard College and the Harvard Divinity School. For a short while he served as a Unitarian minister at the Second Church of Boston, but resigned his post in disillusionment in 1831 after refusing to participate in the administration of the Lord's Supper. Following a tour of Europe during which Emerson became fortified with the doctrines of German idealism and romanticism, he settled in Concord, where he acquired a reputation as one of America's leading philosophers, essayists, and lecturers.[20]

As a Transcendentalist Emerson scrutinized and challenged some of the most sacred beliefs of Christianity. He accepted Jesus, not as a divine savior, not even as a perfect human being, but as a great moral teacher. To Emerson and other Transcendentalists, faith in Jesus was not a christological prerequisite; more important was Emerson's faith in the ultimate perfectability of human beings. Emerson's tendency to deify the individual set him apart from New England Calvinists and many Unitarians as well. His declaration that "the history of Jesus is the history of every man, written large," was viewed as heretical even by liberal New Englanders.[21]

Emerson's intellectual reputation was such that most American writers and thinkers, including a few Jews, acknowledged his preeminent standing in American letters and sought an audience with him. During her youth, the Jewish poet Emma Lazarus developed a friendship with Emerson and corresponded frequently with the New England essayist. Emerson read her poems and counseled her about matters of style. "I should like to be appointed your professor," the aging Emerson wrote to Lazarus affectionately in 1868, after receiving an inscribed book of her poems, "you being required to attend the whole term. I should be very stern & exigeant, & insist on large readings & writings & from haughty points of view."[22] At the age of seventy-three Emerson traveled to New York in order to visit Emma Lazarus and her family. She had previously spent a week with his family at Concord, a visit she long remembered as the highlight of her life. [23]

It was a select group of assimilated, well-established Jews who were eager to meet with and learn from Emerson. Felix Adler, who eventually drew away from his Jewish heritage to found the Ethical Culture movement, was attracted by Emerson's idealism. In 1875 Adler also visited Concord and later confessed the great influence Emerson had upon his thinking. Adler read and reread the New Englander's essays, recalling on one occasion that, "The value of Emerson's teaching to me at that time consisted in the exalted view he takes of the self. Divinity as an object of extraneous worship for me had vanished. Emerson taught that immediate experiences of the divine power in self may take the place of worship. His doctrine of self-reliance also was bracing to a youth just setting out to challenge prevailing opinions."[24]

Emerson's attraction for Lazarus and Adler, and they for him, should not be interpreted as a sign of his consistent friendliness to American Jews. Actually, Emerson displayed a typical patrician contempt toward most Jews, particularly toward those who had more recently arrived from eastern Europe. Writing in his journal in 1837, Emerson explained the disappointment he felt when he first saw some paintings of Polish Jews at a Boston art gallery. "The Polish Jews are an offence to me; they degrade & animalize. As soon as a beard becomes anything but an accident, we have not a man but a turk, a Jew, a satyr, a dandy, a goat."[25] He informed his brother in 1831 that the Jews were a usurious lot, and two years later wrote to him that he had not yet paid a debt which he owed, but will just "as quick as I can find a banker or a Jew that will trust." While in England in 1847, he commented to an acquaintance that an individual he had met "must be a Jew: his manners are of Monmouth Street."[26]

Emerson's anxiety about Judaic, primarily biblical ideas, however, revealed much more about his inner anxieties. From his theological training Emerson had inherited a typical package of notions about the Jewish people at the time of Jesus. These included the conviction that Jews had sought the death of the Christian founder and that Christian truth was far advanced from that possessed by the ancient Israelites. Such ideas constituted the fodder of his early sermons.[27] Eventually, this early negative outlook became intertwined with his antiscriptural thinking.

Emerson strenuously attacked the role that the biblical Jews played in bequeathing religious discipline and moral authority to later generations. Emerson, as Robert J. Lowenberg perceptively observes, resented the "Jewish Idea." Like other Christian liberals of his day and of later generations as well, Emerson saw Judaism as the final obstacle against human liberation. Christianity, he believed, only partially reformed Jewish morality, a morality based upon and limited by the "God of the Jews." Emerson's aspirations were aimed toward the deification of the human being, a process that could be achieved only by freeing conventional morality from the limitations imposed upon it by Jewish teachings. To be sure, such troubling thoughts also drove Emerson to oppose traditional Christianity as well, but in the latter process he never forgot that Christianity's principal core, the chief villain in the drama of Western religious values, was Judaism.[28] Contemplating the achievements of the creative minds of Western civilization, Emerson complained in his journal: "These old giants are still under the grasp of that terrific Jewish idea before which ages were driven like sifted snow, which all the literature of the world . . . tingle[s] with."[29]

It was not unusual, as Lowenberg reminds us, for benevolent, but limited Protestant minds of the early nineteenth century to see Judaism as a restrictive system of belief, parochial, retrogressive, and repressive of modernity. Like Jefferson, Emerson believed that the God of the Jews was cruel, barbaric, in need of reformation. Unlike New England Calvinists he displayed little adulation for the biblical figure of Moses, who transmitted God's law from Sinai to the people of Israel. Jewish Law represented to Emerson the stifling authority of God from which he sought to free mankind, a major impediment to human individuality. Rather than Moses, Emerson preferred the heroic figure of the tyrant Nebuchadnezzer, the biblical villain who destroyed the Jewish Holy Temple in 588 B.C., laid waste the city of Jerusalem, and drove its inhabitants into exile and slavery. The act symbolized for Emerson, not evil, but liberation, a heroic gesture of defiance of God's law. Clearly, Emerson's choice of Nebuchadnezzer as liberator underscores his resentment of, and contempt for, that which was most sacred to Judaism.[30]

5

Like Emerson, Theodore Parker, who was born in 1810, graduated from Harvard's Divinity School and in 1837 was ordained at the Unitarian West Roxbury Church in Massachusetts. Unlike Emerson, however, Parker, although he veered to the extreme left of the Unitarian movement and emerged as its leading voice, remained a practicing minister until his death in Florence, Italy, in 1860.

An outspoken critic of Protestant orthodoxy, Parker often proclaimed his acceptance of those who were committed to other faiths. "One thing I prize above all others," he informed a colleague in 1854, is "fidelity to a man's own sense of the true and the just, the lovely and the holy; then it is of small consequence to me whether the man be a Jew or a Christian."[31] One year before his death, he again remarked that "I never found fault with men for faithfully adhering to their opinions, however diverse from mine. . . . I have known Catholics and Jews deeply religious in the highest sense of the word."[32]

Such tolerance, however, ended at the doorstep of Protestant orthodoxy, whose notions of "miraculous revelation," belief in the "existence of the devil," "the total depravity of man," "the wrath of God," "the eternal torment of the immortal soul," or "the salvation of men by belief," Parker viewed as "monstrous doctrines," barriers to a genuine religious experience. For such fundamental beliefs of evangelical Protestantism—the incarnation of God in a miraculous baby, the death of God by crucifixion, the resurrection of a dead God, Parker announced that "There is nothing which can be called circumstantial or personal evidence for these things."[33] Although he did not recognize Jesus' divinity, still Parker considered himself a Christian, as did Emerson. In 1846 he commented to a friend that he believed Jesus to be "a perfect man—perfect in morality and religion, a religious genius, as Homer was a poetical genius."[34]

As a serious biblical student with roots in New England, Parker had inherited an interest in the Hebrew language and its literature. Early in his life he aspired to become a Hebrew scholar, and he made it a point in his later European travels to visit Judaica book stores. He enjoyed not only browsing, but also purchasing Hebrew religious tomes for his growing collection of Hebrew and rabbinic texts. When in 1844 he visited a Jewish book dealer in Prague, he remarked that "the little old man was attentive, and pleased that a stranger took interest in Hebrew literature. He had a fine copy of the Talmud, twelve volumes, large paper, for forty gulden!"[35]

Yet Parker's interest in, even affection for, the Jews was reserved chiefly for their past. His periodic visits to Europe's Jewish cemeteries, where he enjoyed examining the aging gravestones and deciphering their Hebrew inscriptions, are symbolic of the chiefly historic place that Judaism held in his imagination. After one such visit he confessed his "inborn affection for the mysterious people, for ages oppressed, yet green and living still. I thought of the services they had done mankind—and the reward they got! . . . No spot this side of Rome or Venice had interested me so much as this."[36] But the Judaism that Parker saw had for him long ago served its usefulness and was now superseded by the religion of Jesus, which its people had sinfully rejected.

Such thoughts are reflected in his sermons. Parker accused the Jews of Jesus' time of refusing to "perceive the greatness of Jesus of Nazareth. His ideas were not their notions," he announced to his listeners. "He was not the man they were looking for; not at all the Messiah, the anointed one of God, which they wanted."[37] The Pharisees of Jesus' time are Parker's greatest villains, for they symbolized not only Jews, but also represented his Calvinist opponents whom he frequently compared to Pharisees. Like Calvinists, the Pharisees were the "moral monsters" whose greatest sin was slavery to the letter rather than to the spirit of the law. They wanted to be applauded, commended, "their traditions praised and flattered." Jesus did not impress them. They "could not understand by what authority he taught. Poor Pharisees! How could they. His phylacteries were not broader than those of another man; nay, perhaps he had no phylac-teries at all. . . . Men did not salute him in the market place, sandals in hand, with their 'Rabbi! Rabbi!' Could such men understand by what authority he taught?"[38] Liberal Parker's assault on the Pharisees differed little from Jonathan Edwards's attack a century earlier. The pastime remained one of the constants in Protestant history.

It is in Parker's attack on the Jewish scripture, however, that he parts roads with New England orthodoxy. Parker's most important sermon, "The Transient and Permanent in Christianity," delivered in 1841, endorsed the views set forth in Emerson's Divinity School address, preached three years earlier. Like Emerson, Parker sought to deliver Christianity from its enslavement to the Jewish Idea. "The theological doctrines derived from our fathers seem to have come from Judaism, heathenism, and the caprice of philosophers, far more than they have come from the principle and sentiment of Christianity," declared Parker to his listeners. "Many tenets that pass current in our theology seem to be the refuse of idol temples, the off-scouring of Jewish and Heathen cities, rather than the sand of virgin gold, which the stream of Christianity has worn off from the rock of ages, and brought in its bosom for us."[39] By his frequent coupling of Jew and heathen, Parker attempted to unbridle the Christian Bible from its Jewish moorings.

> Did Christ ever demand that men should assent to the doctrines of the Old Testament, credit its stories, and take its poems for histories, and believe equally two accounts that contradict one another? Has he ever told you that all the truths

of his religion, all the beauty of a Christian life, should be contained in the
writings of those men who . . . were sometimes at variance with one another,
and misunderstood his divine teachings?[40]

In this exposition Parker was not merely displaying an appreciation for the
new science of biblical criticism, but an undisguised resentment of Jewish
biblical authority. In a sermon entitled "Relation of the Bible to the Soul,"
Parker thundered: "The soul shudders at the awful and revolting character
ascribed to Jehovah of the Jews, a God jealous and revengeful, partial and
unlovely." Neither did the Christian scripture escape his scrutiny. The New
Testament, he announced, should not be allowed to "hold the soul in bondage." It "is not the foundation of religion. . . . The Bible or the New Testament are not the sole and exclusive foundations of Christianity."[41] But it was
the Law of Moses that caused Parker the greater dissatisfaction; for mankind,
he asserted, had outgrown its teachings. Simply put, the laws of Moses were
outdated. "Why appeal to his old text-books, as if they were the limit of human
progress?" asked Parker.

Parker attacked the most sacred pillars of the Jewish tradition. An example
of this is seen in the way he chose to respond to New England's evangelical
demands for stricter Sunday laws. Together with other liberal leaders, Parker
joined an "anti-Sabbath" crusade to prevent the passage of laws that would
impose a rigid observance of Sunday on the citizens of New England. But while
lecturing to an anti-Sabbath convention in 1848 Parker drew from his New
Testament studies an unflattering portrait of Jewish Sabbath observance, an
example which he held up for Christians to view and avoid. The Jewish
Sabbath, he argued, was a day that, by the time of Jesus, had deteriorated into
one of religious rigidity, riddled with a host of senseless observances and
ceremonies. "It was not unlawful to eat, drink, and be merry on the Sabbath. . . . It was lawful to perform the rite of circumcision on the Sabbath,
but unlawful to cure a man of any sickness. . . . Such was the Sabbath with
the Hebrews." Christ, Parker declared, rejected such Jewish inconsistencies.
His teachings humanized and universalized the meaning of God's holy day.
Unfortunately, explained Parker, with the arrival of the Puritans to New
England, a spirit of reaction, one which duplicated the degenerate style of the
Jewish Sabbath observance, was reintroduced. The New England Puritans
"made Sunday a terrible day, a day of fear and of fasting, and of trembling
under the terrors of the Lord. They even called it by the Hebrew name—the
Sabbath. . . . Their Sabbath was like themselves, austere, inflexible . . . not
human, but Hebrew and like that of the Jews, stern, cold and sad."[42] He asked
Americans to cleanse from their Sunday "the superstition and bigotry which
have so long been connected with it; I would use it freely, as a Christian not
enslaved by the letter of Judaism. . . . the Sunday is made for man. . . . Let

us use it, then, not consuming its hours in a Jewish observance; not devote it to the lower necessities of life, but the higher."[43]

Parker's anti-Judaism was biblical, but this did not make it any less real. He viewed the ancient Hebrews as a cruel lot, "more savage than the Comanche Indians." Most important, Parker considered the Jewish system of belief out-moded, reactionary, and obsolete. "The Hebrew cleaves to his ancient ritual and ancient creed, refusing to share the religious science which mankind had brought to light since Moses and Samuel went home to their God."[44] Like Emerson, whom he greatly admired, Parker wished to liberate mankind from the outmoded inhibitions imposed upon it by the Jewish Idea.

6

Christianizing Antebellum Society

1

Protestant hegemony during the first half of the nineteenth century owed much less to the liberal currents that I have examined than to the resurgence of orthodoxy. Even in New England, Unitarianism and Transcendentalism were not representative of the popular religious sentiment. More striking was the reaffirmation of Calvinist values, the beginning of which can be traced to a series of religious revivals known as the Second Great Awakening. These were far more successful in captivating the national religious mood and in reshaping the character of American Protestantism.

The Second Great Awakening was a response of pious Americans to the diminished vitality of American Protestantism during the revolutionary era. The many years of political tension and belligerency weakened the religious enthusiasm of the First Great Awakening. Because of the War for Independence, church organizations were disrupted and religious attendance declined. Victory over Great Britain, confidence in the newly devised democratic institutions, accompanied by the disestablishment of churches and the ascendancy of rationalism as a philosophical doctrine, infused a dangerous expectation in the human ability to shape the future. Little time, or need, was left for the fear of God. The religious revivals of postrevolutionary America, which lasted from 1795 to 1835, represented an attempt by American Protestant leaders to restore what they perceived as waning Christian values, and to stem the liberal agitation threatening American Christianity.[1] As a by-product of their efforts a host of evangelical organizations and services were born—the American Bible Society, the American Sunday School Union, the American Tract Society, and the American Home Missionary Society, to name but a few. Together these created a semblance of unity in an otherwise splintered Protestantism.[2]

The Second Great Awakening left in its wake a heightened tone of evangelical fervor from which few Americans were able to escape. Growing up in western New York during the 1840s, the well-known American preacher Washington Gladden recalled that

> The conversion of sinners was supposed to be the preacher's main business. Respecting the eternal punishment of those who die impenitent, and the impossibility of repentance beyond the grave, there was no difference of opinion among evangelical Christians. . . . That hell was a veritable lake of fire and brimstone was hardly questioned by any one. My memory holds many such representations. . . . I shall never forget . . . descriptions of the burning pit, with the sinners trying to crawl up its sides out of the flames, while the devils, with pitchforks, stood by to fling them back again. . . . the terrors of the future were steadily held before our minds. That fear was always haunting me in my childhood; my most horrible dreams were of that place of torment. . . . I do not think that subjective conditions such as I have described were rare in those days; they were the natural product of the prevailing teaching. The business of religion was to fill the hearts with fear.[3]

On the western and southwestern frontier, to which thousands of Americans were lured by the prospects of cheap land and economic opportunity, the Second Great Awakening was marked by an intense religious emotionalism, one which left an indelible imprint on the region's religious experience. Here the pioneers were largely uneducated, socially untamed, and unchurched. Here circuit-riding preachers, usually Methodists, Baptists, or Disciples of Christ, would collect large numbers of men and women, all of whom were by their own admission sinners worthy of the severest punishment, for an intense religious exercise. After an orgy of preaching, screaming, stomping, and jerking, during which time, as Bernard Weisenberg describes so colorfully, those in attendance were informed "that man, sinful by nature since Adam's fall, deserved damnation eternally," that "the death of Christ made atonement for the sins of men and opened the prospect of heaven to the human race—not as a matter of justice, but as a free act of God's sovereign grace," they were ready for a Christian rebirth.[4] No subtle theological doctrines were expounded on the frontier. Christian doctrines were simplified, tailored for the uncultivated minds of the frontiersmen and women. Yet frontier revivals were less exclusive, more democratic in spirit than were the religious experiences of New England Calvinists. On the western frontier all sinners, without distinction, were eligible for the highest heavenly rewards. This explains why denominations preoccupied with frontier religion outpaced all others during the nineteenth century.[5]

In the Northeast, few people helped shape the character of the new style of Christianity more than did the preacher Charles Grandison Finney. Finney's striking achievement was his ability to introduce revivalistic techniques, which the Methodist circuit riders brought to the frontier, to the emerging middle classes of America's cities. Born in Connecticut in 1792 and raised and educated in western New York and Connecticut, Finney began his professional life as a lawyer. In 1821, following two years of legal practice during which he underwent what has been described as an "intense conversion experience," Finney decided to prepare for the ministry. He was ordained as an evangelist by the Oneida, New York, Presbytery in 1824 and remained a member of the Presbyterian church until 1838, at which time he accepted a post with the Congregationalist Church of New York. The many revival meetings that he organized, from New England to Washington, D.C., earned him the reputation as the leading innovator of antebellum Christian revivalism.[6]

Finney's achievement was his ability to communicate religious ideas to the "common man" and woman of his day. As Edward Pessen, the historian of Jacksonian America, observes, Finney's "great accomplishment—achieved through magnetic presence, forceful gestures, glittering eyes, vivid imagery, mastery of a 'scientific psychology' that first opened the sinner's heart through a demonic emotional attack and then reached his mind through force of logic— was to win over and recruit persons to Protestant Christianity who previously had been impervious to its appeal."[7]

Unlike many revivalists of a later day, Finney was a postmillennialist. Like many of the contemporary Christian leaders, Finney believed that through the spread of the Protestant faith the world would be gradually transformed into the one-thousand-year period of heavenly bliss, which would pave the way for the return of Christ and the establishment on earth of the Kingdom of God. Like Jonathan Edwards, he was convinced that the millennium would begin in the United States.[8] In order to hasten that day, nonbelievers and Jews would have to be gathered into the body of Christ.

Finney had incorporated into his thinking many Calvinist notions about the biblical Jews, and he viewed them frequently in typological terms. "Under the *Jewish* dispensation," he wrote in 1835, "there were particular forms enjoined and prescribed by God himself, from such it was not lawful to depart. But these forms were all *typical,* and were designed to shadow forth Christ, or something connected with the new dispensation that Christ was to introduce."[9] He erased Jewish history, leaving in its place a prophetic hint whose function it was to explain the Christian future. Finney also shared with Christians the conviction that Jewish biblical law had been superseded by Christianity. "When Christ came," he declared, "the ceremonial or typical dispensation was abrogated, because the design of those forms was fulfilled, and therefore of themselves of no further use. He, being the anti-type, the types were of course done away at his coming." Jews, according to Finney, were angry at Jesus for they "did not comprehend what was transpiring"; they did not realize that he came to "teach mankind the true religion."[10]

The millennial hopes of early nineteenth-century Protestants, inspired by the Second Great Awakening, also generated thoughts about the role that Jews would play in the final drama of history. Evangelical Protestants reexamined biblical prophecy in the light of contemporary events. In 1797, when war between the United States and France seemed imminent, Timothy Dwight, a leading Calvinist and president of Yale, turned his thoughts to the sixteenth chapter of the Book of Revelation. It appeared clear to this respected preacher "that the prophetic writers of Scripture had the closing decades of the eighteenth century in mind when they uttered many of their dark sayings." The upheavals caused by the French revolutionary wars also produced important signs. Dwight's predictions were firm. The spread of the gospel would result in the gradual Christianization of the world. "The missionary spirit was being manifested everywhere, and the Jews would be converted, in all likelihood, in the near future."[11]

Jedidiah Morse, a Congregationalist pastor and a zealous defender of the Protestant faith, also announced his expectations of the outcome of the Napoleonic Wars. In a sermon based upon the text of *Daniel* 12, which he preached in 1810, Morse foretold that the eastern and western Antichrist, that is, the Turkish empire and the papacy, both of which had risen in 1606, would shortly be obliterated. This would pave the way for a Jewish return to Palestine, their collective conversion, and the coming of the Millennium. Protestant periodicals of the early nineteenth century announced frequently the impending conversion and restoration of the Jews, and in order to hasten these events, their readers were urged to preach the gospel to the Jews.[12] The Second Great Awakening not only strengthened the fabric of American Protestantism, increased its numbers and its institutions, but also enhanced its determination to gather the Jews into its fold as a precondition for the arrival of the Kingdom of God.

2

Despite the denominational diversity of American Protestantism, students of American religious history would agree with Robert T. Handy that "the middle third of the nineteenth century . . . was a period in which conservative, sectarian, evangelical Protestantism was a dominant force on the American scene."[13] This should not be taken to mean that American Protestants were so politically conservative as to demand a halt to the progress of church disestablishment. While some Americans had mixed feelings about matters of church and state, especially when it concerned their own church in their own state, they were quick to prescribe disestablishment for the rest of the nation. Most Americans viewed any government attempt to provide political support, which could conceivably lead to denominational endorsement, as a positive evil. Voluntarism was a key plank in the national Protestant structure.

What American Protestants sought was a more subtle union of church and state; a Christian commitment from its nation's leaders; a spiritual, rather than a political bond, one which would proclaim the Christian character of the

United States. As John Bodo suggests, "The first aim of the theocrats was to make certain that the separation of church and state would not be interpreted to mean that America was no longer a Christian nation."[14]

This was particularly important to American Christians imbued, as were the majority of Protestants, with postmillennial hopes. To evangelicals of the early nineteenth century, the Republic itself became an "object of eschatological fulfillment." Horace Bushnell, a Congregationalist minister born early in the century and one of the leading theologians of the pre–Civil War era, traced the history of Christianity from the days of Constantine to what he saw as its culmination in postrevolutionary America. "Only in the United States," writes Sacvan Bercovitch, "has nationalism carried with it the Christian meaning of the sacred. Only America, of all national designations, has assumed the combined force of eschatology and chauvinism."[15]

The powerful grip that the Holy Bible continued to maintain upon the American mind was one manifestation of this deeply ingrained Christian sentiment. Although splintered into denominational divisions, evangelical, and to some degree even liberal, Protestants were held together by a common allegiance to the Bible. "It would be hard to imagine a nation more thoroughly biblical than the United States between the American Revolution and the Civil War," writes Mark A. Noll. Statesmen and political leaders, along with Protestant preachers, relied upon Old Testament metaphors to clarify the swiftly changing events of the nineteenth century. "Well into the national period," writes Noll, "the public Bible of the United States was for all intents the Old Testament." George M. Marsden likewise states that "The prestige of the Bible in the United States reached its apex in the mid-decades of the nineteenth century. Leaders as diverse as Nat Turner, Stonewall Jackson, and Abraham Lincoln" spoke "in biblical cadences."[16] Superimposed upon creedal diversity, a condition which many Protestants viewed with ambivalence, biblical authority cemented Protestant pluralism.

The antebellum Lutheran minister and church historian Philip Schaff detected little virtue in the multiplication of sects in the United States. "It contradicts the idea of the unity of the church; which we can no more give up, than the unity of God, the unity of Christ, the unity and inward harmony of truth." Schaff believed that America's destiny, to become a Christian nation, would be impeded by sectarian multiplications. He was pleased that America's commitment to Protestant Christianity had not been forced upon it from above, but that it grew out of the very freedom from government control which religion enjoys. He was happy that in his adopted country "religion is left to the free will of each individual, and the church has none but moral means of influencing the world." Still, he recognized that "most of the states have laws for the observance of the Sabbath, monogamy, and other specifically Christian institutions. Thus the separation of the temporal and spiritual powers is by no means absolute." Like many Christians of his day, Schaff accepted, even welcomed, the constitutional principle of separation of church and state more in theory than in actual practice. He cautioned his readers that the idea of separation of church and state should not be taken to mean "a renunciation of Christianity by the nation."[17]

Neither did Lyman Beecher, one of the most popular Presbyterian ministers of antebellum America, detect a conflict between the evangelization of the United States and its democratic institutions. Not Protestantism, but Roman Catholicism, Beecher was convinced, posed a threat to American freedom.[18] Unlike Schaff, Beecher was not particularly enamored with the idea of religious democracy. He argued against the disestablishment of the Congregationalist church in Connecticut; and he was in favor of rigid Sabbath laws. Tolerance in religious matters made him uncomfortable.

For a while it was not at all certain if the principle of separation of church and state would even survive in the new nation. The courts were far from sympathetic to the idea. Leading jurists considered Christianity, if not Protestantism, as part of the common law and viewed America as a Christian nation. Joseph Story, a professor of law at Harvard and an associate justice of the Supreme Court, a post to which he was appointed in 1811, saw nothing incongruous between the idea of Christian America and the principle of religious equality. "There never has been a period, in which the Common law did not recognize Christianity as lying at its foundations," he wrote in 1829.[19] In his *Commentaries on the Constitution of the United States*, which first appeared in 1833, Story asserted that

> it is impossible for those, who believe in the truth of Christianity, as a divine revelation, to doubt, that it is the special duty of government to foster, and encourage it among all citizens and subjects. . . . Indeed, in a republic, there would seem to be a peculiar propriety in viewing the Christian religion, as the great basis, on which it must rest for its support and permanence, if it be, what it has ever been deemed by its truest friends to be, the religion of liberty.[20]

Some Protestant ministers even called for the formation of a Christian political party, as did the Congregationalist minister Ezra Stiles Ely in an Independence Day sermon in 1827. Ely urged all political leaders to dedicate themselves to the teachings of Jesus Christ and requested American voters to support only those candidates who did so. He exhorted Americans to prevent "Jews and Infidels" from winning public office. He urged his listeners to "support no man as a candidate for any office, who is not professedly friendly to Christianity." Ely detected nothing peculiar in his requests. After all, he argued, "I should not wonder if a conscientious Jew should prefer a ruler of his own religious faith; but it would be passing strange if a Christian should not desire the election of one friendly to his own religious faith. . . . surely all sects of Christians may agree in opinion, that it is more desirable to have a Christian than a Jew . . . in any civil office."[21]

The ultimate desire of American politico-evangelists was to amend the Constitution of the United States so that it would incorporate in its body a recognition of the Christian faith. It was not until the 1860s that such a request earned national attention. The movement to bring this about was sponsored by the National Reform Association, organized in 1863. Its magazine, *The Christian Statesman*, published in Philadelphia, and its national conventions, where its amendment to the Constitution was framed, generated enormous popular attention and considerable support.[22]

Evangelical proponents of a Christian America were firmly convinced that only Protestant religious and moral values could guarantee the survival of democratic institutions. They saw the principle of religious liberty as an outgrowth of Protestantism's commitment to freedom of conscience. They drew a clear distinction between freedom in religion, which they considered a positive good, and freedom from religion, which they agreed was an unmitigated evil. Only the spread of Protestant beliefs, they insisted, would guarantee the survival of American civil liberties. For Schaff there was "no liberty without virtue, no virtue without religion; no religion without Christianity." Christianity was "the safeguard of our republic and hope of the world."[23]

3

So long as Christian America remained confined to Protestant churches, Jews could reside comfortably besides it. But when its champions began to translate their millennial aspirations into legislation, such as Sunday laws and compulsory Bible reading in the common schools, Jews felt threatened.

Sunday laws, or Sabbath laws as they were sometimes called, were especially irksome, because they constituted not only a religious but also an economic imposition. Yet it was upon Sunday legislation that many evangelicals focused with particular sharpness. The Protestant Sunday, like the Holy Bible, represented an ecumenical symbol that crossed denominational boundaries, and its protection provided all of Christendom with a common purpose. Desecration of the "Lord's Day" was an affront to Protestant civilization. Legal prohibitions to prevent such an occurrence seemed logical and appropriate. William Lee Miller reminds us that the same Virginia Assembly which legislated Jefferson's statute for religious liberty also enacted a Sabbath law.[24]

Sabbath laws were widespread in nineteenth-century America. With the growth of a non-Protestant, laboring population living in large urban and industrial complexes, where the work week was long and the pace hectic, laws protecting the "Lord's Day" assumed a special urgency. The traditional Sunday, fashioned in the communities of a bucolic and homogeneous America, appeared in danger of disappearing. The question of mail delivery on Sunday, which first arose in 1818, served as the catalyst for the defenders of Sunday. A decade later, the first national organization for the observance of the Sabbath, the General Union for Promoting the Observance of the Christian Sabbath, was formed in New York. In 1844 a national convention of Sunday observers was held in Baltimore. Later in the century a Lord's Day alliance offered the movement organization and leadership.[25]

Sunday observance statutes and ordinances varied in their severity from one state or city to another. It was on the state level, however, where Jewish interests clashed most sharply with those of the theocrats. These conflicts resulted in a number of Sunday-observance court cases whose arguments and decisions constituted a mirror for Protestant thinking in regard to Jewish religious rights. A number of court decisions imposed a severe economic hardship upon antebellum American Jewry. By requiring Jews to abstain from business dealings on Sunday, Jews, who observed their own Sabbath on Saturday, were compelled to close their commercial establishments for two days.

In 1817, for example, Abraham Wolf, a resident of Philadelphia, was convicted and fined four dollars for "having done and performed worldly employment or business . . . on the Lord's Day." Despite his counsel's efforts to explain to the court that the Jewish Sabbath was not Sunday, and the meaning of constitutional guarantees of freedom of conscience, the court's decision stood. The judge's reasoning was clear: "The invaluable privilege of the rights of conscience, secured to us by the Constitution of the Commonwealth, was never intended to shelter those persons, who, out of mere caprice, would directly oppose those laws, for the pleasure of showing their contempt and abhorrence of the religious opinions of the great mass of its citizens."[26]

In another case, in 1833 Alexander Marks was prosecuted by the Town Council of Columbia, South Carolina, for having kept his store open on Sunday, violating a local statute that prohibited business from being transacted on that day. Marks's contention that the federal Constitution guaranteed him freedom of conscience so that, being a Jew, he was not required to observe a Christian Sunday, did not convince the court. The court argued that the Sunday law did not exact or "impose a religious duty or obligation. It requires no sacrifice on the part of anyone. . . . It enjoins no profession or faith, demands no religious test, extorts no religious ceremony, confers no religious privilege or 'preference.' " The ordinance, the court argued, designed for the common social good, should not be viewed exclusively in religious terms. "No member of society has the right to pursue any trade, occupation or pursuit from which society suffers a positive injury . . . and it is for those in authority to decide on the policy of prohibiting or removing such evils."[27] Even residents of the nation's capital were not immune from such ordinances. On November 18, 1859, Washington D.C.'s mayor, James G. Berrett, wrote that Sunday "has become consecrated over the civilized world for more than eighteen hundred years, and the best interests of morality, of society and of humanity require that it should be kept 'holy' according to sacred injunction."[28]

The most rigid of Sunday statutes were first found in New England, but their letter and spirit were soon inherited by western states as well. In California's volatile climate of the gold rush era, the historian Morton Bordon recounts in a recent book, Protestant settlers from the East were appalled at the church's impotence to counteract the quick-paced and lawless life-style of the frontier society. They found in the desecration of the Christian Sabbath, a day usually spent in gambling and drinking, a glaring example of the decline of Christian standards. They blamed Jews and foreigners for this state of affairs and induced the California legislature to enact a Sunday law in 1858. Although at first the Supreme Court declared the statute unconstitutional, it later reversed itself and the law was upheld.[29]

The theocrats of Protestant America did not stop with Sunday, but extended their efforts to Christianize other American holidays. Washington's Birthday and the Fourth of July, the new nation's first holidays, were singled out early as candidates for Christianization. A day of fasting and prayer was proclaimed by President Madison at the outbreak of the War of 1812 and a day of thanksgiving at its closing.[30] Since Thanksgiving Day was already associated with the New England Pilgrim experience, every effort was expended to underscore its religious, primarily Christian meaning.

Pres. George Washington's yearly Thanksgiving proclamations were notable for the absence of any reference to Jesus or Christianity. His wording was designed to accommodate all religious groups, proclaiming, for example, in 1795, that "I George Washington, President of the United states, do recommend to all Religious Societies and Denominations . . . to set apart and observe Thursday, the Nineteenth day of February next, as a Day of Public Thanksgiving and prayer."[31] The neutral, non-Christian character of Washington's proclamations displeased orthodox Americans. They considered a nonsectarian proclamation an affront to Christianity. "To leave Christ . . . out of the account, in so important a matter as a National Thanksgiving, must be an unpardonable neglect," declared a New England Congregationalist official.[32]

American Jews disliked the attempt to incorporate a Christian meaning into such national holidays as Thanksgiving Day. Their resentment was evident when James Hammond, governor of South Carolina, called on the citizens of his state early in the century to observe Thanksgiving by uniting in special prayers "to God their Creator, and his Son Jesus Christ, the redeemer of the world." To dramatize their annoyance, members of the two Jewish synagogues in Charleston announced their decision to remain closed for the holiday.[33] To impress upon the governor the gravity of his act, Charleston's Jews dispatched a series of letters to the state executive, explaining in one that his proclamation was "so utterly repugnant to [our] feelings—so violative of [our] accustomed privileges—so widely variant from the ordinary language of such papers—so exclusive in its tone and spirit," that they were forced to close their houses of worship. "Nor could they, with a proper reverence for the hallowed faith of their fathers, have acted otherwise."[34]

Hammond replied that it had never occurred to him "that there might be Israelites, Deists, Atheists, or any other class of persons in the State who denied the divinity of Jesus Christ"; he had been laboring under the impression that he "lived in a Christian land." His reply only aggravated South Carolina's Jews' sense of isolation. Yet they were not alone in their opposition to the Christian tone of Thanksgiving proclamations. Such messages served as a constant reminder of the gulf that continued to divide Jews from their Protestant neighbors in antebellum America.[35]

4

The theocrats of the early nineteenth century did not overlook the importance of common schools in molding the moral outlook of the nation's youth. It mattered little to them that the ideal of a free and publicly supported educational system was not designed by its originators, one of whom was Thomas Jefferson, to assume a sectarian obligation. But for the champions of Christian America to allow the control of the nation's schools to fall into the hands of those who were indifferent to the values of Protestant Christianity would be to abandon the providential purpose of the Republic and the souls of the young to the devil.

The movement to Christianize American public education was born in Jacksonian America and was driven by the same concerns that motivated Sunday laws: the imagined threat to traditional values of changing America. The early public schools were designed to inculcate Protestant values and to ward off the influences of Roman Catholicism.[36] The imagined threat to Christian values was especially acute in New England, not only because of urbanization and Irish Catholic immigration, but also because of rebellious Protestantism, as manifested by the growth of Unitarianism and Transcendentalism. The demand for the disestablishment of the Congregationalist churches in New England was viewed by some clerics, by Lyman Beecher, for example, as a potential religious disaster. By 1840 educators agreed that the salvation of democracy and the preservation of Christian morality were mutually intertwined and dependent upon the common school.[37] As Prof. Timothy L. Smith observes, the Jeffersonian ideal of separation of church and state found difficulty in averting the pressure imposed upon it by the popular demand to inculcate Christian values in the education of its youth. The majority of Americans could not imagine how children could be educated without the fundamental doctrines of Protestant Christianity. Pre–Civil War common schools were imbued with religious instruction. Protestant ministers served as teachers and examined and certified prospective teachers. After all, writes Timothy Smith, Protestant "sects identified their common beliefs with those of the nation, their mission with America's mission."[38]

Ruth Miller Elson's study of nineteenth-century common school textbooks suggests that tolerance for Jews was not one of their conspicuous characteristics. Schoolbooks divided the world's faiths into true and false. The Mosaic or Jewish religion was pictured in many as being only partially developed, awaiting its fulfillment in Christianity. Generally, American textbooks limited true religion to Protestantism; and they made little effort to teach youngsters an understanding, or even tolerance, of other faiths.[39] Jews were regarded with ambivalence; as an ancient religious people, their contribution of monotheism was viewed as laudable, but a failure when compared to the achievements of Christianity. In a number of texts Jews were denigrated, their suffering attributed to their disobedience toward God. Rarely was a Jew, biblical or contemporary, mentioned favorably.[40]

Religious bias served as a foundation upon which Protestant-oriented schoolbooks supplied their young readers with an introduction to the Jewish role in contemporary society. The Jews' alleged greed for money and material possessions was frequently underscored in the nation's schoolbooks. While hard work and perseverance were the accepted prescriptions for American economic success, Jewish achievements were rarely attributed to honest toil but to sinister activities. Elson notes that in most antebellum school texts, Jewish accumulation of wealth was described as the product of greed. "All of the vices normally ascribed to the city slicker in a rural culture are attached to the Jews. They are sly, crafty, and prone to cheat in money matters." The image of the Jew conjured up in the unformed mind of the school child was of an individual different from most Americans, one who was to be feared, avoided, not a typical American.[41]

It is hardly surprising that many Jews of the early nineteenth century were reluctant to send their children to the common schools. At first, in New York and in other large centers of Jewish population, the Jewish community assumed the responsibility of educating its young. While parents would have preferred to send their offspring to the city's public schools, which by law were required to provide a nonsectarian course of study, they were aware that in practice conditions were otherwise. In 1843 a group of New York Jews complained to the city's educational authorities about the Christian orientation of the public school programs. They pointed to the textbooks used, including the New Testament, as examples of material that, in accordance with educational guidelines, did not belong there. The board of education rejected their complaint on the ground that the inculcation of Christian material was, in their opinion, not incompatible with the city's educational goals. While the board acknowledged that New York State law prohibited denominational instruction, that prohibition, they contended, did not include a rejection of the teaching of Christian values.[42]

Jews faced a serious dilemma in confronting the need for public education in the nineteenth century. On one hand, they aspired to integration with their fellow Americans; but on the other, they feared the consequences that the teaching of an alien faith might have on the unformed minds of their children. Even so, not all parents wished to isolate their children from their non-Jewish neighbors, and they dispatched their children to the nation's common schools despite their Protestant orientation. The recollections of Louis Marshall, who would later become one of the most prominent Jewish leaders, though far from bitter nevertheless convey an unhappy youthful experience.

> When I attended the public schools of Syracuse, and I can assure you that ordinarily the relations between the Jews and non-Jews were most friendly, the Bible was read every morning by the teachers in charge of the various grades. Ordinarily the readings were from the New Testament, and I usually enjoyed them, although there were times when they were not what they should have been. . . . On Good Fridays, however, the reading always related to the crucifixion and the teachers seemed to have the habit of intoning their reading, and especially when the word "Jew" was mentioned in such a manner as to convey the idea not only of contempt, but also of hatred.[43]

The entire question of public education was debated vigorously in the pre–Civil War Jewish community. It was an issue that did not subside until a more general secularization of public education materialized during the latter years of the century.

5

In conformity with the spirit of Protestant America, efforts to convert Jews to the Protestant faith were intensified during the early nineteenth century. In fact, for the first time, missionary activity aimed especially at Jews became well organized and adequately funded. Such organizations as the American Society for Meliorating the Conditions of the Jews (ASMCJ) and the Baptist Society for Promoting Christianity Among the Jews spearheaded such efforts. By the end of the nineteenth century, according to the findings of one historian, there were more than thirty Protestant missions in the United States whose efforts were directed exclusively at Jews.[44]

Prominent Americans, eager to hasten the Christianization of America, offered their support and encouragement to these groups. Elias Boudinot, a close friend of George Washington, president of the Continental Congress in 1782–84, and a member of Congress during Washington's administration, was also elected in 1815 as the first president of the American Bible Society.

Boudinot also supported the founding of the ASMCJ, the largest of the American missionary groups. He remained an active supporter of the ASMCJ until his death in 1821 and willed a portion of his wealth for the use of that organization specifically for the support of indigent Jewish converts.[45] Other distinguished individuals who served on the ASMCJ's board of managers included Peter Wilson, former president of Columbia University, and John Quincy Adams, secretary of state, who had a long record of interest in the conversion of Jews. For a while, Adams, who became president of the United States in 1824, served as ASMCJ's vice president, while James Monroe, another national chief executive, served as one of the directors of the society.[46]

In their approach to the Jews, evangelists frequently employed Jewish converts to Christianity, or Hebrew Christians as they were commonly called. American evangelicals believed (as it turned out, quite erroneously) that Jewish resistance to conversion would dissipate more rapidly if confronted by their own converted brethren. Remembering that Christ and his apostles were Jews, Protestant missionaries also attributed a special scriptural role to the Jewish convert. The Hebrew Christian was more than a mere believer; he was, as Zvi Sobel writes, "a believer with a pedigree"; he was "twice chosen," once by God himself, and then by Jesus.[47]

American missionaries were aware of Jewish resistance to conversion. Jewish reluctance to become Christians, missionary leaders reasoned, was due less to theological factors than to their mistreatment, a condition which many had for centuries endured at the hands of Christians. William Craig Brownlee, a Presbyterian clergyman and a prominent antebellum leader in missionary circles, who served at pulpits in Pennsylvania, New Jersey and New York, admitted in 1847 that despite the religious and scientific contributions that Jews had offered to the Western world, they had been treated "As the offscouring of the earth—despised, condemned, and persecuted—abused, reviled, and charged with the most abominable crimes, without evidence, unheard, and contrary to all probability. Nay, they have been treated like the wild beasts of the forest—have been proscribed, banished, murdered, or driven from one nation to another, but found safety in none."[48] Brownlee, an orthodox Calvinist and a leader in the anti-Catholic movement as well, urged Protestants to help reverse this deplorable record of Jewish-Christian relations. He prescribed a program of "religious improvement," which would confer upon the Jewish people "the blessings of the gospel."[49]

Presbyterians were particularly active in efforts to bring the Jews to Christ. In October 1849 the New York Synod of the Presbyterian Church appealed to the Jews of New York to join them in what they conceived as the completion of God's work. Both faiths, the Presbyterians explained to their Jewish neighbors, evolved from the ancient synagogue, an institution which the Christian correspondents insisted represented God's efforts to spread religious truth throughout the world. "We humbly claim that we are, to some extent, advancing this object, and that the true spirit of the synagogue is among us." They called their own houses of worship "baptized synagogues"; and they were disappointed that Jewish synagogue practices had made, unlike their own, few religious advances. "It is a fearful sign of prevailing degeneracy in the synagogue, when the Scriptures and prayers are read in the ancient language, and the words are not understood, and those who read without understanding think they have been really worshiping."[50]

Christian ministers were, indeed, urged to study the Hebrew language and the history of the Jews as well, so they would be fortified when witnessing to Jews. B. B. Edwards, a professor of Hebrew at Andover Theological Seminary, a chief nursery of missions to the Jews, insisted that all missionaries should master the Hebrew language. It "is not a dead language," he explained. In promoting such study "we are taking a most direct means to spread the glorious Gospel of Christ."[51] Hannah Adams, who until her death in 1835 lived in Boston, was the first American to write a history of the Jews. Entitled *The History of the Jews from the Destruction of Jerusalem to the Nineteenth Century*, the work, completed in 1818, was driven not only by reasons of scholarship, but by a deep desire to witness the conversion of the Jewish people. Two years earlier, Adams and a group of women under her direction created the Female Society of Boston and Vicinity for Promoting Christianity among the Jews. It was the first organized attempt to witness to Jews in the United States, and it formed the basis for the subsequent formation of the larger and longer lasting ASMCJ.[52]

Although Adams's *History* did not measure up to later historiographical standards, for its time it filled a void, serving as the first useful, sympathetic introduction to postbiblical Jewish history. Even so, Adams made no effort to conceal her missionary intentions. Her account is tinged with regret that Jews have so long denied the truth of Christianity. She had little doubt about their future destiny and prayed that their conversion would be hastened.[53]

By 1861 numerous denominational missionary organizations had emerged, each eager to claim its share of Jewish conquests. Among the most active were the American Baptist Society for Evangelizing the Jews, formed in 1844; the Reformed and United Presbyterians, which commenced its missionary work in 1858; and the Evangelical Synod of North America, which began a Jewish outreach program in 1861. The Mormon church also showed a vigorous interest in converting Jews. To these were added numerous nondenominational efforts, such as those of the Pennsylvania Society, the New York City Tract Society, and the Hebrew Christian Brotherhoods.[54] By midcentury American Jews faced an array of Protestant evangelists eager to offer them immediate salvation and hasten the Christianization of their adopted land.

7

Fashioning an American Judaism

1

Jews devised a variety of defenses in their confrontation with Christian America. On one hand, they rebutted and exposed missionary arguments and activities, while on the other, they reshaped their religious practices to conform better to the democratic and voluntaristic ideals of the mid-nineteenth century.

Their task was eased somewhat since resistance to missionary activity found support within the Protestant community. Christian opposition to proselytizing Jews began as early as 1816 and continued throughout the nineteenth century. It emanated chiefly from smaller groups, both conservative and liberal, such as Primitive Baptists, Regular and Separate Baptists, Reformed Methodists, and Hicksite Quakers, on one hand, and Freethinkers, Unitarians, and Universalists, on the other. Despite their differences these groups were united by the common fear that one Protestant denomination might gain ascendancy over the others and in the process threaten the principle, so important to the smaller sects of Christendom, of separation of church and state. Christianizing America was as much a threat to the smaller Christian sects as it was to American Jews.[1]

Christian objections to missionary activity among Jews did not imply opposition to the conversion of Jews. What some Christians resented was the method employed by missionaries rather than their goal. Even liberal Christians argued, as one did in the *Unitarian Miscellany*, that missionary endeavors were counterproductive, that the harassment of Jews had only driven Jews further away from Christianity. Also, as the nineteenth century progressed, organized missionary activity faced an increasingly hostile secular press. Such periodicals as the *Nation*, the *New York Times*, the *New York Sun*, the *New York Evening Post*, and other city newspapers offered few hospitable gestures to missionary societies.[2]

Even so, mid-nineteenth-century American Jews had good reasons to be concerned about missionary activity. Few in number, they felt vulnerable in the face of an energetic determination to convert the unwary among them. A New York historian recalls that one of the reasons New York Jews decided to erect a Jewish hospital in 1850 was because of rumors that missionaries were engaged in preaching the gospel to Jewish patients in the city's hospital wards.[3] New York Jews viewed the ASMCJ with a mixture of anxiety and contempt when they learned of its deceptive efforts to trap vulnerable immigrants. Its practice of offering monetary bribes to recent arrivals from abroad in exchange for their conversion shocked the Jewish community. Smaller Jewish settlements were also targeted by missionaries. To counteract the missionaries' influence, the Baltimore Hebrew congregation contributed three dollars each month to its poorer congregants so that their children would not be tempted by the bribes of local missionaries.[4]

The founding of the ASMCJ motivated a number of forceful responses from the American Jewish community. In 1820 an anonymous author, who called himself "an Israelite," produced a work entitled *Israel Vindicated: Being a Refutation of the Calumnies Propagated Respecting the Jewish Nation: In Which the Objects and Views of the American Society for Meliorating the Condition of the Jews Are Investigated.* The small book consisted of thirty-two letters purportedly written by "Nathan Joseph" of New York to his friend, "Jacob Isaac" of Philadelphia.[5] *Israel Vindicated* represented the first outspoken antimissionary response that emanated from the American Jewish community. Its author, who argued that for Jews to submit silently to defamation would be unseemly, challenged the distortions about Jews spread by the agents of ASMCJ. With an unprecedented boldness he refuted the existence of the Christian Savior and scoffed at Christian interpretations of Old Testament messianic "prophecies" and the typology which their theologians employed to explain the Jewish past and the Christian future. Such biblical readings, he argued, were contrary to rabbinical teachings. Neither was he willing to accept the account of the Resurrection. "Thus you see, dear Isaac," he wrote his imaginary friend, "that the dogma of the resurrection, that corner stone and only support of the Nazarene faith, is founded upon testimony of interested men, who could not even agree among themselves as to the evidence they were to give."[6] He also insisted that witnessing to the Jews contradicted the spirit of the Constitution and was relieved that American laws prohibited zealous missionaries from employing force in their attempts to draw Jews into the Christian fold.[7]

Another reaction came from Solomon Henry Jackson, an English-born Jew, whose rebuttal of the ASMCJ's work resulted in the publication of a newspaper, *The Jew,* which first appeared in New York in 1823. Jackson, its editor, published one issue each month until its demise in 1825.[8] *The Jew*'s purpose, clearly stated on its front page, was to defend "Judaism Against All Adversaries." Jackson classified missionary activity with other forms of antisemitism, a threat to Jewish existence, which he urged Jews to confront with boldness.[9] "The right of defense, when attacked," wrote Jackson in an opening editorial, "is considered a first law of nature. . . . In the present enlightened age, not to defend Judaism, would be considered a tacit acknowledgement that it was indefensible. . . . Not to defend our character as a people, as Jews, by repelling detraction, would be a dereliction of duty."[10] Unlike many of his contemporaries, Jackson, like the anonymous author of *Israel Vindicated*, was willing to strike hard at missionary distortions of Judaism, even if it aroused a measure of Christian anger. Despite its short existence, *The Jew* stands as an important milestone in the history of American-Jewish defense against the encroachments of Protestant America.[11]

Among the individuals who tried to neutralize the Protestant missionary threat, none was more colorful than Mordecai Manuel Noah. He was born in Philadelphia in 1785, resided for a while in Charleston, but spent most of his adult life in New York City. Here Noah achieved prominence as a journalist, playwright, diplomat, and politician. Despite his professional success and social standing, as his biographer Jonathan Sarna observes, Noah sensed no conflict between his Americanism and Judaism. He did not allow himself or his family to forsake their commitment to the Jewish heritage. His ability, not common in early nineteenth-century America, to explain to Christian audiences the Jewish views of Christianity made him an invaluable representative of early American Jewry.[12]

Noah is best remembered for his attempt in 1825 to establish a colony for Jews in western New York State. In an age when land was undeveloped, plentiful, and cheap, colonizing schemes designed to bring about social and religious reforms were numerous. Noah was not the first Jew to see in America an ideal location for the colonization of European Jews, but he carried his scheme further than did any of his contemporaries. In 1819 he petitioned the New York legislature, unsuccessfully, to sell him Grand Island, a neglected piece of real estate in the Niagara River, to serve as a Jewish immigrant colony. Despite the project's rejection by the New York lawmakers, Noah continued to pursue his dream to settle Jews in an American colony. "I have long been persuaded," he wrote to Secretary of State John Quincy Adams, "that this is the only country where the Jews can be completely regenerated, where in the enjoyment of perfect civil & religious liberty . . . under the protection of the laws, their faculties could be developed, their talents & enterprise encouraged; their persons & property protected and themselves respected and esteemed, as their conduct and deportment shall merit."[13] Noah's persistence succeeded. By the time the New York legislature had decided to sell the island in 1824, Noah had already collected around him a group of willing investors, most of whom were non-Jews, which enabled him to purchase the property. Noah renamed the island "Ararat" and hoped to create upon it a temporary resting place, a retraining station for the preparation of Jews for their ultimate journey to the Promised Land.[14]

Needless to say, the visionary Ararat scheme earned more ridicule than immigrant support. Yet one of its motives, to counteract Protestant missionary influence, should not be overlooked. Throughout most of his adult life, Noah wrestled with American missionaries, especially those associated with the ASMCJ. He was also aware of the group's efforts to establish a colony in New York for Jewish converts. Both projects, Noah's and the ASMCJ's, were scheduled to materialize in 1825, and as Joshua Kohn reminds us, both schemes failed to attract enough people to sustain them, and both collapsed simultaneously in the year of their birth.[15]

Despite Ararat's demise Noah's struggle with missionary activity did not cease. He continued to urge Christians to refrain from witnessing to Jews, explaining to them, as he did in 1845, that apart from their faith in Jesus, there was little else that separated the two religious systems; that there was no point, therefore, in Jewish conversion. "Our law is your law, our prophets are your prophets, our hope is your hope, our salvation is your salvation, our God is your God. Why should we change? Why surrender that staff of Jacob which has guided our steps through so many difficulties?"[16] By diverting Christian efforts from evangelizing Jews to work for their restoration to Palestine, Noah played upon Christian millennial hopes. "My friends," Noah asked a Christian audience, "why not ask yourself the great and cardinal question whether it is not your duty to aid in restoring the chosen people as Jews to their promised land?"[17] At this stage the question commanded greater interest in Christian orthodox circles than it did among American Jews.

2

In the religious sphere Noah's secular leadership was matched by that of Isaac Leeser, the most important religious spokesman of antebellum American Jewry. Born in Westphalia, Germany, in 1806, where he pursued but did not complete his rabbinic education, Leeser arrived in Richmond, Virginia, in 1824. Here he worked in his uncle's country store, and in his spare time he offered instruction to Jewish children and conducted religious services for adults. His forthright response to an antisemitic slur that was printed in the Richmond *Whig* in 1828 brought his name to national attention. In 1829 Leeser was invited to assume the position of cantor at Philadelphia's Congregation Mikveh Israel. He accepted and remained in Philadelphia until his death thirty-nine years later. During his tenure Leeser became the leading defender and outstanding spokesman of the American Jewish community.

Leeser's name has been associated with numerous religious and social innovations. He was the first to preach his sermons in English; he was a founder of the American Jewish Publication Society, and he published the first English translation of the Hebrew Bible. His educational contributions included the founding of the first institution of Jewish higher learning, Maimonides College, and support for Rebecca Gratz in the creation of the first Jewish Sunday school for younger students. He wrote schoolbooks for children, prayerbooks for his congregation, and learned treatises on Judaism. Leeser defended traditional Judaism against the rising tide of religious liberalism. But he was probably best known for his monthly Jewish magazine, *The Occident and American Jewish Advocate,* which first appeared in 1843.[18]

In the pages of *The Occident* Leeser exchanged ideas with Protestant ministers, defended Jewish civil and religious rights, published articles written by Christian clergy, and explained Jewish religious beliefs to them. Leeser proclaimed what one might call a Monroe Doctrine of Jewish rights, suggesting on one occasion that if the Gentile majority ceased referring to the Jewish people as "despised" and "degraded," Jews would look upon Christians in a more favorable light.[19] He challenged the conventional belief that the United States was a Christian country, and that the Christian faith was an integral part of the law of the land. Firmly convinced that the United States Constitution granted equality to Jews and Christians, Leeser objected to the treatment of Jews as "tolerated aliens."

He followed closely the progress of civil and religious rights of American Jews. He frequently criticized officially endorsed Thanksgiving Day proclamations that were Christian in tone, and he challenged the legitimacy of Sunday laws. He considered such ordinances not only unethical but unconstitutional, comparing them on one occasion to mandated baptism or forced church attendance. He believed that as a religious minority American Jews had but one resort, and that was to agitate for the abrogation of such laws from the nation's statute books. Leeser rejected the prevalent notion that Sunday laws were justified on the ground of health and social welfare. To Leeser, such laws were theologically inspired and their institution elevated one religious system over another.[20] When in 1855 the speaker of the California legislature employed defamatory language while criticizing a Jewish merchant for conducting his business on Sunday, Leeser wrote in *The Occident:*

> It is in the nature of the vulgar to hate those who differ from them, but it was not to be expected that a man who, from his position as presiding officer of a deliberative assembly, should so far forget himself as to utter sentiments so adverse to the spirit of the Constitution under which he was chosen to his position. Such a man is not deserving of being handed down to notoriety and infamy even; utter forgetfulness would be his just due.[21]

Leeser was equally disturbed by the injection of Protestant religious instruction in the nation's common schools, and his *Occident* was the first organ to grant the subject a public airing. He warned parents in 1843 to beware of teachers who "implant the peculiar tenets of Christianity clandestinely." But he was most preoccupied with efforts to thwart the insidious work of missionaries. Through the pages of *The Occident* he conducted discussions and debates with ministers and missionaries; he lashed out at the ASMCJ, accusing its agents of spreading lies and distortions about Jews, and urged Jews to organize defensively against them.[22]

Much of his literary output was designed to counteract missionary misrepresentations about Judaism. Christians, he asserted, had misread and misinterpreted the Bible. On one occasion he countered a Presbyterian call for the conversion of Jews by inviting the Presbyterians to adopt Judaism. Leeser did not conceal his conviction that with time the Christian world would learn to appreciate the truth of monotheism; and, as a traditionalist, he instructed Christians that the Sinaic revelation had not been displaced by a new Christian dispensation. "At a time when the Jewish community was virtually leaderless," observes George L. Berlin in his recent book, "Leeser shouldered the responsibility of serving as its defender."[23] Yet, as Jonathan Sarna notes, unlike other Jewish opponents of missionary activity, Leeser avoided harsh polemical tones. Wherever possible he employed language that was measured and reasonable. His targets were missionaries, not American Protestantism.[24]

3

A more aggressive response to Protestant orthodoxy and its missionary crusade came from Isaac M. Wise, who claimed to be an ordained rabbi (rare in antebellum America), who migrated to the United States from Bohemia in 1846. After a short stay in Albany, Wise accepted a pulpit in Cincinnati, where he organized and from where he led the Liberal or Reform movement in American Judaism until his death in 1900. Wise founded two weekly journals, one in German and the other an English newspaper, *The Israelite*, which first appeared in 1854.[25]

The Israelite was designed in part to disseminate Wise's progressive Jewish ideas, a task in which he succeeded beyond his wildest dreams. For many years it was the principal newspaper read by American Jews and, like Leeser's *Occident* but even more contentiously, a leading defender of their religious and civil rights. Like Leeser, Wise believed firmly that public exposure of any abridgement of Jewish rights was the most effective weapon with which to defend liberty. An enlightened rationalist, he urged Jews to air their grievances through the press in sound, well-reasoned arguments. That such protests might make American Jews conspicuous and vulnerable did not concern Wise, for he had great faith in the ultimate fairness of the people of his adopted land. As citizens of a constitutional democracy, Wise believed, Jews differed from their neighbors only in matter of faith and were, therefore, entitled to the rights and immunities accorded to all other American citizens.[26]

As a defender of Jewish rights and an outspoken critic of antisemitism, Wise aired his views about Christianity with surprising bluntness. His attacks on the theology of Protestant orthodoxy, engendered by his irritation with missionaries, made some of his coreligionists uncomfortable. But Wise persisted, since he believed "the conversionist craze of American orthodox Christianity" was a problem more serious in the United States than anywhere else in the world. When asked by some Jews to attenuate his attacks, Wise responded that he would do so when Christians agreed to cease their attempts to convert Jews and cast aspersions upon Judaism. Wise's willingness to challenge openly the doctrines of Christianity, something his European contemporaries would have refrained from doing, was a measure of his unfaltering confidence in American democratic institutions.[27]

Wise believed that his training as a rabbi equipped him to evaluate Christian beliefs with objectivity. He minimized the religious significance for Christians of such events as the Crucifixion and Resurrection of Jesus. He described the life and martyrdom of Jesus as a fictitious myth concocted by his disciples. Neither was he impressed with the person of Jesus. "Jesus was neither philosopher nor statesman, neither genius nor prominent talent, and in all excellencies or reason he stood far below other great men of history."[28] A product of the enlightenment, Wise, Rabbi Walter Jacob reminds us, could not abide irrationality in any faith, including his own. Although he recognized the high moral standards that grew out of Christianity, he considered them inferior to those of Judaism. Paul's abrogation of the Law, Wise was convinced, weakened the moral strength of Christianity.[29] Wise reversed the traditional Christian charge that Judaism's chief purpose was to provide a corridor between paganism and Christianity. His theological position was that "there is but one revelation, that at Sinai, and that all men must return to it in the end, Christians as well as Jews."[30]

For Wise to voice such views publicly, in an age dominated by evangelical Protestantism imbued with the idea that the Jews had been dispersed as a punishment for their sinful behavior and that Protestantism was destined to be the universal faith, took an unusual degree of self-confidence. No doubt Wise was aware of the existence of anti-Jewish sentiments in his adopted land. He had experienced a measure of these during his early years in Albany, but his rational optimism convinced him that anti-Judaism was an aberration, destined to be eradicated from the United States.[31]

He displayed little patience, therefore, with any civil or social disqualifications imposed upon Jews. He fought against any attempt to Christianize the Constitution or the nation's public schools. "We are not a Christian People," he declared, "we are people of the United States." In regard to Bible reading in the schools, he declared in 1869: "We want secular schools and nothing else. Nor has any state a shadow of right to support any other. As Jews we do not want any one to teach our young ones the religion of our fathers. We do it all ourselves. . . . The public schools are institutions for the education of free, intelligent, and enlightened citizens. That is all. To this end we need good secular schools and nothing else."[32]

He became annoyed with missionaries shortly after his arrival in America. He was irritated at their nagging persistence and their ignorance of Judaism. He found their activities crude and humiliating for American Jews, and he was incensed at the dishonest tactics that they employed. His irritation was aggravated by the conviction that missionaries were reversing the inevitable destiny of America's religious progress. He believed that Christianity in the United States would eventually adopt the monotheistic ethical standards of liberal Judaism. "The Jews cannot be Christianized; this is beyond the question. The spirit of the age goes against trinitarianism and favors monotheism." He was appalled at the presumptive belief of missionaries that they were capable of instructing Jews, a people who had advanced so far beyond them religiously. "Your religion is good enough for you," he informed one missionary, but "worthless for us. . . . we cannot assimilate anything that sounds, looks or smells like polytheism, idolatry or heathenism in any shape or form. . . . Let us alone, as we never interfere with you."[33] In an age of triumphant Protestantism, Wise's rhetoric fashioned a protective barrier between Christians and Jews.

4

The threat of Christian America was compounded by the weakened hold that Judaism maintained on the small Jewish community. Like other Americans, Jews were engrossed in economic pursuits that left little time for religious practice and contemplation. By the 1840s, many drifted westward, away from the populated centers of the eastern seaboard. Pittsburgh, Cleveland, Cincinnati, Louisville, Chicago, and St. Louis were communities captivated by a spirit of enterprise. Their Jewish inhabitants found little time for, nor did they have any interest in, traditional observance. Isaac Wise recalled, perhaps with some exaggeration, that in 1846, apart from one or two individuals, no Jew in the United States "could read unpunctuated Hebrew" or had the "least knowledge of Judaism, its history and literature."[34]

Jewish leadership was dominated by individuals who were poorly educated in the traditions of their faith. A Jewish visitor from Germany observed in 1859 that "not infrequently . . . he, who at home enjoyed not even the benefits of a superficial education, in this country holds his head high and proud and makes a lot of noise, like an empty ear of grain."[35] When a trained rabbi found his way to American shores, his stay was lonely and frustrating. Few Jews living in nineteenth-century America were prepared or willing to abide by the customs and laws of the Jewish tradition. The first ordained rabbi in Baltimore wrote to his friend in 1849: "I dwell in complete darkness, without a teacher or companion. . . . The religious life in this land is on the lowest level, most people eat foul food and desecrate the Sabbath in public. . . . Thousands marry non-Jewish women. Under these circumstances my mind is perplexed and I wonder whether it is even permissible for a Jew to live in this land."[36]

Even the leading Jewish layman Mordecai Noah, according to Jonathan Sarna, was not a scrupulous observer of Jewish laws. He labored on the Sabbath and observed only those holidays and practiced only those rituals which he found convenient. Noah was not averse to placing a Christmas tree in his home or distributing gifts to his children on Christmas Day.[37] It was hardly surprising behavior in view of the educational preparation of America's Jewish leadership. Traveling throughout the Midwest in midcentury, Rabbi Wise was appalled at the quality of Jewish knowledge. "Outside of Detroit," he wrote, "I had not, in the whole course of my journeying, found one teacher, *Chazan*, reader, or congregational official who had enjoyed even a common-school education. . . . The whole section of the country through which I had traveled . . . appeared to me, as far as Judaism was concerned, like a dead sea."[38]

The openness of nineteenth-century American society, the lack of social distinctions of its citizens, mitigated further the development of strong Jewish commitments. America beckoned to its newcomers to adopt the customs of the land and it made no effort to thwart their assimilation. In isolated communities of the South and West, where Jewish organized life was weak or nonexistent, the temptations to adopt the ways of the majority were irresistible. On the edge of the wilderness some Jews abandoned their faith altogether, while a few adopted the religion of the majority—Protestantism.[39] For many of those who remained within the Jewish fold, the lack of inspiring leadership or an adequate education left them confused about their own heritage. Wise noticed that Jews found it difficult to distinguish between Jewish and Christian beliefs. American Judaism became "tinged with Christian thought. [Jews] read only Christian religious literature. . . . they substituted God for Jesus, unity for Trinity, the future Messiah for the Messiah who had already appeared, etc. There were Episcopalian Jews in New York, Quaker Jews in Philadelphia, Huguenot Jews in Charleston, and so on. . . . It was but a step from Judaism to Christianity."[40]

Well-educated Jewish laypeople, such as Emma Lazarus, for example, during her earlier years, felt at home with the symbols of Christianity. Lazarus wrote of Jesus with empathy. She included both Christ and Saint Paul among the great spiritual minds of Jewish history. She found little satisfaction in organized Jewish religion and had little patience with its antiquated ceremonial practices. Lazarus preferred instead the unstructured and, what she perceived to be, the more universal values of such liberal Christians as Ralph Waldo Emerson and Theodore Parker.[41]

Jonathan Sarna writes eloquently about Mordecai Noah's struggle to reconcile Judaism with Christianity. The New York Jewish leader tried to convince himself that the differences between the two systems of belief were minor, and he hoped that with time his Christian friends would also recognize the thin boundary that separated the two faiths. Like other enlightened Jews who had been removed from the deeper currents of Judaism, Noah spoke highly of Christianity and Jesus and their contributions to civilization. He, too, hoped for a future age in which all religious differences would disappear and all people would be united in a common faith, one more akin to Judaism.[42]

5

By 1860 Protestant aggressiveness and Jewish laxity constituted a dual threat to the survival of Judaism in the United States. While the former could be faced and challenged, the latter demanded religious innovation and theological alterations, so that the ancient heritage would appear more inviting to American Jews. Yet, paradoxically, while Protestantism was a threat to American Jews, it also served as a model upon which they would shortly pattern their own religious practices.

There was much, after all, in the Protestant pattern of religious practice that was not at all hostile to Judaism. In fact, an imperceptible process of religious adaptation had been going on since the middle of the eighteenth century. The close social and economic associations that developed between the two groups enabled Jews to see how Christians lived and worshipped. Under the circumstances a degree of protestantization of Judaism was bound to occur from the very early years of American history.

When the *hazzan* Gershom Mendes Seixas led his New York congregation in special services to mark the adoption of the new federal Constitution, to commemorate Thanksgiving Day, or to observe a special day of fasting, humiliation, and prayer at the outbreak of the War of 1812, he was acting no differently than other Protestant ministers.[43] The very office of rabbi underwent radical change. While in Europe the rabbi wielded considerable power over the entire Jewish community, in the United States his influence was confined to his own congregation; and even there he became increasingly subservient to its lay officers. While on the Continent rabbis were esteemed for their knowledge of the rabbinic texts, in the United States, at least prior to the mid-nineteenth century, rabbis were neither learned nor ordained; rarely did they earn public adulation. Like their Protestant counterparts, rabbis served as administrators, cantors, conductors of religious services, preachers, and teachers of children, who shared their authority with laymen. Actually, the designation of "rabbi" was rarely employed before 1860. In accordance with Protestant practice, Jewish religious leaders assumed the title of "reverend," "minister," or even "pastor." In short, the development of rabbinical practice in the United

States was unique, substantially different from what Jews had experienced abroad.[44]

The American political environment, shaped by revolution and Enlightenment ideas, influenced synagogue administration. Some congregations drafted constitutions and bills of rights, while many widened their franchises and democratized their organizations. The American Protestant model was followed, for example, in the distribution of pews, which in a number of instances were assigned to families and even sold, as in Protestant congregations. Wherever possible, decorum that was deemed respectable in the Christian community was adopted by American Jews.[45]

Isaac Leeser, although a traditionalist, was not averse to the adaptation of Protestant religious forms in his religious practice. An admirer of the customs of the Episcopalian church, he was influenced by its practice. He was impressed by the character of the Protestant sermon. According to Lance Sussman, Leeser altered the office of *hazzan* into a Jewish ministry patterned upon a Protestant model. After arriving in Philadelphia to assume his duties at Congregation Mikveh Israel, he was quick to employ preaching as part of his own religious exercises. He made the sermon a cornerstone of the Jewish religious service in the United States, and he considered preaching the central responsibility of Jewish religious leadership.[46]

Even more important, appreciating the symbolic value of scripture in American Protestantism, Leeser worked vigorously to make American Judaism also a Bible-centered system of belief. He sensed the diminished role that rabbinic studies were destined to play in the hurried, materialistic American environment, and he concluded that by shifting the emphasis toward biblical readings Judaism would be more spiritually satisfying and at the same time would conform better to Protestant standards. No doubt Leeser's relatively limited Talmudic education made the task even more palatable. As a student of Judaism Leeser had focused on biblical literature; he had little training in advanced Jewish thought. Not surprisingly, his most important literary achievement was an English translation of the Hebrew Bible, a task which he completed in 1854. Leeser's English Bible became the standard work for nineteenth-century American Jews.[47]

Leeser's bibliocentric theology was in part an attempt to synthesize traditional Judaism with Protestant religious standards. He was acquainted with Protestant biblical scholarship and his completed work, patterned linguistically after the King James Bible, was praised by American Christian scholars such as Princeton professor of theology Charles Hodge, a Presbyterian, and Silas Weir Mitchell, a physician and author of religious books. By Americanizing Jewish religious practices along Protestant lines, Leeser's translation of the Bible hastened the acculturation of American Jews. The transformation both altered and helped to perpetuate the Jewish heritage in the United States.[48]

For similar reasons Leeser became the leading proponent of the Jewish

Sunday school movement, the educational vehicle which would shortly become the chief transmitter of Jewish ideas to the young. Here, too, Leeser was strongly influenced by the development of the Protestant Sunday school movement, which was transported from London to Philadelphia shortly after the American Revolution. Here it was discovered by Leeser and Rebecca Gratz, who adopted it for Jewish use in 1838.[49] In an address delivered in Philadelphia in 1840, Isaac Leeser admitted that the Sunday school idea came from "our Christian neighbors." Nevertheless, determined to counteract evangelical missionary activity, Leeser saw the Sunday school as a protective shield against missionary incursions.[50]

Nevertheless, because of the lack of appropriate textbooks, Leeser and his staff first utilized teaching material published by the American Sunday school Union, a Protestant organization. By blotting out portions of the Christian books, Leeser modified the Protestant publications to suit the religious requirements of Jewish children. Because of the absence of an English translation of the Hebrew Pentateuch, students were assigned readings in the King James Bible and selected Protestant hymnals. Permission to delete those passages that did not conform to Jewish beliefs was granted to Leeser by the American Sunday School Union. "This, too, is a highly gratifying fact," declared Leeser, "and it speaks loudly and emphatically of the enlightened views of the board of publication of that powerful institution."[51]

The success of the Philadelphia Sunday school experiment inspired Jewish communities in New York, Charleston, and Richmond to open their own schools. Demand for curricular material encouraged Leeser to develop his own textbooks, a number of which were patterned after similar Christian publications. His *Catechism For Younger Children*, published in 1840, a title clearly of Christian influence, was adopted in Philadelphia and other American cities. Concerned that the Hebrew Sunday School Society (as it was eventually designated) not be confused with its Protestant counterpart, Rebecca Gratz, who administered the Philadelphia program, cautioned her niece on one occasion to "not call your Sunday *Sabbath* school, my dear Miriam, lest some should mistake your meaning."[52]

The Jewish Sunday school was an important manifestation of the Americanization of the nation's Jewish life. Inspired by Protestant cultural practice, it introduced into American Judaism a new religious institution and practice (such as, for example, the confirmation ceremony). Most important, however, it provided early American Jewry an instrument for survival in a Protestant environment.

6

Even so, for a number of American Jewish leaders, Leeser's liturgical and educational reforms did not go far enough. His efforts to conserve traditional values, his literal reading of the Scriptures, and occasional millennial musings left those who were more liberal uncomfortable. Some Jews sought a more drastic reformation of Jewish life, one as sweeping as was the Protestant Reformation in Christian life. Eventually such demands gave rise to what would be called the Reform movement in Judaism.

The roots of Reform Judaism were not American, but grew out of the currents of rationalism that swept across the Western world during the middle of the eighteenth century. Rationalism, a result of Enlightenment thinking, granted each individual the right to think independently, even about the most sacred matters. It challenged traditional religious authority and practice that could not withstand the test of reason. Its optimistic and democratic ethos captivated the imagination of young Jewish intellectuals in western and central Europe. Yearning for admittance into non-Jewish society, Jewish rationalists sought to divest themselves of all outward signs that stamped them as different.[53]

Admittance into civic equality was only one part of the motivation of reformers. Many, such as Moses Mendelssohn who translated the Pentateuch from Hebrew into German in 1783, were also driven by the desire to conserve Judaism by making it more meaningful to their contemporaries. Talmudic law, which for centuries controlled every facet of Jewish existence, had by the mid-eighteenth century either fallen into disuse or was being increasingly disregarded. Some Jews were embarrassed by what they saw as undignified religious behavior, one which had not kept up with that of their Christian neighbors.[54]

As German Jews entered the United States after 1830, they carried with them a disdain for traditional forms; and their new home provided a most appropriate environment for the reformation of religious practice. Not surprisingly, Reform Judaism achieved its greatest gains and most spectacular conquests in the United States. Prof. Lucy S. Dawidowicz explains why this was so.

Reform's success in nineteenth century America may be credited in part to its compatibility with the American scene, especially with developments among Protestants. The most vigorous Protestant denominations then in America had grown out of the English dissenting churches, which had repudiated European Christian orthodoxies and the authority of established churches. These churches, it turned out, were best adapted to survive under the rigors of life on the frontier or the vast prairie.

Few learned ministers or theologians were available to guide these Methodists, Baptists, Presbyterians, evangelicals, and revivalists, even if they would have wanted such guidance. . . . That ethos infected also Jews, who having left behind them in the Old Country the distinctions of class and status, were happy no longer to endure their indignities. In America, where their private and public conduct could no longer be monitored as it had been in the closely knit communities of small towns, Jews became their own authorities . . . deciding which commandments they would or could observe and which they would discard. The rabbis who shaped the Reform Movement legitimated the conduct of the lay people.[55]

Although the Reform movement was born in Germany, it was in the United States that it achieved its fullest development. Here efforts to modernize traditional practices were evident even before the arrival of German thinkers and preachers. In 1824 in Charleston, the home of the largest and most cultivated Jewish community in the United States, forty-seven members of the Congregation Beth Elohim, inspired by Protestant practice, dispatched a memorial to its vestry requesting that its worship services be changed. They asked that a "more rational means of worshiping the true God" be adopted, suggesting that worship services be abbreviated and that prayers be recited in English.[56]

Liberal Protestants were pleased at the Charleston Jewish rebellion. The aging Thomas Jefferson wrote one Charleston congregant approvingly from Monticello that "Nothing is wiser than that all our institutions should keep pace with the advance of time." "Reformation in church and state is always attended with difficulties," wrote another enlightened Protestant, suggesting to Charleston's Jews that the "success which has crowned the boldest leaders in . . . these departments warrants you to proceed."[57] One writer in the *North American Review* declared with surprise that "Little was it suspected, that in the bottom of that [Jewish] denomination itself, there were any who were so far surmounting the proverbial prejudices of their sect, and so far imbibing the liberal spirit of the age, as to admit the possibility of improvement within their pale."[58] The events in Charleston signaled the beginning of a trend that was difficult to check. By 1842, with German liberals flocking into the United States, the Reform congregation Har Sinai was organized in Baltimore. Three years later, Temple Emanu-El was established in New York, and in the following decade, in 1855, Knesseth Israel was organized in Philadelphia. By 1858 the foundation for a Reform congregation was also laid in the growing city of Chicago.[59]

The American leaders of this crusade were disciples of German Reform theoreticians. All were convinced that Reform was a legitimate outgrowth of rabbinic teachings, and they shared the view that if Judaism was to survive and thrive in America, it must adopt itself to the Protestant religious milieu. Rabbi Gunther Plaut, a historian of Reform Judaism, writes that the early reformers patterned their religious services along Protestant lines. "Responsive prayers—quite unknown in this form to Jewish tradition—silent meditation, the inclination of the head by the devout worshippers, the centrality of the sermon—all these are instances of the protestantization of the Reform service. The abolition of the cantor, the introduction of organs and Christian choirs, made the picture rather complete."[60]

No single individual believed in and promoted the new Judaism more energetically and successfully than did Rabbi Isaac M. Wise. Shortly after his arrival in the United States he became convinced that orthodoxy would not take root in the New World; that if Judaism was to stay alive it must refashion itself in accordance with America's free and open society. Wise hoped to achieve a synthesis of Americanism and Judaism. He was convinced that the United States provided the ideal conditions for the growth of Judaism. For Wise the United States was the long sought after Promised Land. He had enormous faith in the democratic institutions of his adopted home. "The United States occupy the same place in modern history as Greece did in antiquity," he announced with pride. "Our country is the heiress of the European civilization. . . . Liberty is our place in history, our national destiny, our ideal, the very soul of our existence."[61] There were also other American proponents of the Reform movement—Max Lilianthal, David Einhorn, Samuel Adler, stand out strikingly. Like Wise they were scholarly immigrants from central Europe who arrived in the United States in midcentury. Individually and collectively they helped advance the fortunes of liberal Judaism. And also, like Wise they sought a synthesis of Americanism and Judaism.[62]

Jewish reformers were not impervious to the favorable impression that their religious innovations made upon Protestant observers. "The non-Jews would sympathize with us," wrote Wise proudly, "since we alone were actuated by regard for the needs and the spirit of the age." As in the case of Jefferson's complimentary utterances regarding Charleston's religious innovations in 1824, the liberal Christian writer Crawford H. Toy wrote some years later that Jews who profess the reform theology are "merely Jews who have reached modern, i.e. Christian, ideas of religion."[63] It was a thought that Jewish traditionalists, such as Isaac Leeser, found particularly threatening. Not surprisingly, the Jewish periodicals of the mid-nineteenth century engaged in a continuous debate between the proponents of traditional values and the champions of modernity.[64] It was a futile contest, from which no decisive victor emerged, for the American environment provided ample room for both.

8

Zionward

1

While Jews were engaged in fashioning an American Zion, a group of evangelical Protestants cast their eyes eastward, to the biblical Promised Land. Throughout the eighteenth and nineteenth centuries Protestant consciousness was preoccupied with the mystery and history of the Holy Land; it was a recurrent theme in Protestant literature. But, at least before 1820, it was largely a mythical and metaphysical concern. For early American Protestants, Palestine as a contemporary geographic reality inhabited by living people was of no social consequence. Their focus was on the biblical Israel, the Zion of the Old Testament. Even Enlightenment thinking, so important in the eighteenth and early nineteenth centuries, was powerless to alter this vision. Samuel Levine, who has examined the religious literature of the period, concludes that even with the decline of metaphysical thinking, postbiblical references to Palestine were almost nonexistent; that throughout the eighteenth century mythical and metaphorical concepts continued to dominate any discussion of Palestine.[1]

With the introduction of quicker and safer transportation in the early nineteenth century, a growing interest in foreign missionary activity, travel, and the incorporation of the Near East as a geopolitical arena of concern for the Western world, a changed attitude toward the Holy Land began to emerge. Yet even in the years that followed, American religious writers were reluctant to separate contemporary Palestine from its biblical images. The spiritualization of the Holy Land, as Moshe Davis suggests, remained an integral part of nineteenth-century Protestant culture.[2]

American Protestantism's attachment to the Bible, which continued to be the most widely read book of the nineteenth century, also helps to explain the nation's preoccupation with the ancient Near East. Families commonly read and studied the Holy Book. Parents gave their sons and daughters biblical names and taught them how to read from the stories of Scripture. The designations of countless American towns and cities founded during the early nineteenth century mirrored the biblical knowledge of their early settlers. As the frontier pushed westward, so did biblical place names, suggesting, as Professor Davis reminds us, the organic relationship that existed between the United States and the land of Israel.[3]

Despite the decline of religious zealousness of the early settlers, interest in the Holy Land did not diminish. As conditions for travel improved, American citizens began to journey to the Near East, eager to see for themselves the land of the Bible, the book upon which they had been reared. As children, they had been expected to study the geography of the Holy Land, to be able to identify with precision its ancient cities and boundaries. They were required to know where the great biblical events had occurred; where Abraham resided in Canaan, where he died, and at what point the Israelites crossed the Red Sea.[4] As adults, some were drawn to those holy places about which they had learned so much, the birthplace of their Christian faith, the land where Jesus Christ had preached, died, and was resurrected.

Biblical geography and archaeology, fields of scholarship that first emerged during the mid-nineteenth century, were inspired by America's bibliocentric culture. Not surprisingly, many of America's early archaeologists, fascinated with the land of the Bible, were ordained ministers.[5] Edward Robinson, a professor of biblical literature and a founder of the field of biblical geography and archaeology, did more than any other American to initiate an interest in the exploration of the Holy Land. Born in Southington, Connecticut, in 1794, where his father served as a Congregationalist minister, Robinson grew up in a home in which biblical Palestine was as real as the city of Hartford. As he matured, so did his interest in biblical scholarship. In 1823 Robinson received an instructorship in Hebrew at Andover Theological Seminary, and a few years later he was appointed to a professorship at Union Theological Seminary. In 1836 Robinson crossed the southern border of Palestine at Beersheba, explored many of the country's lesser-known areas, identified for the first time many biblical sites, and published a seminal three-volume work about his explorations, *Biblical Researches in Palestine*. The work reconstructed forever the map of Palestine.[6]

Reminiscing about his professional life and his early biblical studies that motivated his explorations, Robinson acknowledged that "As in the case of most of my countrymen, especially in New England, the scenes of the Bible had made a deep impression upon my mind from the earliest childhood; and afterwards in riper years this feeling had grown into a strong desire to visit in person the places so remarkable in the history of the human race." In his own New England region, he recalled,

> From the earliest years the child is there accustomed not only to read in the Bible for himself, but also reads or listens to it in the morning devotions of the family,

in the daily-village school, in the Sunday and the Bible-class and in the weekly ministrations of the sanctuary. Hence, as he grows up, the names of Sinai, Jerusalem, Bethlehem, the Promised land, become associated with his earliest recollections and holiest feeling—with all this, in my own case, there has subsequently become connected a scientific motive.[7]

Robinson had a profound impact upon the lives of his students, many of whom followed in his footsteps and became well-established biblical geographers and archaeologists in their own right. Horatio B. Hackett, for example, who studied with Robinson at Andover, became an ordained Baptist minister and toured the Holy Land in 1852. As a professor of Bible and Hebrew at Brown University and later at Newton Theological Institute in Massachusetts, Hackett traveled to Palestine to collect physical illustrations with which to illuminate his teaching and to collect testimony that would "reconcile scriptural statements with geographic reality." He gathered his findings in a book that appeared in 1857, *Illustrations of Scripture: Suggested by a Tour Through the Holy Land.*[8]

Not only biblical scholars and ministers were gripped by the image of the Holy Land; laypersons, too, brought up in a Protestant environment, hungered to learn more about the Near East. Catering to public curiosity, popular magazines grabbed at every opportunity to describe the journeys of eastern travelers. The experiences of U.S. Navy Lt. William F. Lynch, who in 1847 was seized with a desire to navigate the Jordan River and the Dead Sea, are an example of the attraction that Palestine held for orthodox laypersons. After considerable effort the forty-seven-year-old explorer persuaded the secretary of the navy to let him mount an expedition to Palestine. After landing in the Holy Land, Lynch and his men lugged their supplies overland from the Mediterranean coast to Tiberias, where they began the unprecedented naval journey from the Sea of Galilee down the Jordan River to the Dead Sea. It was the first time that any American had explored the region or had unfurled an American flag over Palestine.[9] Lynch's journal shows, writes David Finnie, who has examined the records of many of these early expeditions, that "like the missionaries, he was a Godly man steeped in Fundamentalist doctrine and Old Testament lore. . . . His self appointed mission to be the explorer of the Jordan and the Dead Sea combined pioneering spirit with religious sentiment."[10]

One could multiply examples of how religious sentiment and curiosity drove a disparate group of Americans toward Palestine during the mid-nineteenth century. William C. Prime, editor-in-chief of the *New York Journal of Commerce*, who explored Palestine in 1855–66, followed up his journey with a well-received book, *Tent Life in the Holy Land.* With his Bible as his "only guide," Prime recalls that "Every step that I advanced on the soil of Palestine offered some new and startling evidence of the truth of the sacred story."[11]

The Holy Land did not live up to every traveler's expectation. Palestine's most famous nineteenth-century lay visitors, Herman Melville and Mark Twain, were both disillusioned with what they saw. Melville, who sailed into Jaffa harbor in January 1857 and spent nineteen days in the Holy Land, left the country with ambivalent feelings. His pilgrimage, according to his biographer, stemmed in part from a desire to learn about the land's biblical and Judaic past. Yet he was not enamored with what he experienced. Jerusalem, which had profoundly moved other travelers, disappointed him. Melville made frequent note of the poverty of Jerusalem's inhabitants and the ancient city's smelly streets strewn with trash. "All Judea seems to have been accumulations of this rubbish," he wrote in his diary.[12] Melville saw Palestine at its very worst, burdened with two thousand years of neglect, not yet touched by the Zionist revolution that in a few decades would begin to transform its landscape beyond recognition. Traveling in the 1850s, however, Melville did not find his journey exhilarating or spiritually elevating. "No country will more quickly dissipate romantic expectations than Palestine. . . . To some the disappointment is heart sickening," he recorded in his journal. Yet he could not drive the memory of his travels away from his mind.[13]

Melville detected faint signs of early Zionist stirring, but was skeptical about its ultimate outcome. He found the efforts of the Anglo-Jewish philanthropist Joseph Montefiore, on behalf of the few Jewish residents in Palestine, admirable, but unproductive. "The idea of making farmers of the Jews is vain," wrote Melville. "In the first place," he reasoned, "Judea is a desert with few exceptions. In the second place, the Jews hate farming," while a third obstacle stemmed from Arab and Turkish hostility. "The Jews dare not live outside walled towns or villages for fear of the malicious persecution of Arabs & Turks.—Besides, the number of Jews in Palestine is comparatively small, and how are the hosts of them scattered in other lands to be brought here? Only by a miracle."[14]

Mark Twain's account of his three-week tour of Palestine exposes even greater disappointment than Melville's. Twain sailed on a steamship from New York in 1867, joining what could have been the first boatload of seventy American tourists to the Near East. He was a thirty-one-year-old journalist whose reputation as an author of fiction was rising. His journey resulted in a widely read book, *The Innocents Abroad, or the New Pilgrims' Progress*, one of the most widely read travel accounts of the nineteenth century.

Together with seven companions Twain traveled overland from Beirut to Jerusalem. The soon-to-be famous American author was not happy with what he saw. The streets were too narrow, too crooked, he complained. "Lepers, cripples, the blind, and the idiotic, assail you on every hand. . . . Jerusalem is mournful, and dreary, and lifeless. I would not desire to live here."[15] The rest of the country, he lamented, was too barren, too small, no larger than an

American county, hardly the biblical land of milk and honey. The people—Arabs, Turks, and Jews, whom he tended to lump together—did not impress him. He could not understand how anyone could be impressed by such a place, and he was glad to leave.[16]

Mark Twain's religious skepticism colored his observations. In a series of lectures that he delivered after his return to the United States, he revealed little of the awe and reverence seen in the accounts of other American pilgrims. Toward pious travelers Twain could barely conceal his contempt.

> It is pretty safe, no doubt, to believe that from Abraham's time till now, Palestine has been peopled only with ignorant, degraded, unwashed loafers and savages. Arabs they were, they are, and always will be. . . . The difference between . . . an Arab to-day and an Israelite of old amounts to nothing, perhaps, than that you spell the nationality of the one with four letters and of the other with nine.[17]

Twain cared little for either the few Jewish inhabitants or the Arabs of Palestine. "Seen afar off," he wrote on another occasion, "the ancient children of Israel seem almost too lovely & too holy for this coarse earth; but seen face to face, in their illegitimate descendants, with no hope of distance to soften their harsh features and no glamor of sabbath-school glory to beautify them, they are like any other savage."[18] Yet in his own perverse way, Twain also could not tear his mind from the Holy Land. But unlike more orthodox observers, he found in the land of the Bible an oppressive burden which, like other liberals, he wished to wash away from America's religious sentiment.

2

It was more than an interest in antiquity, however, that drew American Protestants toward Zion. In some instances, a vigorous crusade to Christianize the Near East assumed an even higher priority. The task of bringing the gospel of Jesus to the non-Christian inhabitants of Palestine dominated the agendas of many Protestant churches of the nineteenth century.[19] The idea of dispatching missionaries to the Holy Land, a concept which first originated in England at the end of the eighteenth century, took root in the United States in 1810. In that year, the American Board of Commissioners for Foreign Missions, with its headquarters in Boston, was organized by New England Congregationalists. Supported by some of the wealthiest families of the region, as well as by other denominations of the Calvinist tradition, the American Board of Commissioners reflected the prevailing conviction that it was the sacred duty of New England's pious to spread the values of Christian America to all ends of the earth, especially to the inhabitants of the Holy Land.[20]

The first two missionaries dispatched by the American Board of Commissioners to Palestine were Levi Parsons and Pliny Fisk. Both were natives of Massachusetts and students at Andover Theological Seminary. Parsons and

Fisk, as well as the other early missionaries to the Holy Land, many of whom were recently ordained, were a dedicated group of young men. When they and their families arrived in Palestine early in the century they were prepared to face hardships and disappointments. They were well educated for their time. Many had attended the finest New England colleges. The majority were graduates of Andover, an institution founded by Congregationalists in 1808 to counteract the dangers of Unitarianism. Andover became the major American nursery for the preparation of missionaries to the Near East. Here, as David Finnie writes, the young seminarians arrived with the anticipation of spending their entire life "in a remote non-Christian land." Here they were taught that "the 'heathen' included not only pagans but Jews . . . and 'nominal' Christians." By 1845 about sixty of them left to reside in the primitive conditions of the Near East. Only two-thirds lived to return to the United States; the rest succumbed to disease and privation at a relatively young age. Levi Parsons, for example, overcome by illness, died in Alexandria in 1822 at the age of thirty.[21]

Since Ottoman law inflicted the death penalty upon any Muslim who converted to Christianity, missionaries soon learned to refrain from preaching the gospel to the Arabs. More tempting subjects were the "nominal" Christians of the eastern churches—the Greek Orthodox, Armenian Orthodox, and the Maronite and Lebanese Roman Catholics; they too were subjects for American Protestant salvation, as were Palestinian Jews.[22]

Missionaries were aware of the growing number of Jews migrating to the Holy Land by the mid-nineteenth century. These newcomers, however, were not the young Zionist pioneers that would shortly stream eastward from the ghettos of eastern Europe, but devout Jews who wished to spend their declining years upon hallowed ground. According to one missionary's report in 1847, many Jews "Old and Young, rich and poor, learned and unlearned, alike share in this fond longing for a final resting-place in Palestine.[23] Missionaries estimated at this time that an increasing number of Jews had entered Palestine following the Egyptian occupation of Syria in 1832: about 40,000 Jews inhabited the Holy Land by 1845, and most lived in the four holy cities of Jerusalem, Hebron, Tiberias, and Sephat. Jerusalem alone counted 10,000 Jews in 1845, prompting the contemporary admission "that the number of Jews now in Jerusalem is greater than at any other period in modern times."[24] One missionary marveled that in Jerusalem alone, of any place upon the earth, is "Hebrew spoken as a conversational language," and that "Most of the Jews are learned, and many spend the principal part of their time in studying scriptures or the Talmud, while others are engaged in discussing the law, and disputing in the synagogue, or in weeping over Jerusalem."[25]

In 1851 the Disciples of Christ, a Protestant movement organized in Kentucky in 1832, dispatched a missionary, James T. Barclay, to Jerusalem to preach to the Jews. However, his efforts to find converts, he lamented some years later, bore no fruit. "On the contrary, several Christians have actually gone over to the Moslem and the Jews!" he complained. Though despondent, Barclay insisted that "notwithstanding all the great discouragements, I can but regard Jerusalem as one of the most important missionary stations on earth."[26]

Barclay's experience with Palestine's pious Jews was typical of the reports received from other missionaries. Some, frustrated by their failures, found it difficult to conceal their annoyance, as did two Rhode Island missionaries who reported that after establishing an agricultural school (whose ultimate aim was to proselytize Jews), "The Jews would come, pretend to be touched & all that, get clothing & then—vanish. . . . they were very deceitful." "Not a single Jew was converted either to Christianity or Agriculture," they griped.[27] Speaking to a missionary in 1857, the American novelist Herman Melville was informed that "the Jews are lazy & don't like work," adding in disgust that the whole idea of converting Jews "is half melancholy, half farcical."[28]

Despite the puny results and the resentment of the Jewish inhabitants, missionary efforts persisted in Palestine. By the close of the 1880s, according to a historian of the missionary movement, American missionaries, anticipating a rapid growth of Jewish population, viewed the Holy Land as the most fertile territory for the conversion of Jews.[29]

3

Pilgrims, travelers, and missionaries were not the only Protestants drawn to the Holy Land in the nineteenth century. Religiously motivated individuals and groups not as easily classified were also pulled eastward. A few came to Palestine to establish permanent Christian colonies. Although most of these did not outlive the enthusiasm of their founders, they mirrored the importance of Zion in nineteenth-century Protestant thought.

One of the earliest of such Protestant adventurers was Clorinda Minor, who founded Mount Hope Colony in 1851. Situated three miles north of present-day Tel Aviv, it was the first American Christian settlement in Palestine. Minor was a disillusioned follower of William Miller, a Protestant visionary who convinced his flock of followers that the world would end in 1843. After turning for a while to Seventh-day Adventism, Minor became imbued with the certainty that it was her duty to help prepare the land of Israel for a Jewish return. It did not take her long to develop a warm and cooperative relationship with the Jewish inhabitants of Palestine.[30] In a letter to Isaac Leeser, with whom she corresponded regularly, Minor explained that the idea for the colony originated during biblical discussions with a few Chicago friends. Together they became convinced that the "time of the Gentiles was expiring, and the set time to favor Zion had come." Her millennial visions, however, did not prevent her from appreciating the physical risk under which Palestinian Jews resided. To survive, she explained to Leeser, the Jewish inhabitants would require the support of a strong power.[31] A short-lived experiment, the Mount Hope Colony established a precedent that other Christian Zionists would emulate.

Of these, one of the best known was the American Colony, established in Jerusalem in 1881. Its founders, Horatio and Anna Spafford, were devout and prominent Presbyterian laypersons from Chicago. They conceived the idea of a religious colony in Palestine in the wake of a series of personal tragedies, which began with the Chicago fire of 1871 and culminated with the drowning of their four daughters in 1873 and the death of their son from scarlet fever two years later.[32] In an attempt to emulate what they imagined was the communal experience of the first Christians and to hasten the Advent, which they believed was linked to a Jewish return, the Spaffords and their nineteen followers divested themselves of their financial assets and organized an association in which all property was to be held in common.[33]

In Palestine they offered their support to both Jews and Arabs, refrained from any aggressive attempts to proselytize among the local inhabitants, and took an interest in the agricultural development of the Holy Land. The American Colony has been credited with the introduction of eucalyptus trees to Palestine in 1883.[34] From the outset a friendly relationship was established between the Jews of Jerusalem and the Protestant residents of the American Colony. As one of the more successful Christian communal experiments, it continued in existence until it was dissolved in 1948, after the founding of the state of Israel.[35]

4

In one of the most unusual and celebrated cases the attraction of Zion proved so overwhelming that it resulted in a Christian conversion to Judaism. The convert was Warder Cresson, who was born in 1798 to a prominent Philadelphia Quaker family. Cresson was deeply affected by the religious and social fermentation of the early nineteenth century. Dissatisfied with the Quaker Community of Friends, whose wealth and social affectations he found hypocritical, Cresson began a search for spiritual answers that eventually drew him into the Shaker, Mormon, and Millerite movements respectively. Around 1840 Cresson met Philadelphia's leading rabbi, Isaac Leeser, whose views had a profound impact upon his own thinking.[36] Leeser's millennial outlook and his stress upon the future restoration of the Jews to Zion excited Cresson, as did the Zionist orientation of Mordecai M. Noah. These prominent Jews, both of whom showed little hesitation in communicating their opinions to Christian audiences, believed that a return of their people to the land of Israel was the only solution to contemporary Jewish problems. Cresson found such thinking compelling, for in his own mind it conformed with Christian millennial beliefs and linked Jewish restorationism to the Second Advent.[37]

Determined to participate in the inevitable eschatological drama and convinced that only by being physically present in the Holy Land could a Christian affect the realization of these biblical prophecies, Cresson left his family in Philadelphia and sailed for Jerusalem. As he indicated some years later: "In the Spring of 1844 I left everything near and dear to me on earth. I left the wife of my youth and six lovely children (dearer to me than my natural life), and an excellent farm, with everything comfortable around me. I left all these in the pursuit of truth."[38]

Cresson spent four years in Jerusalem, where from the very first he took an intense dislike to those Christian missionaries who preyed on unsuspecting Jews. Throughout his life Cresson waged a relentless battle against Christian zealotry. Unlike many missionaries to the Holy Land, he did not come to Palestine to witness to Jews, but to behold the Jewish restoration in accordance with God's promise. His ambition was, as Abraham Karp notes, "to participate in the Zionist fulfillment."[39]

Cresson's conversations with devout Jewish residents of Jerusalem and his growing knowledge of Judaism convinced him by 1847 to convert to the Jewish faith. In Judaism he found a religion that "satisfied his heart and was acceptable to his mind," a faith which he believed was superior to what he had gleaned from Christian teachings. "Why then the need of the vain attempt to set up a New Testament, or a New law," Cresson wrote some years later, "when the whole Marrow and principle has been set up for thousands of years before, in that most Holy and Divine law that can never be abrogated and finished, any more than God can be abrogated and finished."[40]

Following his conversion in March 1848, Cresson, who now adopted the new name of Michael Boaz Israel, decided to return to Philadelphia to settle his affairs and to attempt to persuade his family to return with him to Jerusalem. He looked forward to his American visit, to seeing his family once again and renewing old acquaintances. He hoped to convince his wife to follow him into his newly adopted faith. He expected some resistance from his family, but the storm that erupted surprised him. "I tried every way I could to convince my wife and family," he recalled, "and to conciliate my views with theirs, but this I found to be impossible, unless I would *abjure* or perjure myself, and deny the very foundation and greatest principle of my faith, which is the *Unity* of God."[41]

During his absence, he learned, his wife Elizabeth had left the Quaker Community of Friends and joined the Episcopalian church, becoming, as he put it somewhat contemptuously, a "believer in 'One God Being Three,' and in 'three *being one*'; that is, in a *Trinity*."[42] Even more ominous for Cresson was the revelation of his wife's efforts to use his conversion to Judaism as a pretext to pronounce him insane, thereby enabling her to assume possession of his property. "Finding the *prejudice* against me, because I was a Jew, increasing more and more every day," he later explained, "I thought it was high time to make some inquiry as to what had become of the proceeds of my farm, stock, and utensils." His wife, he discovered, to whom he had trustingly granted full power of attorney over their common holdings during his absence, refused to give him an accounting of his possessions. To restrain him further and to divest him of his property, his wife and son brought a charge of lunacy against Cresson, a charge which was upheld in a subsequent trial and proclaimed publicly in a court of law. The charge was supported not only by his immediate family, but also by the members of Philadelphia's Episcopal church, whose minds could not fathom how anyone who was not deranged would voluntarily convert to Judaism.[43]

Warder Cresson appealed the decision that declared him a lunatic, incompetent to handle his own affairs. Two years later, in 1851, the charge was overturned in a new court trial in Philadelphia. Despite his family's and its counsel's vigorous pleading to prove that Cresson's religious behavior was proof of mental instability, the jury handed down an acquittal. Pennsylvania's newspapers were almost unanimous in their support of the results of the new trial. The *Pennsylvanian* thought it strange that if a Jew turns to Christianity "It is all natural and proper . . . but if a Christian turns Jew, the man must be insane!" Likewise, the *Sunday Dispatch* commented that "We do not understand why a person who, after investigation, turns to the Israelitish faith, should not be permitted to do so without imputation of lunacy." The *Public Ledger* considered it important that the decision established once and for all "that a man's 'religious opinion' never can be made the test of his sanity."[44]

In 1852 Warder Cresson, more appropriately Michael Boaz Israel, now a devout Jew, returned to Palestine to work for its agricultural renaissance and to prepare for the return of the Jews to their ancestral home. Michael Boaz Israel lived in Jerusalem, where he remarried, raised a family, and emerged as a prominent member of the Jerusalem Sephardic community. When he died in 1860 he was buried on the Mount of Olives, a burial place reserved for prominent rabbis.[45] Cresson's life was symptomatic of the powerful pull that Zion had exerted upon the Protestant imagination.

5

An offshoot of evangelical Protestantism, the Church of Jesus Christ of Latter-day Saints, better known as the Mormon church, differed drastically in its structure and religious outlook from mainline Protestantism; yet its sense of the Holy Land's place in the culmination of human history had much in common with that of other evangelicals. This is not surprising, since its founder and Prophet, Joseph Smith, grew up early in the century in western New York, where he and his family were swept up by the religious enthusiasm of the Second Great Awakening. While his family, Smith recalled, "was proselyted to the Presbyterian faith," he, still in his teens, experienced a series of religious revelations that caused him to reject all of the known Christian creeds. Smith was also mysteriously directed to find and translate a message engraved upon a series of ancient plates, from which he composed the *Book of Mormon*, upon which the Mormon church was founded.[46]

From the very first the new American church, with its eclectic theology, proved to be enormously attractive. As Stanley Hirshson observes,

> the Saints borrowed doctrines from almost every available source. From Masonry came the Endowment, and from the Old Testament came plural marriages, the emphasis upon temples, and the belief in the gathering of all true believers in Zion, not Palestine but a suburb of Kansas City. The New Testament contributed Christ, who emerged from Mormon theology a polygamist, and the Twelve Apostles. And from idolatry the Saints took offerings for the dead and the supposedly magical power of Mormon rites. Here was a religion with something for everybody.[47]

But Smith's prophetic claims also generated suspicion and hostility from his Protestant neighbors. This forced him and his followers, who multiplied rapidly, to flee from their persecutors from place to place, generally in a westerly direction. Violence followed the Mormons wherever they planted their church. They escaped to Kirtland, Ohio, and from there to Independence, Missouri, and to Nauvoo, Illinois. While in jail in Carthage, Illinois, Joseph Smith was murdered. The mantle of leadership fell to his lieutenant Brigham Young, who marched his Saints further westward until they arrived at the valley of the Great Salt Lake. Here they established their settlement of Deseret.[48]

From the very first Mormons detected similarities between their own tragic history and that of the Jews. Like the Jewish people, the Mormons saw themselves as a peculiar people, persecuted and driven from their homes by the Gentiles. Like the Jews, they persisted in their religious convictions, determined to survive. Their eventual settlement in the desert of Utah, as Eldin Ricks notes, "adjacent to a saline lake . . . presented to their minds such an obvious parallel to the Dead Sea and the Sea of Galilee connected by the Jordan that the Mormon colonists named the river Jordan."[49] Such similarities between Mormons and Jews were not lost on their Protestant detractors, who derided the Mormon theocratic ecclesiastical organization, with its Temple and prophet at its helm, as "Judaic rather than Christian," a resurrection of the society of the ancient Israelites.[50]

Like the early Puritans, Mormon leaders were determined to master the Hebrew language and looked for Jewish teachers to instruct them.[51] "My soul delights in reading the word of the Lord in the original," Smith wrote in his diary, reminiscent of the exaltations of Cotton Mather or Ezra Stiles. "I am determined to pursue the study of the languages until I shall become a master of them."[52] In 1835, while the Mormons were in Kirtland, he and the Elders

engaged a Sephardic Jew, Daniel Maduro Piexotto, to teach Hebrew to the
Saints. Piexotto did not retain his post long and was followed by Josua Seixas,
an apostate son of Gershom Mendes Seixas of New York's Shearith Israel
synagogue. Seixas, a trained Hebrew scholar who had held academic posts at
Andover, Western Reserve, and Oberlin and was also the author of a well-
received Hebrew grammar, agreed to hold classes for forty Mormon students.[53]

Theologically, Mormon interest in Judaism was rooted in the *Book of Mormon*, the sacred document which lay at the heart of the Mormon church. It
purports to be a record of the dispersion of the Jews to America following the
destruction of their First Temple in Jerusalem in 588 B.C.E. It speaks of a Jewish
longing to be restored to their ancestral home in Judea and prophesies a Jewish
restoration to the Holy Land in accordance with God's covenant with the
children of Israel. And it exhorts all Gentiles to recognize the importance that
such a return portents for their own salvation. It also admonishes non-Jews to
refrain from anti-Jewish actions. "Yea, and ye need not any longer hiss, nor
spurn, nor make game of the Jews. . . . ye need not suppose that ye can turn
the right hand of the Lord unto the left."[54]

Interest in Jewish restoration received a high priority on the Mormon
agenda, and it was not dampened by the tribulations that they experienced
during their formative years. During the dedication ceremony for the completion of the Mormon Temple in Kirtland in 1836, Joseph Smith offered a prayer
for the Jews, beseeching Heaven that "the yoke of bondage may begin to be
broken off from the house of David and the children of Judah may begin to
return to the lands which thou didst give to Abraham, their father." Like other
Christians, Smith anticipated a Jewish restoration to Palestine as a prelude to
the coming of the Messiah.[55]

The Prophet's urge to hasten the restoration of the Jews accounts for his
desire, as stipulated in the *Book of Mormon*, to preach the gospel to them. In
this sense Mormons differed little from other Christian evangelists. The importance of witnessing to Jews first occurred to Smith in 1823, even before he had
formed his church. During the church conference of 1840 the Mormon Elders
agreed to dispatch one of their members, Orson Hyde, a close associate of
Joseph Smith, with instructions to establish a mission to the Jews in Jerusalem.
Stopping in England on his way to Palestine, Hyde contacted Solomon Hir-
schell, leader of the British Jewish community, to convince him of the importance of a Jewish return. Some weeks later, after seeing Jerusalem for the first
time, Hyde was overcome with emotion, recalling that "a storm of commin-
gling emotions suddenly arose in my breast, the force of which was only spent
in a profuse shower of tears." World conditions persuaded Hyde that a Jewish
return to Palestine was imminent, and he ventured the prediction in 1842
"that by political power and influence," the Jews "will be gathered and built up;
and further, that England is destined . . . to stretch forth the arm of political

power and advance in the front ranks of this glorious enterprise." That shortly after these utterances Hyde's daughter eloped with a Jewish lover to California may not be unrelated to her father's obsession with the future destiny of the Jewish people.[56]

Interest in a Jewish return did not abate after the murder of the Prophet. In 1845, a year after Smith's death, Brigham Young and the Council of Twelve Apostles of the Church of Jesus Christ of Latter-day Saints circulated a letter to world leaders, including those of the United States, informing them that Jews had been commanded to prepare for their restoration to Zion. Mormon prophecy continued in this vein throughout the remaining years of the nineteenth century. In 1879 Wilford Woodruff, a leading member of the church, observing the early stirrings of the Zionist movement, declared publicly that "the time is not far distant when the rich men among the Jews will be called upon to use their abundant wealth to gather the dispersed of Judah . . . and rebuild the holy city and temple. For the fullness of the Gentiles had come in, and the Lord has decreed that the Jews should be gathered from all the Gentiles' nations where they have been driven, into their own land."[57]

Mormons drew a distinction, however, between the Zion of America, which according to the *Book of Mormon* was reserved for the Saints, representatives of the tribe of Ephraim, and the Zion of the Jews, the land of Israel. As one Mormon put it, "The places of assembly are America and Palestine, the former . . . as the gathering of 'Ephraim and his fellows,' " while the "dispersed of Judah" will "migrate to and rebuild Jerusalem." Both events were linked in the unfolding drama of world salvation. As Rudolph Glanz writes, the return of the Jews to their homeland "would give the signal for the gathering of the Gentiles in the American Zion."[58] Providence had prepared different roles for Jews and Mormons.

6

Clearly, there was a significant segment of American Protestant thought, from the Puritans on, strongly influenced by the prophecies of the Old Testament, which linked the coming of the millennium with the restoration of the Jews to Zion. While the majority of early American Protestants saw themselves as the New Israel transplanted to the New World, the stage upon which the New Zion was destined to emerge, an articulate evangelical minority insisted on greater scriptural precision. For this group of Christian believers the Kingdom of God required the return of the Jews to their Promised Land. These Christian proto-Zionists, who might more appropriately be called restorationists, defined a new level of Jewish-Christian relationship in American Protestant culture.[59]

Restorationists, like premillennialists in general, believed that Christ's return will signal an abrupt end to this world and usher in the Last Judgment.

Although premillennialists disagreed about the details of the future scenario, they nevertheless shared a common outline of future events. Timothy Weber, a leading student of premillennialism, describes it as follows:

> Human society will grow worse and worse until the Antichrist will gain control, throwing the world into a reign of terror (the "tribulation") mainly directed against all those who will not recognize the divine pretensions. At the end of the tribulation, the reign of Antichrist will be destroyed at the Battle of Armageddon by the triumphant return of Christ. Having disposed of Antichrist and his forces and having bound the power of Satan, Christ will establish his millennial kingdom, which will end after a thousand years with an easily subdued revolt by Satan, the resurrection of the dead, the judgment, and the creation of a new heaven and a new earth.[60]

Because the restoration of the Jewish people to their homeland constituted a sign that the Second Advent was at hand, restorationists viewed it as an event of signal importance.

Restorationist ideas were not new, having evolved from the Reformation, the pietistic and Puritan movements of the sixteenth century. From Holland and England they were transmitted to the American colonies a century later, where they haunted the minds of religious thinkers. Jonathan Edwards, although he and other colonial theologians did not subscribe to a premillennialist eschatology, frequently speculated about the return of the Jews to their traditional homeland, in accordance with God's promise.[61] John Wesley, too, prayed that each Jew, "impelled by secret grace, His way to Canaan find."[62] Ezra Stiles speculated about the approximate year that the Jews will return to the Holy Land, build their third temple, and adopt Christianity in preparation for the Advent.[63] When in 1799 Napoleon Bonaparte, following his march into Palestine, offered to restore the Jews to their homeland, the evangelical imagination was electrified. Even the American secular press debated the Messianic implications of Napoleon's plans for Jewish restoration.[64] Missionaries dispatched to the Holy Land by the American Board of Commissioners for Foreign Missions frequently imagined themselves playing a role in the events about to unfold.

Thoughts about the expected restoration generated interest about the history of the Jewish people. Ethan Smith's *View of the Hebrews*, published in 1823, was a work designed to explore the biblical roots of the Jewish past and "the present state of the Hebrews," in order to better comprehend the significance of the impending restoration. A missionary from Vermont, Smith was certain that in accordance with biblical assurances, "the Jews are to be restored to Palestine as Jews. . . . And that the ten tribes of Israel will there be united with them."[65] *Niles' Weekly Register,* one of the most widely circulated early American periodicals, commented frequently on Christian millennial hopes.

In 1816 the *Register* predicted that should the Jews decide to migrate to the Holy Land, they would make its deserts blossom and its city of Jerusalem "rival the cities of the world for beauty, splendor and wealth." Almost anticipating the Zionist dream of Theodore Herzl more than a half century later, the *Register* urged Jews to "raise yourself from a thousand years' slumber. . . . Take your possession of the land of your Fathers; build a third time the temple of Zion, greater and more magnificent than ever. Trust in the Lord, who has led you safely through the vale of misery thousands of years, He also will not forsake you in your last conflict."[66]

Liberal-minded Jews, acculturated into American society, did not encourage such Christian prophetic musings; many even resented them. The more traditional minded, however, such as Isaac Leeser and Mordecai M. Noah, themselves given to messianic speculations, were less disturbed. Noah's Zionist exertions served as an inspiration to Christian millennialists. They sympathized with his appeal in 1824 that the United States take the lead in bringing about a Jewish return, thereby setting an example for the nations of the world. It is a Christian obligation to offer such support, declared Noah to a group of Christian listeners. "Are we not the only witnesses of the unity and omnipotence of God?" He reminded his audience of "the predictions of your apostles— you who believe in the second coming of the Son of Man—where is he to come to? By your own showing to Jerusalem, to Zion, to the beloved city of hope and promise."[67] Noah argued

that the great events connected with the millennium so confidently predicted in the Scripture, so anxiously desired by liberal and pious Christians, so intimately blended with the latter days—that consummation of a great and providential design in the union of the Jews and Gentiles —can alone be looked for *after* the restoration of the Jews to the land which the Lord gave them for an everlasting possession. It is your duty, men and Christians, to aid us peaceably, tranquil, and triumphantly to repossess the land of your Fathers, to which we have a legal, equitable, perpetual right, by a covenant which the whole civilized world acknowledges. . . . You believe in the second coming of Jesus of Nazareth. That second advent, Christians, depends upon you. It cannot come to pass, by your own admission, until the Jews are restored, and restored in their unconverted state.[68]

Jewish response to Noah's plea was far from enthusiastic. Some greeted it with ridicule and contempt. Isaac Leeser objected to a linkage of a Jewish messianic destiny with the hope of evangelical Christianity.[69] Noah, however, recognized quicker than most of his contemporaries the opportunity that grew out of Christian millennialism and exploited it for the benefit of his own Zionist objectives.

Noah presented his Zionist ideas to the Protestant world at a propitious moment, for by 1845 the evolution of millennial speculation had entered a new and important stage. In part, this was due to the innovative efforts of the Christian visionary William Miller. Born in Pittsfield, Massachusetts, in 1782, Miller, a close student of the *Book of Daniel*, calculated in 1818 that the world would end in twenty-five years. As a Baptist preacher, Miller delivered thousands of sermons, published numerous tracts, and organized a number of conferences designed to prepare believers for the Advent that was about to take place. Unlike other premillennialists, however, Miller rejected the prevailing notion of a Jewish return to Palestine, either before or after the Advent. Miller differentiated between the "natural" and "spiritual" Jews, viewing the former as the physical Jews who, because of their rejection of Christ, had forever forfeited their claim to the land of Israel. Only the latter, the New Israel, he contended, had inherited the biblical promises. This interpretation generated a vigorous debate among American Adventists, a good many continuing to insist on the physical restoration of the Jews as a precondition for the Second Coming.[70]

Unlike many Millerites, however, most premillennialists did not abandon the idea of a Jewish restoration. This was true of the largest group of all, which achieved prominence during the last quarter of the nineteenth century, the Dispensationalists.[71] Dispensationalism, founded by John Nelson Darby, an Englishman who died in 1882, grew out of a small Protestant sect in England and Ireland active during the 1820s, the Plymouth Brethren. Dispensationalists divided history into seven periods of time, or dispensations, each of which, in accordance with God's plan, was judged by different standards. Unlike Protestant postmillennialists, Dispensationalists were pessimistic about the world's future and lived with an anticipation of God's imminent return and intervention in world affairs. From the perspective of Jewish-Protestant relations, however, Dispensationalists drew a sharp distinction between the earthly people of Israel, the Jews, and the church, the spiritual Israel. While the former, they argued, were born into the covenant, the latter must undergo a new birth through conversion. Each of the two religious communities, they explained, was subject to a different destiny. During the millennium the spiritual church will be "raptured" away and will reign as the bride of Christ, while the Jews will be restored to their Promised Land and inherit the earthly kingdom. Before the Second Coming, however, all the nations, including the Jews, will be judged during the period of tribulation, after which Jesus and the Jewish remnant, who will recognize him as their Savior, will rule over the world from Jerusalem. From a spiritual perspective, therefore, Dispensationalists were sympathetic to a restoration of the Jews to Palestine and, not surprisingly, in later years developed a pro-Zionist outlook.[72]

Dispensationalism was introduced into the United States during the late 1840s. Darby, its founder, journeyed frequently to America and for a few years resided in the United States. While here he conducted religious discussions and organized Bible study groups with laypersons and clergy. He made numerous converts, especially among Presbyterians and Calvinist Baptists, both of which groups contributed the largest numbers to American Dispensationalism.[73]

Dispensationalist influence widened in the United States through the sponsorship of a series of "Prophetic" and premillennial conferences, five of which were convened before the outbreak of World War I. At each the issue of Jewish restoration was offered serious attention. Among the participants were some of the leading theological minds and church leaders of the orthodox Protestant community. Joining the first Prophetic Conference, which gathered in New York City in 1878, was Bishop W. B. Nicholson, of the Reformed Episcopal Church of Philadelphia. Nicholson spoke about "The Gathering of Israel" and raised the rhetorical question: "Is this restoration of Israel a foreshown fact in prophecy?" His affirmative response was underscored with the assurance that it "lies at the very centre of God's gracious purposes concerning the world."[74] He warned that before that momentous event would transpire Jews would be required to undergo a period of severe "chastisement and suffering," which when ended "will have reduced them to a remnant." That remnant will be returned securely and in a state of unbelief to Palestine, where the Jews would undergo a collective conversion to Christianity.[75]

Other speakers dilated on this theme. A few, such as Charles K. Imbrie, a minister from New Jersey, was unable to conceal a note of ambivalence about Jews, harping upon their collective guilt for the slaying of the Messiah, a sin which would soon be "blotted out" with their restoration and conversion. News of a Jewish return was particularly important to those in attendance, since their own and the entire world's redemption hinged upon that great event. "Israel's day of joy must first come in order for the coming of the day to the whole earth."[76]

The latter point was repeated at the Second International Prophetic Conference, held in Chicago in 1886. Here, Nathaniel West, minister of the First Presbyterian Church of St. Paul, Minnesota, delivered the keynote address, entitled "Prophecy and Israel." "The fortunes of the chosen people decide the fortunes of the world," thundered West as he set the theme of his talk.[77] As a Dispensationalist, West rejected the idea that the New Israel had displaced the chosen people, the Old Israel. No conditions were attached by God to his covenant with Abraham and his descendants, asserted West. Christians have not and never will take Israel's place, for the Jewish covenant with God is perpetual. "Israel, as such, can never be amalgamated or lose his right of primogeniture in the Kingdom of God." Yet Israel alone, underscored West, commands the power to bring salvation to the world. "The New Testament Kingdom of God, on earth, can not come in the shape foretold, until Israel's conversion." The obligation to draw the Jewish people into the body of Christ, which West imposed on those who came to hear his message, was clear.[78]

Later prophetic conferences in 1895, 1901, and 1914 coincided with the growth of the world Zionist movement and Theodore Herzl's efforts to organize a political program for Jewish restoration. These revolutionary activities generated enormous interest among Dispensationalists, who interpreted them in accordance with their own eschatological perceptions. Dispensationalists saw the Jewish national movement as a step toward the fulfillment of biblical promises and as concrete evidence that God had not forsaken the Jewish people.[79]

In at least one case a Dispensationalist, William E. Blackstone, imbued with Zionist fervor, attempted to put theology into practice by implementing a return of the Jews to Palestine. A successful Chicago businessman, Blackstone revealed his thinking regarding these matters in a small book, *Jesus is Coming*, which appeared in 1878. A Dispensationalist-premillennialist tract, it emphasized the Second Coming and the restoration of the Jews. As to be expected, Blackstone was also active in missionary activities and a founder of Chicago's Hebrew Mission in 1887. He was also a participant at the Second International Prophetic Conference in 1886.[80] A deeply religious man, Blackstone visited Palestine in 1888 and took an active concern in the desperate plight of the Jews of Russia. He concluded that nothing less than their immediate resettlement in the Holy Land would extricate them from the danger that they faced in Europe.

Upon his return to Chicago from Palestine, Blackstone organized a large mass meeting of Jews and Christians, the first such gathering ever held in the United States, to formulate a plan to restore the Jews to Palestine. On March 5, 1891, Blackstone visited Pres. Benjamin Harrison at the White House, where he presented to him a memorial which outlined his plan of resettlement. The memorial, signed by many prominent citizens, included such names as Melville W. Fuller, chief justice of the U.S. Supreme Court; Chauncey M. Depew, U.S. senator from New York; Thomas Reed, speaker of the House of Representatives; and William McKinley, representative from Ohio, later president of the United States. The document, sent to America's and Europe's heads of state, requested bluntly that Palestine be returned to the Jews "According to God's distribution of nations, it is their home—an inalienable possession from which they were expelled by force." The memorial went on to request that the president and his secretary of state use their good offices to invite the monarchs of Europe to join in an international conference to consider the plight of the Jews and their just claims to Palestine.[81]

Blackstone's proposal, however, did not receive the wide support of American Protestants, who, with some justification, wondered if Jews were at this time prepared to settle in Palestine. Actually, Zionist sentiment among American Jews was still in an embryonic stage in 1891; and Blackstone was disappointed at the unenthusiastic reception that his plan received in the American Jewish community. Understandably, even those Jews attracted to the call of Zion found it awkward to link their own aspirations with those of Dispensationalists seeking redemption through a Jewish restoration.[82] For all its intensity, Blackstone's efforts notwithstanding, the Christian yearning for a Jewish return had little to do with the Jewish search for cultural regeneration and national security.

9

At Ease in the
Gilded Age

1

During the closing decades of the nineteenth century, American Jews settled into what appeared to be a benign religious environment. The imperial ascendancy of American Protestantism, with the determined efforts of its evangelical wing to Christianize the nation, produced a bark more threatening than its bite. Religiously splintered, American Protestantism had reconciled itself, with a measure of reluctance to be sure, to a condition of spiritual divisiveness. "Is the existence of so many religious types and sects and creeds regrettable?" asked William James, the nation's most distinguished thinker, in 1902. "To this question I answer 'No!' emphatically."[1] No doubt, as Prof. John Higham writes, popular opinion was not yet prepared to embrace an idea of cultural "pluralism," assimilation being the ideal of the Gilded Age.[2] Still, the notion of religious diversity as a positive good was not unknown to nineteenth-century Americans. Historians of American religion, such as H. Richard Niebuhr, Sidney E. Mead, Will Herberg, Andrew M. Greeley, and Franklin H. Littell, have documented the pluralistic character of American religion. Andrew M. Greeley's assertion "that denominationalism is a central characteristic of American religion" and Will Herberg's comment that "The unity of American life is indeed a unity of multiplicity" recognize the importance of this principle in American culture.[3] It was a deeply imbedded liberal ideal with which Jews were able to live comfortably.

Even more so than American Protestants, Jews were well versed in the meaning of religious differences. As a minority Jews had long been surrounded by alien faiths with which they were forced to learn to live. Neither was religious debate altogether shunned within their own community. Judaism had never been a monolithic system of belief, even though, as in Protestantism, a few of its adherents would have liked to make it so. Generally, the more enlightened Jewish leaders encouraged an examination of the sacred sources of the tradition and the search for independent conclusions. Differences of opinion about religious and ethical matters that had caused controversy and divisiveness abounded throughout Jewish history.[4] The splintered American religious condition, the independence enjoyed and cherished by many Protestant groups, and the fierce religious individualism of many of its members made good theological sense to many American Jews.

The Liberal, or Reform, movement in American Judaism matured during the Gilded Age. Under the leadership of Isaac M. Wise an organizational structure had been erected that stood the test of time and guaranteed to the movement permanency. It included the founding in 1873 of what would shortly become its national organization, the Union of American Hebrew Congregations. Two years later, Hebrew Union College was established in Cincinnati, which began to prepare a pool of Liberal rabbis. To provide a forum for the movement's leadership, the Central Conference of American Rabbis was founded in 1889.

Throughout the latter years of the nineteenth century, Reform Judaism continued to conform to the religious conditions imposed upon it by its upwardly mobile, rapidly Americanized membership. With the Jewish community numbering nearly 250,000 by 1880, and a growing amount of it dispersed throughout the small cities of the Middle West, rigorous observance of traditional standards declined. As in Protestantism, new intellectual currents in evolutionary thought and biblical scholarship further weakened traditional observance.

It is ironic that while American Judaism declined in orthodox standards it saddled itself with unprecedented prophetic responsibilities. Reform rabbis of the Gilded Age became increasingly conscious of their "mission" to transmit to the world the moral and ethical values of monotheism. The dispersion of Israel, long considered a heavenly burden to be patiently born, was now inverted into a providential opportunity, a blessing to Israel for the sake of mankind. By the end of the century some Reform rabbis even suggested that Jews, like Christians, should undertake missionary work.[5]

No document expressed more succinctly the ideology that guided Liberal Judaism during the late nineteenth century than the one produced by eighteen American rabbis who gathered near Pittsburgh in November 1885. For the next fifty years their eight-point declaration, known as the Pittsburgh Platform, was considered the most authoritative statement of the theology and practice of Reform Judaism.

In one respect it was an optimistic document, reflecting the confident, almost euphoric, mood of the Gilded Age. That the statement was drafted near Pittsburgh was symbolic of the westward, progressive tilt of Reform. Centrally located, the conference was designed to bring together Jewish representatives from all geographic regions.[6] Kaufman Kohler, rabbi of New York's

Temple Beth El and a leading theoretician of Reform Judaism, was the chief engineer behind the conference. In large part it was because of his initiative that the gathering convened, and much of the substance of the final statement was based upon Kohler's introductory proposals. Kohler arrived at the meeting determined to persuade his colleagues that only through drastic adjustments would Judaism continue to thrive on American soil. His dissatisfaction with the state of late nineteenth-century Judaism was evident in his opening lament. "Every one," he declared, "who has watched the condition of affairs of Judaism in general and in our country in particular, must have been impressed with the urgent need of decisive action in view of the appalling indifference which has taken hold of the masses. . . . Our younger generation grow daily more estranged from our sacred heritage. . . . We are visibly losing our prerogatives as a holy 'nation.' "[7]

Following his jeremiad Kohler presented ten proposals that after deliberation were reduced to eight principles. That the authors were well versed in modern biblical science was evident in their rejection of the divine authorship of the Holy Scriptures and other supernatural biblical assertions. Neither did they accept as binding the biblical ceremonial laws, "except those that elevate the sanctity of our lives." Jewish dietary laws were dismissed as outmoded, for, as the rabbis put it, they failed "to impress the modern Jew with a spirit of priestly holiness; their observance in our day is apt rather to obstruct than further modern spiritual elevation."[8] The formulators of the Pittsburgh Platform referred frequently to Israel's sacred obligation to convey a moral light to the world. "In view of the messianic end and object of Jewish history, we feel bound to do our utmost . . . to make our religious truth and our sacred mission understood to all and appreciated by all, whether Jew or Gentile," read the ninth principle. Although no reference was made to the prospect of launching a crusade to convert Christians to Judaism, a logical expectation of those who believed themselves bound by a missionary obligation, the subject, to which one afternoon was devoted, did occupy the minds of the participants. It dramatized the rabbinical confidence in the potential attractiveness of their revised faith, and in the security of the American religious milieu, which found such considerations socially acceptable.[9]

2

These radical suggestions, however, were not universally welcomed. The theology of the Pittsburgh Platform was particularly distasteful to the newer arrivals, the thousands of eastern European Jews who flocked to the United States at the end of the nineteenth century. Reform Judaism's radical break with tradition represented a breach with the past too drastic for their comfort. Even the more enlightened among them, although prepared for religious change, preferred to move more cautiously. Raised in traditionally orthodox homes, their practice of Judaism demanded a greater continuity with the past than that which was being made available in the Liberal agenda. Caught between their loyalty to traditional forms and the social requirements of the new era, they devised what would shortly be known as the Conservative movement, or the Historical School, in American Judaism.

Anti-Reform sentiment had been visible earlier in the century; it was reflected in the writings of Isaac Leeser and his Philadelphia successor, Rabbi Sabato Morais. Alexander Kohut, a Talmudic scholar from Hungary who arrived in New York in 1884, added his warning of the danger that such radical departures presented to the integrity of Judaism. "A Reform which seeks . . . progress without the Mosaic-rabbinical tradition," declared Kohut, "is a deformity—a skeleton without flesh and sinew, without spirit and heart. It is suicide." While opponents of Reform recognized that the times required religious change, still they demanded that religious alterations not break the historical continuity that Judaism maintained with its rabbinic past. Proponents of Conservatism did not believe that conformity with a Protestant environment necessitated the uprooting of Judaism from its *Halachik* (legal and biblical) moorings.[10]

The foundation for the Conservative movement was laid in 1886 when a group of traditionalist leaders joined by a number of disillusioned Reformers established the Jewish Theological Seminary. Located at first in Cooper Union in New York City, the school was designed to offset the influence of Hebrew Union College by training rabbis and teachers in the more traditional beliefs of Judaism. Its early presidents, Sabato Morais and especially Alexander Kohut, helped fashion a new curriculum that within a few years promulgated what would be known as the Conservative movement in American Judaism, although its educational mission clearly bore the imprint of the Jewish Theological Seminary of Breslau, a nursery of great European rabbis and historical Judaism. Like the Breslau institution, whose name it bore, the New York seminary stressed not only Talmudic learning but also biblical studies, Jewish history, and philosophy. With the founding of the movement's lay organization in 1913, the United Synagogue of America, and its professional organization, the Rabbinical Assembly, in 1918, a new and separate bureaucracy had emerged within American Judaism.[11] Even more so than Reform, despite its Germanic roots, Conservative Judaism represented an attempt by more traditional-minded American Jews to conform to a society permeated with Protestant religious practices.

It was not until 1927, however, that a unifying plan for the Conservative movement was overwhelmingly endorsed by the members of the Rabbinical Assembly. Its spirit was revealed in an address given that year by Louis Finkelstein, president of the Jewish Theological Assembly. Finkelstein explained why Conservatism found itself compelled to straddle past and present: "Because on the one hand we regard the laws of the Torah as prophetically inspired and because on the other we regard the legalism of the rabbis as the finest and highest expression of human ethics, we accept both the written and oral Law as binding and authoritative on ourselves and on our children after us." At the same time, Finkelstein conceded that the rabbinic codes were not cast in stone, that fresh innovations and new interpretations were bound to arise. "There is none of us," he declared, "so bigoted as to refuse to cooperate with those who are attempting them, provided always that the ultimate purpose of the change is to strengthen the attachment of Israel to the whole of the Torah, and that it does not defeat its own end by striking at the fundamentals of Judaism."[12] Finkelstein's comments signified a sharp departure from the premises of Reform. Although he accepted the need for change, he also gave good reasons for Conservatism's hesitancy to pursue it.

3

Orthodoxy was not uncommon in early nineteenth-century American Judaism, but as a by-product of the heavy immigration of the late nineteenth century, the most traditionally oriented dimension of American Judaism came into its own during the 1880s. Beyond New York and Philadelphia, Orthodox congregations with an eastern European orientation were relatively inconspicuous during the earlier years of the nineteenth century. The founding of Beth Hamidrash Hagadol in New York City in 1852 by a small group of Russian Jews represented one of the early exceptions. By 1900, however, 300 eastern European Orthodox synagogues were in existence in New York City alone, although many had only a handful of members.[13] Orthodox immigrants brought with them traditions and customs, including the Yiddish language, which had been part of their evolving culture for a number of centuries. Their religious and theological outlook differed profoundly from that seen in Reform and Conservatism. Robert Gordis's succinct distinction among the three branches of Judaism is illuminating: "Reform declared that Judaism has changed throughout time and that Jewish law is no longer binding. Orthodoxy denies both propositions, insisting upon the binding character of Jewish law and negating the view that Judaism has evolved. Conservative Judaism agrees with Orthodoxy in maintaining the authority of Jewish Law and with Reform that Judaism has grown and evolved through time."[14]

Like their rivals, Orthodox Jews developed an institutional structure that maintained a semblance of ecclesiastical order. In 1887 they established the Etz Chaim Talmudic Academy, and in 1897, the Rabbi Isaac Elchanan Theological Seminary, the first center for advanced Torah study in the United States. The two educational institutions merged in 1915 to form the nucleus of Yeshiva University, the chief center of higher learning for American Jewish Orthodoxy. In 1902 American Orthodox rabbis formed their own professional organization, the Union of Orthodox Rabbis of the United States and Canada. Unity, however, was no more assured to Orthodoxy than it was to other American religious constituencies. After 1912 the ultra-Orthodox organization Agudath Israel branched out from Poland, where it was founded, to the United States, where it quickly divided the Orthodox movement.[15]

Of the three divisions in American Judaism, Orthodoxy found it most difficult to accept the reality of American life. It tried desperately, at first, to insulate itself from the openness, voluntarism, and religious laxity with which it found itself surrounded. The first Orthodox rabbis who arrived in the United States from eastern Europe were repelled by the thought of religious compromise, preferring rather to isolate themselves from the world around them. The renowned scholar Rabbi Jacob Joseph, who was brought to New York from Vilna in 1887 by a group of traditionalists, found it almost impossible to adjust to American conditions. Even Orthodox Jews were reluctant to accept his rigorous rulings.[16] This was equally true of another outstanding Talmudic scholar, Russian-born Rabbi Jacob David Willowski, who was called to Chicago in 1903 by its Orthodox community. Willowski was unable to sympathize with the reluctance of Americans to transport Europe's religious patterns unchanged to America's Midwest. At one time Willowski rebuked a gathering of rabbis for migrating to America, a country which he described as an "unclean land." Disillusioned, he left the United States one year after his arrival.[17]

Yet, with time, Orthodoxy learned to make compromises with American culture. Such accommodations began with the earlier Sephardic leadership and continued with the work of Isaac Leeser and, later, with the efforts of Rabbi Bernard Drachman, who in 1889 assumed the pulpit of New York's small congregation Zichron Ephraim. Drachman believed that traditional Judaism should and could live harmoniously in the United States. He assisted eastern European youngsters to learn to exist both as Americans and as Jews, being convinced that uncompromising orthodoxy would inevitably fail to survive in the American environment. It was not until the 1920s, however, that Orthodox Judaism learned to make the necessary adjustments that enabled it to grow into an acceptable branch of American Judaism.[18]

4

If one considers the distance that many Jews traveled from traditional Judaism by 1900, Orthodox anxieties were not unfounded. Despite the growth of Jewish population, which increased to about one million by 1900, American Judaism was also marked by apathy and indifference.[19] In the middle-class neighborhoods of New York, Christmas trees adorned many Jewish homes, which prompted Felix Adler to complain in 1869: "Let us speak plainly and without metaphor. To celebrate a day which has cost us so much pain, so much blood, so many sorrowful experiences with joy and merriment—is this not a bitter and cruel mockery? However much we may esteem our Christian neighbors, however highly we may honor their institutions, we are Jews and we have our own history, our own remembrances of the past."[20] Jewish indifference was even more striking outside New York City. In Rochester, New York, by the end of the century, Jewish holidays were ignored and the bar mitzvah (male confirmation) ceremony was abolished. In Atlanta dietary laws were disregarded, and every effort was made to strip Judaism of its "foreignness."[21]

The Pittsburgh Platform of 1885 was in itself an illustration of the burden that an ancient faith had imposed upon a group of American Jews pulled by the currents of their age. A few presented a serious challenge to the integrity of traditional Jewish values. George L. Berlin reminds us that Josephine Lazarus, sister of the poet Emma Lazarus, agreed with liberal Protestants that Judaism had outlived its usefulness, that it had lost its spiritual strength. Much to the annoyance of her coreligionists, Lazarus had accepted the Christian dichotomy between Law and Love. She proposed that Judaism and Christianity merge into a new faith, one in which Christian Love would serve as a moderating influence upon Jewish Law. In another instance, Harris Weinstock, a California Jewish communal leader, requested the Central Conference of American Rabbis to include the life and teachings of Jesus in the curriculum of its religious schools. As an outstanding Jewish teacher of his generation, argued Weinstock, Jesus belongs in Jewish history. Weinstock reflected a tendency on the part of a group of Liberal rabbis to adopt Jesus as their own. Their motive was to universalize and Americanize Judaism. "The stress on the Jewish nature of Jesus and on his ethical message," according to Berlin, "was the means by which the Reformers undermined the liberal Protestant claim for the uniqueness and superiority of Christianity." Now that the Jewishness of Jesus was clearly advertised, Judaism could claim equality, if not superiority, to Christianity, and it could qualify as an American religion.

A handful of rabbis went further. On Reform's radical fringe some wondered if to remain Jewish was in their own or society's best interest. Like radical Protestants they aspired toward a universal religion. Solomon Schindler, for example, rabbi of Boston's congregation Adath Israel, dreamed of a new religion, neither Christian nor Jewish, but one which would encompass elements of all the major faiths. Judaism, he believed, because of its rationalism and flexibility, would flow easily into this new faith. In accordance with his radical idealism, Schindler encouraged his congregants to intermarry with liberal Protestants, a recommendation which divided his congregation. Strongly influenced by the transcendental and democratic ideals of Emerson and Parker, Schindler resigned his rabbinical post in 1893 to form an interdenominational church where he could preach and practice these ideals. Although in 1911 Schindler recanted his extreme behavior, others, such as the Boston Reform

Rabbi Charles Fleischer, who stepped out of Judaism also in 1911 to devote his time to social and other universal concerns, did not.[22]

The most celebrated apostate of the Gilded Age was Felix Adler, the son of Samuel Adler, esteemed rabbi of New York's Temple Emanu-El. In 1876 Felix Adler decided to leave Judaism and establish a universal and creedless faith, stripped of its theism and ceremonial and ritualistic trappings, one which was more consistent with the ethical and moral requirements of modernity. He saw no point in the continued existence of Judaism, which he viewed as obsolete. Judaism, he argued, as did many liberal Protestants of his day, had served its usefulness. Even its prophets, he observed, "predicted the time when their people would be relieved of their separate mission." For Adler, religion's principal purpose was not to obey God, but to inspire its followers to live ethical lives and perform acts of redeeming social value. Accordingly, he named his new faith, which he founded in 1877, "Ethical Culture."[23]

It is quite probable that Ethical Culture reflected the outlook of many assimilated American Jews who were embarrassed by their tradition. Membership in the society, which included many Jews, offered those who were eager to hasten the process of assimilation and Americanization an ecclesiastical endorsement, without having to undertake a full-blown commitment to Protestantism. Prof. Benny Kraut points out perceptively that by ridding Judaism of its ancient religious forms, by doing away with its theism, rites, and ceremonies, and by inviting Jews to leave its tradition, Ethical Culture brought the work of Reform Judaism to its logical conclusion.[24]

Jewish indifference to hallowed forms during the Gilded Age was also evident in their readiness to adopt a Sunday-Sabbath, a radical practice that began among Reform Jews in Germany. The idea generated even greater interest after it was introduced into the United States. Here, religious freedom, coupled with a six-day work week, made Sunday services appear as an appropriate solution to declining synagogue Sabbath attendance. First introduced in 1854 at the Har Sinai Temple in Baltimore, the practice spread to other communities. In 1870 Sunday-Sabbath services were conducted by Rabbi Samuel Hirsch at the Kenesseth Israel Temple in Philadelphia. Felix Adler helped to popularize the idea by offering a series of Sunday lectures to an overflowing crowd during the mid-seventies in New York's Carnegie Hall. Indeed, with the rising popularity of the sermon, rabbis preferred to preach to larger audiences that were unattainable on the Jewish Sabbath. Some of the leading Reform rabbis—Kaufman Kohler, Joseph Krauskopf, David Philipson, and Emil Hirsch—supported the movement, although the first three did so with some hesitancy, during the closing decades of the century.[25]

Sunday worship generated debate and soul-searching within the lay and clerical Jewish community. Traditionalists were alarmed at the trend and viewed it as a threat to the very existence of Jewish identity in the United States. On this matter even Isaac M. Wise parted company with his more radical colleagues. Yet both the president and secretary of the National Council of Jewish Women denounced the traditional Sabbath service as antiquated and urged that it be replaced by Sunday, so that Jews would conform to a universal day of worship and rest.[26]

The debate, which was carried to the Pittsburgh Conference in 1885, also reflected a divided mind. An opinion frequently voiced by Sunday supporters was that American Jews had reached such a deplorable state of religious decline that only Sunday worship-services would effect their spiritual regeneration. However, not enough votes were mustered in Pittsburgh for the idea to achieve official approval. Rabbi Emil G. Hirsch, one of the most persistent defenders of the Sunday-Sabbath, who had moved from Philadelphia to Chicago's Har Sinai Temple, saw Sunday worship as an opportunity to make the Jewish Sabbath more intelligible to non-Jews, many of whom, he reported, had become regular listeners to his sermons. "Judaism is not known by our neighbors," pleaded Hirsch in 1895. "The Sunday service has in our experience in Chicago been a most potent factor in this campaign of education." He had spoken on Sundays, Hirsch claimed triumphantly, "to hundreds of non-Jews about Judaism."[27]

Lacking dynamic rabbinical leadership, or confronting a determined opposition, other communities were unable to emulate Chicago's success. In Rochester, New York, a weekly newspaper, *Jewish Tidings* (the title had a christological ring), first published in 1887 to represent the voice of radical Reform, launched a vigorous crusade on behalf of the advocates of the Sunday-Sabbath. To its critics the *Tidings* replied that "The sentiment of Jews today demands such a change in the day of worshipping the Almighty as will best conform with their habits of life and business. Hence the change must come in spite . . . of the foolish veneration for an antiquated day."[28]

Despite its efforts, the *Tidings* failed to persuade many prominent Jews, including Louis Marshall, a well-known Syracuse attorney, and Cyrus Adler, who became president of the Jewish Theological Seminary. Adler regretted that Jews, in their eagerness to acculturate, were so quick "to yield the religious tie." "It is in my mind a fatal mistake," he told Reform Jews, whom he blamed largely for this tendency.[29] Although for a while the movement appeared to be heading toward victory, the arrival of many Russian Jews and the introduction of the five-day week shortly after persuaded even its strongest supporters to return to the traditional Sabbath.[30] The entire controversy symbolized in a dramatic way the distance American Jews were prepared to travel from their traditional practices in order to conform to a Protestant model.

An intense desire to integrate also explains the attraction that membership in the Masonic fraternity held for many American Jews during the Gilded Age.

In his study of San Francisco's Freemasonry, Tony Fels underscores the unusual opportunity that such membership provided for Jews and Protestants to mingle socially. Few clubs in the United States, other than Masonic fraternities, admitted Jews. For a variety of reasons, explains Fels, Jews felt at ease in this fraternity. The monotheistic and moral dimension of the Masonic Order, an organization that was not particularly Christian or evangelical, appealed to Jews, as did its religious outlook, which was more akin to rational than evangelical Protestantism. In its ceremonial language and ritualistic practices Freemasonry identified itself with biblical Israel; and its humanitarian, universal, and cosmopolitan outlook, as well as its anti-Catholicism, supplied ingredients not altogether unappealing to liberal American Jews. Not surprisingly, although Jews comprised about eight percent of the Bay City's population at the end of the century, Fels found that twelve percent of the city's Masonic fraternity was Jewish.[31]

The enthusiastic approval with which many Jews greeted the American declaration of war against Spain in 1898 can also be seen as a measure of the progress of their acculturation, and their desire for acceptance. Isaac M. Wise considered the Spanish-American War a crusade for American values, a necessary sacrifice which pitted enlightened, democratic forces against a medieval, backward, Roman Catholic civilization. "If nothing else comes of this turmoil," editorialized the Cincinnati rabbi in his *American Israelite,* "it has shown that Anglo-Saxonism, Protestantism, Americanism, Free-Masonry, and Judaism are common objects of hatred in Paris and Vienna and St. Petersburg, just as they are in Madrid and Havana. It is the lower civilization against the higher." His was the kind of rhetoric that was frequently duplicated in Protestant magazines; for many Protestants continued to nurture the Black Legend of Spanish-Catholic corruption. They saw the war as an opportunity to evangelize a backward Spanish empire. Like many Protestants, Wise interpreted the quick defeat of the enemy as a vindication of American ideals. He attributed Spain's capitulation to its established Roman Catholic church, and America's victory to its free religious environment.[32]

The pride and patriotism that American Jews evinced at the turn of the century was dramatized in 1905 when they celebrated the 250th anniversary of their settlement in America. Held in New York's Carnegie Hall, the celebration included a major address by ex-President Grover Cleveland, in which he assured his listeners that Jews have "been more influential in giving shape to the Americanism of to-day" than any other ethnic group. This sentiment was confirmed by a message forwarded to the gathering from Pres. Theodore Roosevelt, who was unable to attend the festivities. Roosevelt's conviction that American Jews "have become indissolubly incorporated in the great army of American citizenship" must have pleased the gathering, whose pursuit of assimilation had always assumed the highest of priorities.[33]

But the integration toward which Jews aspired possessed its impassible limit. Robert Gordis, a leading voice of Conservative Judaism, explains that "From the days of the French Revolution to the present, the ideal which most modern Jews have sought, and not always found, is integration without assimilation and acculturation without absorption."[34] The problem that Jews faced was inherent in the very nature of Jewishness itself. In the process of their quest for acculturation, American Jews were unprepared to deny their own uniqueness, their own chosenness. Yet the concept of a special election, as Arnold M. Eisen, professor of Jewish religious thought at Stanford University, so ably reminds us, has never sat too comfortably in a democratic context. "It was one thing to call oneself a 'chosen people' when religious barriers or ghetto walls reinforced the collective sense of being 'a people that must dwell alone.' But it was quite another to claim chosenness in the new chosen land of America, where Jews wanted nothing so much as the chance to be a part of the larger society."[35]

Yet chosenness was hardly an alien doctrine for non-Jewish Americans. The Puritans had inherited this biblical notion and had bequeathed it to all Americans, who, like the Jews, believed that their nation was chosen by Providence for a special destiny. "What better way was there for the promotion of Jewish integration into American life," asks Eisen, "than by trumpeting a symbolic definition of self which Jews and Americans shared?" The difficulty Jews faced "was to arrive at a balance between exclusivity and participation, continuous with Jewish tradition and acceptable to America."[36]

American Jews found their way out of this dilemma by redefining the meaning of election, the central thought in Jewish theology. For American Jews of the Gilded Age, chosenness came to represent a harmonious relationship between the ideals of democracy and the values of Judaism. Jews denied that any conflict existed between the two. As they saw it, both Jews and American Protestants inherited a common election, a shared responsibility, a mission, to transmit their lofty ideals to all of mankind.[37]

5

Assimilated American Jews viewed with suspicion any event that might retard the progress of their acceptance as equal partners in their adopted land. Consequently they viewed ambivalently the arrival of 500,000 Jews from eastern Europe between 1881 and 1900. The newcomers' poverty, lack of secular learning, religious orthodoxy, or socialist leanings appeared to them as obligations, a threat, and an embarrassment. Isaac M. Wise at times sneered at their Yiddish "jargon" and their comportment, which he categorized as "semi-Asiatic" and "medieval." In one of his most intense diatribes, Wise fulminated: "It is next to an impossibility to associate or identify ourselves with that half-civilized orthodoxy. . . . We are Americans and they are not. . . .

We are Israelites of the nineteenth century and a free country and they gnaw the dead bones of past centuries."[38]

Wise's sentiments were to some degree shared during the 1880s by other leaders of America's German-Jewish well-heeled establishment. Some even sided with New England patricians in a demand to place limits upon eastern European immigration. The United Hebrew Charities, organized in 1874 for the purpose of providing economic relief to needy American Jews, recommended that recent arrivals who appeared to be unemployable be returned to their country of origin or repatriated to other countries. Similarly, the Hebrew Emigrant Aid Society of New York City, formed in 1881 and also staffed by older settlers, requested that limits be set upon Jewish immigration. *The American Hebrew*, one of the most widely read Anglo-Jewish weekly magazines published in New York City at the end of the century, supported such recommendations.[39]

In expressing such views Americanized Jews exposed their fear of the danger that a large number of new arrivals might pose to the progress of their integration. The presence of a mass of unassimilated Jews, so unlike themselves in their religious and social habits, caused them discomfort. They feared that their own social ascent would be imperiled by the new arrivals and were concerned that non-Jewish Americans might mistake the appearance and behavior of these newcomers as being typical of all Jews. It was not until the mid-nineties, when American Jews became deeply aware of the extent of the Russian brutality to which their European coreligionists were being exposed, that their sense of obligation toward them was awakened. By 1900 many American Jews had reversed their initial support for immigration restriction.[40]

The emergence of political Zionism, buttressed by the ideological fervor of new immigrants, also made assimilated American Jews uneasy. The reason was clear: they feared that a national movement could invalidate their ultimate desire to achieve full integration in their adopted land. They were concerned that Zionism might cast a shadow of doubt upon the genuineness of their intention to amalgamate. Furthermore, for those attuned to the ideology of Reform, and in some cases even Conservatism, Zionism collided with their efforts to universalize the image of Judaism, to strip away any remnants of its particularity. Israel's "great messianic hope," declared the authors of the Pittsburgh Platform in no uncertain terms, was "the establishment of the Kingdom of truth, justice, peace among all men." Its current mission transcended its national past, which Reformers believed they had outgrown. "We consider ourselves no longer a nation but a religious community, and therefore expect neither a return to Palestine . . . nor the restoration of any of the laws concerning the Jewish state."[41]

Ever since the genesis of the Reform movement, its leadership had insisted that America was its Promised Land. The United States, the finest sovereign specimen to appear on the stage of modern history, was the most fitting land to qualify as Israel's new Zion. Liberal Jews were distressed at the suggestion that they should think of the Holy Land as a political haven. In his old age, Isaac M. Wise characterized modern Zionism as an unfortunate mutation, an outgrowth of European antisemitism, which he insisted was a transient tendency. The dispersion of the Jews (whom he did not consider a nation, but a religious community), traditionally viewed as a misfortune, was to Wise and other Reformers a blessing and an opportunity to spread the idea of ethical monotheism. Wise considered the frequently repeated prayer for the restoration of a Jewish kingdom sinful.[42]

Not only political Zionism, but cultural Zionism, the idea that Zion would serve as the spiritual and cultural source for universal Judaism, was equally threatening to some American Jews. To admit that American Judaism would require cultural direction from Palestine, observes Michael A. Meyer, "amounted to an admission of failure." America, not Palestine, was "the leading edge of the Judaism of the future, the focal point of spiritual development."[43]

Cultural or political Zionism was an anathema to a number of Liberal rabbis. David Philipson confessed in his autobiography that "The two main articles of my life's creed have been liberal Judaism and Americanism. I have constantly defined myself as an American of the Jewish faith." Jewish nationalism was an unacceptable doctrine to this Liberal leader. "To my mind," he writes, "political Zionism and true Americanism have always seemed mutually exclusive. No man can be a member of two nationalities." To Philipson, the Jewish nation had come to an abrupt end with the destruction of the Second Temple by Roman armies in 70 A.D. At that moment "the nation's work was finished. . . . when the day of dispersion came Israel ceased to have a national existence, it began its Messianic career."[44]

This kind of thinking was not uncommon among American Jewish Liberals. Jacob Voorsanger, a leading rabbinical figure in San Francisco and a close friend of Wise, was in full agreement with the anti-Zionist views of his colleagues. Like Wise, Voorsanger categorized Zionist sentiment as an "oriental" aberration transported to America by recent immigrants. He considered the Jewish people "a spiritual concept rather than a physical reality," whose primary function was to convey a prophetic message to mankind, a task which would be sabotaged by misguided Zionists. He also feared that the Zionist movement would obstruct the Americanization of recent immigrants and expose Jews to the unpatriotic charge of dual loyalty. Zionism, he believed, was a dangerous doctrine that would retard the full integration of Jews into American society. When the opportunity arose, Voorsanger never failed to assure his non-Jewish friends that American Jews were not sympathetic to the idea of Jewish nationalism.[45]

The appearance of Theodore Herzl's *Der Judenstaat* (*The Jewish State*) in 1896 and the convening of the First Zionist Congress in Basel, Switzerland, in the following year were disquieting events for Liberal American Jews. The Central Conference of American Rabbis denounced Herzl's proposals, proclaiming that "the object of Judaism is not political nor national, but spiritual."[46] Some months later, the lay wing of American Reform, the Union of American Hebrew Congregations, expressed similar sentiments at its annual meeting. "We are unalterably opposed to political Zionism. The Jews are not a nation but a religious community. . . . America is our Zion." Such sentiments included not only Reform opinion but a segment of Conservative Judaism as well. Sabato Morais urged his coreligionists not to endanger their American security by generating suspicion about their loyalty.[47]

Even so, opinions about Zionism, even among the most liberal, were never unanimous; there were always those who exercised an independent judgment. The poet Emma Lazarus, who in the past had regarded Jewish immigrants with patrician aloofness, was so moved by the news of Russian brutality in 1881 that she concluded that Zionism was the only antidote to antisemitism. Shortly before her untimely death in 1887, Lazarus explained to American readers that "When our race shall have an organic center the outraged Jews shall have a defense in the court of nations, as the outraged Englishman or American . . . all suggested solutions other than this of the Jewish problem are but temporary palliations."[48]

Religious reformers such as Bernhard Felsenthal, Gustav Gottheil, Stephen S. Wise, Judah Leon Magnes, Joseph Krauskopf, and Gotthard Deutsch represented a group that did not share in the anti-Zionist feelings of their clerical colleagues. Felsenthal tried to reconcile the idea of Zionism with Reform's mission idea. In 1897 he contended that a Jewish center in Palestine would enhance Israel's role in the world. Gustav Gottheil, Temple Emanuel's senior rabbi, made no effort to conceal his Zionism from his well-to-do congregants. Gotthard Deutsch, a professor at the anti-Zionist Hebrew Union College, frequently lectured his colleagues on the spiritual meaning of a Jewish national rebirth.[49]

Rabbi Stephen S. Wise, a social and religious reformer, recalls the isolation that Zionism earned him in the Liberal Jewish community. "To be an American Zionist in the last decade of the last century," he wrote before his death, "was to be the son or grandson of east European Jewish Immigrants. One could count on the fingers of two hands the numbers of sons and daughters of Portuguese-Spanish and German Jews who were ready at the outset to avow themselves disciples and supporters of Zionism."[50]

By the early twentieth century a segment of liberal opinion, both lay and clerical, shifted from a position of anti-Zionism to what might be more accurately designated as "non-Zionism." What surfaced was a willingness on the part of some Americanized Jews to support efforts to colonize Palestine so that other Jews not as fortunate as themselves might settle there in a productive capacity. For such an enterprise they were prepared to offer fiscal support and diplomatic counsel, even an occasional admission that Palestine served a Jewish spiritual purpose. For a while Emma Lazarus assumed this position. A fully assimilated Jew, she could imagine no other life for herself but in America. "For ourselves, personally," she wrote, "we have nothing to ask or desire, neither our national or domestic happiness is bound up with the existence of any other Government in the world than that of the United States."[51] Kaufman Kohler's eventual turn toward Zionism was similarly marked. As one of the authors of the anti-Zionist plank in the Pittsburgh Platform of 1885, he nevertheless agreed some years later to "Let Palestine, our ancient home . . . again become a center of Jewish culture and a safe refuge for the homeless. We shall all welcome it and aid in the promotion of its work. Let the million or more of Jewish citizens dwelling there . . . be empowered and encouraged to build up a commonwealth. . . . We shall all hail the undertaking and pray for its prosperity."[52]

No doubt, by the early years of the twentieth century, a number of assimilated American Jews had moved a considerable distance from their formerly unbending anti-Zionist position. To be sure, their change of heart was due in part to Great Britain's issuance of the Balfour Declaration of 1917. The declaration's acceptance by the American government signified an important endorsement that offered political legitimacy to the idea of a Jewish homeland. Neither were American Jews impervious to the rising tide of antisemitism abroad and at home. Even so, by the second decade of the twentieth century, many of the most influential Jewish Reformers and lay leaders remained unalterably opposed to political Zionism, which they continued to view as an ideology opposed to Judaism's religious principles, and unalterably committed to the indivisibility of their American loyalty.[53]

10

Liberal Crusade

1

By the 1880s mainline Protestantism was undergoing a liberal transformation. Having for years accepted and lived complacently with the orthodox assumptions of its predecessors and the social and political standards of America's rising business leadership, espousing its slogans of individualism and free enterprise, it now became increasingly conscious of the needs of the less privileged. The explosion of scientific and sociological knowledge, theories of organic evolution, fresh economic and political insights, coupled with dramatic demographic and economic changes within the United States, had a profound impact on contemporary religious thought and behavior. These conditions provided to liberal voices in American Protestantism a period of unprecedented ascendancy and respectability that they had not enjoyed previously.[1]

On its surface this trend was accompanied by an unusual degree of tolerance between Christians and Jews. Some liberal theologians such as James Freeman Clarke and Crawford H. Toy treated the Jewish historical experience with more esteem than was ordinarily seen in liberal Christian writings. Toy, a Southern Baptist who became a Hebrew scholar with a liberal Christian tilt, wondered about the persistency of Judaism. "No other religion in the world has enjoyed so long a recorded life," he exclaimed, concluding in 1882 that "This persistency is to be ascribed, in part, to its elevated conceptions of God and man, which gave it the advantage over its rivals; but in part, also, to the vigor of the Jewish race, which has maintained the separate existence of the people for so many centuries in the midst of strangers."[2]

For a while, the founding of the Free Religious Association (F.R.A.) in 1867 by a group of radical Unitarians who objected to the phrase "the Lordship of Jesus Christ" in the Unitarian constitution provided a forum for the mingling of liberal Jews and non-Jews in religious fellowship.[3] One of its founders and first president, Octavius Brooks Frothingham, came from a celebrated New England Unitarian home where Ralph Waldo Emerson and other Transcendentalists were frequent guests. Disillusioned with the creedal divisions and Christian authoritarianism of his Calvinist neighbors, he saw in the F.R.A. an opportunity "to unite all religious men in bonds of pure spirituality, each one being responsible for his own opinion alone."[4] A commitment to theism was the foundation upon which the new organization was established, and it included in its initial small but diverse roster individuals of all faiths, and those of no faith at all.

Liberal Jews, too, such as Max Lilienthal, Isaac M. Wise, Felix Adler, Emil G. Hirsch, Bernard Felsenthal, Solomon Schindler, and Charles Fleischer, were included among its early officers and members.[5] F.R.A.'s liberal and rational outlook and its encouragement of a free religious expression were appreciated by many Jews, as was Frothingham's open and liberal mind. Doubt about religious matters and theological principles, he explained, constituted a much healthier religious posture than orthodox certainty. "In *honest doubt*," Frothingham wrote, "there lives more faith than in all the creeds." Frothingham was also convinced that "neither Judaism nor Romanism, nor the established forms of Protestantism . . . will constitute the coming faith."[6] Liberal Jews were comfortable in the presence of such ideas, although few were willing to travel his distance. But even some Christian liberals contended that Frothingham, who made little effort to conceal his conviction that historic Christianity had served its usefulness, had placed himself beyond the pale of Christianity.[7]

Frothingham was not alone in his unorthodoxy. One of New England's most commanding Unitarian voices, Charles W. Eliot, president of Harvard University, also announced his anticipation of a creedless future. Like Frothingham, Eliot believed that the coming faith would transcend the Christian standards of his own day. It would be guided by no single system of belief. Rather, it would form a composite derived from a multitude of world religions.[8] Unlike other New England Brahmins of his generation, Eliot displayed no anxiety about the arrival of hundreds of thousands of Jewish immigrants from eastern Europe. He was thankful for the beneficent gifts bestowed upon humanity by this ancient people. "I say that the highest conception of God, man, and nature are all Jewish," he told a New York gathering in 1906. He compared Jewish synagogue organization to that of New England's Congregationalism. Like the Congregationalist churches, he declared, synagogues "are all independent, or autonomous." They are "places of training for self-government and the wise exercise of liberty."[9]

The latter years of the nineteenth century were also characterized by the growth of an unprecedented interfaith relationship between the liberal wings of the two faiths. The experience manifested itself through an exchange of pulpits, participation in common religious exercises, and theological discussions. American Jews welcomed the opportunity to join in religious fellowship with liberal Protestants. In 1878 Gustav Gottheil proposed that Jews and Christians correct "their views of their respective religions, a thing . . . much needed on either side." After all, observed Gottheil, "nothing strengthens faith in the Father more surely than the growing sense of the brotherhood of his children."[10]

As the number of Jews increased through immigration, Christian curiosity about them grew also. Gottheil and others welcomed any opportunity to describe Jewish beliefs and practices to their American neighbors. In the pages of *The North American Review* Gottheil explained to his readers that Jews, although tied together by culture and history like Protestants, hold diverse theological positions. While most Jews preferred liberalism to orthodoxy, there were those among them who professed no religious sentiment at all. He assured his readers that although the Jew resisted conversion, he "is no adversary of Christianity, no enemy to the Church." Gottheil rejoiced "that the chasm which separated the daughters from their mother is narrowing, and that bridges are being thrown across it on which those who were, but never ought to have been, estranged from each other, may meet for the exchange of assurances of restored friendship."[11]

A similar effort to narrow the rift between Jew and Protestant, and in the process to explain Judaism to non-Jews, prompted Max Lilienthal, a pioneer in American Reform Judaism, to accept an invitation in 1867 to preach in a neighboring church. Lilienthal was probably the first American rabbi to preach in a Protestant church, a practice which he repeated in later years in various cities throughout the country.[12] Lilienthal's reasons for doing so were clear: "I always cheerfully seize the opportunity of stating before a Christian audience the sublime doctrines of our religion," he wrote.

> To Christians they are a "terra incognita." They read our religious papers as little as we read theirs. But few ever visit our temples and hear there our doctrines expounded. The greatest and most advanced modern scholars, even a Buckle, have no understanding either of the Jewish religion or Jewish history, and the old prejudice is lurking out from every loophole. . . . Hence I always seize the opportunity whenever offered to preach in churches and to speak on Judaism and its liberal tendencies.[13]

David Philipson, Lilienthal's student and successor, was equally inspired when a few years later he was beckoned by the Cincinnati YMCA to deliver a course of lectures to its Christian members on the biblical Prophets. "I believe that this was the first time that a rabbi had been thus requested," recalled Philipson. "I gladly accepted the invitation, for I recognized therein a great opportunity for bringing the Jewish interpretation of the messages of these great spirits to a Christian audience."[14] Philipson spoke frequently from non-Jewish pulpits and was proud of the experience, to which he often referred in his autobiography. He considered his participation in interfaith services a highlight of his rabbinical career. He recalled proudly that "Christians of all sects sought my companionship." Like other Reform leaders, Philipson believed that American Jewry had entered a new era of interreligious understanding, that his own universal outlook was shared by the most enlightened Americans of all faiths.[15]

As the foremost spokesman of Reform Judaism, Isaac M. Wise felt especially obligated to explain his theological position to non-Jews, and he frequently accepted invitations to speak to Christian audiences. Through such exercises he also hoped to gather friends for Judaism, to win for Reform an accepted, if not a dominant, place in American society. A similar motive accounts for his early, energetic support for the F.R.A. He viewed his membership in this organization as an opportunity to indoctrinate his liberal, non-Jewish colleagues, with the ideas of Liberal Judaism. Prof. Benny Kraut argues that Wise found in the F.R.A. "a highly desirable public platform among the best educated and most liberal American religious elite [from which] to preach his own brand of Jewish religious triumphalism."[16]

The interfaith activities initiated by such liberal leaders as Wise, Lilienthal, and Philipson inspired similar practices in Jewish communities throughout the country. In Rochester, New York, Jews and Protestants began exchanging pulpits in 1870. Isaac Cohen, rabbi of Concord Temple, offered biblical instruction in the neighboring city of Rochester to a group of Sunday school teachers representing "nearly every church in the city." In Chicago, Rabbi Felsenthal organized in 1874 the Society for the Promotion of the Study of the Old Testament in the Original Languages, which met on alternate Sundays at the First Methodist Church. Chicago's ecumenical spirit continued when Emil Hirsch arrived from Philadelphia a few years later. He and other rabbis lectured frequently from the pulpits of Chicago's Congregationalist and Methodist churches.[17]

Carl Herman Voss writes about the friendship that developed in the early years of the twentieth century between Rabbi Stephen S. Wise, founder of the Free Synagogue of New York, and the Unitarian minister John Haynes Holmes, pastor of the Church of the Messiah. Wise, already well known in progressive circles as a social activist, and Holmes, a Protestant liberal and social reformer, had arrived in New York in 1907, where they met and formed an instant friendship. In 1910 both agreed to exchange pulpits periodically and to conduct interfaith services, activities which grew widely in popularity.[18]

For Stephen Wise the purpose of these union services was "to show that Jew and non-Jew could meet from time to time in the spirit of common worship of the universal Father." It was a sentiment shared by Holmes. "How could a church be true to its faith," asked Holmes, "and not seek within itself and in the larger community of souls, the universal brotherhood of man?" Wise recalled that in arranging for such activities "each of us was meticulously scrupulous to avoid giving offense to the congregations of the others. We were of one mind and of one spirit in being utterly vigilant that no word be uttered, no prayer be offered up, no hymn be chanted that did not include within itself the spirit of . . . the congregations worshipping together."[19]

Even more unusual was the introduction of interfaith activities into the heart of New York's immigrant Jewish neighborhood. Here, on the fringe of the Lower East Side, a former Columbia University professor, Charles Sprague Smith, established an ecumenical church in 1899. Called the People's Church, his creation was described by Smith as "a creedless church for creedless people." It convened weekly in Cooper Union Hall with an overflow crowd. Smith invited to its pulpit representatives of all religious faiths, imposing upon them only two limitations: they were forbidden to proselytize or to attack any creed. Smith hoped to limit the church's religious teachings "to those ethical principles that are fundamental and universal" and consequently to help usher in "that church of the future dreamed of by many." Protestant ministers and Reform rabbis appeared frequently in the pulpit of the People's Church. "That a nucleus of the church universal of the future . . . actually exists and flourishes in New York today is a fact," commented an observer when he discovered the People's Church in 1907. By that date it had become a flourishing institution, providing standing room only for its growing congregation.[20]

It was not an isolated example. The New York State Conference of Religion, consisting of Protestant ministers and rabbis, met periodically to determine "what is common in their various faiths." Early in the century it appointed a committee of Christians and Jews to prepare *A Book of Common Worship*, which would enable men of widely diverse religious creeds to assemble in worship. *The Outlook* reported in 1910 that frequent use was being made of the little volume at interfaith gatherings.[21]

2

The convening of the World's Parliament of Religions in Chicago in 1893 served as a significant catalyst for interfaith activities. Held in conjunction with the World's Columbian Exposition, the idea was initiated by Charles Carrol Bonney, a Chicago educator, jurist, and member of the Swedenborgians, a small Protestant sect also known as the Church of New Jerusalem. Concerned that the forthcoming Chicago Exposition might descend merely to extolling humanity's mechanical and material victories, he suggested in 1889 that an opportunity be provided for international authorities of arts and letters to gather and converse. From this suggestion evolved the idea of a parliament of the world's faiths. The task of planning, developing, and implementing the idea was placed in the hands of forty-six-year-old John Henry Barrows, pastor of the First Presbyterian Church of Chicago. Of New England heritage, son of a preacher and abolitionist, and a former student at Yale, Union, and Andover, Barrows surrounded himself with an energetic committee of Christians and Jews.[22]

Barrows and his team hoped to gather in Chicago "the leading representatives of the great historic religions of the world" to examine what truths each held and taught, to observe their differences, and to inquire what light each might shed upon the other. That such aspirations were met with a general approval in academic and religious circles was in many cases due to reasons that went beyond the stated aims of the committee. For one thing, a growing interest in the study of comparative religion was, according to Chairman Barrows's own admission, a vital factor that lay behind the widespread endorsement of the idea. "The Congress at Chicago will give thousands a coveted opportunity to hear such a series of lectures as no university in the world could furnish," wrote one commentator.[23] Also, there were those who visualized the coming event as they would a vast arena in which the giant faiths would battle, like gladiators, for supremacy. Protestants who followed this line of thought did not doubt the victorious outcome of their faith and welcomed the coming contest eagerly. As Sylvester F. Scovel, president of the University of Wooster, put it: "Personally I have no fear that the religious congresses will accomplish the vicious equalization of the good and the bad. . . . I welcome the comparison which these congresses are sure to bring about . . . and that the superior power of those which have vital conceptions of God and the future will be clearly shown as against those so-called religions which have neither."[24]

The hope that the parliament would promote the Christian faith was foremost at least in the rhetoric of its leading American supporters. A leading educator, W. F. Warren of Boston University, who played a key role in originating the parliament, was anxious for the world to discover the "Perfect Religion"—Christianity.[25] "Many favored the parliament," recalled its leading architect, "from the profound conviction that it would show forth the superiority . . . of Christianity." In accepting a position on its advisory council, Bishop John H. Vincent of the Methodist Episcopal church divulged his dream of "a great Christian union in a great hall. . . . It will be the most magnificent spectacle the Christian world has ever seen," he wrote, almost with a note of ecstasy.[26]

Although not all American Protestant leaders responded to the parliament with enthusiasm, a good many did. Philip Schaff, Lyman Abbott, Washington Gladden, and Theodore T. Munger, a few of the more prominent names, consented to read papers. Despite the parochial motivations of a few, the parliament's chief administrators and supporters were driven by a desire to unite men of different creeds in a common bond of enduring friendship. "The religious faiths of the world have most seriously misjudged each other," declared President Bonney in his address of welcome on the opening day. "Such errors it is hoped that this Congress will do much to correct." He assured the gathering that all were there to learn rather than to pronounce judgment upon each other.[27] Bonney extolled religious pluralism as the ideal for a democratic society. There is no single religious answer, he declared; each faith captures a portion of the ultimate truth. "As the finite can never fully comprehend the infinite," stated Bonney, "each must see God with the eyes of his own soul; each must behold Him through the colored glass of His own nature; each must receive Him according to his capacity of reception." The support of such ideas by many of the delegates made the congress unique in the history of American Protestantism. Like Bonney, Chairman Barrows also assured the heterogeneous gathering that "the speakers will not be ambitious for short-lived, verbal victories over others. . . . We are here as members of a Parliament of Religions, over which flies no sectarian flag, which is to be stampeded by no sectarian war-cries."[28]

American Jews were eager to plunge into the ecumenical atmosphere of the parliament, and happily, the leadership of the conference worked to remove all obstacles from their path. Barrows welcomed the cooperation of "these friends, some of whom," he declared, "are willing to call themselves Old Testament Christians, as I am willing to call myself a New Testament Jew."[29] Bonney assured the Jewish representatives that the parliament was ready to offer the Jew the reverence which he demanded for his Christian convictions. "Our differences of opinion and belief are between ourselves and God, the judge and Father of us all . . . and if we part at the threshold of the Gospels, it shall be, not with anger, but with love, and a grateful remembrance of our long and pleasant journey from Genesis to Malachi."[30]

American Jewish leadership, primarily Reform but also Conservative, was eager to participate in the event. Indeed, it has been suggested that Cyrus Adler, an authority on Semitic languages when he was associated with the Washington Smithsonian Institution, was among the first to propose the idea of a religious parliament.[31] Being invited to join in the proceedings of the religious conference was an important symbolic event for Jews, an indication of their acceptance as religious equals. The Central Conference of American Rabbis, the only American rabbinical organization existing in 1890, assumed the responsibility of coordinating American-Jewish participation. Papers to be presented, which included biblical, historical, and ethical subjects, were assigned to a wide spectrum of Jewish religious opinion, liberal as well as traditional; but the primary perspective offered was Liberal.[32]

A significant number of papers presented by Jewish scholars and rabbis stressed the interrelationship of Christianity and Judaism rather than their differences. Kaufman Kohler hammered away at the heavy dose of Jewish knowledge in which Jesus and his disciples were steeped. "Jesus was the true son of the synagogue," he explained, acknowledging, however, that he "belonged to no school. He was the man of the people," in whom, "the Essene ideal of love and fellowship took a new and grander form."[33] Alexander Kohut demanded that "not theory but *practice,*" not creed, but deed be the watchwords of humanity. He lamented that Judaism and Christianity "imbibed the water of enlightenment from the virgin spring of truth," but continued to remain distinct, "estranged from each other by dogmatic separation, and a fibrous accumulation of prejudice."[34] "John, Paul, Jesus himself, we can claim them all for our own," pleaded Josephine Lazarus, one of the few women speaking for Jews at the parliament. But "we do not want 'missions' to convert us." "We cannot become Presbyterians, Episcopalians. . . . Christians as well as Jews need the larger unity that shall embrace them all, the unity of spirit, not doctrine . . . the times are full of signs. On every side there is a call, a challenge, Hath not one God created us?"[35]

The key Jewish speaker was Chicago's Emil Hirsch, a rabbi and professor at the University of Chicago. A member of the parliament's planning committee, Hirsch played an active role in organizing the parliament. A prominent voice in Liberal Judaism and committed to the progress of Jewish-Protestant relations, Hirsch stressed the common elements that underlay the two historic religions. His emphasis, one that was underscored by liberals of both Christianity and Judaism, was upon mankind's need for one true faith, one which would transcend human diversity and unite all of mankind. Hirsch asserted that "The day of national religion is past. . . . Race and nationality cannot circumscribe the fellowship of the larger communion of the faithful, a communion destined to embrace in one covenant all the children of men." What was now required, Hirsch insisted, was a single religion which will "teach the solidarity of the race that all must rise or fall as one."[36] The plea for the obliteration of religious particularity, heard repeatedly from the Liberal representatives of Judaism, exceeded the demand of even the Pittsburgh Platform.

In a sense the Jewish demand for the eradication of religious differences concealed a deeper desire, a hope that the gathering would strike a death blow at antisemitism. Accordingly, some of the Jewish presenters were critical of Christian teachings about Judaism. "Popular Errors about the Jews" was the title of one such paper. Rabbi Joseph Silverman, its author, reminded his listeners that

> a dense ignorance exists about Jews regarding their social and domestic life, their history and literature, their achievements, their religion, ideals and hopes. And this ignorance is not confined merely to ordinary men, but prevails also amongst scholars. Ovid, Tacitus, Shakespeare, Voltaire, and Renan, most heathen and Christian writers, have been guilty of entertaining and, what is more culpable, of disseminating erroneous ideas about the descendants of ancient Israel.[37]

Generally speaking most Jewish observers and participants were elated with the entire event, viewing it as an important milestone in Jewish-Christian relations. Even the more traditionally oriented participants were visibly enthusiastic. Rabbi Alexander Kohut considered the parliament "a triumph of nineteenth century genius," one which "conclusively demonstrates that our country is at the head of the great pilgrimage to the goal of truth."[38] Isaac M. Wise welcomed the opportunity to display his theological views to the world, "to proclaim the God of Israel and his ethical law in that august Assembly." Recalling the event years later, David Philipson exclaimed: "Happy [were] we who were privileged to live at that time and to participate in those stirring days of brotherhood and religious amity."[39]

Protestant participants were equally encouraged with the outcome of the parliament and left confident about humanity's spiritual future. Such sentiments did not preclude a measure of Christian triumphalism. Some viewed the parliament as a major victory for American Christianity. According to Barrows, "no religion excepting Christianity put forth any strong and serious claim to universality."[40]

Protestant theologians and ministers were generally pleased with the universal message of the parliament. Minot J. Savage, one of the first to edit a volume of the parliament papers, considered the gathering "a surrender of all assumptions of infallibility—that one baseless claim that has ever stood in the way of progress, that has treated with contempt those outside the pale."[41] F. Max Muller, the renowned Oxford University professor of comparative religious systems, followed the proceedings, which he could not personally attend. Muller considered the gathering "unique." "It is unprecedented," he wrote to his American friends. "Nay, we may truly add, it could hardly have been conceived before our own time."[42] A Minneapolis Methodist called the event "a love feast of the world's great faiths," who met together to discover that they had much in common. A doctor of divinity from Marietta College in Ohio was certain that because of what had happened in Chicago, Christians had at last discovered "the common brotherhood of man."[43]

The experience left a mark on the thinking of Washington Gladden, the innovative Social Gospeler, who in the following years remained sharply critical of those who divided religions into categories of true and false. Lyman Abbott, Brooklyn's popular preacher and editor of one of America's most widely read periodicals, *The Outlook,* agreed that "the first effect of this parliament of Religions must be to correct the opinion . . . that all forms of religion but our own are a mixture of ignorance and superstition."[44] The existence of Christian denominationalism disturbed Abbott, who was forever on the lookout for signs of its impending demise. Christian unity became with him a hope, almost an obsession. He rejoiced in 1897 when he thought he sensed that religious divisions were ceasing to be of consequence. "They are not, as they used to be, the themes of conversation. . . . We have grown more catholic, that is, more large minded."[45]

One of the immediate consequences of the conference was the calling in

1894 of a "Congress of Liberal Religious Societies." Initiated by a group of
clergymen and endorsed by 600 ministers from throughout the United States,
the congress was designed to perpetuate the spirit of religious liberty, pluralism, and universalism engendered by the Chicago parliament. Its object,
declared its founders, was "to develop the church of humanity, democratic in
organization, progressive in spirit . . . hospitable to all forms of thought . . .
but keeping itself open to all new light and the higher development of the
future." Conspicuous among its chief organizers was the name of Emil Hirsch,
who hosted its first gathering of 3,000 people, mostly liberal Protestants, in
Chicago's Sinai Temple.[46]

A rhetoric of ecumenism also pervaded the atmosphere outside of the
clergy, for the parliament had left an imprint upon American intellectuals and
reformers as well. The parliament's distinguishing characteristic was that it
belonged to laypersons as well as the church, women as well as men, professors
as well as clergy. Julia Ward Howe, one of the nineteenth century's distinguished women, former abolitionist, poet, suffragist, and pacifist, who had
confronted the parliament with a paper entitled "What is Religion?," believed,
as she looked back at the event, that it vindicated the vanguard of the
Christian church that had challenged the view of the futility of all other
beliefs.[47] The best-selling novelist Edward Bellamy, who stood at the head of
the column of late nineteenth-century reformers, was not present at Chicago;
yet one would barely suspect this by thumbing the pages of *Equality*, which
appeared shortly after the gathering. "It is a very long time since it has been
customary for people to divide themselves into sects and classify themselves
under different names on account of variations of opinion as to matters of
religion," the somewhat stupefied hero, Julian West, is informed in the fictitious
year 2000. " 'Do you actually tell me that human beings have become capable
of entertaining opinions about the next world without becoming enemies in
this? . . . How long is it since people ceased to call themselves Catholics, Protestants, Baptists, Methodists, and so on?' queried West in amaze-
ment."[48]

Scholars, too, could not put the event out of their minds. Writing for the
International Journal of Ethics in 1900, Prof. Morris Jastrow, a Jewish philosopher at the University of Pennsylvania, conceded that prejudices and misun-
derstandings would not be swept away by "a single assembly of this kind." Yet a
decision of many nations and peoples "To consider calmly the religious views
with which they were not in sympathy . . . was an augury that the hopes and
dreams of the visionaries in ancient and modern times might at some remote
period be at least partially fulfilled."[49]

3

Coupled with dreams of religious unity was a surge of social consciousness
that overwhelmed American Protestantism between the 1880s and the out-

break of the First World War. It engendered a style of Christianity known as the Social Gospel with which many Jews found sympathy. Although it represented a theological ethos difficult to define with precision, its arrival tended to shift Protestantism's focus from individual to social salvation. Sin, Social Gospelers contended, was a collective rather than an individual malady. It was "not a private transaction between the sinner and God," wrote one of its leading theoreticians; rather "humanity always crowds the audience-room when God holds court."[50]

The movement, if one may so call this tendency, although it was never formally organized, is as important for the understanding of the few decades that preceded World War I as was the evangelical awakening for the earlier years of the nineteenth century. Nourished by evangelical roots, the Social Gospel was shaped by the intellectual climate of its time, drawing its energy from the latest findings in economics, sociology, and biology. In some respects, too, the Social Gospel can be seen as Protestantism's response to urbanization, industrialization, and immigration. Its social and political crusades introduced a new style of religious activism into American Reform. Imbued with a post-millennial and patriotic outlook, the Social Gospel was an optimistic movement, aspiring toward a gradual spiritual and moral improvement of mankind, convinced of the ultimate triumph of the "American way."[51]

Its pioneers included some of the most articulate Protestant voices of the late nineteenth century. With the establishment of the Federal Council of Churches in 1908, their efforts were endorsed by thirty-three Protestant denominations. The council's statement of aims reflected Protestantism's social concerns and included requests for "equal rights and complete justice for all men in all stations of life," "the abolition of child labor," a minimum wage, old-age pensions for all working people, and other demands not ordinarily associated with mainline Protestantism.[52]

To be sure, Social Gospelers were not all of one mind. While some crusaded for improved housing, women's rights, and better working conditions, others continued to pursue the quest for a Christian America, immigration restriction, and temperance. While some continued to espouse an evangelical Protestantism, others tilted their theology leftward, toward secular humanism. Despite these differences, however, all shared a common rhetoric, if not a mood for social reform, and labored to hasten a never precisely defined "Kingdom of God" on earth, a social order which one writer described as a "gradual Christianization of all human relationships."[53]

The movement's most commanding theological voice was that of Walter Rauschenbusch. Of German Baptist heritage and a professor of church history at the Rochester Theological Seminary, Rauschenbusch had also acquired some firsthand information about the life of the poor. As a young man Rauschenbusch had served as a missionary in New York's Hell's Kitchen, where he had witnessed the deprivation and hardships of the city's underclass. The experience left a deep impression upon him, as did his advanced religious studies abroad. Enamored of such American reformers as Edward Bellamy, Jacob Riis, and Henry George, Rauschenbusch also perused the works of Karl Marx and Leo Tolstoy. But for moral and religious inspiration he turned to the biblical prophets, who served as examples and guides for his subsequent social endeavors.

A deeply religious man, he became convinced that American society was in a condition of social decay unparalleled in its seriousness and scope. Only a reformed polity, an altered economy guided by socialist principles and biblical values, he was convinced, would lead mankind out of the corruption bred by modern acquisitiveness.[54] Most importantly, Rauschenbusch viewed the salvation of society as a precondition for the salvation of its individuals. Human sinfulness, he believed, was transmitted collectively, "from generation to generation." Sin, he explained, "is lodged in social customs and institutions and is absorbed by the individual from his social group."[55]

Like Rauschenbusch, Washington Gladden, a Congregationalist minister, also rejected the traditional, evangelical interpretation of salvation. Serving congregations in Brooklyn, North Adams, and Columbus and editing a popular religious weekly, the *Independent*, Gladden became one of the most popular interpreters of the Social Gospel. He had grown up in pre–Civil War central New York, where the dogmas of orthodox Calvinism and the conversion of sinners were the primary concerns of the local pastor. "The appeal was . . . almost wholly individualistic," he recalled. One's personal religious welfare was the only issue that mattered.[56]

As he matured Gladden determined that neither a religion of fear nor an obsession with individual salvation would guide his life. Addressing a group of Yale divinity students in 1902, Gladden confessed that he was "unable to understand how Christianity . . . can be intelligently or adequately preached or lived in these days without a constant reference to social questions. No individual is soundly converted until he comprehends his relations and strives to fulfill them."[57] Gladden urged ministers to acquaint themselves with economic and sociological theories, for it was the "religion of politics, of economics, of sociology that we are going to teach." To Gladden, as to other Social Gospelers, religion was the key to social reform, and social reform was the key to human salvation.[58]

For this reason theoreticians of the Social Gospel displayed a deepened interest in the sources of ancient Judaism, in biblical history, especially in the prophetic books of Scripture. It was a kind of back-to-the-Bible movement that America witnessed during these years, wherein the solution of modern social problems, problems of poverty and affluence, capital and labor, freedom and exploitation, were sought in the Jewish Scripture. A Yale Divinity School lecturer went so far as to rename *Exodus* in 1905, calling it "The Story of an

Ancient Labor Movement," a title which he believed would more appropriately "serve to indicate what is really the main theme of the narrative."[59]

The tendency for Christians at this time to link the social message of Jesus to the thoughts of the Hebrew prophets generated a renewed curiosity about these moral and ethical writings. It was in the prophetic literature that Walter Rauschenbusch sought a clue to a better present. Such an examination, he believed, was an indispensable part of any inquiry into Christian social reconstruction. "They are an integral part of the thought life of Christianity," he observed in 1907. "What other nation" but that of the Jews, he remarked with surprise, "has a library of classics in which the spokesmen of the common people have the dominant voice. It would be hard to find a parallel to it anywhere."[60] He viewed the prophets, not as "religious individualists," but rather as "public men" with interests in "public affairs." "The morality which they had in mind was not the private morality of detached pious souls but the social morality of the nation. This they preached, and they backed their preaching by active participation in public action and discussion."[61] Their concern was always for the poor, the widows, and the fatherless, never for the landed aristocracy. The prophets reflected the essence of Jewish law, which was so different from the Roman law, observed Rauschenbusch. It was this difference that made their theology useful for the Social Gospel.[62]

Lyman Abbott also evinced an interest in the literature of the ancient Jews. Pastor of Brooklyn's Plymouth Congregational Church, popular religious author, and editor of the widely read magazine *The Outlook*, Abbott was also one of the leading voices of the Social Gospel. To the Old Testament heroes Abbott attributed the beginnings of democratic institutions. "Moses was a great statesman, the father of civil liberty for all humanity," he wrote. He was struck by the consistently strong moral element in biblical history. It always predominates over the "the merely political," as does "the religious over the merely ethical."[63]

Democracy, Abbott exclaimed, was the child of "Hebrew ancestry." The democratic society upon which American institutions were based "stemmed from the Hebrew Commonwealth, twelve centuries before Christ." Surrounded by absolute despots, the Jewish nation organized a government with separation of powers, ruled by a "constitutional monarch."

> In the Hebrew Commonwealth no hereditary caste or class was permitted; there was a state church, but the priesthood were forbidden to become landowners, and were made dependent for their support on the voluntary offerings of the people. . . . private ownership in land was allowed, but only for a limited tenure; labor was honorable and idleness a disgrace; slavery, though not prohibited, was hedged about with such conditions that in the course of a few centuries it disappeared; women's position, if not absolutely equal to that of men, was one of unexampled honor in that age; provision was made for the educa-

tion of all . . . out of which grew the first popular school system in the known world.[64]

Like Abbott, Charles Reynolds Brown, pastor of the First Congregational Church of Oakland, California, sought his social inspiration in the Old Testament. Invited to deliver the Lyman Beecher Lectures at Yale in 1908, he chose the Book of Exodus as his text, because, as he put it, "it bears upon the social message of the modern pulpit." For Brown the Egyptian exploitation of the Hebrews was analogous to the impositions imposed by modern industrial capitalism upon urban labor. He considered the Fourth Commandment, which instituted the Sabbath, as the first piece of labor legislation in history: "So far as history records, the first attempt ever made to regulate the hours of labor by law was made at Sinai."[65]

Jewish Liberal leadership, flattered by these comparisons, was in accord with many of the humanitarian objectives of the Social Gospel. Its ideas were not alien to Judaism. For years Felix Adler, who had been a Reformer before he moved into Ethical Culture, had been convinced that the mission of Judaism was "to rehabilitate the prophetic ideal of social justice"; and his attack on unbridled individualism antedated those of most Social Gospelers. Adler was one of the first to launch a campaign for improved housing for the poor of New York, for improving working conditions, for the abolition of child labor, and for the enhancement of public health.[66] The theologian Octavius Frothingham, who knew Adler well, was hardly surprised at the social crusade launched by the founder of the Ethical Culture Society. "Jews are unencumbered by the mysteries of Christian theology," he wrote in his autobiography. "Their genius is for social organization, and the moral element is very large in their religion."[67]

During the few decades before the First World War Liberal Jews shared many of the cheerful, optimistic theological presumptions current at that time. The heavy emphasis placed by numerous American Christians upon the ethical and moral aspects of religious belief was not incongruent with their traditional sentiments. Thoughtful Jews would have not disputed the prevailing belief that "the concrete problems of our day are social problems. . . . the overshadowing question of our day is the social question," or that people must be judged by their works, rather than by their beliefs. "It is not enough that we believe; we must do." "Our relations with God cannot be right, if our relations with our fellow men are wrong." These were propositions that Jews universally accepted.[68] Rauschenbusch's assertions that the sins of mortals could be understood only in relation to the doings of present and preceding generations made good sense to Jews. His contentions that "sin is lodged in social customs and institutions and is absorbed by the individual from his social group," that the evils of one generation are caused by the wrongs of the generations that preceded it, and will in turn condition the sufferings and temptations of those who come after," appeared as a repudiation of the doctrine of Original Sin, an unacceptable premise in Jewish religious thought.[69]

Many of the humanitarian principles of the Social Gospel were lodged in the core of Judaism. Kaufman Kohler, who formulated a systematic study of Jewish theology, understood the essential ingredient of Judaism to be the individual's consciousness of his or her social responsibilities, his or her obligations to those who surrounded him or her. Judaism "looks to the *deed* . . . not to the empty creed and the blind belief," he wrote. "The life of the recluse is of little use to the world at large and hence of no moral value. . . . Only in devotion to his fellows is man made to realize his own godlike nature." "The soul of the Jewish religion is its ethics," wrote Kohler. "Its God is the fountainhead and ideal of morality." Like Social Gospelers, Jews yearned for the Kingdom of God to materialize in historical time. They hoped for a "complete moral order on earth, the reign of truth, righteousness and holiness among all men and nations."[70] Such ideas, incorporated in the Pittsburgh Platform, were supported universally by the Liberal rabbinate. Emil Hirsch noted in 1893 that the religion of the future "will be impatient of men who claim that they have the right to be saved . . . while not stirring a foot or lifting a hand to redeem brother men from hunger and wretchedness."[71]

Few rabbis displayed a more energetic dedication to social betterment than did New York's Stephen S. Wise, founder of the Free Synagogue. Wise immersed himself in a variety of projects of social improvement. His Free Synagogue became a center of humanitarian activity and civil reform. "More than any other rabbi of that time," notes his biographer, Melvin Urofsky, "Wise was an active and important figure in American progressivism." Like his Christian counterparts, with whom he worked closely in progressive endeavors, Wise was a Jewish Social Gospeler.[72]

This is not to suggest that the impact of the Social Gospel was not felt in more traditional Jewish circles. Solomon Schechter, who early in the century was lured from his professorship at Cambridge University to the presidency of the Jewish Theological Seminary, reflected substantial agreement with its aspirations. Unlike his more liberal colleagues, however, Schechter viewed the search for modern altruists among biblical and postbiblical figures to be somewhat unhistorical. Yet, like the Social Gospelers of his day, he stressed the idea of God's immanence and believed that for people to work toward the establishment of "the visible Kingdom of God in the present world" was "the highest goal religion can strive to reach."[73] The Kingdom, explained Schechter, is inconsistent with "bad government," or a "state of social misery engendered through poverty and want. . . . All-wise social legislation in this respect must help towards its special advent."[74]

To what extent such rabbinical jeremiads influenced American Jews is impossible to gauge with accuracy. Yet one must differentiate between the enthusiasm displayed for social reconstruction in clerical rhetoric and its reception by congregational memberships, both Jewish and Protestant. Jewish ardor for the Social Gospel was also dampened by the persistence of a deep strain of ambivalence within it toward them and their traditions. With some justification, the christological foundations upon which the Social Gospel rested cast a cloud of suspicion upon the efforts of some of its most energetic practitioners.[75]

11

Anti-Judaism and
the New Theology

1

Despite their social compassion and ecumenical outlook, liberal Protestants did not succeed in obliterating the vestiges of Christian antisemitism. On the contrary, their frequent reference to the Jewish past was a subject to which they turned primarily to highlight their own triumphant entry on the stage of history.

End-of-the-century liberals often contrasted Christianity's universal vision with the constricted perspective of Judaism. Crawford Toy, a professor of Hebrew at Harvard, was fond of comparing the intolerant nationalism of ancient Judaism with Christianity's universalism. "National particularism was too deeply ingrained in Jewish life to permit the emergence of a purely religious principle of universal character," he wrote in 1892.[1] James Freeman Clarke, whose writings during the latter half of the nineteenth century reflected a deeply ingrained progressivism, faulted Judaism for being too "ethnic." In contrast to Christianity, asserted Clarke, Jews failed to achieve a holistic perspective.[2] Walter Rauschenbusch put it succinctly when he stated that in the hands of Jesus Judaism became "human and therefore universal."[3] He counseled his readers to sift out of the New Testament "what is distinctively Christian in origin and spirit," to remove from it all narrow Jewish ideas. Christianity, he declared "has to struggle hard with the stubborn nationalistic pride of Judaism which claimed either a monopoly of messianic salvation or at least special privileges within it."[4]

Liberals thought they recognized in Christianity a force that could liberate humans from Jewish parochialism. According to Octavius Frothingham, whose writings were inspired by New England's Transcendentalists, the task of liberal Protestantism was to aspire toward a heightened liberation, a more fulfilling universal ethic. Like Ralph Waldo Emerson and Theodore Parker, Frothingham wished to see Christianity, the only system of belief that he believed could qualify as a candidate for a "Religion of Humanity," liberated from the limitations of the Old Testament, a book that spoke to too few.[5]

It was a desire endorsed by others. Minot Savage, a Unitarian minister whose writings commanded attention during the Progressive Era, asserted that only Unitarianism could qualify as a universal faith. If and when that day should arrive, glowed Savage, "we shall occupy a position absolutely impregnable, one that will ultimately bring the whole intelligent world to our side."[6] Lyman Abbott frequently dilated upon this theme, as he did in 1903 when he asked, "What, then, did Christ add to Judaism?" His response, that "Christ added breadth," was in keeping with the opinions of his liberal colleagues. "Theologically, ethically, sociologically, Judaism was racial," while "Christ's theology, ethics, sociology, was human, not Jewish."[7] Abbott defended this demeaning portrait of early Judaism by noting that in biblical times "humanity appears to Israel to be required only toward Israelites; the Jew must not permanently enslave a Jew, but may so enslave a pagan; he must not take usury of a Jew, but may of a pagan; he must not eat unclean, but may reserve them for the stranger in the land."[8]

That Judaism was seen in its earlier years as a narrow, self-serving system of belief was a typically unhistorical perspective reflected in the writings of Charles David Williams, bishop of the Michigan Protestant Episcopal Church and one of the most outspoken proponents of Christian universalism. Like Frothingham, Abbott, and Rauschenbusch, whom he greatly admired, Williams had acquired by the early twentieth century a reputation for liberality and social empathy, qualities which were not, however, extended toward Jews and their faith. He considered Judaism a "religion of isolation and separation," and his description of its early years was far from flattering. Jews, he wrote,

> Held scrupulously aloof not only from the Gentile, but from the ignorant and depraved. . . . The Pharisee drew aside his robe as he walked the street, lest he should be defiled by the touch of one of the "amhaaretz," the "groundlings." . . . Now compare with that Christ and His Christianity—the Christ who shunned no contacts with an evil world, who ever flung Himself with the very heart of human society and mingled without restraint in all its associations.[9]

Judaism's alleged inadequacy was bolstered further with an indictment of its legalism; it was frequently described as being enslaved to the letter of Old Testament and rabbinic law. Believing their law to be God's final revelation, progressive Christians argued, Jews became obsessed with its observance. To their overlegalistic minds Jesus' desire to select from the holy codes only those elements that contained universal implications appeared as a dangerous threat. The unfortunate consequence of such a narrow devotion was, according to Toy, "the extremism which it tended to produce. The natural result of complete devotion to an external law was the breaking up of life into minute details, the loss of unity and the loss of spirituality."[10] To the pious Jew, according to Toy, every particle of law, be it of ceremonial or moral significance, was of equal importance. What is more, "casuistry came in as the natural accompaniment of this outward scheme of righteousness." The whole tendency, according to the Harvard theologian, was to "depress spirituality. It obscured the fundamental principle of life, that goodness consists in the attitude of the soul toward the right. It metamorphosed God into a list of commands, and life into a chaos of obediences. It was slavery to the letter of the Law. It dwarfed the liberty of the soul by repressing the instinct of love."[11]

Rauschenbusch also viewed the early rabbis, the Pharisees, with disdain, as he watched their irrelevant devotion to ceremonial and ritualistic details. The Pharisees, wrote Rauschenbusch with a surprising inaccuracy, "even nullified the fundamental obligation of the child to the parent by teaching that if a man gave money to the Temple, and thus supported the ritual warship of God, he was free from the duty of supporting his parents." Jesus' attack on the Pharisees, according to Rauschenbusch, was fully justified. After all, they were "blind leaders who fumbled in their casuistry, and everywhere missed the decisive facts in teaching right and wrong. Their piety was no piety; their law was inadequate." Like his early nineteenth-century liberal ancestors, Rauschenbusch wished to liberate Christianity from the confining regulations of the Old Testament. "We are under no obligation to accept the mythical ideas and cosmic speculations of the Hebrew people," he wrote at the close of his life.[12]

To liberal Protestants Jewish legalism constituted the trap from which Jesus freed Christianity. This emancipation was Christ's singular achievement. According to Charles S. Macfarland, one of the founders of the Federal Council of Churches, it was for this reason that the Christian Savior leaned more heavily upon the prophetic books than he did upon the Pentateuch, the more legalistic volumes of the Old Testament. Unlike the Jews of his day Jesus took a more expansive approach to the Scriptures, extracting only those passages that had a greater moral purpose. "The questions which concerned the scholars of his time were not such as concerned Christ," wrote Macfarland. "He used Scripture, not to set forth matters of casuistry, but great ethical and spiritual principles."[13]

The Episcopal priest Charles D. Williams was even more direct in his indictment of Jewish legalism. He described those who were enslaved by its practice as "men infinitesimally scrupulous and yet absolutely unprincipled." How does one account for their "ethical monstrosity, this moral contradiction"? asked Williams. The culprit, he was assured, was the Pharisaic "ecclesiastical conscience" of the Jewish obsession with minute details of the codes of law, yet unconcern with their larger ethical and moral implications.[14]

Neither did liberals shy away from flinging the ancient charge of crucifixion upon the Jews. It is surprising that even the Unitarian reformer John Haynes

Holmes on one occasion pictured the Christian Savior hanging upon the cross with "Jewish priests hooting at his agony." He was convinced of the Jewish culpability in the crime. It was quite understandable, he declared, "in view of Jesus' admonitions of the Jewish leadership."[15] Similarly, for Rauschenbusch it was the bigotry of the Jews "which pushed Jesus toward death."

> The traditional zeal of Judaism, the solemn injunctions of their most sacred books, and the punishments the nation had incurred by slackness and tolerance in the past, seemed ample justification of the vigor with which they set themselves against a man who seemed to flout the Sabbath, to disregard the laws of fasting, to eat with profane and unwashed hands, to overthrow the entire doctrine of clean and unclean food, and to confuse all moral distinctions between good and bad by associating with irreligious men. . . . So they counteracted by innuendo and direct charges, and tried to entrap him. . . . They were the active agents in the legal steps which led to his death.[16]

Rauschenbusch's imaginative description of Jewish involvement in the most "heinous crime of all human history" was frequently repeated in even the most enlightened religious writings of this period. Indeed, the martyrdom of Jesus took on a fresh meaning for liberal Protestants as they placed it against the background of the social concerns of Progressive America. According to Charles D. Williams, death upon the cross was the penalty the Christian Savior paid, it seemed, when he attempted to rebel against the rigid and backward views of a corrupt establishment. As the greatest social reformer in history, Jesus proved a threat to the conservatism of the Jewish leadership, "the faithless priests of the temple," to whom he correctly referred as "hypocrites, blind leaders of the blind, serpents, generation of vipers, the children of hell," who "under the guise of religious service," with "punctilious solicitude for the nonessentials of religion" represented reaction at its worst.[17]

Deicide served also as a vehicle with which liberal Protestants could attack legal conservatism, another charge foisted upon the ancient Hebrews. In an era of sociological jurisprudence, the trial of Jesus took on a new clarity. How can one explain, asked one Protestant theologian, why "Jerusalem's most prominent citizens" proceeded to commit "the most diabolical and heinous crime of all human history, a crime about which the civilized world has shuddered ever since?" Clearly, the answer was linked to the stubborn adherence of the Jew to the letter of the law, which allowed the rabbis of that day to ignore the deeper meaning of justice.[18] It mattered little whether Christian liberals disagreed with their more orthodox colleagues about the divinity and resurrection of Jesus. Their view of the Jewish responsibility in Jesus' execution differed little from that of their more conservative counterparts.

From a practical standpoint neither did the liberal position on the theology of supersessionism differ in its essentials from that of orthodoxy. Even the most liberal minds, according to Robert Everett,

> supported the idea that Christianity had superseded Judaism, and they all tended to regard the religion of Israel as a relic of the past which refused to die. . . . What is evidenced here is the on-going process of Christians seeking their self-identity by the negation of Judaism. While the . . . liberals did not talk in terms of the Old Israel vs. the New Israel, their method of proving Christianity's superiority was similar to the traditional arguments. They all saw the truth of Judaism passing over to Christianity.[19]

With the arrival of Christianity, liberals argued, a higher and more advanced stage of religious experience had been introduced. In the process it had displaced Judaism as the appropriate religion of mankind. "Judaism is Christianity in the bud; Christianity is Judaism in the flower," declared Lyman Abbott in 1911.[20] Rauschenbusch was even more emphatic: "The Christians were the real Israel," he wrote. "By one daring act of expropriation of the Jewish people, the Jewish people were thrust out of their historic heritage," while Christianity "gained a profound sense of historic dignity and importance." Even the liberal Crawford Toy asserted that the Jews of antiquity had long ago completed their work in the world; and that their ideas which found their way into the Old Testament had achieved their full expression in the more elevated ideas of Christianity.[21]

Protestant liberals found it difficult to avoid the conclusion that as a religion Judaism had long since served its essential function; that it had reached a stage of obsolescence. It is revealing that a course of study in Hebrew sociology offered at Tufts College proposed to trace "The origin and development of social, political and religious institutions from the rise of Judaism to its decay."[22] Shailer Mathews, dean of the Divinity School of the University of Chicago, stated in 1910 that in regard to family life, property rights, and the relationship between individuals, the moral standards of the New Testament were far above those accepted by the Jews of Christ's time.[23] Such were the stock ideas transmitted to seminarians at the end of the nineteenth century.

Liberals did not limit themselves to a criticism of the Judaism of antiquity, its primitivism, parochialism, and legalism, but extended their attack to contemporary Jewish religious and social practices. This prompted the editors of *The American Hebrew* to dispatch a series of questions in 1890 to a select group of non-Jews, many of whom were Protestant ministers of various ideologies, requesting reasons for the persistence of anti-Jewish feeling in the United States. "We admit," the editors prefaced their questionnaire, "that Jews, like all human beings, have their ignoble as well as noble types, but this difference is as between members of the human family, and is not due to their faith." The editors wished to know how American Christians justified antisemitism; whether it was an outgrowth of religious instruction offered in church schools—instruction that, for example, magnified the story of the Crucifixion? Or was it a defect in Jewish behavior that made Jews unappealing to Christians? The editors also invited suggestions that might minimize anti-Jewish feeling.[24]

Twenty-five ministers replied. All condemned antisemitism and disclaimed any personal ill-feeling toward Jews. With the exception of one pastor, Washington Gladden, all denied that religious instruction was in any way responsible for fostering antisemitism. Yet most insisted on the importance of teaching the story of the Crucifixion. "The judicial murder of Jesus Christ is rightly held up . . . as the great crime of mankind," declared Morgan Dix, a doctor of divinity from New York City. After all, "we must teach our children the facts of history."[25]

A number of those polled attributed the persistence of antisemitism to Jewish religious and social behavior. The practice of unfamiliar religious rituals, such as "keeping their Passover," Jewish snobbishness—"Have you not held yourself apart from the life of this New World in a nook of your own . . . looking down from your fancied eminence as the chosen race?"—and the contradictory charge of a Jewish refusal to intermarry with Gentiles were typical objections. One minister remarked that the "Jew goes to Summer resorts as a Jew; is found in parties of his own people," and "becomes an irritant in the social structure of American life."[26]

Materialism and commercialism were also assigned as causes. "They [Jews] live only for this world. The greed of gain is the one absorbing passion," stated one reverend. "I have no personal grievance," declared a Yonkers minister, "but I often hear the remarks from careful business men that the Jew does not consider it wrong to cheat a Gentile."[27] W. H. P. Faunce, president of Brown University, listed Jewish "indifference to popular opinion, often amounting to open defiance, a want of public spirit, a lack of genuine patriotism, a want of human sympathy and breadth of view, [and] a class spirit in place of real love of humanity" as causes for Jewish unpopularity. Rev. J. R. Day of New York City believed "that Jews as a class are somewhat 'loud' in talk, 'flashy' in dress and offensive in display of jewelry."[28]

Two decades later, *The American Citizen*, a magazine launched to combat antisemitism, again polled a selected group of American clergy about their views toward Jews and Judaism. The responses revealed that few notions had changed during the intervening years. In answer to the question "How a more kindly relation between Jews and Christians may be furthered?" a New York minister suggested that Jews must first "abandon the notion that this is not a Christian Commonwealth." An Episcopal clergyman believed that prejudice against the Jew was an outgrowth of "Chauvinism, his race-pride, race-conceit, race-exclusiveness, race-aloofness." A Brooklyn minister linked the cause of antisemitism to the "rigid observance of the dietary laws" and the Jewish reluctance to marry Christians.[29]

The depth to which such attitudes were ingrained in the heart of liberal Protestantism becomes even more evident by an examination of the utterances of Stanton Coit, a close friend of Felix Adler and a cofounder of the Ethical Culture Society. In view of his background it is surprising to learn of Coit's demand in 1914 that Jews publicly deny their claim to chosenness. Jewish particularity annoyed Coit, who was also a founder of the University Settlement House in the heart of New York City's Jewish neighborhood. He was an admirer of Ralph Waldo Emerson, whose fantasies and fears about the "Jewish idea" held a special appeal for him. What seemed to trouble Coit most, however, was the Jewish claim to a "spiritual monopoly," which, he insisted, was responsible for the persistence of antisemitism.

Coit admitted that not all modern Jews shared in this claim, but those who did he considered a grave menace "to the religious originality and autonomy of every nation in which they sojourn." Because of that handful, he believed, contemporary Jewry "cannot much blame the Gentiles for believing that the descendants of Israel are spiritually race-proud and still think that no other nation can compare with them in religious, moral, political, and economical insight."[30] No end to the historic antagonism between Jew and Gentile would materialize, he warned, unless Jews collectively repudiated their claim to spiritual superiority. "The first step must consist in the removal of the notion from the Gentile mind that the Jew of to-day is spiritually arrogant. Unfortunately, in all that I have been able to read of the writings of the most humanistic and catholic Jews of our time, I have found no sufficiently unequivocal repudiation of the claim to spiritual supremacy over all other peoples of the world."[31]

For Coit, Jewish triumphalism appeared to be a more menacing defect than any form of Christian jingoism. While other nations, he admitted, were tainted with a similar vulgarity, unlike that of the Jews, "no other nation's cruder self-deification has ever taken the form of the highest insult to other peoples—the claim to a spiritual monopoly."[32]

Like Emerson and Parker, Coit accused Jews of obstructing the moral development of Western civilization. Jewish biblical teachings have discouraged Christians from exploiting their own creative spiritual resources. In all its needs, argued Coit, Christendom has become a captive to Jewish moral ideas, "a parasite to the Jews." He urged the nations of the Western world to put an end to this parasitism "by extracting the initial falsehood that caused it, the deadly microbe that has paralyzed the highest spiritual centers of the brain of every Christian."[33] Clearly, Coit, a leading representative of liberal Christianity, had managed to churn up in his own mind a way to cleanse from the world all vestiges of a Jewish uniqueness. By a simple assignment, which would require a collective Jewish confession of culpability, an age old malady—antisemitism—would be eradicated once and for all.

2

Protestantism's New Theology, fashioned by the theories of Darwinian evolution and Higher Criticism, which gripped progressive religious thinking during the late nineteenth century, provided additional fodder for negative thinking about Jews. These new ideas, transported in the mid-nineteenth century from German universities, forced liberal Christians as well as Jews to reassess their traditional beliefs and practices, causing debates and divisions within their ranks. They also provided Christianity with new weapons for its war against the Jews.

While it made orthodox Christians uncomfortable, evolutionary thought was readily accepted by liberal Protestants. The Darwinian idea of natural selection, which proposed that a process of evolution rather than God's command determined the origin of species, did not disturb progressive-minded Christians. Its challenge to such sacred concepts as the act of Creation and the Last Judgment, now displaced with the conviction that history was a process of improvement, fitted well into America's optimistic ethos. The New Theology enshrined a belief in the inevitability of progress, "in the ultimate triumph of good."[34] Such ideas were welcomed by a number of religious leaders, such as Lyman Abbott, who acknowledged his acceptance of the principle of evolution as a theological truth. "The evolutionist believes that God's processes are the processes of growth, not of manufacture," declared Abbott in 1897.[35]

Evolutionary thought also provided intellectual legitimacy to those biblical scholars who employed in their analysis the tools of historical criticism. The sacred books of God were seen by them as products of an evolutionary process, collaboratively crafted over a period of many years. Knowledge drawn from archaeological discoveries and new theories of comparative linguistics enabled scholars to acquire new insights into biblical literature. Evolutionary thought, concerned with lower and higher stages of cultural development, stimulated an interest in the comparison of one religion with another. This was evident by the widespread curiosity generated by the presentations at the World's Parliament of Religions, and the opportunity they afforded to display Christianity's superior development in respect to other faiths. John W. Buckham, a graduate of Andover Theological Seminary and the author of a number of important theological works, wrote in 1909 that the study of comparative religions "is disclosing the inherent strength and superiority of Christianity as it could appear in no other way." Such a study persuaded Buckham that Christianity qualified as the most appropriate candidate for a universal faith. Other religions, he believed, lacked "the power of development and adaptation" or, as he put it, the "moral and spiritual vigour and resources to meet the multiplying demands of advancing humanity."[36]

However, to those Americans accustomed to a literal reading of the Bible, who had grown to accept what they suspected was its clear and simple truth, the application of Darwinian theories and critical scrutiny of God's Word were seen as forms of blasphemy, and their proponents as enemies of Christianity.[37] Evolutionary thought and Higher Criticism also generated debate within the Jewish community. This was particularly evident, as Naomi Cohen shows, among Liberal Jews. The Reform movement had from its very inception characterized Judaism as an evolving system of religious practice and belief. Its emphasis upon the adaptability of Judaism to altered challenges conformed to the Darwinian concept of natural selection. Emil Hirsch, for example, marked 1859, the very year Charles Darwin's *Origin of Species* first appeared, as a significant turning point in humanity's intellectual history. He told a group of rabbis that "Darwin taught us a truer appreciation of the function of the past as a conditioning, yet stimulating preparation for the future." He urged his colleagues to scrutinize their sacred texts with a fearless, historical perspective. "Biblical criticism has come to our aid," he declared, warning that "woe unto a theology that is so little sure of its truth as to dread the searchlight of scientific investigation."[38]

Some Liberal Jewish scholars, however, voiced a concern that Protestantism's critical focus upon the literature of the Old Testament might distort the sacred history and mission of the Jewish people. When in 1903 Kaufman Kohler assumed the presidency of Hebrew Union College, he launched a program of studies that would produce rabbis and scholars equipped with the tools of biblical criticism, and with the skill to employ them for Jewish ends. He and others had become painfully aware of the danger and the dilemma that evolutionary doctrines and biblical criticism, especially if such exercises were left exclusively in the hands of Protestant theologians, presented to the future of Judaism. The Anglo-Jewish leader Claude G. Montefiore put his finger on the problem in 1893 when he noted that "To ignore criticism altogether is to run a tremendous risk. It is likely to make the chain of development in Judaism snap off altogether" and to drive future generations away from their ancestral faith.[39]

The problem was that Protestant scholarship had opened new corridors for the old contention that Christianity, which had evolved from the more primitive Jewish spiritual experience, had reached a higher, if not final, stage of religious development. Lyman Abbott, who was enamored of evolutionary studies, argued on one occasion that "The history of sacrifice in the Old

Testament is the history of the process by which the pagan conception was transformed into the Christian conception." Such exercises elevated the New Israel above the Old and offered fresh confirmation to the Christian theology of displacement.[40]

By attacking the Jewish Scriptures, Protestant scholars launched an assault against the foundations of Judaism. Throughout Jewish history, write Jonathan and Nahum Sarna, "It appears to be an incontrovertible fact that the ultra-Orthodox and the ultra-Reform, as well as those who represent the variegated shadings of religiosity between these poles, together with the secular Jew, all accept the Hebrew Scriptures as the bedrock of Jewish civilization."[41]

Montefiore complained in 1882 that the Jewish Scripture "must bear the whole attack" of the new biblical critics. He was disappointed that he was unable to discover among Christian theologians "an equal readiness to assimilate and accept the higher criticism of the New Testament."[42] Isaac M. Wise was also unable to conceal his anger at what he viewed as the arrogance of the proponents of Higher Criticism and their attack upon the Hebrew Bible. "We do protest most emphatically," he wrote, "against the alleged results of that negative Bible criticism which uproots the veracity and integrity of the inspired writers and reduces the ancient history of Israel to a record of rude barbarism." With some justification Wise detected a vindictive tone in Old Testament Protestant scholarship, one which he found absent in the treatment of New Testament literature. "They go to the New Testament blindfolded, and hurl their superlative learning, ingenuity and wit at the Old Testament," complained Wise.[43] Under the guise of scientific objectivity proponents of the New Theology contributed a significant plank to the spiritual foundations of antisemitism.

3

In the light of the New Theology and the liberal tracts produced by the most progressive representatives of American Protestantism, one might well ask how a serious meeting of minds between Protestants and Jews could have possibly occurred by the opening years of the twentieth century. If social reform and human betterment were earnest objectives of the representatives of this era, there is little evidence that the elimination of hostility toward Judaism was a significant part of their goal. The New Theology, with its weighty emphasis upon Immanence and the future Kingdom, with its scholarly interest in the origin of the sacred texts, accomplished little in improving the relationship between the two faiths. Indeed, the liberal stress upon the need to universalize the modern religious outlook saw in Jewish religious and ethnic existence an obstacle to modernity. No doubt some elements of liberalism's rejection of traditional Judaism were also present in Jewish progressive circles. Liberal Jews, too, separated themselves from the ceremonial and ritualistic practices of their Orthodox coreligionists, preferring to impose their emphasis upon what they imagined were the purely moral and ethical elements of their faith. In so doing, however unwittingly, they joined forces with and supplied an endorsement for Protestantism's behavior.

12

Defending the Evangelical Tradition, 1880–1915

1

Although diminished in its intensity, the voice of Protestant orthodoxy was by no means stilled in the few decades preceding the First World War. The very elements that nourished Protestant liberalism, for opposite reasons, provided evangelical orthodoxy renewed vigor. The threat of the New Theology united evangelicals into a defensive alliance. While the theories of Darwinian evolution encouraged liberals to reassess the precepts of historic Christianity, to those inclined toward orthodoxy they were seen as the clever work of Satan, ever ready to ensnare the unwary and self-deluded. Higher Criticism was accepted as nothing less than a sinful attack upon the Holy Bible, a defiance of that which was most sacred and meaningful to Christians. It threatened the evangelicals' commitment to biblicism and robbed the pious of their conviction that scriptural truth was available to all who read the Word of God.[1]

The social and demographic changes that encouraged liberals to launch works of social reconstruction motivated the orthodox to withdraw from the sinfulness about to engulf them. They were wary of the temptations of modernity: the city, its problems, its foreign and non-Protestant multitudes. They remained unimpressed by the challenges of a pluralistic America. Comparative religious studies held few attractions to the evangelic mind. The World's Parliament of Religions, which had generated profound excitement among liberals, left them cold, if not angry. American Baptists refused to participate in its activities, and the Northern Presbyterian General Assembly condemned the entire principle of ecumenism. Some called it "treason against Christ." Morgan Dix, rector of Trinity Church in New York City, characterized the entire proceedings as "a masterpiece of Satan."[2]

By the end of the nineteenth century the most rapidly growing group within American Protestant orthodoxy was that of the premillennial Dispensationalists. Adherents to this group had fashioned a world view that was diametrically opposed to the more fashionable, more optimistic postmillennialism of their liberal coreligionists. Society, according to the Dispensationalists, was not gradually improving, nor would it be improved by human effort. On the contrary, one need only observe the events of the world to see the moral corruption and social deterioration that surrounded mankind. To premillennialists, the single certainty was that a day of reckoning and judgment was imminent.

Jews played a special role in premillennial Dispensationalist thought. God, argued the members of this evangelical wing of Protestantism, had prepared one plan, a separate covenant, for his earthly people, the Jews, and another for his heavenly people, the Christians. Jewish suffering, a punishment for their rejection of Christ, was a temporary condition. It will cease, they predicted in accordance with their reading of prophecy, with Christ's return to earth after an intervening period of great difficulties for unbelievers. With Christ's Second Advent the biblical prophecies concerning Israel will be fulfilled as promised. Christ will then rule for a thousand years from Jerusalem over a restored Jewish kingdom.[3]

It was a theology that gained acceptance in evangelical circles during the last quarter of the nineteenth century; and it differed sharply from the beliefs of liberal Protestants who saw in Dispensationalism an unappealing anti-intellectualism. Still, by the end of the century a growing disillusionment with postmillennialism had attracted some leading Christians to its ranks. While Dwight L. Moody was the most striking, it also counted A. T. Peterson, editor of the influential *Missionary Review of the World*; James H. Brooks, a leading Presbyterian from St. Louis; Adoniram Judson Gordon, a prominent Baptist pastor in Boston; W. J. Erdman, an influential Presbyterian minister who had held pulpits in Chicago, New York, and Boston; and Cyrus I. Scofield, a Congregationalist pastor and one of the most important Dispensationalist voices of the late nineteenth century. Most significant, as Timothy Weber observes, is that included among these premillennial converts were many successful and energetic Christian teachers and administrators of the growing number of Bible colleges. These religious institutions, with Moody's Bible Institute in Chicago serving as their flagship, were responsible for popularizing Dispensationalist theology in the United States.[4]

Protestant attraction to premillennial Dispensationalism was in part an outgrowth of contemporary social and political conditions. With the changing tone of American society, coupled with deteriorating international conditions that culminated in the outbreak of the First World War, an event which assumed in Dispensationalist minds an "apocalyptic character," many Protestants became disillusioned with the postmillennial optimism that had dominated the religious scene during the latter half of the nineteenth century. Many came to believe, as did the evangelist Dwight L. Moody, that society was doomed. They did not anticipate, as did the postmillennialists, the conversion of mankind to Christ within historical time. Premillennialism, with its expectation of the end of history, offered to many a more satisfactory scenario that would result from the social and international unrest erupting throughout the world.[5]

Moody, the most popular premillennial revivalist of the late nineteenth century and the most articulate exponent of its theology, stressed to his large audiences that only with the coming of Christ would the world's fundamental problems be solved. All human endeavors to find solutions to these problems were not only immature and futile, but sinful. The world, Moody explained, was beyond the efforts of mankind to repair. The conversion of sinners was the only worthwhile task for human beings to pursue.[6]

Moody's life mirrored a significant era in evangelical Protestantism. It spanned an age in which Christian revivalism shifted its focus from the Western frontier to America's new frontier, the city. Moody's personal significance stems from his being an innovator in the techniques and administration of urban revivalism. Moody's objectives were clear: to Christianize the city, the nation, and if possible, the world. To accomplish these ends Moody organized mass revivals, founded two secondary schools at Northfield, Massachusetts, and his Bible Institute in Chicago, which would become a model for America's Bible colleges. His biographer, James F. Findley, Jr., admits that Moody's success and enormous popularity resulted not only from his personal magnetism and Christian message, but also from the financial support he received from millionaires. Among his backers were John Wanamaker, J. P. Morgan, William E. Dodge, George and J. F. Armour, and Cyrus McCormick. His alliance with the captains of Industry did not seem to him incongruent with his premillennial Christian message. His appeal was also strong among America's growing middle class. Moody's conviction that social unrest grew out of unbelief and his personal dislike for social reform endeared him to America's conservative classes.

Although his life was dedicated to saving souls, Moody was not a theologian. He had no formal theological training and, like the business elite of his day, he was self-made and self-educated. The newer currents of Higher Criticism, comparative religious studies, and the Social Gospel repelled him. Faith to Moody was viewed primarily as a personal relationship between the individual and Christ. Christ remained throughout his life the center of his theology, and the Old and New Testaments were his sole guides. By his own admission, he read no other books.[7]

Moody viewed the Jewish people as a separate and unique nation, an eternal people, with a special destiny. "When I meet a Jew I can't help having a profound respect for them [sic], for they are God's people," he declaimed in a sermon in 1877.[8] Like other premillennialists he believed that Jews were destined to be restored to the Promised Land, where those who had not yet received Christ would be collectively converted. In 1892 Moody traveled to the Holy Land to see with his own eyes the site of the future Kingdom of the Jews.

The program of study at Moody's Bible Institute reflected the founder's attitude toward the Jews. According to David Rausch, "The founders and leaders of the Moody Bible Institute consistently supported the restoration of the Jewish people to the Land of Palestine. . . . They deplored the persecution and bigotry that surrounded the prevalent attitude toward the Jew and proclaimed the view that the Jewish people were indeed God's Chosen People."[9]

Such a view of Jews and Judaism differed drastically from that of liberal Protestantism, but it also left some troubling questions about its impact upon the future of Jewish-Christian relations in the United States. Premillennial Dispensationalism's irrational approach to serious religious questions, its anti-intellectual appeal, was difficult to reconcile with Jewish religious sensibilities. Its theologization of the Jewish people as Old Testament characters hardly conformed to the reality of the living Jews of the late nineteenth century. Such thinking made it possible and convenient for Christians to explain away the tribulations of contemporary world Jewry as predetermined by biblical prophecies and as a punishment for their subsequent sinful behavior. Jewish existence was transformed by Dispensationalist preachers into an instrument in God's hands for the purpose of Christian redemption. Jewish individual identity became irrelevant, subordinated to a collective destiny in the Dispensationalist drama.

No doubt Dispensationalism contributed to the psychological comfort of Protestants estranged from the pace of modern times or confused by world events that were beyond their comprehension. Theirs was a theological achievement earned at the expense of Judaism and the Jewish people. Like their liberal competitors, although for different reasons, premillennialists saw Jews as betrayers of Jesus and Judaism as an incomplete system of belief, one which required the fulfilling and culminating experience of the Second Advent. Neither did the Dispensationalist theology succeed in insulating eastern European immigrant Jews from the American Protestant establishment's verbal assaults that greeted them when they arrived at America's shores.

2

Between 1881 and 1920, 2,117,000 Jews migrated from eastern Europe to the United States. Five years later, 3,800,000 Jews resided in the country, constituting 3.25 percent of the total American population. If one considers that in 1880 Jews numbered only 275,000 and comprised only 0.55 percent of the nation's inhabitants, their growth in numbers within the next few years was clearly dramatic. From a relatively inconspicuous minority, Jews, chiefly immigrants from Russia and Poland, congregating primarily in the nation's urban enclaves, were transformed in the few decades preceding World War I into a conspicuous ethnic group. By 1925 New York City counted 1,600,000 Jews, while Philadelphia and Chicago claimed 250,000 and 270,000 respectively.[10]

Not all American Protestants, liberal or orthodox, viewed these newcomers from an eschatological perspective. Outside the Dispensationalist camp Jewish immigrants were greeted quite differently. To some older, well-established residents of Protestant heritage, life in the urban ghettos became an object of curiosity. To others, Protestant patricians more inclined toward nativism and xenophobia, new arrivals generated anxiety and resentment.[11] Their attitudes, publicized in books and articles that were widely circulated, also helped to mold an ambivalent American Protestant outlook toward recent Jewish arrivals.

Henry Adams, a descendant of two presidents, a historian, and a novelist, was a glaring example of America's patrician elite. Brought up in New England as a Unitarian, Adams became increasingly embittered about the Jewish invasion of his ancestral home. American destiny, he believed, was incompatible with Jewish values. "We are in the hands of the Jews," he wrote to an acquaintance in 1896. "They do what they please with our values." Adams associated the Jews with all that he found distasteful with modern America, its materialism, acquisitiveness, and crassness. As he aged he also began to attribute to Jews an inordinate amount of sinister power and influence.[12]

The popular fiction of the Gilded and Progressive ages was permeated with unflattering stereotypical images of the Jew. In the most widely read dime novels, stories, plays, songs, and humor sheets, according to a study by Michael N. Dobkowski, it was almost impossible to find a Jew who was not a social misfit, ugly, morally obtuse, cowardly, or unpatriotic. Even the authors of the best of America's novels, high-brow or low-brow, were enslaved to some degree of contempt for the Jew. Among them were the most celebrated and talented of America's literary figures—Horatio Alger, Henry James, Frank Norris, Theodore Dreiser, Hamlin Garland, and the list goes on—who each displayed in their work a varying degree of distortion and animosity toward Jews.[13]

It was rare to find in late nineteenth- and early twentieth-century America Protestant voices raised in defense of the Jewish minority. That of Madison C. Peters, a New York Baptist minister, was an exception. A popular author of twenty-five religious books, several written on Jewish-American themes, who ministered to unchurched immigrants, Peters admitted in 1902 that although America "grants liberty to the Jew, she nevertheless to a great extent denies him fraternity and equality."[14] It was not a typical acknowledgment heard in the clerical guild. Peters complained that American Jews were rejected from polite society; that "At many of the clubs, social, professional, and even political—[they are] ostracized"; that their children are denied access to the schools and universities; that on the stage they are "caricatured, burlesqued, and lampooned"; that hatred of the Jews has even been allowed "to enter the public school and thus poisons the mind of Young America," and that this condition reflected one which was becoming acceptable in American society.[15]

John Higham and Barbara Miller Solomon have observed that America's Protestant elite was found at the forefront of the movement to restrict immigration from eastern Europe.[16] One of the most influential of this group was Edward A. Ross. He was born in 1866, studied at the University of Berlin, earned a doctorate in political economy from Johns Hopkins, and taught at the universities of Stanford, Nebraska, and Wisconsin. A prolific writer (he authored twenty-seven books and more than three hundred articles), Ross was a founder of the field of American sociology. Prior to the 1930s Ross espoused the supremacy of the Anglo-Saxon race and was a supporter of extreme nativist causes. Typical of his generation and class, Ross was fearful that the huge influx of immigrants would destroy the racial character of the American Anglo-Saxon heritage. He was particularly disturbed about the influence of America's two million Jews. "Easily one-fifth of the Hebrews in the world are with us," he wrote in alarm and with some contempt in 1914. "America is coming to be hailed as the 'promised land.'"[17] His sociological imagination and training did not prevent Ross from accepting every unsubstantiated rumor about Jews, no matter how repulsive it might be.

The fact that pleasure-loving Jewish business men spare jewesses but pursue Gentile girls excites bitter comment. The insurance companies scan a Jewish fire more closely than any other. Credit men say the Jewish merchant is often "slippery" and will "fail" in order to get rid of his debts. . . . "the readiness of the Jews to commit perjury has passed into a proverb.". . . Physicians and lawyers complain that their Jewish colleagues tend to break down the ethics of their professions. It is certain that Jews have commercialized the social evil, commercialized the theater, and have done much to commercialize the newspaper. . . . The truth seems to be that the lower class of Jews of eastern Europe reach here moral cripples. . . . Pent within the Talmud and the Pale of Settlement, their interests have become few, and many of them developed a monstrous and repulsive love of gain.[18]

Ross's thinking about Jews was not unusually extreme for his age; it was reflected in the writings of many social scientists of American Protestant heritage. Some of them, such as John R. Commons, Richard Ely, William Z. Ripley, and including the most blatant racist of them all, Madison Grant, supported the efforts of Boston Brahmins to stem the Jewish tide from Europe, one which they feared would destroy the ideals and values of the Protestant, Anglo-Saxon society that had taken more than two centuries to build.[19]

America's Protestant churches, as we have seen, did not remain unaffected by the intellectual currents of their age. The New Theology was complemented by the nativist and anti-Jewish sentiments of America's leading scholars, whose foreboding thoughts legitimized and reenforced traditional christological biases against Jews. A striking example of the link forged between nativism and Protestant orthodoxy can be seen in the writings of Josiah Strong. A descendant of Massachusetts Puritans, Strong rose to become one of the most respected Congregationalist leaders of the late nineteenth century. He was particularly disturbed about the condition of his nation's cities, and he aspired to both reform and evangelize America's metropolises.

His writings at the end of the century warned repeatedly of the "Perils of the City." They reflected a popular obsession with urban evils and a concern that the growing foreign character of the nation's cities would endanger the higher values of America's Protestant culture. Although Strong's primary anxiety concerned the rising number and influence of Roman Catholics, he did not ignore the increasing number of Jews.[20] Strong contended that Christianity, in its most advanced (that is, Protestant) form, was a product of the genius of Anglo-Saxonism. "It is no accident that the great reformation of the sixteenth century originated among a Teutonic, rather than a Latin people," he wrote in 1885.[21]

Strong's convictions were infectious. In 1887 at a national Christian conference whose theme was focused upon America's "Perils and Opportunities," the immigrant-urban dweller emerged as one of the conference's key concerns. One speaker, Daniel Dorchester from Boston, whose presentation was entitled "The City as a Peril," made it clear at the outset that the nation's cities were "moral battlegrounds"; that their problems were "the leading problems of civilization."[22] Dorchester explained that unlike the virtue and intelligence that resulted from a rural upbringing, "corrupt elements" concentrate in cities, which "produce hideous congestions of evil." Such places become "the strongholds of devildom, where 'Satan's seat is.' "[23] Simon J. McPherson, a minister from Chicago, elaborated upon the same theme, agreeing that "the city has always been the decisive battle-ground of civilization and religion." The city, he announced "is an artificial congestion of population." Here crime and vice are rampant, materialism and greed dominate, and Protestant churches are disappearing.[24]

It was the unassimilated foreign population that disturbed the Christian gathering most. "A Citizenship unassimilated into the national, moral and religious life of any people is a peril," declared one speaker.

Those heterogeneous masses, with habits, sympathies, political and religious predilections, so unlike and positively antagonistic to those of our native population, have weighed heavily against us. Coming in large crowds, pouring into the principal cities often as new and distinct nationalities, keeping up Old World customs, introducing their crude and sometimes revolutionary opinions onto our elections, massing their forces, and effectively controlling them, they have set aside the American Sabbath, opened Sunday theaters . . . infidel clubs, communistic societies and anarchistic leagues, inaugurating mobocracy, and copiously filling up the ranks of the social outcasts.[25]

Prof. H. H. Boyesen of Columbia College reminded the gathering that the nation's liberal immigration policies had been drafted with the understanding that Americans would remain a predominantly Protestant people. Boyesen argued that "the immigrant of to-day is not the same as the immigrant of ten and twenty years ago. He is, as statistics prove, largely drawn from a lower stratum of European society."[26]

The conference ended on a militant tone, with the delegates agreeing on the need for an aggressive program of evangelization. One speaker demanded that a commitment to lead a Christian life should be demanded of all those who wished to reside in the United States. A church leader from Buffalo suggested that "By a stricter legislation, by a stronger police oversight, by a surer punishment of offenders, our American Sabbath can be, and ought to be, as beautiful a possession as it was to the founders of the James River Colony, in 1607."[27]

3

By the early twentieth century concern about the increasing number of Jewish immigrants became a central issue among Protestant missionaries. Howard B. Gross, a Baptist and a writer on missionary topics, wondered if the new immigrant could ever be fully assimilated into American Protestant culture. He feared the negative impact of a large number of non-Christians upon American Christianity. He warned in 1906 that "whatever would make the country less distinctively Protestant in religion tends to destroy all the other social and civilized characteristics which . . . we wish to preserve."[28] Neither did Protestant liberals ignore the issue. The immigrant problem emerged as a leading item on the agenda of the initial gathering of the Federal Council of Churches in 1908. Here, too, the necessity for an intensified campaign of evangelization among the nation's newcomers was supported by a general consensus.[29] On this matter, it seemed, there was little conflict between Protestantism's Right and Left.

From the standpoint of Protestant missionaries, the large number of Jewish immigrants represented an unprecedented opportunity, a sacred obligation to draw them into the gathering of Christ. "No such opportunity ever came to a nation before," wrote Howard B. Gross early in the century. "The Christian Church must seize it or sink into deserved decadence and decay." What is more, the conversion of newcomers was equated with their Americanization, their acceptance of Christianity with their introduction to democratic values.[30]

Efforts to evangelize Jews increased with intensity during the years of their greatest immigration. According to David Eichhorn, between 1880 and 1910 twenty-nine American denominations established missions for Jews, a number which did not include hundreds of independent organizations and individual efforts launched for the same purpose.[31]

A premillennial Dispensationalist theology motivated many of the most aggressive missionary efforts. The special place that conservative Protestants attributed to Jews in the final phase of history, so important for Dispensationalist eschatology, was frequently acknowledged by American Protestant missionaries. They saw the future condition of the Jewish people as the key to Christianity's future. One missionary put it this way in 1902: "The Jewish question, so momentous to the world at large, is of vital importance to the Christian. The Church must face it. Self-preservation will soon compel an interest. . . . in the light of their covenant promises, their increasing influence, and their power against the cause of Christ, surely their salvation should call forth the best effort of the Church."[32]

One of the most articulate Dispensationalist missionaries, Arno C. Gaebelein, emigrated from Germany to the United States in 1879, where he was ordained as a Methodist minister. After preaching the gospel in Baltimore, Gaebelein moved to New York City, where in 1887 he discovered the truth of Dispensationalism. He taught himself Hebrew and Yiddish so he could discuss and debate religious issues with the Jews of the Lower East Side, where he established his missionary headquarters. Years later Gaebelein recalled how he arrived at his decision to work among the Jews of New York.

> I knew that the Lord wanted me to turn aside from the regular ministry and devote myself to work among God's ancient people. Now all seemed to become clear as to why the Lord prevented my going to the regions beyond. He had work for me to do among the thousands who were arriving month after month in our great American Metropolis. They come mostly from Russia where they were so cruelly persecuted and were indeed "like sheep without a shepherd." Misery and want were seen everywhere on the East Side of New York where they mostly settled. And my heart was deeply moved with compassion.[33]

In terms of numerical success, Gaebelein's efforts to bring Jews into the church were hardly spectacular. Jews, it seemed, viewed him at best with sympathetic curiosity, at worst, as a dangerous influence upon their families. To neutralize or at least to minimize such resentment, Gaebelein proposed, as would other Christian missionaries after him, that the conversion of the Jews did not necessarily require that they break their ties with Judaism. "From the very start of my work among the Jewish people," he wrote, "I felt that they should not be Gentilized" or separate themselves from their people.[34] As a premillennialist, Gaebelein was unable to comprehend the contradiction—indeed, from the Jewish perspective, the impossibility—of being both Jew and a Christian at once. It did not occur to him that the acceptance of Christ as the Messiah was the very negation of Judaism.

The frustration that Gaebelein and other missionaries experienced in their attempt to witness to Jews and the suspicion and hostility with which they were greeted were understandable. The entire record of Christian witnessing to Jews was tinged with antisemitism. Few Jews cared to exchange their recent escape from the pogroms of Russia for a spiritual death granted to them by American evangelists.

It would be wrong to assume that premillennial Dispensationalists maintained an exclusive hold upon Jewish missionary activity. Liberal evangelicals were also involved, although with somewhat less religious enthusiasm. Also active in immigrant neighborhoods were institutional settlement houses, established in congested immigrant neighborhoods by mainline churches and socially concerned Americans. Founded primarily for the improvement of the physical and cultural well-being of their constituents, a number were not above preaching "Christian values" to their Jewish visitors. The suspicion that Jacob A. Riis, a muckraker and social worker, aroused when it was discovered in 1903 that he was engaged in proselytizing Jewish children who attended his New York settlement house, the Jacob Riis Home, was one of the celebrated instances of the suspicion such endeavors aroused among Jews. For Riis, the resentment that the incident created among the Jewish residents of the surrounding neighborhood, as for many enlightened Protestants, was unintelligible. From Riis's point of view, Americanization could not possibly succeed without a dose of Christian indoctrination.[35]

In this sense, the spiritual threats that newly arrived immigrant Jews and their families faced early in the century came from both the right and the left wings of the Protestant community. But the most determined efforts to remove them from their Jewish heritage and draw them into the Christian fold came from the orthodox evangelical wing of American Protestantism.

4

The large influx of Jews during these years renewed demands for a reaffirmation of the idea that the United States was a Christian republic. James M. King, a speaker at the Washington, D.C., Christian Conference in 1887, summed up the commonly held view that "we are a Christian nation" and that the "Christian religion, and the morality that it teaches, in one way or another, permeates all our institutions."[36] To be sure, King continued to defend the establishment clause of the Constitution's Bill of Rights, as did other Protestants, but they hedged their defense with the claim that Protestantism had been voluntarily and spontaneously adopted by the American people as the Republic's religion.[37]

That Protestantism had fashioned a strong, voluntary link with the American nation was an argument employed by one of America's leading nineteenth-century church historians, Philip Schaff. Schaff denied the existence of an "absolute" separation of church and state, a condition which he considered an "impossibility." Such division as "exists in this country," wrote Schaff in 1888, "is not separation of the nation from Christianity."[38] Even contemporary legal authorities supported this train of thought. David J. Brewer, an associate justice of the U.S. Supreme Court, insisted, when addressing the Supreme Court in *Holy Trinity vs. United States* in 1892 and again in 1905, that America was a Christian nation; "not in the sense that Christianity is the established religion," he explained, "or that the people are in any manner compelled to support it." On the contrary, the Constitution specifically provides that "Congress shall make no law respecting an establishment of religion." Nevertheless, argued Brewer, "We constantly speak of this republic as a Christian nation—in fact, as the leading Christian nation of the world."[39]

Having accepted Brewer's premise, then it made good sense to many Protestants to employ the nation's public schools as vehicles for the transmission of Christian values. Their concern was aimed less at the nation's colleges, which by the mid-1880s were lodged securely under denominational influence. Christian anxiety over the future of American education was focused chiefly upon the condition of the nation's common schools, whose body of students was increasing in religious and cultural diversity.[40] Philip Schaff recognized that in their need "to please the Roman Catholics, who opposed every *Protestant* version, and the Jews and infidels who oppose Christianity in any form," some common schools minimized their religious instruction. He was pleased, however, that most states acknowledged the need for some religious teaching and reported in 1888 that four-fifths of the nation's schools permit "reading of the Bible, the singing of a hymn, and the recital of the Lord's Prayer, or some other prayer, as opening exercises of the school." His observation that the majority of American school teachers, "especially the ladies, are members of evangelical churches" was comforting for those who wished to Christianize America.[41]

The link that the nation's public schools had established with Christian practice presented a critical problem to the parents of Jewish school children. They saw American public education, which they had been conditioned to respect for its nonsectarian character, threatened by the introduction of religious exercises into its curriculum. They were also aware that late nineteenth-century common schools, frequently under Protestant administration, did not provide a hospitable environment for Jewish students. One Jewish observer complained that "at the public school the disadvantages of the disciples of Moses are so great as to cause many a little heart, burning with ambition, to dread the approach of the Mosaic festivals. With the recurrence of each season, examinations are arbitrarily fixed on the very holiday of the Jew; absences for religious purposes [are] punished as offense."[42]

The putative nonsectarian curriculum, wrote Nina Morais with disappointment in the *North American Review* in 1881, attributed all of mankind's advances to Christian civilization, while the achievements of Judaism were ignored. While "Christian values" received a special place of prominence in the curriculum, the ethical contributions of Judaism were relegated to a place of insignificance.

> Under the instruction of the unsectarian school mistress, invention is the result of Christian civilization; the geography of India is the triumph of Christian progress; the science of morals is inseparable from Christian dogma. Hymns to the Trinity, readings from the Testament, resound in the halls of secular learning, and the Jew, perhaps excused by special permission from denying the teachings of his home, is marked with the sign of an invidious separation.[43]

It was an observation that did not escape other Jews, who continued to support public education while wondering about the ultimate damage this education might inflict upon the integrity of the Jewish commitment of their sons and daughters.

13

Liberalism and the Genesis of Political Zionism

1

Before 1914 the American Zionist movement was small and uninfluential. Its vital center was found on the European continent where the ideology of Jewish nationalism was born. Whatever popularity Zionism did possess among American Jews was confined to a small group of immigrants who resided in the urban ghettos where European developments possessed greater relevancy. As a rule, the Reform rabbinate and its following devoted more time attacking than supporting the aspirations of American and European Zionists.

Nevertheless, just as the leadership of the World Zionist Organization (WZO), founded in Basel, Switzerland, in 1897, was lodged in the hands of assimilated western European Jews, in the United States the leadership of the American branch, the Federation of American Zionists (FAZ), organized in 1898, was drawn from Americanized Jews. However, in both Europe and in the United States, the rank and file of the movement's membership was eastern European.[1]

The early leadership of American Zionism was recruited from a select group of unrepresentative Reform and Conservative Jews. A prominent Reform rabbi, Gustav Gottheil, helped to initiate the FAZ, while his son, Richard Gottheil, a professor of Oriental studies at Columbia University, became its first president. Richard Gottheil's early writing helped to formulate the philosophy of American Zionism. Gottheil rejected the charge of dual loyalty that some Jews feared they would be accused of if they attached themselves to Zionism. Zionism, he contended, was a solution for European antisemitism, which was not an American problem.[2] It was an argument that would increase in popularity among American Jewish supporters of Jewish nationalism. Stephen S. Wise, who became a convert to Zionism after attending a European Zionist congress in 1898, shared Gottheil's sentiments. Wise served as the first secretary of the FAZ. In their attachment to Zionism, Gottheil and Wise did not typify the attitudes of most of their Reform colleagues.

From the ranks of Conservative Judaism early Zionist leadership was supplied by such individuals as Judah Leon Magnes, who would later become the first chancellor of the Hebrew University of Jerusalem; Harry Friedenwald, a physician who grew up in a traditional household; and Henrietta Szold, who later founded the Hadassah Woman's Organization. Like Reform Zionist leaders these individuals were not representative of the membership of American Conservative Judaism, although they were more in tune with the interests of the Yiddish-speaking, eastern European supporters of Zionism.

It was only after World War I that recent immigrants began to assume positions of authority in American Zionism.[3] With the outbreak of World War I, the center of the world Zionist movement shifted from Germany to England, while the importance of the United States, a more neutral location, was also elevated. These changes, coupled with the election of the prominent jurist and Progressive reformer Louis D. Brandeis to the presidency of the FAZ, altered the faltering fortunes of American Zionism.

Brandeis, who maintained the leadership of the American Zionist movement until 1921, centralized its administrative structure, changed its name to the Zionist Organization of America (ZOA), and attracted new talent and prestige to the movement. An assimilated Jew, Brandeis gave little indication in his early years that he would someday assume a role of leadership in American Zionism. Born in Louisville, Kentucky, in 1856, of Bohemian immigrant parents who fled the aborted Revolution of 1848, Brandeis, at the age of nineteen, with no previous collegiate experience, entered Harvard Law School, where he was shortly recognized as the leading student of his class. After his graduation in 1877 he launched a successful legal career, drawing many of his early clients from Boston's business elite. Throughout these early years Brandeis's attachment to Judaism remained unimpressive. He was not a member of a synagogue, was not associated with a particular branch of Judaism, and made few contacts with Jews before he was fifty-four years of age, devoting his energies chiefly to his successful legal practice. Attracted by the Progressive and reform currents of the early twentieth century, Brandeis turned his focus increasingly toward the needs of labor and the poor. It was in this capacity that he came to understand Jewish immigrant life.

During the presidential campaign of 1912 Brandeis's interest in reform and his growing humanitarian reputation drew him into the inner circle of Woodrow Wilson's close advisors. He played an important role in forging the Democratic party's program and campaign strategy that brought victory to Wilson. Brandeis's eventual nomination to the U.S. Supreme Court in 1916 by President Wilson was in part a reward for his party loyalty. This nomination leading to his eventual appointment to the court was the culminating achievement of his long and successful legal career.

It was also the first time an American Jew received such consideration, and for this reason was resisted by leading members of America's Protestant establishment. Fifty-five Boston Brahmins, including A. Lawrence Lowell, president of Harvard, and Charles Francis Adams, brother of the xenophobic Henry, petitioned Wilson to withdraw his nomination of Brandeis. The debate over Brandeis's appointment lasted almost five months. The antisemitic undercurrents that were responsible for the delay left a deep impression upon Brandeis.[4]

Professional and political success did not inhibit Brandeis from assuming a role of leadership in the American Zionist movement, an involvement which did not begin in earnest until 1913. By that time he had become increasingly conscious of growing antisemitism, both in Europe and in the United States. Melvin Urofsky, who has examined Brandeis's career, concludes that his devotion to Zionism grew out of his commitment to Progressivism and his attachment to American ideals, rather than to Judaism and the Jewish people. It was an attitude shared by many American Jews who joined him in his Zionist work. They too viewed Zionism as an aspect of Progressive reform, a logical reaction of decent Americans to Europe's mistreatment of its Jewish minority, one no different than they might have assumed toward any other social evil.[5]

Brandeis did not believe that Zionism compromised his loyalty to the United States. An opponent of the "melting pot" concept, Brandeis did not believe that Jews, or for that matter, any minority, were obligated to assimilate into American society. On the contrary, he supported a pluralistic model and viewed ethnic and religious diversity as conducive to a healthier America. According to Urofsky, Brandeis accepted Zionist idealism as "complementary and supportive of American democracy." On one occasion he told a Jewish audience that *"To be good Americans, we must be better Jews, and to be better Jews, we must become Zionist."*[6]

Yonathan Shapiro, an Israeli student of Brandeis's Zionist career, adds that American Jews also saw in Zionism a solution not to American, but to Europe's mistreatment of its Jews. It made good sense for them to support what Shapiro calls "Palestinianism," that is, the building of a homeland in Palestine, not necessarily for themselves, but for the Jewish people in need of a home. Prior to 1918 few American Jews saw in Zionism, as did their European brethren, a source of cultural and national renaissance for Judaism.[7]

2

American Protestants did not remain indifferent to the rise of political Zionism. The events of World War I, the Balfour Declaration of 1917 which committed Great Britain to the support of a Jewish national homeland in

Palestine, and Great Britain's emergence as a mandatory power over Palestine catalyzed both interest and activity among Protestant preachers and scholars. As was the case in the earlier years, the Holy Scripture and the land of its birth continued to be central concerns of many evangelical Protestants. Accounts of pilgrimages to Palestine and of biblical archaeological expeditions led by prominent ministers or writers continued to circulate in American Christian circles from the 1890s through the 1920s. Because physical and political conditions in Palestine improved substantially under British rule from what they had been under the Turks, opportunities for travel and exploration also increased.

A growing interest in biblical archaeology coincided with the growth of Jewish nationalism. The two events were not unrelated. The American School of Oriental Studies was founded in 1900 for the pursuit of research and instruction in biblical archaeology, geography, and history. Its student body consisted largely of ministers and American rabbis, while within its faculty a close relationship developed between Christians and Jews. The school's annual report for 1929 observed that its director, William Foxwell Albright, "frequently lectures before Jewish audiences in Hebrew on archeological and biblical topics." A son of a Methodist missionary, Albright, who earned a Ph.D. from Johns Hopkins University in 1916, maintained a close academic relationship with the Hebrew University of Jerusalem. The 1929 report also noted that "Every year some twenty young scholars, Christians and Jewish, return from the school in Jerusalem to disseminate in America the new international and interconfessional ideals of scholarship which they have learned to know in Jerusalem."[8] Melvin Grove Kyle, an associate of Albright and a clergyman of the United Presbyterian church, led an expedition in 1921 to the Land of Moab to probe the mystery of the destruction of Sodom. Kyle's conclusion, that "geologists have found in nature exactly what the biblical record describes in Providence," was an inspiring confirmation of conservative Protestant biblicism.[9]

It was more than scientific interest or the desire to confirm biblical texts that attracted Protestant clergymen to the Jewish national homeland. A few, such as Adolf A. Berle, a Congregationalist pastor who also served as a professor of applied Christianity at Tufts College, were driven toward Zionism by humanitarian interests. Berle, who had been interested in the Zionist movement for a number of years, was particularly aroused by the promise of the Balfour Declaration. In a book published in 1918, *The World Significance of a Jewish State,* Berle discussed the political and religious benefits that he believed a Jewish state would confer upon the world. Even before the First World War had ended he was persuaded that a Jewish state, "perhaps under the protectorate of the great powers," was bound to materialize; and once achieved it "will have significance to the world far beyond, probably, what even its ardent advocates dream."[10]

Christianity itself, Berle wrote, with an unusual degree of optimism, would undergo a transformation in its attitude toward the Jews. The new Jewish state, predicted Berle, will serve as "mediator between East and West," since "there is no race in the world more capable for this task than is the Jewish race. The Jew has become more Oriental and Occidental." What is more, according to Berle's utopian projections, the new Jewish state would emerge as a center of arts and letters, law and religion, toward which the international community would turn for intellectual stimulation.[11]

To those skeptics who might doubt the accuracy of his scenario, who would insist that all this was "mere conjecture," Berle retorted that it stands to reason that if Jews were able to achieve as much as they had in science and the arts under the adverse conditions to which they had been subjected for centuries, how much more could be expected of them under more favorable circumstances. A Jewish national home, he was sure, was bound to activate the dormant creative energies that had been arrested for many years. "Here we shall see one of the oldest races of history literally born again."[12] Judaism itself would undergo a revival, for during the many years of dispersion the religious creativity of the Jews had been dampened. "His [the Jew's] capital may well become the clearing house of religious ideas," declared Berle. And as a final dividend, Berle anticipated that "The old prejudices would perish, the Jew will change, and the Gentile will see him once more in greatness and glory."[13]

In his Zionist vision and enthusiasm Berle was unusual among liberal Protestants. More typical was the reaction of the New York Unitarian John Haynes Holmes, who sailed for Palestine in January 1929 as a guest of Nathan Straus, the New York merchant and philanthropist. Holmes was a prolific author and active reformer involved in a staggering variety of social projects. Although a pacifist with a universal outlook typical of many liberal Christians, he was sympathetic to the Jewish national idea, in part because of the influence of his close friend Rabbi Stephen S. Wise. His trip to Palestine grew out of a desire to learn about Zionism firsthand.

Throughout much of his three-week tour of Palestine, Holmes was accompanied by his friend Judah Magnes, who was now chancellor of the Hebrew University. He spoke to a variety of people from all walks of life: scholars, young men and women, laborers, pioneers, professional people, Arabs and Jews. He was impressed with "the quiet confidence of the leaders of Zionism," and he learned to appreciate the enormous difficulties with which they were confronted. "I came away from Palestine knowing a darker side of Zionism than I had ever dreamed before, but with an assurance as to its future as firm-rooted as the everlasting hills."[14] He was impressed with the heroic endeavors of the *chalutzim* (pioneers), many of whom had left prosperous careers in order to recapture their heritage for themselves and their children. They reminded

him of "the early English settlers who came to the bleak shores of Massachusetts. . . . Here is the same heroism dedicated to the same ends."[15]

Holmes did not minimize the problems which the early Zionists faced. "Not
to see these problems is not to comprehend that nature of the Palestinian
adventure, not to estimate these problems at their full weight of delay, discouragement, and defeat is to miss altogether the challenge and the peril of the task
to which modern Jewry had set its hand. . . . The job of Zionism is colossal.
The problems involved seem many of them to be insuperable."[16] The problems
to which Holmes referred were in part technological, agricultural, and fiscal,
results of the poverty of the neglected land as well as of the exorbitant prices
charged for small parcels by absentee Arab landlords. "Unwilling or unable
themselves to develop their land, these feudal barons propose that it shall be
developed by the Jew only at a price which will give them wealth beyond the
dreams of avarice."[17]

Holmes also recognized the resentment that Jewish settlement in Palestine
created among the local Arab population. Its cause Holmes attributed to the
Arab belief that the country belonged to them and that the Jews were "undertaking deliberately to take it away from them." Arab agitation, Holmes gleaned
from his conversations with Arab leaders in 1929, had been growing since the
issuance of the Balfour Declaration, the failure of their own nationalistic
ambitions, and the increasing Jewish immigration. These accounted for a series
of Arab uprisings against the Jewish settlers during the 1920s. "To-day, as in
recent years, the situation is one of tension, with lines drawn taut and thus
liable to break at any time."[18]

Holmes recognized the difficulty of bridging the gap between Arabs and
Jews. Racial and religious differences exacerbated the economic problems.
"These constitute the most dangerous point of strain, since they stir the
fiercest passions, and lead to the most sudden and ghastly outbreaks of violence." Holmes was fearful, at times almost pessimistic, about the outcome of
competing nationalisms.

> The problem of Jew and Arab seems dark. And it is dark when the world in which
> the two races live side by side is looked at from the standpoint of its two poles.
> The tragedy of the situation is the dominance on both sides of extremist pro-
> grams which allow of no adjustment or reconciliation. Thus, there are Arabs
> who would stop all Jewish immigration, kill or expel all Jews now inside the
> borders of Palestine, destroy Zionism, and then, if possible, overthrow the
> Mandate, establish their own government, and join hands with their brethren
> throughout the Moslem world in the formation of an Arab state. In the same way
> there are Jews who would open wide the ports of entry, overwhelm the present
> Arab majority by a sudden flood of immigrants, set up their own constitution and
> laws, and bend the English sword to subdue the native population to the rule of

the Jewish state. From the extremist of this type nothing is to be gained. The only hope is from moderates who can see that both races may live together in a land which is their mutual heritage.[19]

Yet Holmes, at least in 1929, unlike many of his liberal colleagues, was impressed with the potential promise of the Zionist experiment. When he returned to New York in February 1929, he addressed various Christian groups requesting that they offer their support to the Jewish homeland.[20]

3

Few Protestant groups, however, greeted the beginning of the Jewish return to Palestine with greater enthusiasm than did the premillennial Dispensationalists. For years they had preached the message that Jews had a God-given right to take possession of the land of Israel, but it was not until the end of the century, it seemed, that people began to listen. At their prophetic conferences of 1878, 1886, 1895, 1901, and 1914, speaker after speaker proclaimed the biblical prophecy of a Jewish restoration.

Dispensationalists followed the progress of the early Palestinian Jewish settlement and took pride in the accomplishments of the early *chalutzim* as if they were their own. They were attentive to the debates, discussions, and progress of the early Zionist clubs, the Lovers of Zion.[21] A. E. Thompson, a prominent voice in Dispensationalist missionary circles and pastor of the American Church in Jerusalem, wrote with pride in 1902 that "Zionism has spread like a prairie fire," that the "oppressed millions of Russia and Rumania, the hated multitudes of Germany and France, the free and happy citizens of the British Empire and the American Republic, ceasing to dream of restoration, have awakened to work out their destiny."[22]

Charles Taze Russell, a Congregationalist minister who formed the movement known as Jehovah's Witnesses, was also an outspoken proponent of the view that modern Zionism was a fulfillment of biblical prophecy. When in 1910 he was invited by a group of New York Jews to offer his opinions about Zionism, Russell reminded the crowd of 5,000 that when "thirty years ago I attempted to tell to Israel the good tidings that God's set time to remember Zion had come," he was ignored. He now added the prediction that "Zionism is about to take on fresh vigor, that its most prosperous days are yet to come."[23] Joining these voices was that of the East Side missionary Gaebelein, who predicted in 1904 that "the day may soon be here, sooner than we think, when the world shall behold the Jewish state."[24]

One of the most energetic Dispensationalist champions of the budding Zionist movement was William E. Blackstone, a successful Chicago real estate promoter, a leading Methodist, and an associate of Dwight L. Moody. Blackstone's book *Jesus is Coming*, first published in 1878 and later revised to conform to the developments in world Zionism, was one of the most influential works in evangelical Protestantism. Much of it was devoted to an exploration of the role Jews were destined to play during the last days and beyond. Seven hundred thousand copies of the book were published, and it was translated into thirty-one languages. [25]

Following Blackstone's first visit to Palestine in 1888–89, he organized a Jewish-Christian conference in Chicago for the purpose of gathering public support on behalf of the Jews of Russia. For both theological and pragmatic reasons, Blackstone believed that a Jewish return to Palestine was the only feasible solution to their plight. The United States government, he proclaimed, was the only nation in a position to initiate such a return. [26]

In 1891 he submitted to Pres. Benjamin Harrison a Memorial signed by more than four hundred Christian leaders, which requested that a way be found to return the Jews to Palestine. "Let us now restore to them the land, of which they were so cruelly despoiled by our Roman ancestors," declared Blackstone. The petition requested that the president and his secretary of state, James G. Blaine, urge the rulers of the world powers to convene an international conference in order to consider the Jewish claim to Palestine. Although the Memorial did not achieve an immediate result, it dramatized the ground swell of support for Jewish restoration that existed in Protestant orthodoxy. [27]

In 1916 Blackstone dispatched a second Memorial to Pres. Woodrow Wilson, reminding the chief executive that the first Memorial had achieved no substantive results, and expressed the hope that the second would stimulate greater administrative effort. It was endorsed by Andrew White, president of Cornell University; John Wanamaker, the celebrated merchant; the Federal Council of Churches; the Los Angeles Baptist Ministers Conference; the Methodist Episcopal Church of Southern California; and the Presbyterian Ministerial Association of Los Angeles. The last three bodies incorporated the Memorial's statement as part of their own organizational policies. American Zionists praised Blackstone's efforts on behalf of their cause, and in 1918 invited him to address their meeting in Los Angeles. [28]

Protestant Dispensationalists viewed the historic events of 1917–18—the Balfour Declaration, the conquest of Jerusalem, and the entry of the British army into the Holy City—as momentous events for Christendom. They saw in these happenings prophetic signs that linked their own destiny with that of the Jews. Dispensationalists, as Timothy Weber observes, saw in these occurrences the signal of the imminent restoration of the Jews and the Second Coming of Christ. Such events were of the utmost importance to them because the key ingredient in the drama of world redemption was the restoration of the Jews. Dispensationalists watched occurrences in the Holy Land, therefore, with as much intensity as did American Jewish Zionists. [29]

None of this takes away from the strong evangelical motivation that accompanied Protestant attentiveness to the progress of Zionism. Dispensationalists especially were in general agreement that the final triumph of Zionism would not materialize as long as Jews remained unrepentant. "It is quite certain," wrote A. E. Thompson, "that restored and reunited Israel will not enjoy her exalted place, according to ancient covenant, until the King appears in His glory."[30]

In paying tribute to Blackstone's efforts on behalf of their cause, American Zionists preferred to ignore his evangelical motive; they chose rather, as Malachy writes, to pay "honor to the man, the Christian friend, without paying attention to the religious motivation which lay behind his positive deeds."[31]

4

Protestant support for Jewish nationalism was far from unanimous; the most striking objections came from its liberal wing. Pres. Woodrow Wilson was surrounded by such a group of enlightened anti-Zionist liberals when he left for the Paris Peace Conference in 1919. One member of his staff, for example, William Linn Westermann, a professor of ancient history at the University of Wisconsin, made little effort to conceal his dissatisfaction with the Balfour Declaration. Westermann suspected that the Zionists' ultimate desire to establish a Jewish state in Palestine would injure the Arab claim to self-determination, a matter with which he was much more concerned than he was with Jewish Zionist aspirations. He wondered also about the plight of Protestant missionaries under Jewish domination. He found the arguments presented by Emir Faisal, who spoke for the cause of Arab nationalism in Paris, much more compelling than those presented by Chaim Weizman, who represented the Zionist position.

Westermann and other members of Wilson's delegation were impressed by the missionary spokesman Howard Bliss, president of the Syrian Protestant College at Beirut and a prominent Social Gospeler. Bliss arrived in Paris and requested that greater consideration be given to Arab nationalist demands. His plea did not fall on deaf ears, for some members of Wilson's staff, such as Charles R. Crane, a liberal theologian and an active Unitarian, were repelled by the idea of a Jewish homeland being lodged in Palestine. One disaffected member was particularly disturbed by the thought that "the tomb of the founder of Christianity" would be placed "under the domination of his murderers." Others who cared little for the Zionist idea and were impressed with the Arab cause included the secretary of state, Robert Lansing, and Wilson's close advisor, Col. Edward M. House.[32]

Zionism was suspect in the American academic community. Unlike the philosopher John Dewey, who remarked in 1917 that "the Zionist state would stand forth to the world as an inspiring symbol of victory against great odds, against seemingly insuperable odds, of the rights of nationality to be itself," those academics who spoke out on the issue revealed more animosity than concern for the collective requirements of the Jewish people.[33] Swept up by the xenophobic winds of the 1920s, a number wondered if Zionism was compatible with true Americanism. Harvard historian Albert Bushnell Hart warned American Jews that "They must either reject their American citizenship or renounce any such dangerous doctrine as Zionism." One writer invited in 1922 "every Jew who does not want to become a Palestinian to say so openly."[34]

While the Zionists were negotiating their collective future in Paris in 1919, the economist Thorstein Veblen remarked that a Jewish homeland tucked away in the Near East would remove Jews from the fertile intellectual soil of Europe, an environment which he believed was necessary for their continued creativity. Turned in upon themselves, argued Veblen, Jews would cease contributing their insights to Europe's intellectual life. It seemed to him that it is only when the Jew "falls into the alien lines of gentile inquiry and becomes a naturalized, though hyphenate, citizen in the gentile republic of learning, that he comes to his own as a creative leader in the world's intellectual enterprise."[35] What appeared to disturb Veblen most was his belief that once isolated in the Promised Land the creative energies of the Jewish people would wither. In Palestine they would succumb to the resurrected religious orthodox standards of the past. To Veblen Jews possessed a universal responsibility, a burden which he imposed on no other national or religious group.[36]

Philip Marshall Brown, a professor of international law and diplomacy at Princeton University, who early in the century was a member of the American legation in Constantinople, argued in 1919 that Zionism would intensify anti-Jewish hostility. He displayed concern about Zionist intentions and, like other suspicious liberals, insisted that Zionists assure the civilized world that the establishment of a sovereign state in Palestine would never be one of their ultimate goals. Typical of Christian liberal anxieties, Brown sounded the alarm that Jews proposed to erect a theocracy in the Near East. He feared that "they desired a political order where it would be possible once again to apply the municipal ordinances of Moses."[37] There was an ominous ring in his warning to Zionists that their behavior was bound to increase world animosity against them: "They do not appear to sense the fierce anger that surges up when it is suggested in a disguised form to give to the Jews the predominant interest and control in the Holy Land. . . . There exists an instinctive religious resentment towards the Jews which they would do well never to excite. . . . the object in view must not be a 'national home' for the Jews, but an *international* home for all who hold Palestine dear."[38]

This desire to universalize Jewish nationalist hopes was common among liberal Protestants who suddenly awoke to the religious significance of the Holy Land. Jewish particularism continued to be an unacceptable option to them, and they sought assurances that Zionism would conform to their own imagined universal ideals. Jewish self-determination was an uncomfortable idea for liberal minds, and it was rarely equated with the needs of other stateless nationalities. Liberals insisted that Jews should behave with uncharacteristic, almost an unnatural, caution when articulating their national and collective desires.

Even John Haynes Holmes, who on earlier occasions had professed admiration of the Zionist experiment, warned in 1929 that the "peril of a reversion to the corruptions and indecencies of nationalism is Zion's greatest problem."[39] Secure in their own national enclaves, liberal Christians took to lecturing Zionists about the corruptions of nationalism. Their expectation for Jews was that they be the first to temper their national hopes with the lovely ideals of universal justice, righteousness, and peace. For Holmes, Jewish nationalism was to be guided by a more elevated standard than that imposed upon ordinary sovereign states. "Is the new Zion to be one more nation added to the other nations now existing upon the earth?" he asked, "Are we to have in Palestine only another confusion of flags, frontiers, languages, coinages, the trappings and attributes of sovereignty, to make existing nationalistic confusion worse confounding? Is Jewry to follow in the path of empire, and become another people feverish with pride and quick to aggression?"[40] Of course not. Jewish nationalism was destined to serve a higher purpose. Zionism, Holmes announced, has "a universal significance. This significance resides at bottom in Zion's vindication of man's insistence upon a spiritual interpretation of life—his belief in the triumph of right over wrong, of good over evil, of the spirit over the flesh."[41] Clearly, one cannot leave Holmes and other commentators on Zionism without the conviction that in their own way liberals had theologized the Jewish homeland every bit as much as did Dispensationalists or Mormons.

The writings of Harry Emerson Fosdick also serve as an important example of how otherwise humanitarian Christian sensibilities displayed little confidence in, or offered little encouragement to, Jewish nationalist desires. A professor of theology at Union Theological Seminary, and for many years the popular minister of the New York's Riverside Church, like Holmes, Fosdick was one of the most prominent voices in liberal social causes. It was a measure of his liberality, according to his biographer, Robert Moats Miller, that Fosdick accepted his call to the pastorate of the Riverside Church only on the condition that it remain creedless and interdenominational in its fellowship. A prolific author of more than fifty books and one of the most skillful preachers of his age, Fosdick exerted an enormous influence on the liberal Protestant thought of his age.[42] When applied to Jewish national interests, however, Fosdick's liberalism became awkward.

One of his books, *A Pilgrimage to Palestine*, which appeared in 1928, exposed a typical liberal discomfort with Jewish national desires. To be sure,

Fosdick, who toured the Holy Land with his family in 1925, was impressed with what he saw of the Jewish efforts to establish a homeland. "The story of folk like this," Fosdick wrote following his journey, "is one of the romances of modern times and one hopes that, whether they win or lose in their venture, they may sometime find a historian worthy to record their exploits."[43] Yet, interestingly, Fosdick preferred during his visits to associate with anti-Zionists. While in Jerusalem he resided at the American Colony, the leading Protestant organization in Jerusalem, whose orientation since the Balfour Declaration had tilted increasingly toward the Arab cause. William Foxwell Albright, the distinguished archaeologist, attributed Fosdick's anti-Zionism to the American Colony's influence.[44]

Despite Fosdick's professed sympathy for the ideals of Zionism, he could not conceal his skepticism about its eventual outcome. He did not believe that Palestine, which at that time included all the territory west of the Jordan River, could provide room for two million Jews; and he displayed pessimism about a possible solution to the conflict between Arab and Jewish settlers. For this clash he placed blame almost entirely upon the Zionists, whom he characterized as "confident and aggressive." He viewed as ominous the rising number of Jews arriving in Palestine during the 1920s. Conversing with Moslem leaders, one of whom was the Grand Mufti of all the Moslems of Palestine, whose hatred of Zionism knew few bounds, Fosdick concluded that the Zionist objective to convert Palestine into a Jewish home would be unworkable. In the course of his dialogues with Arab leaders Fosdick was informed bluntly that rather than see a Jewish homeland develop in Palestine, all of Islam was prepared to rise against the Zionist invasion.[45]

Fosdick's concluding analysis was that only a "moderate" Zionist program might have a chance for success; that is, a Zionism that would be willing to forgo a large immigration of Jews and would not press for a conspicuous Jewish identity in Palestine. He warned that should "a chauvinistic, arrogant, political Zionism win control," it would end in the "greatest Jewish tragedy in history."[46]

Fosdick saw a Zionism of magnanimity as the only solution to Jewish nationalistic hope. Unlike the experiences of other national endeavors, the Jewish variety was expected to be nobler, more altruistic in its outlook and behavior. Fosdick put it this way: Zionism "must forgo grasping ambition for political dominance and turn its back on chauvinistic nationalism. It must cease its absurd pretense that into this poor land as a place of refuge millions of persecuted Jews from southeastern Europe can be poured. . . . But if the partisans of political Zionism, as now seems probable, are allowed to force the issue, I am willing to risk my reputation on prophecy: Zionism will end in tragedy."[47]

5

Neither did all American Jews embrace the Zionist cause, its principal opponents being those who were found in the leftward fringe of the Reform movement. Reform's opposition to Jewish nationalism had roots deeply imbedded in the movement's history. It was an antipathy that dominated a core of Reform's leadership through the 1920s, one which detected in Zionism's particularism a negation of the religious universalism toward which it aspired. Anti-Zionism, therefore, was an ethos that Reformers shared with their liberal Protestant counterparts.[48] But it was a segment of American Judaism that by the 1920s was beginning to decline in influence.

Disturbed by the announcement of the Balfour Declaration, Rabbi David Philipson, a key member of this group, attempted to organize in October 1918 an anti-Zionist conference in New York. Even Liberal Jews, however, hesitated to offer him support. Louis Marshall, president of the prestigious Jewish defense agency, the American Jewish Committee, although not a champion of Jewish nationalism, refused to participate and persuaded Philipson not to proceed with his plan. "I do not see what can be gained by embarking on a campaign of controversy and polemics, especially at this time," he wrote to Philipson. "To combat Zionism at this time is to combat the Government of England, France and Italy, and to some extent our government." Besides, observed Marshall, "The rank and file of American Jewry will not participate in your conference."[49]

Even so, Marshall was not a supporter of the cause of Zionism. "I am not in favor of a Jewish State and never have been," he wrote to an acquaintance in 1919. Like many assimilated Jews, Marshall feared that Zionism, given the nativist mood of the postwar decade, might raise public suspicions about the genuineness of Jewish loyalty to their adopted country.[50] It was a concern that some, such as David Philipson, were intent on allaying.

More importantly, for Philipson, Zionism threatened the very essence of his theology, a fear that drove him to battle against Zionists as if they were dangerous enemies. In April 1922 Philipson appeared before the Foreign Relations Committee of the House of Representatives to protest the Lodge-Fish Resolution, a bill which would stamp an American endorsement upon the idea of a Jewish national home in Palestine. Representing a decreasing constituency of Liberal Jews, Philipson argued on this and subsequent occasions that Judaism, as a religious movement, should not be engaged in a political program. "Judaism for me spells a religion and not a political program or a nationalistic separatism."[51] By the mid-1920s, however, Philipson's voice was becoming a lonely one, not only among American Jews in general, but within the ranks of Reform as well. Yet his hostile pose toward Zionism coincided with the ideology of Christian liberalism.

14

The Triumphant Twenties

1

The years between the wars were not pleasant ones for many American Jews. Zionist hopes notwithstanding, domestic and world events converged to intensify hostile feelings toward them. More than ever antisemitism became socially acceptable even in the United States.

The new mood was in part an outgrowth of the war and its aftermath. Victory over their adversaries in 1918 brought only a temporary elation to Americans. The initial euphoria was quickly swept aside by feelings of anxiety and disillusionment. Some of it was related to the pent-up concerns about religious and ethnic discord that had surfaced earlier in the century. These concerns coalesced during the years of World War I into an obsession with national unity and "100 percent Americanism." Tolerance of ethnic and religious diversity, signs of which were evident before the war, dissipated. An urgent desire to hasten the assimilation process of the yet unintegrated aliens overtook American society.[1]

Allied victory did little to restore national confidence. Many expressed frustration with the fruits of Wilson's Great Crusade. A desire to withdraw into a protective cocoon that might provide safety from social and religious subversion pervaded the environment of the 1920s. Postwar economic dislocation, the triumph of Bolshevism in Russia, and the mounting threat of a non-Protestant and non-Christian immigration were the perceived dangers to the integrity of American life.

American Jews were not the sole or even chief targets of those who rose to defend the American way, but they were among the most obvious and vulnerable. To those inclined toward paranoia, the Jew represented not only an economic threat, that is, one who was untrustworthy in his commercial dealings, but also an agent of conspiracy and subversion, a purveyor of Bolshevik ideas.[2] Testifying before a congressional committee after his return to the United States in 1921, George S. Simons, a Methodist minister who had resided in Russia before the Revolution, announced that half of the Russian

Bolsheviks were "Yiddish" and that they were exerting influence upon their coreligionists in New York City. It was common journalistic practice during the postwar "red scare" to couple the term "Jewish" with "Bolshevik," conveying to newspaper readers the impression that most Jews would gladly join in the destruction of American institutions. Not surprisingly, Attorney General A. Mitchell Palmer's raids upon and deportation of aliens suspected of radicalism shortly after the Great War seized most of their victims from Jewish immigrant neighborhoods.[3]

The successful campaign that immigration restrictionists waged against America's traditional open-door policy was in part designed to limit the admission of Jewish aliens from East Europe. The literacy test, included in the Immigration Act of 1917, did little to stem the postwar tide of immigration. In 1921, pogroms in East Europe drove almost 120,000 Jews to the United States, a figure which constituted twenty-one percent of that year's total number of arrivals. Postwar economic uncertainties, doubts about America's assimilative capacity, and anxieties generated by the red scare convinced restrictionists that stronger barriers against outsiders should be erected. A temporary immigration act was passed by Congress and signed by President Harding in 1921. His successor, Pres. Calvin Coolidge, gave his blessing to a more permanent law, the Reed Johnson Act of 1924. With unmistakable racist and antisemitic overtones, this new legislation provided that future arrivals to the United States not exceed 150,000 each year, and that they be selected on the basis of predetermined national quotas based upon the white American population counted in the census of 1920. Among its chief victims were eastern European Jews, since the smallest quotas were assigned to their regions of Europe. The passage of the Act of 1924 marked the virtual end of Jewish immigration to the United States.[4]

It was a victory for a select group of self-appointed custodians of American Protestant culture. That the Jewish presence weakened the racial and cultural character of American civilization was a complaint frequently voiced during the hearings and public debates that preceded the passage of these restrictive immigration measures. The popular literature of the 1920s both reflected and inspired such attitudes. One of the most notorious of such works, which became a best seller during the postwar decade, was Madison Grant's *Passing of the Great Race*, a racist interpretation of history and an antisemitic tract of the intellectual caliber of *Mein Kampf*. Grant's hostility toward Jews was infectious. His warning about Jews was clearly recognizable, for example, in the words of one Methodist minister who lashed out at Jewish newcomers with unconcealed disgust. "For a real American to visit Ellis Island and there look upon the Jewish hordes, ignorant of true patriotism, filthy, vermin infested, stealthy and furtive in manner . . . is to awaken in his thoughtful mind desires to check and lessen this source of pollution."[5]

Somewhat less given to an anti-Jewish polemic, but similar in its intent, was Burton J. Hendrick's widely read *The Jews in America,* reprinted from a series of articles in the nondenominational *World's Work* in 1923. Hendrick, a well-known investigative reporter, a muckraker associated with *McClure's Magazine* during the Progressive Era, and a winner of three Pulitzer Prizes for his biographical writings during the 1920s, stands as a reminder that an enlightened liberal mind was also capable of anti-Jewish hostility.[6]

Conceding that the earlier Jewish immigrants of Iberian or German ancestry were capable of becoming fully Americanized, Hendrick saw little hope for the recent hordes from Poland and Russia. They were incapable of adapting to America's political and economic environment; their prospects were "about as promising as a similar inflowing stream of Hindus." The orthodox Polish Jew received the brunt of Hendrick's disdain. He described him as living by preference in crowded ghettos. His dress "emphasizes his Jewish particularism. His long beard and the ringlets about his ears are also part of his religion." And so was his propensity for involvement in seditious activities.[7]

Hendrick warned that if the influx of Europe's Jews continued, hostility toward them was bound to increase. "There is only one way in which the United States can be protected from the anti-Semitism which so grievously afflicts the eastern sections of Europe," he wrote, with the pretended concern so often evoked by those who did most to spread the virus of Jew-hatred, "that is by putting up the bars against these immigrants."[8]

The danger that a vast number of Jewish arrivals presented to American institutions was similarly stressed in a series of articles by a young journalist, Kenneth L. Roberts, who would later emerge as a popular writer of historical fiction. As a reporter, Roberts traveled to Europe to observe the immigration process firsthand. He returned disenchanted with immigrants in general, but with a special animosity toward the newest and most numerous arrivals, the Polish Jews. His account of his experiences and views appeared first in the *Saturday Evening Post* and in 1922 in a book entitled *Why Europe Leaves Home.*

Roberts pictured Polish Jews, to whom he referred as "human parasites," as incapable of ever becoming Americans. Inferior biologically, their presence would eventually destroy the higher racial character of the American people. Their immoral habits were well known, explained Roberts. "Even now, in Central Europe, when a thing is accomplished in a dishonest or illegal manner, it is spoken of as being done *Judischer Weise,* or in the Jewish manner."[9] Roberts, like Hendrick, warned Americans, especially those "sentimentalists and individuals whose interest in immigration arises from non-patriotic reasons," of the dangers of an open-door policy toward those who are "inassimilable, undesirable, and incapable of grasping American ideals."[10]

Significantly, the writings of Grant, Hendrick, and Roberts were not found

on the fringes of the journalistic world, but were the presentations of prominent minds, widely circulated and widely read.

2

During the First World War a typewritten translation of an anonymous
document, full of hatred and falsehoods about the Jews, which among other
things accused world Jewish leaders of conspiring to overthrow Christian
civilization, generally known as *The Protocols of the Elders of Zion*, was privately
circulated among prominent citizens of Washington, D.C., and New York.
Boris Brasol, an antisemite and Russian Czarist sympathizer who arrived in
New York as part of a Russian military mission in 1918, initiated its distribution.[11] Given the concern about "loyalty" that dominated American society
during the years of war and the postwar suspicion of Jewish radical inclinations,
the work found fertile soil. Publishers, such as New York's George Haven
Putnam, who in 1921 sensed the profitability of its publication, produced a
book based upon the *Protocols*, entitled *The Cause of the World Unrest*.[12] After
reading it, Louis Marshall, president of the American Jewish Committee,
informed Putnam that "To say that I was shocked that your honored name
should be made the vehicle of disseminating among the American people these
outpourings of malice, is merely to confess the poverty of my vocabu-
lary."[13]

It was not Putnam the publisher, however, but Henry Ford the automobile
manufacturer who succeeded in bringing the *Protocols* to public attention.
Beginning on May 22, 1920, through the pages of the *Dearborn Independent*, a
weekly magazine that he owned and distributed nationally, Ford commenced
an unprecedented assault on American and world Jewry. His editorials, the first
of which was entitled "The International Jew—the World's Problem," proceeded to expose to his readers the alleged power and influence that Jews had
acquired and, because of it, the threat they posed to Christian society. Every
element that Ford found distasteful in the modern world his magazine laid at
the feet of the Jews. Urbanism, unbridled capitalism, political corruption,
alcoholism, Higher Criticism, liberalism, socialism, and Bolshevism were all
alleged to be hatched by Jewish conspirators whose ultimate design, he
charged, was to deceive, destroy, and enslave the world.[14] Periodically Ford
reprinted from the *Independent* collections of such articles in book form, which
he distributed free of charge to friends, clergymen, college faculty, school
teachers, editors, and legislators throughout the United States.[15]

American Jews were stunned at Ford's attack upon them, never before
having been confronted with an onslaught comparable in scope. Louis Marshall informed the Detroit millionaire that his articles constituted "a libel
upon an entire people who had hoped that at least in America they might be

spared the insult, the humiliation . . . which these articles are scattering throughout the land and which are echoes from the dark middle ages."[16]

The remonstrance, however, did little to persuade Ford to discontinue his series of hate. It was not until 1927, after the threat of a court suit and a boycott of his automobiles, that the Detroit manufacturer offered a formal apology and agreed to discontinue the odious series.[17] Observing this reversal, which took seven years to accomplish, David Philipson wondered if the harm that Ford had perpetrated during that time could ever be undone. "The minds of hundreds of thousands have been poisoned. The propaganda of hatred has born terrific fruit," he wrote in dismay.[18]

3

Grant, Hendrick, Roberts, Ford, and other Protestant nativists of the 1920s were not pillars of the church, nor did they speak for any denomination or group of American church attenders. One might argue that their hostility toward Jews was less a result of any reasoned theological position than a product of modernity, its secular and pseudo-scientific by-products, such as Social Darwinism and racism. Yet, in their own way, secular antisemites shared with the more religiously committed an ominous uncertainty about the future of Protestant culture in America.

Much has been written about the ascendancy of evangelical Protestant orthodoxy, "fundamentalism," as it was referred to during the postwar years. Evangelical Protestantism, as we have seen, was hardly a novel religious expression in the 1920s; its roots were deeply planted in early American history. By 1900 fundamentalism, as Ernest Sandeen observes, "though still unchristianed, was already a significant force in American life." At that early date it was still centered in the urban areas of the Northeast, where it was engaged in challenging its modernist opponents. By the 1920s, however, with some justification, fundamentalism was perceived as a religion of rural America and was increasingly linked in the public mind with the forces of social and political reaction.[19]

Fundamentalists were disquieted about the inroads that the New Theology had made into Protestant thought. The prevailing belief that good works of well-meaning Christians, technological and scientific advances, would usher in the Kingdom of God, contradicted the most sacred assumptions of their theology. The sciences of evolution and biblical criticism, they insisted, had corrupted Christian faith.[20] They pointed to the disappointing results of the First World War as evidence of man's futile efforts to remake the world. Like their secular counterparts, evangelical Protestants were disillusioned with the results of the Great War and the peace that followed. Christianity, they concluded, had derived little value from these years of bloodletting. It had not captured the world; humanity had imbibed few Christian lessons from the crisis, the Bible had not been restored to a central position in human affairs.

More than ever, fundamentalists were determined to prevail in their contest with Protestant liberals. The religious debates that they waged with their opponents ranged over subjects which were hardly new to American Christians. These included arguments about the doctrine of inerrancy and infallibility of Scripture, the divinity of Christ and his virgin birth, and the inherited sinful nature of human beings, a destiny from which they could not escape by moral exertion, but only through a belief in Christ's sacrifice and forgiveness. Especially now, viewed against the threat of the sins of modern society, these issues took on a new and desperate urgency.[21]

Fundamentalists crystallized traditional Christian beliefs. They collected them in an arsenal of doctrines with which to challenge their liberal opponents. This is not to suggest that fundamentalists agreed with each other on all theological points; they did not. However, they were united about a commonly perceived threat to the survival of American Christianity. Indeed, as William P. Hutchison observes, to fundamentalists, liberal Christianity was not even accepted as Christianity.[22]

Neither should it be assumed that fundamentalism's rigidity in theological matters necessarily led to anti-Jewish feelings. Many of the essays included in *The Fundamentals*, in accordance with premillennial Dispensationalist thinking, emphasized the importance that the Jewish experience held for Christians and their salvation. The authors of this multivolume work, which established the foundation of postwar evangelical Protestantism, challenged the conclusions of scholars of Higher Criticism who contradicted the testimony of the Hebrew Scripture. More than most Protestants, fundamentalists made a point of stressing the Jewishness of Jesus; they displayed a deep reverence for the Jewish Scripture and accepted Jews as the Chosen People of God.[23]

To be sure, fundamentalist writings also repeated traditional Christian attacks upon Jewish ritualism and legalism in Pharisaic times. Evangelicals continued to warn Jews that their road to salvation would be temporarily blocked because of their rejection of the Christian Messiah, and that the Old Israel had been superseded by the New. Yet their writings also cautioned that Christendom's cruelty toward the Jewish people would not go unpunished. They frequently emphasized the centrality of the Jews in God's universal plan.[24]

Liberal Protestants, such as Harry Emerson Fosdick, saw fundamentalism as the chief threat to America's religious life. To Fosdick and other liberals, as well as to those of the newer and less rigid school of neo-orthodoxy and Christian realism, fundamentalism was guilty of the sin of intolerance and intellectual blindness by its rejection of advanced scientific learning.[25] Still, it should not be assumed that Jews felt more secure within the theological framework of liberal Protestantism or neo-orthodoxy than they did with fundamentalism. One need only glance at the writings of such enlightened opponents of fundamentalism as Helmut Richard Niebuhr and Shailer Mathews to conclude otherwise.

Niebuhr, who together with his brother Reinhold helped to fashion a Protestant theology of Christian Realism, displayed (unlike his brother) little appreciation for the persistence of Judaism as a separate, autonomous faith. His widely acclaimed book *The Social Sources of Denominationalism,* which first appeared in 1929, is a polemic against religious separatism. Niebuhr's message is clear in its reminder that "The spirit of Jesus revolted against Jewish class distinctions between the righteous few and unhallowed many"; that Jesus saw "the typical child of God is a Samaritan who knew the meaning of human solidarity; ignoring the nationalism of Jews and Romans, he found faith superior to that of the chosen people."[26]

Niebuhr's accusations against the early Jews concern primarily their "racial loyalty," as distinct from Christianity's "Catholic culture," its "religious and cultural cosmopolitanism," which was far removed from the "separistic spirit which Judaism represented."[27] No doubt Niebuhr was lamenting the excesses of nationalism that were about to cast a spell of darkness upon the Western world. But seeking in the sources of Jewish history the spiritual ancestor of a contemporary evil and juxtaposing his findings against the universal and transcendent message of the gospel were conducive neither to truth nor to interreligious harmony.[28]

Shailer Mathews, whom we had first met among the Social Gospelers, also detected in Protestantism a perfect solution with which to heal the religious uncertainties that had befallen America during the postwar era. The spiritual confusion, according to Mathews, was brought on by the vast and diverse immigration for which, as he put it, "Protestantism is needed if for nothing else than its power to arouse a pride in American democracy."[29]

He was saddened to learn, however, that Jews resisted the imposition of such spiritual benefits. "Whatever the motive such proselytism is bitterly opposed by Jewish leaders," complained Mathews. He was disappointed at the thought that American Jews might respond to the growing antisemitism by withdrawing further from the beneficent lessons of Christianity.[30] While the seemingly tolerant tone of such progressive religious thinkers as H. Richard Niebuhr and Shailer Mathews did not appear at first glance to possess the imminent threat to Jewish security that the intensity of fundamentalism did, it would be an error to assume that theirs was a blueprint for interreligious harmony.

4

It was fundamentalist extremism, however, that inspired the first organized antisemitic movement in the United States, the Ku Klux Klan. Founded in

1915 by William J. Simmons in Atlanta, the secret hooded order blossomed, reaching about four million members by 1924. By that time it had spread nationally, with most of its membership residing outside of the South. With its expansion the Invisible Empire gained increasing influence and political power in state and local government. At its height, the KKK claimed chapters in almost every state of the United States.

Posing as a patriotic organization, as a defender of "100 percent Americanism," prohibition, racial purity, immigration restriction, especially of Roman Catholics and Jews, and as a self-proclaimed defender of evangelical Protestantism, it appealed to numerous Americans who had succumbed to the mood of social anxiety and boredom of the postwar generation.[31]

Jews were viewed by Klan theoreticians as a danger to American stability, and their elimination from American life became one of the Klan's key objectives. Any individual seeking membership in the Klan was expected to respond affirmatively to the question "Do you believe in the tenets of the Christian religion?" Yet, at the same time, Jews were accused of separating themselves from their Christian neighbors. One Klansman explained that his resentment of the Jew stemmed from "the amazing tenacity with which he resists absolute Americanization." Grand Wizard Hiram Wesley Evans contended that by resisting intermarriage with Gentiles, Jews had automatically excluded themselves from becoming Americans. Jews were also accused by the Klan leadership, who must have read Ford's *Dearborn Independent* with care, of planning the destruction of the American economy in order to enrich themselves, of promoting racial strife between whites and blacks so that they could profit by the ensuing social chaos, and of conspiring for the destruction of organized Christian life.[32] Edward Y. Clarke, Imperial Giant of the Klan, explained his order's view of Jews this way: "The Ku Klux Klan stands primarily for the principles of Jesus Christ and that explains why it is impossible for us to take the Jews in . . . Now the Christian white men are bound to band themselves into one great Klan and to give the Jews some of their own medicine."[33]

The powerful links that the Klan forged with Protestant fundamentalism suggest that the hooded order was much more than an organizational dimension of secular antisemitism. The KKK envisioned itself as the defender of American Protestantism, and it was from the ranks of fundamentalists that it drew much of its membership and leadership. The Klan's founder and Imperial Wizard, William J. Simmons, had been a preacher of the gospel before he transferred his religious energies to fashioning christological symbolism for the Klan. The Protestant ministry served as a nursery for Klan executives. Evangelical Protestants felt a familiar comfort in the mystic rituals of the Ku Klux Klan, and in the personal moral standards which it espoused. Like evangelical Protestants, Klansmen were disappointed with the declining social values of the postwar generation—bootlegging, crime, sexual promiscuity, movies—and wished to restore the centrality of the Protestant faith as an antidote to the anti-Christian influences around them. After observing 80,000 Klansmen and Klanswomen march through the streets of Washington, D.C., in August 1925, one Protestant minister wrote: "There was not an individual among its white-robed tens of thousands who were not Protestant, not one who had not declared his faith in Christ. . . . Ministers were in considerable numbers. . . . The favorite selection (of its fifty bands) was *Onward Christian Soldiers!*"[34]

Every effort was made by the KKK leadership to recruit the support of evangelical clergy. Protestant ministers were offered free membership in the Klan, an offer which many readily accepted. According to Wyn Wade's excellent study of the Klan, 40,000 fundamentalist ministers joined the hooded order, many of them achieving high positions in its ranks. They preached pro-Klan sermons in their churches and helped draw from their congregations new members into the movement. It was a reciprocal relationship that developed between church and Klan. The KKK invigorated the fundamentalist crusade; it crossed denominational lines, helped to unify diverse sects within the evangelical movement, and increased the numbers and frequency of church attendance. Klansmen and clergy supported each other in their common endeavor to strengthen evangelical Protestantism and restore the health of a Christian America.[35]

No event pictured more dramatically the link between church and Klan than did the visitations that groups of Klansmen periodically paid to their local churches. Arriving usually unannounced but not unanticipated, a robed and hooded contingent approached the pulpit and handed the preacher a monetary offering. Such gifts were seen as important tokens of the Klan's appreciation of the pastor's Christian work. They symbolized an offering of love and solidarity that bound together the two groups. Impecunious preachers were flattered by the Klan's attention and appreciation of their humble work for which they were otherwise poorly rewarded.[36]

Equally significant was the element of mystery and virility that the hooded order, with its rituals, dress, and ceremonies, injected into evangelical Protestantism. Wade describes the emotional intensity of a Klan rally:

> Though similar to the pagan fire festivals of central Europe during the middle ages, the Klan's cross burning in the 1920's were invariably constrained by a strict Christian ritual. The ceremony opened with a prayer by the "Kludd," or Klavern minister. The multitude then sang "Onward Christian Soldiers." After the hymn, the cross was lit, and the explosion of the kerosene and the rush of flames over the timbers was thrilling, to say the least. . . . Bathed in warmth, left arms outstretched toward the blazing icon and voices raised to "The Old Rugged Cross," Klansmen felt as in one body. These were moments they would always remember.[37]

Efforts by some historians to disassociate the rise of the KKK with the fundamentalist crusade of the 1920s have not been convincing. After examining the American Protestant press, Robert Miller, for example, could find no evidence for linking Protestantism with the Klan. No doubt, his perusal of nondenominational, liberally oriented magazines, such as the *Christian Century*, *World Tomorrow*, *Christian Work*, *Christian Herald*, and similar independent Protestant weeklies, unearthed no editorial support for the KKK. This was also true of his search of official denominational pronouncements, statements of Protestant leaders, reports of conventions and assemblies. The same cannot be said, however, of the Southern Baptist press, which, as a rule, upheld the principles and aims of the Klan.[38] Neither can the approval offered by the rank and file of evangelical Protestants be discounted, including, as we have seen, that of thousands of rural preachers who offered their allegiance to the Invisible Empire.

To be sure, no detectable organic connection existed between the Klan and the church, certainly not one comparable to that which had existed between the Spanish Inquisition and the Roman Catholic church. Neither was the support for the KKK espoused by the most thoughtful spokesmen of American Protestantism. Indeed, a number of prominent Protestant leaders, such as Harry Emerson Fosdick, Charles E. Jefferson, Lynn Harold Hough, and Sherwood Eddy, warned publicly of the danger that the ideas and tactics of the KKK held for democratic institutions.[39] Nevertheless, it is difficult to avoid the conclusion that during the 1920s the Klan's program of racism and antisemitism conformed to a view that was shared by millions of pious American Protestants.

5

The rise of the Ku Klux Klan, Henry Ford's anti-Jewish ravings, and the general public enmity toward Jews that was becoming increasingly evident made some thoughtful Christians wonder if the full measure of European antisemitism was about to take root in the United States; and if so, they asked, what was the church's responsibility? As one form of response they promoted "interfaith" discussions, or dialogues, a practice which would increase in frequency and importance in future decades.

The Federal Council of Churches (FCC) was one of the first to introduce the practice. Founded earlier in the century as a consequence of the ecumenical optimism of the Progressive Era, the FCC had paid little attention to the problems of Jewish-Christian relations before World War I. But with the growing evidence of antisemitism, the council established in 1923 a Committee on Goodwill between Jews and Christians. Its founders admitted that while Europe had been infected with "passions, strife, persecutions, and pogroms . . . America has not yet been wholly free from prejudice and injustice and recent tendencies have seemed to bring the peril nearer."[40] With its typical optimism, the committee declared that its goal was to determine and remove the causes of antisemitism in the United States, to promote understanding and goodwill, and to counteract the dissemination of false propaganda about the Jews. In the following years it organized numerous conferences and dispatched teams of rabbis and ministers on speaking tours throughout the country.[41]

Meanwhile, the Central Conference of American Rabbis had established its own Committee on Goodwill, which worked cooperatively with the FCC. Similar steps were taken by other Jewish organizations, such as the International Order of B'nai B'rith and the National Council of Jewish Women. Individual efforts added to these goodwill programs. Edward Hunt founded the American Goodwill Union in 1924, and Rabbi Isaac Landman founded a Permanent Commission of Better Understanding Between Christians and Jews in 1927.

Yet, as Benny Kraut observes, some Jewish leaders wondered if the real aim of some of these Christian endeavors was goodwill or a desire to convert Jews to Christianity. Indeed. executives of the FCC, such as Alfred Williams Anthony, a Northern Baptist, drew only a thin line between goodwill and evangelization. Understandably, Jews were concerned whether the FCC was capable of ignoring the evangelical demands of many of its constituents.[42]

Such troublesome thoughts prompted a group of Jews and Christians to form a nonecclesiastical interfaith organization, one which would remain unaffiliated with either the FCC or any other religious body. One of the leading promoters in this movement was John W. Herring, a Congregationalist minister and executive secretary of the FCC. In 1926 his work led to the formation of an organization eventually to be known as the National Conference of Christians and Jews (NCCJ).[43]

Although American Jews, representing a wide variety of theological opinions, offered the NCCJ wide support, many continued to remain cautious about its ultimate purpose. The efforts of one individual, Everett R. Clinchy, however, went a long way in allaying such anxieties. No individual labored harder than Clinchy during these early years to improve the interreligious, yet nonsectarian, reputation of the NCCJ. An ordained Presbyterian minister, Clinchy had served pulpits at Fairmount, New Jersey, and at Wesleyan University in Middletown, Connecticut, and had been a member of the secretarial staff of the Federal Council of Churches. His life and work exemplified the deep concern about the growth of Christian antisemitism in the United States. A Jewish acquaintance characterized Clinchy as "nominally a Protestant but in reality a man rising above creed and sectarianism, a man who recognizes in every fellow man a brother and a child of God."[44]

Through its "round table" discussions and "seminars" with Christians and Jews, the NCCJ performed a badly needed educational function. Its endeavors provided both faith communities an opportunity to learn about each other, an exercise that was rarely performed before the 1920s. Clinchy believed that the prompt reaction exerted by concerned Protestants weakened the effectiveness of the growing antisemitic movement in the United States.[45]

The NCCJ was the first organized effort to endorse the concept of religious pluralism in the United States. Inspired by the writings of such philosophers as Horace Kallen and John Dewey, religious pluralists challenged the Christian triumphalism and ethnocentricism of the postwar years. The NCCJ granted a spiritual equality to both Christians and Jews. Clinchy admitted that human relationships in the United States might have been much simpler if the nation's inhabitants had all come from the same heritage and tradition. Although he believed that the differences in doctrine and religious practice that "divide men are neither foolish, nor inconsequential," nevertheless, "though men may be separate in conviction as the fingers of their outstretched hand," they must remain "as compact as a clenched fist in their attack upon the enemies that threaten the life of organized society." No other solution was possible for the survival of American democracy, wrote Clinchy, but "to accept the fact of cultural pluralism and to adapt our patterns of behavior to it."[46]

6

Ironically, the ethnocentric 1920s were also the years in which the Protestant biblical authority George F. Moore offered the first scholarly challenge to Christian triumphalism. Unlike Clinchy, Moore was not an activist in the battle to improve interfaith associations. His attack upon antisemitism was a contemplative one, launched through the publication of a series of studies that enabled Christian biblical scholars to view Judaism from a fresh perspective. A graduate of Union Theological Seminary of New York in 1877 and ordained a Presbyterian minister in the following year, Moore went on to teach at Andover Theological Seminary until 1902, and then at Harvard as a professor of Hebrew, the Bible, and rabbinics. A careful, meticulous, and dedicated student, he did more than anyone else of his generation to disabuse his academic colleagues of the accumulated misinformation about the Jewish religious heritage. Although not an active crusader against antisemitism, Moore sympathized with those who sought to eradicate it. Jews "have small reason to admire Christian ethics in application, whether ecclesiastical, political, social, or individual," he wrote in 1923. "Judging the tree by the fruit it has borne in eighteen centuries of persecution, they not unnaturally resent Christian assertions of its preeminence."[47]

Moore was chiefly a scholar, a student of talmudic literature, who labored a lifetime to disengage the Jewish historical record from Christian sources and interpretations. His primary effort was to convince the historians of early Christianity that their vision of Judaism was faulty, since it was based upon a foundation of ignorance of rabbinic literature. He complained in 1921 that Christian writing about Jews has been primarily "apologetic or polemic rather than historical."[48] He was critical of Catholic and Protestant scholarship that for centuries saw little else in rabbinic literature beyond a mine in which to search for superstitions, "unholy rites," and "blasphemies against Christianity."[49] Moore lamented that even recent and contemporary scholars found little else beyond "legalism" in the sacred Jewish sources. The argument that runs consistently throughout his work is that Judaism can be understood only on its own merits, by a study of its own sources, not by an attempt to find its relationship to the Christian faith. He urged his readers to approach rabbinic literature with the same reverence which they accorded the synoptic Gospels.[50]

He was also critical of Old Testament scholarship; here, too, Moore recognized the inability of Christian biblicists to accept the Jewish Scripture on its own terms, but only as they believed it to be related to the Gospels. He was appalled, for example, at Christian efforts to seek in the Hebrew Bible and its commentaries "a figure corresponding to the Son, or the Word (Logos)" or "a divine being, intermediary between God and the Father and the world."[51] It was clear to Moore that no such figure or symbol could be discovered in sacred Jewish literature, and he urged Christians not to spend their time searching for it.

Moore's two-volume work *Judaism in the First Centuries of the Christian Era*, published in 1927, continues to remain among the clearest expositions of rabbinic Judaism produced by an American Christian scholar.[52] His emphasis upon the formative years of modern Judaism stands in sharp contrast to the traditional practice of Christians to disregard postbiblical Jewish history. He was not disturbed by the thought that the completion of the New Testament was of no significance to the early rabbis, that it had no impact on their own achievements. He recognized that any meaningful comprehension of "the creation of a normative type of Judaism" will fail to materialize without a thorough study of the creative accomplishments of the early talmudic sages.[53]

Moore's view of the Pharisees as the most significant religious body in the Judaism of the early Christian period grew out of his familiarity with the rabbinic sources. Unlike other Christian writers Moore does not capitulate to the deprecation of the Pharisees found in the Gospels. He understood that Jewish survival depended upon their intelligent guidance; that because of the groundwork which they laid, "unity of belief and observance among Jews in all their wide dispersion has been attained in later centuries."[54]

Aware of the differences that have evolved between Christians and Jews, Moore warned his readers that "Judaism must be allowed to speak for itself" and should not be viewed as "a background, an environment," or "a contrast" for Christianity.[55] Christian ignorance about Judaism has produced confusion and misunderstanding about such important designations as "law," a term which Moore considered "a poor English rendering for *Torah*, or "original sin—an alien doctrine" for believing Jews. Their employment, Moore explains, served no useful purpose in enhancing Jewish-Christian relations.[56]

Moore represented a lonely voice in a generation glued to the idea of triumphant Christianity when he suggested that both Judaism and Christianity, each in its own unique way, represented a valid road to God. "Both Rabbis and Church Fathers," he writes, were "convinced that they were showing men exactly how to conform to the revelation of God."[57] Moore stopped short of demanding a reevaluation of Christian theology in regard to its relationship with the Jewish people, a task which would be left to theologians of a later generation.

It is difficult to gauge precisely the extent of influence that Moore's scholarship had upon American Protestant thought. The noted Jewish biblical scholar Samuel Sandmel believed that Moore's "eminence had been such that it has created a new tone in the Christian assessment of Judaism," but that its influence has been most pronounced among "Christian Biblical scholars."[58] How far it extended beyond this exclusive guild, or filtered down from it, is another question; it was probably not very far. Moore's writings, found primarily in specialized journals with small circulations, possessed limited popular appeal. Still, as a Christian student of Judaism, Moore towered above his contemporaries. Together with the activists of the NCCJ, Moore injected a thoughtful, redeeming note into the otherwise discordant religious temper of the 1920s.

15

Hear No Evil,
See No Evil

1

The decades of economic collapse and shattered world peace of the 1930s and 40s had a profound effect upon the relationship of Protestants and non-Protestant faiths. In part this was a result of the relative decline of Protestantism's numerical status. By the end of the 1950s, for example, Roman Catholics, who constituted more than 22 percent of the population, compared favorably to the 35.5 percent claimed by the combined denominations of Protestantism. By that time Jews had also increased their numerical strength to 5.5 million. With unemployment dogging its membership in the 1930s, and its fiscal support in a state of decline, Protestantism showed little growth beyond the 40 million that it counted during the years of the Great Depression. To some observers, Protestantism's relative drop gave legitimacy to the suggestion that America had ceased to be a Protestant nation.[1]

Even so, from a theological perspective, American Protestantism continued to display an unusual vigor. On one hand, neo-orthodoxy had penetrated deeply into the nation's intellectual life. With Reinhold Niebuhr as its leading American interpreter, neo-orthodoxy provided a theological alternative for those who stood uncomfortably between fundamentalism and liberalism. While avoiding the rigid biblicism of the Dispensationalists, neo-orthodoxy's "Christian Realism" could escape from a capitulation to the trappings of modern culture.[2] On the other end of the ecclesiastical spectrum, neoliberals continued to apply the doctrines of the Social Gospel to the needs of a world crippled by unemployment and economic despair. The leadership of the Federal Council of Churches was particularly noted for its social activism during this troubled decade, although few of its efforts activated a corresponding reaction from, or even proved inspiring to, the rank and file of its millions of congregants.

Actually, a large segment of the Protestant laity opposed even the economic

innovation of the New Deal. Neither did they approve of any military involvement against European dictators. Despite a growing threat to America's security, pacifism was a marked characteristic of American Protestantism on the
eve of the Second World War. At the same time, throughout the thirties,
fundamentalism, now a dissenting minority, continued to challenge the underlying assumptions of any new theological trends and reemphasized the urgency
of a Christian personal salvation in a world whose values appeared in a
deplorable state of regression.[3]

2

The intensity and frequency of American antisemitism continued to climb
during the 1930s, reaching a peak shortly before America's entry into World
War II. Prior to Japan's attack upon Pearl Harbor, hundreds of antisemitic
organizations were actively engaged in spreading their message of hate
throughout the United States. The persecution of the Jews of Germany did not
seriously move American public opinion. Polls conducted during the late
thirties indicate that the majority of the American people perceived Jews as
possessing objectionable traits—dishonesty, greed, aggressiveness—and constituting a greater menace to American society than any other single ethnic
group. A small minority, twenty percent of the respondents of one poll,
recommended that Jews be expelled from the United States.[4]

A combination of domestic and foreign events conspired to intensify anti-
Jewish hostility in the United States. Some of it, as manifested for example by
the diabolical activities of Fritz Kuhn and his German-American Bund, was
linked directly to the rise of Nazism in Germany. As Hitler's designs for world
conquest became manifest, a Jewish tilt toward American interventionism in
the European war exposed Jews to further popular hostility. American isolationism, a much more acceptable public stance in the 1930s, added fuel to the
flames of anti-Judaism. Americans who had not yet psychologically recovered
from their last European crusade were reluctant to repeat the adventure.
Advocacy of intervention in European difficulties became viewed as an exclusively Jewish desire, whose purpose was to serve Jewish ends. The American
First Committee, organized by conservative isolationists to prevent America's
entanglement in the Allied war against Adolf Hitler, warned about Jewish
desires to drag Americans into battle.[5]

Franklin D. Roosevelt's New Deal experimental programs were also attributed by his conservative opponents to Jewish socialist designs. According to
E. Digby Baltzell, "The anti-Semitic and racial undertones which marked so
many of the anti-Roosevelt stories and which soon became an obsession among
members of the country-club establishment were not accidental." Much of the
anti-Roosevelt rhetoric was mingled with antisemitism. Haters of the New
Deal dubbed it "The Jew Deal" and described it, according to one historian, as

"a Jewish trick contrived to betray the United States into the clutches of international conspirators who were plotting a world state under Jewish domination." The president himself was accused of being a Jew, who was descended from Sephardic Hebrews who arrived in New York in the seventeenth century.[6]

American-Jewish defense agencies were kept busy monitoring the progress of the hate campaign. The 1935 Report of the Secretary of the Anti-Defamation League indicated that some of the hate groups about which it was collecting information included the Silver Shirts, Black Shirts, Khaki Shirts, Homesteaders, the Vigilantes, Ku Klux Klan, the Defenders, and the Crusader White Shirts. The American Jewish Committee estimated that by 1939, 500 antisemitic groups, encouraged by the success of German Nazism, were active in the United States. Nazi antisemitic propaganda, distributed through German consulates, provided continuous encouragement for these extremists.[7]

3

Nazi antisemites and their American imitators, thriving in an environment of social and economic dislocation, produced a climate of normalcy for Jew hatred. Liberal intellectuals and academics vied with one another to produce explanations and antidotes for the aberration. In the process, however, it became clear that many American humanists and social scientists were themselves infected with the disease. Their learned treatises frequently pointed to Jews as the chief cause for their own victimization. Jewish materialism, cultural parochialism, and their insistence on separating themselves from their Christian neighbors were explanations frequently offered for the terrible malady that had befallen the Jews in Europe and was threatening their security in the United States. A few examples of such academic work will suffice.

English-born and Oxford-educated Basil Mathews, a prolific writer on religious themes, widely read in the United States, where he also served as a professor of Christian world relations at Andover Theological Seminary, displayed early in his career a typical British admiration for the Judaic contributions to civilization.[8] By 1935, however, he lamented the drift toward secularism and the pursuit of gain that he discovered dominated the Jews of New York and elsewhere. But it was within their parochialism that he detected the clue to their tribulations. "The Jew's refusal on religious grounds to share the social festivities of the people among whom he is, his worship on a different day from that of Christian neighbors, his standard of values that challenge and often contradict that of his nation of his adoption, his very beard and curls, costume and greetings, language and occupation, have always emphasized not only that he was different, but that his difference savored of a feeling of superiority."[9]

The healing and civilizing qualities of Christian universalism became a popular theme in enlightened academic circles. William Earnest Hocking, one of the most respected philosophers of the early decades of the twentieth century, was not pleased with the arguments of cultural pluralists. Religious diversity, a condition which he admitted served a useful purpose at times, was not one, however, that he found particularly inspiring. Writing in 1939 while serving as Alfred Professor of Philosophy at Harvard, Hocking looked forward to the time when humanity would be liberated from its particularistic religious chains and begin to embrace the all-encompassing truth of Christian universalism.[10]

Even social scientists, who gathered together shortly after America's entry into the war against the Axis in 1941 to explore the persistence of antisemitism, agreed that its solution could be uncovered by eliminating Jewish exclusivity. Raymond Kennedy, a professor of sociology at Yale, prescribed for the malady a more rapid assimilation for American Jews. He counseled Jews to distance themselves from orthodoxy and adopt the standards of Reform Judaism, which, as he put it, "had adopted many of the features of . . . the more progressive of the Protestant churches."[11]

Jessie Bernard, a sociologist at Lindenwood College who also grappled with the causes and cures of antisemitism, envisioned a synthesis of Judaism and Christianity as the only feasible solution. He described his suggestion as "A new synthesis of beauty, an attempt to assimilate what was lovely in both heritages." He admitted that "Only strong personalities can make the transfer," and that it would be "a major spiritual operation to uproot an old value and graft a new one in its place. It is not a process that can be carried on en masse. Every Jew must do it for himself."[12]

J. O. Hertzler, chairman of the Department of Sociology at the University of Nebraska, went even further in his desire to make Judaism disappear. As he saw it, the "provincial spirit" and "exclusiveness" of Judaism was its principal failing. Even assimilation, he complained, had not enabled the Jews to cast off their "tribal spirit"; nor has conversion solved the problem of antisemitism. The convert, he observed, "is hated by both the Christian and the Jew—as a pretender who can never be an enthusiastic Christian in the one case, as a renegade in the other."[13] Like Stanton Coit before him, Hertzler pointed to the Jewish claim that they are "God's Chosen People" and to their insistence on living apart from their Gentile neighbors as the chief reasons for antisemitism. The ghetto, he argued, was a Jewish invention; it satisfied the Jewish desire to live separate and isolated from their Christian surroundings.[14]

Writing on the eve of Germany's extermination of Europe's Jews, the Nebraska professor saw little hope for the eradication of antisemitism so long as the Jew continued to resist complete assimilation. "To cease to be a cultural irritant," he writes,

> the Jew must be completely assimilated. Any old allegiance to his "chosen people" idea will have to disappear; he must consciously remove characteristics of

behavior which are recognizably Jewish; he must deliberately mold himself and his life on Gentile patterns. . . . He will have to be completely absorbed ethnically, that means he will have to marry with non-Jews, generation after generation, until he has no grandparents who were considered as Jews and no children who by chance might have any distinguishing "Jewish" characteristics.[15]

Hertzler's formula, which prescribed the spiritual obliteration of Judaism, was not rejected by all American social scientists. Ellis Freeman, for example, a professor of psychology at the University of Tampa, dubbed the Jewish desire to perpetuate its traditional ways with the unflattering term *Judaeocentricism.* His studies convinced him "that the most certain way of abolishing anti-Semitism would be to abolish Judaism."[16] Another prewar psychologist, J. F. Brown, of the Menninger Clinic in Topeka, Kansas, and a professor at the University of Kansas, agreed that the solution to the problem of antisemitism was a total biological absorption of the Jews into Christian society. He advised haste in this matter, so that the annihilation of the Jews, which had begun in Europe, would not spread to the United States. Jews must realize, he cautioned, "how deep seated is the problem of anti-Semitism, and not rely too greatly on an unwarranted trust in the essential goodness of human nature."[17]

4

As the Nazi noose tightened around the fate of Europe's Jews, American Jews found themselves desperately alone, surrounded by a noncaring Gentile world. Neither did they find much comfort in the official actions of the nation's policymakers. Paralyzed by immigration restriction laws and, as Richard Breitman and Alan Kraut document, a State Department bureaucracy paralyzed by an unimaginative interpretation of its responsibilities, compounded by the reluctance of a president to assume risks on behalf of Europe's Jews, the fate of world Jewry appeared bleak.[18]

Obviously, one could not know if Germany's desire to humiliate and crush its Jews might have been stemmed by early American intervention, since even relatively minor signals of disapproval from Washington to the Third Reich were nonexistent. To what degree antisemitism had permeated America's Department of State and the Foreign Service has been debated by American historians. Henry Feingold's pioneering work *The Politics of Rescue* carefully documents the paralysis that gripped the United States by the late thirties in respect to Germany's Jews. The State Department, he contends, was riddled with antisemitism, while immigration restriction laws formalized during the preceding decade were welcomed by those who wished to prevent the entrance of refugees from Nazism. David Wyman's study *The Abandonment of the Jews* substantiates the thesis that the strong anti-Jewish sentiment among American policymakers inhibited more creative rescue efforts.[19]

Neither can one discount the indifference that prevailed in the halls of

Congress on the eve of the Second World War. It was a sentiment motivated in part by a fear that Jewish anti-Nazi agitation might draw the United States into the conflict with Germany. In this sense Congress was echoing the public's reluctance to exert any special effort to save Europe's Jews. Deborah Lipstadt's study of American press opinion, *Beyond Belief,* finds that throughout the thirties much of the nation's press opposed any relaxation of immigration laws. Even news of *Kristalnacht* (Night of Broken Glass) in November 1938, the most vicious outburst of violence against the Jews to occur in Germany before the war, did little to alter American public opinion regarding immigration.[20]

What the Nazis had in store for the Jews was no secret in Washington by 1941. Throughout the late thirties Jews were suspecting the worst. Even so, the efforts of Jewish organizations to budge the president and his State Department into relaxing immigration laws were of no avail. Jews were a relatively small minority who lived in a world that displayed little sympathy for their plight. Neither did the growing public fear of a "Trojan Horse," a "Fifth Column," which would allow Nazi subversives masquerading as refugees from Nazism to enter the United States, help the Jewish case. It produced instead a public hysteria that further sealed the fate of Europe's Jews.[21]

A political realist, FDR was not about to upset the nation's immigration policies. Breitman and Kraut observe that between 1933 and 1936, the president approached the refugee issue with circumspection, offering "a symbolic humanitarianism," while at the same time continuing "to meet with Jewish spokesmen but largely in an effort to mollify the American Jewish community without making any promises." For pragmatic reasons, since Roosevelt preferred not to associate his administration too closely with Jews, he avoided making Jewish rescue a centerpiece of his foreign policy. While "Hitler found it valuable to publicize the Jewish identity of his victims, Roosevelt found it equally expedient to obscure the religious identity of those he would have liked to rescue."[22]

5

Generally speaking, Protestant reaction to European events did not differ appreciably from that of most Americans. William E. Nawyn, who has examined the American denominational attitude toward Nazi persecution, concludes that "Protestants, acting as individuals, in a denominational or inter-denominational capacity, showed remarkably little outrage and all too often failed to do more than express pious injunctions opposing the destruction of German Jewry, and solicitude over the desperate circumstances of the Jewish refugee."[23] Any effort to protest Nazi behavior in liberal Protestant circles was neutralized by pacifist sentiment. Liberals were reluctant to condemn Nazi atrocities so long as social imperfections, such as Jim Crow laws, continued to exist in the United States. Their inability to differentiate between Nazi and other social evils destroyed their ability to mount an effective campaign of protest against German behavior. Protestant leaders failed to offer their co-religionists moral direction during these trying times. To be sure, some isolated voices were raised in protest. But, Nawyn concludes, "viewed in the context of Protestantism's vast numbers, wealth, and potential influence, its response was meager."[24]

What is more, in those instances where ethnic and denominational links existed between American and German Protestants, as in the case of the Lutheran and Mennonite denominations, both conservative in their theological views, they remained either silent or apologetic about Germany's barbaric behavior. This was evident in the responses of the two largest divisions of the Lutheran church, the United Lutheran Church of America (ULCA), and the Lutheran Church–Missouri Synod (LCMS). Both groups understood their mission to be primarily to preach the gospel rather than to involve the church in social and political issues. Both divisions remained either silent about Germany's persecutions or skeptical about the accuracy of the reports from Germany.[25]

The *Lutheran Witness,* the leading organ of the LCMS, remained sympathetic toward Germany until 1940, insisting "that it is not the obligation of the Church to express itself on the moral issues involved in the current international situation." Such spiritual aloofness did not prevent it from attributing the growth of German antisemitism to Jewish failings. It also exposed its isolationist position in 1940 when it commended Charles Lindbergh's efforts to keep the United States out of the European conflict.[26]

Mennonites, who traced their origins to the German Anabaptists of the sixteenth century, envisioned the world as divided into two kingdoms, God's and the earth's. True Christians, Mennonites insisted, lived in the former and, apart from offering obedience to it, avoided any involvement with the latter. Mennonites contributed no official response to Germany's persecution of Jews. Their journals did not condemn Nazi atrocities, nor did they conceal a pro-German, antisemitic attitude.[27]

Kansas Mennonites offered their financial support to the Reverend Gerald B. Winrod of Wichita, Kansas, a blatant antisemite and an apologist for Nazism. Professing to be a premillennial Dispensationalist, Winrod managed to extract from biblical prophecies a much more negative image of Jews than was customarily expounded by Dispensationalists. Like other supporters of the Ku Klux Klan, Winrod was impressed with the message of *The Protocols of the Elders of Zion.* As a critic of modernism, evolution, liberalism, the New Deal, Communism, and atheism, Winrod appealed to the pious, conservative temperament of the Mennonites. His journal, *The Defender,* fundamentalist in tone and full of invective against the Jews, was published at the Mennonite printing office and enjoyed a wide circulation in the Mennonite community.[28]

Winrod was not the only native fascist of 1930s who claimed to have a deep commitment to Protestant values. Gerald L. K. Smith was another who, like Winrod, was a Protestant minister. Smith was born near Madison, Wisconsin, in 1898 to impoverished and devout parents, members of the Christian church. Smith became a preacher of the gospel while still a student at Valparaiso University, a calling in which he excelled within a few years following his graduation. By 1929 he had moved to Shreveport, Louisiana, where he remained a respected member of the clergy until he became entangled in politics and an associate of Huey Long. By the mid-thirties Smith had acquired the reputation of a prominent demagogue, a Jew-baiter, and a close companion of Henry Ford. Smith was also excited by the ideas of *The Protocols* and was an admirer of the Jew-hating radio priest Father Caughlin.[29]

Protestantism's efforts to convert Jews to Christianity during these trying years may be classed among its most insensitive gestures. Evangelical periodicals were among the most consistent in reporting about the tragic European events; but missionaries saw little in these reports except an opportunity, even an obligation, to preach the gospel to Jews. Conrad Hoffmann, Jr., director of the International Missionary Council's Committee on the Christian Approach to the Jews, considered Nazi mistreatment of Jews a new and important challenge for Christians. Jesus Christ, asserted Hoffmann in 1935, "is the key to the solution of the problem of the Jew, here as in Germany and elsewhere." It was a message he and other missionaries continued to transmit through the thirties. Evangelists saw in their outreach efforts a unique opportunity granted to them by Providence, one which allowed them to perform the ultimate act of Christian compassion.[30]

Throughout the decade premillennial Dispensationalists distributed a quarter of a million New Testaments to the Jews of America. They tried to extract Christian prophetic meaning from the tragic events that had befallen the Jews. They wondered if Hitler's wrath upon God's Chosen People and his hatred of the Western democracies were signals that the world was about to end in disaster. They had long been convinced that Jews were determined to play a central role in Dispensational eschatology, and they now wondered if Jews were being punished for their rejection of the Christian Messiah. Evangelicals saw in Germany's persecution of the Jews a sign of God's plan to drive Jews either to the Holy Land or to conversion.[31]

While Dispensationalists were forbidden to participate in acts of antisemitism, which they classified as the work of Satan, yet, as William Glass observes, neither were they offered the theological tools with which to counteract such work. Indeed, as part of God's plan, antisemitism's onward surge and hidden purpose, they believed, could not and should not be obstructed. "Antisemitism was an inescapable part of God's manipulation of events to consummate His program," and any mortal efforts to alter the course of events were futile. Clearly, American evangelists could not be counted among those who would offer any significant support to the Jews during the 1930s.[32]

Neither was the Federal Council of Churches a dependable agency during this hour of crisis. Representing a collective liberal Christian commitment to social justice and ecumenism, the FCC nevertheless failed to provide the necessary moral leadership to oppose Germany's diabolical activities. Its occasional and puny pronouncements for the defense of Jewish rights in Germany proved of little value in offsetting Germany's Protestantism's cooperation with Nazism. Indeed, the ties that many of the FCC's constituent denominations maintained with their German coreligionists tended also to limit its effectiveness as a voice for Jewish survival.[33] Stephen Wise recalled with disappointment how Christianity's indifference to the plight of the Jews affected his own thinking about Jewish-Christian relations: "It is because of my deep disappointment over the failure of American Christendom to bestir itself and to arise against the brutal foes and destroyers of the people of its Christ that my interest in the so called interracial and interreligious good-will movement has become attenuated. It failed, deliberately chose to fail, in the hour of our greatest need."[34]

Wise was not unaware, however, that among liberal and neo-orthodox Protestants a few unrepresentative voices were raised on behalf of Jews during the 1930s. One of these was Wise's companion and co-worker in good deeds, John Haynes Holmes, who for more than a generation had been an outspoken foe of antisemitism. But the events that he witnessed after a visit to Germany, he admitted, were unprecedented. "My thoughts are still confused, even as they are harrowed and tortured, by what I saw and heard in Germany this summer," he wrote in the mid-thirties. Upon his return to the States, Holmes announced that the Jews in the Third Reich were doomed. Just like criminals "condemned to execution," they are "allowed to exist . . . in death houses," awaiting the inevitable end.[35]

Holmes explained to Americans the unique nature of contemporary German barbarism. "The attack on the Jews in Germany is no mere Ku Klux Klan excursion of a gang of heedless hoodlums." Jew-hatred was the very essence of Nazi ideology. If the Jews were to be spared, the whole structure of National Socialism would crumble; the very soul of the Nazi cause would wither, explained Holmes. Nazi Jew-hatred was not only a political policy, but a popular mania, and its virus had contaminated the entire German population. "When Hitler inaugurated his campaign against the Jews, he released a gas attack which had poisoned and therewith corrupted an entire nation." By 1937 Holmes predicted ominously that if the Nazi regime endured, it would ultimately exterminate the entire Jewish people.[36] The solution to the impending catastrophe that Holmes proposed was both simple and unprecedented. "There is only one thing that can be done about the Jews in Germany, and that is to *get them out*. They must be rescued, as the residents of a burning house."[37] Needless to say, few of his listeners were persuaded.

Despite his pacifism, which he refused to repudiate even after the Japanese attack in 1941, Harry Emerson Fosdick was also a leading critic of Germany's policy toward its Jews. In 1933, shortly after Hitler had been elevated by his people to leadership, Fosdick met with a group of Christians and Jews to draft a public protest against Germany's anti-Jewish measures. That year he also delivered a scathing denunciation of Nazism at a meeting of the FCC. Fosdick was annoyed at the feeble response toward Nazi behavior voiced by American Christians. In order to make Germany's repugnant behavior clear to the world, he urged Americans to boycott the Berlin Olympic Games of 1936, again to no avail. The United States chose to honor Germany by participating in the international athletic event. Throughout the thirties Fosdick cooperated with various Jewish organizations to offer assistance to German-Jewish refugees.[38] But, like Holmes, he was an isolated voice in Protestantism's liberal establishment.

6

Reinhold Niebuhr, the leading American exponent of neo-orthodoxy, who many continue to regard as the outstanding American Protestant theologian of the twentieth century, differed considerably in philosophical temperament from Holmes and Fosdick. But Niebuhr's voice was also prominent among the group of defenders of Jewish rights during the 1930s; and like Holmes and Fosdick, his was an isolated voice that did not speak for the Protestant majority.

At first glance there appears little in the evolution of Niebuhr's theology that American Jews would have found particularly exciting. Niebuhr's reaffirmation of Christian orthodox values and his rejection of the utopian aspirations of the liberal Christianity of the Social Gospel contained little meaning for American Jews. Like Niebuhr, even more so, they found the events of the 1930s and 1940s, both international and domestic, disheartening. Yet they were not as quick as he was to discard their faith in liberal idealism.

Niebuhr's focus on the centrality of sin, his conviction that evil was pervasive and incurable, was not a palatable notion for most Jews.[39] Despite all that would occur to them during the 1940s, Jews clung to the belief that sin was not inevitable. Niebuhr's grim and gloomy view of humanity upset Jews. In 1945 (while the ovens of Auschwitz had yet not cooled), Milton Steinberg, one of the most prominent Conservative American rabbis, was critical of Niebuhr's "reaffirmation of the reality of evil" in humans and society. A decade later, Levi Olan, a leading spokesman of the Jewish Reform movement, instructed Niebuhr that humanity, torn between bad and good, is always free to choose. Niebuhr's theology, remarked Olan, is "Paulinian, Augustinian, Calvinistic and Reformationist," but not Judaic.[40] Even those more sympathetic to Niebuhr's ideas, such as the Jewish theologians Emil Fackenheim and Abraham Heschel, found deep flaws in his religious thought. Heschel, a friend of Niebuhr and an admirer of his "depth of insight" and "fullness of vision," acknowledged that Niebuhr's view of sin was essentially alien to the Jewish intellectual tradition.[41]

Yet, interestingly, Niebuhr's orthodoxy, which grew more from his observation of the tragic world around him than from theological speculation, enabled him to assess society's behavior with a piercing accuracy. He was quicker than most of his generation, for example, to conclude that humanity's iniquity found its ultimate expression not in individual but in collective behavior. This insight sharpened his awareness of society's indifference to its own brutality.[42]

More importantly, however, the disenchantment that Niebuhr experienced did not drive him into monastic seclusion. On the contrary, it molded within him a "Christian Realism," which suggested that in spite of all that was amiss with the world, it was incumbent upon Christians to strive, not for society's perfection, a futile endeavor because the Kingdom would not materialize in historical time, but for its improvement, a more realistic possibility.[43] Christian Realism quickened Niebuhr's sense of social consciousness and provided him with a "depth of insight" into the realities of human and social behavior which liberalism had failed to inspire. It also sharpened his perspective of the plight of the Jews as a minority in a Christian civilization.

Niebuhr was among the first of the leading Protestants to direct attention to the rising wave of antisemitism in Nazi Germany. Throughout the decades of the 1930s Niebuhr warned of the threat to Jewish survival in Germany. As did many others, Niebuhr tended at first to minimize the central role that antisemitism played in the mythology of the Third Reich. By 1938, however, as the Nazis goose-stepped into Vienna, Niebuhr was assured that "the ultimate in man's sadistic tendencies" was being unveiled.[44] In the next few months he helped to initiate the Volunteer Christian Committee to Boycott Nazi Germany and urged Americans to refrain from traveling on German ships, buying German products, or "setting foot on the territory of the Third Reich."[45]

Niebuhr had long been aware of the antisemitic tendencies in the German Lutheran establishment, but he found its hasty capitulation to the Nazi racial doctrines inexcusable. The source and reason for such behavior preoccupied his attention. A fear of Marxist revolution, he reasoned, explained in part the overwhelming support Adolf Hitler received from the nation's Protestant churchgoers. The Nazi revolution, he learned, had even stimulated growth in church attendance; and many of the nation's pious looked upon the recent political transition as a "gift of God."

More importantly, Niebuhr surmised, the Nazi victory over Germany's spiritual life was enhanced by a theological disposition in Lutheranism to maintain, as he put it, "an attitude of pious reverence toward the State even when the latter violated the precepts of Christianity." Clearly, Nazism flourished upon the fertile "soil of Lutheran Protestantism." Martin Luther, he recalled, had little faith in the behavior of human beings and placed an inordinate reliance upon secular government, "the Kingdom of God's left hand," as Luther called it, to prevent anarchy and social conflict. The logical result of Germany's spiritual foundation, Niebuhr observed, was officially sanctioned state violence.[46]

The complacency of America's churches toward Nazism and antisemitism, however, represented a moral failing on his own turf, one which he personally felt obligated to address. His primary objection was directed at what he believed was the ethical miscalculation of the Christian pacifist. Despite Niebuhr's early flirtation with pacifism, his antipathy toward the sentiment was never completely absent. During World War I he wrote in his notebook: "I cannot bring myself to associate with pacifists." The belief that all conflict could be abated or all crises resolved through rational discussion and an appeal to reason and justice, a view popular in liberal Christian circles, he concluded, constituted a serious misunderstanding and in the present crisis might result in dangerous consequences. In 1934 Niebuhr publicly announced his resignation from the Fellowship of Reconciliation, a Christian pacifist organization that had the strong support of Fosdick and other prominent ministers. Recognizing that the world of politics was full of "demonic forces," he declared, as only a Christian Realist could, that he had decided "to support the devil of vengeance against the devil of hypocrisy."[47]

Throughout the 1930s Niebuhr continued to mount his campaign against pacifism. His frequent comments suggest a deepening concern about democracy's ability to meet the challenge that engulfed civilization. "Is liberalism . . . not too simple a creed to suit the complexities of our tragic era?" he asked in 1939. He was dismayed at a style of Christianity that would prompt the archbishop of Canterbury to hail the victory of Hitler in Austria because it was "bloodless." Nonviolence, he argued, was not a scriptural concept. Peace under tyranny does not have any relationship to the "peace of the Kingdom of God." Those who believed otherwise he advised to remove their crucifixes "from their altars and substitute the three little monkeys who counsel men to 'speak no evil, hear no evil, see no evil.' "[48]

Owing to its reluctance to take a forceful position against Nazi aggression, he broke his association with the *Christian Century* in 1940, a magazine with which he had been actively involved as a contributing editor for many years. He immediately launched a new periodical, *Christianity and Crisis*, a journal which from the very outset became a formidable opponent of all pacifists, isolationists, and advocates of appeasement of dictators.[49]

Despite the admirable efforts of Niebuhr and other selected Protestant leaders, the future destruction of Europe's Jews was not averted. Generally speaking, the American Christian public remained apathetic about Jewish problems. The Olympic Games of 1936 were not boycotted, Jewish refugees from Nazism were not permitted to enter the United States, and immigration laws were not relaxed for the emergency. On the contrary, they were rigidly enforced so that even their meager quotas were not filled. American antisemitism did not decline until after the end of the Second World War, but by then it was too late for the millions who had perished.

7

Early reports about the systematic annihilation of Europe's Jews, which appeared in the American press by 1942, were met with skepticism. Only a few of the more prominent newspapers, according to recent studies, offered the news substantial coverage.[50] According to Deborah Lipstadt, the incredible nature of these accounts relegated them to the realm of the unbelievable, or to wartime propaganda. Even when accepted, the mass killing of Jews was seldom divorced in the public mind from the usual German cruelty toward conquered civilians.[51] It was difficult for most Americans to accept the notion that the Nazis were engaged in a separate but parallel war of destruction against a defenseless population, a war which did not seem to serve any strategic purpose.[52]

Most Americans knew little about the plight of Europe's Jews during World War II. Despite the mounting information made available to them, the secular press, news magazines, and radio newscasts offered little prime space or time to the killing of Jews. A 1944 poll indicated that the majority of Americans refused to believe that Hitler was systematically putting millions of Jews to death. The news of such brutality had never been officially confirmed by the Roosevelt administration. It was the progress of the war against the Axis that most Americans were concerned about, not the plight of the Jews.[53]

Actually, the progress of Hitler's war against the Jews was more consistently reported in the Protestant denominational press. Attentive Protestants were not ignorant about Germany's Final Solution. Denominational periodicals provided detailed reports, buttressed by editorial comment, about Nazi brutalities. Throughout the war the Geneva office of the World Council of Churches knew as much as it was possible to know about Germany's ultimate intentions; and it transmitted reports about its incredible findings to American religious periodicals. However, these were reported to American readers with considerable caution and skepticism.[54]

The *Christian Century,* for example, the nation's most prominent liberal Protestant weekly magazine, had from the very first remained suspicious about reports of Hitler's intentions. Its persistent journalistic reticence was exemplified in 1942, when Rabbi Stephen S. Wise provided information to its editors about Hitler's plan to kill all the Jews of Nazi-occupied Europe. The *Christian Century* accused Wise of exaggeration, instructing him "to exercise some rhetorical restraint in speaking of a crime so vast and foul."[55] The *Century's* skepticism about the Final Solution did not abate until the end of the war. In 1944 it referred to the Russian army's discovery of the death camp Majdanek, near Lublin, as the "atrocity story of the year." It was not an uncommon reaction. Journalistic reserve persisted even after American armies broke into the death camps. Even with the evidence in front of their eyes, few religious periodicals were willing to accept the truth of Germany's brutality.[56]

Neither did revelations about Nazi killings diminish the numerical growth or dampen the spirit of American Protestantism. The emergence of the World Council of Churches in 1937 was heralded by some as the beginning of a new era in Protestantism. By the end of the war in 1945, the worldwide organization, according to one historian, had emerged "stronger in almost every respect." Indeed, the Second World War proved to be a decisive and "beneficial turning point in the history of the international Protestant community." With the defeat of the Axis, American Protestants emerged more confident than ever that the future of their prophetic role in the world was assured. Church membership had been steadily increasing, and an ecumenical spirit pervaded international Protestantism. Peter Ludlow writes that "the Second World War revitalized the international Protestant community."[57] There is little indication, however, that revelations about the Holocaust produced any signs of contrition or remorse in either American or European Protestantism.

In this respect Protestantism mirrored the condition found on most levels of the nation's political and social life. Wyman recalls that "it seems unbelievable that in Roosevelt's press conferences (normally held twice a week) not one word was spoken about mass killing of European Jews." It was not until 1944 that the American government created a War Refugees Board to coordinate rescue operations, but by that date the Final Solution had almost achieved its objective. Clearly, as historians of the Holocaust have stressed, America's desire to save European Jews failed to match the determination of the Nazis to destroy them.[58]

8

Revelations about the Holocaust had little appreciable impact upon American society in the decade following the Second World War. When the fighting ceased in Europe, recounts Leonard Dinnerstein, Jewish displaced persons, survivors of the horrors of the Nazi death camps, were herded together by the United States Army in make-shift camps under deplorable conditions. With little concern about the psychological effect, many were lumped with their former Gentile concentration camp guards. American military officials, including some high-ranking officers, showed little sympathy for the Jewish D. P.'s, and they ignored executive orders that required the former victims to be housed and treated with dignity.[59]

On the domestic postwar front, the Eightieth Congress, meeting in 1947–48, showed little inclination to admit victims of Nazism to American shores. Imbued with nativism, both houses of Congress were adamant in their refusal to pass an emergency D.P. immigration bill that would allow Jews to enter the United States. Patriotic organizations, such as the American Legion and the Daughters of the American Revolution, lobbied fiercely against its passage. The Displaced Persons Act, which eventually passed in the 1948 session, was so constructed that Jewish refugees were deliberately excluded from the United States.[60]

Indeed, it was easier for ex-Nazis to enter the United States in 1948 than it was for Jewish D.P.'s. A demand to liberalize the D.P. Act was incorporated in the Democratic Party Platform of 1948. With the support of Pres. Harry Truman and such lawmakers as Hubert Humphrey, Paul Douglas, and Margaret Chase Smith, a new Displaced Persons Act was passed in 1950. It paved the way for the entry of more than 400,000 European D.P.'s. Few of these were Jews, however, since by that date most had found homes in the new state of Israel and elsewhere.[61]

While Jewish organizations insisted that the perpetrators of Nazi crimes be punished, Christian opinion remained cool. Callousness toward the victims of Nazism was also reflected in the rapidity with which some ministers counseled forgiveness to Nazis. One Lutheran periodical explained to its readers that they should not assume that "the people responsible for these shocking crimes against humanity [Jews specifically were not mentioned] have ceased to be human beings, that they have become obnoxious reptiles and simply must be exterminated." The editorial warned that a spirit of retribution was un-Christian and should not be permitted to eclipse the law of love.[62]

Despite all that had happened to world Jewry, antisemitic groups, the Ku Klux Klan, and others professing fundamentalist Protestant association continued their malevolent activities in the postwar years. Their continued existence remained as a lingering symptom of a chronic malady that would not be healed. Some of the names included among these Christian extremists had already reached notoriety before the war. One of the most infamous was the Kansas evangelist Gerald Winrod. Through the pages of his journal, *The Defender Magazine*, which by 1950 was being mailed to 100,000 homes, Winrod continued to transmit his message of hatred against the Jews. Affiliated with no single denomination, Winrod envisioned the whole of America as his congregation. He had visited Germany in 1934 and returned profoundly impressed by the achievements of Nazism. Fortified with Nazi ideology, Winrod decided to run for the U.S. Senate in 1938 on a platform of isolationism, antisemitism, and Christian Americanism; but, despite his elaborate campaign, he was defeated. His *Defender Magazine* continued to praise the virtues of Nazism and antisemitism until America's entry into the war. Between 1941 and 1945, although never convicted, Winrod was indicted three times on the charge of sedition.[63]

At the end of the war, surrounded with former Nazi sympathizers, Winrod resumed his antisemitic crusade. His circle of friends included Col. E. N. Sanctuary, who had authored a number of antisemitic monographs and who was one of his strongest supporters. Sanctuary had taught Sunday school classes at the Broadway Presbyterian Church in New York City. Elizabeth Dilling, an Episcopalian whom Winrod described as a "true Bible believing child of God," was another of his dependable allies. Her primary talent was casting aspersions on the Talmud, a task which she consummated in an "exposé" published in 1953 entitled *The Plot Against Christianity*.[64]

Winrod's supporters included a number of important Christian leaders. One was W. B. Riley, a founder of the Northwestern Bible Schools, a co-organizer of the Baptist Bible Union of North America, and a major force behind the World Christian Fundamentalist Association. Riley's home was in Minneapolis, where he served as pastor of the prominent First Baptist Church and where he ran a small string of Christian bookstores celebrated for their collection of antisemitic literature.[65]

Riley's Minnesota neighbor, William D. Herrstrom of Fairbault, was in complete accord with Winrod's teachings. To disseminate his ideas Herrstrom edited two journals, the *Bible News Flashes* and the *Americanism Bulletin*. His insistence that Jesus was not a Jew was a popular doctrine in antisemitic groups, as was his equation of communism with Judaism. Herrstrom's statement that "We're not against the Jews—only the Kommunist Kikes," pretty much summed up his philosophy, as it did the point of view of most postwar Christian antisemites.[66]

With the postwar red scare of the 1950s, the crusade against communism became a convenient umbrella under which antisemites could find shelter. This was true of Gerald L. K. Smith, a key individual in the Winrod circle of Christian extremists.[67] Smith was disappointed that America had entered the war against the Axis. America's involvement, he believed, was unnecessary and resulted only because of pressure from international Jewry. In the presidential election year of 1948, Smith helped to create the Christian Nationalist party, with himself at its helm. Its platform called for the deportation of Zionists, the "dissolution of Jewish Gestapo Organizations," the shipping of Negroes to Africa, and the liquidation of the United Nations. The platform also posed the question: "Shall the lovers of Jesus Christ or the enemies of Jesus Christ determine the destiny of America?" Smith portrayed Christ as the world's greatest antisemite. On one occasion he remarked: "When I am cursed by a Jew, when I am hated by a Jew, when a Jew seeks to kill me, or smear me, or brand me as an evil force, then I have fellowship with Jesus Christ." He had already compiled a prewar record of antisemitism, but he now became obsessed with the desire to dislodge the United Nations, an organization which he claimed was run by Jews and communists. To achieve this end he organized a national conference in San Francisco and a pilgrimage to Washington, D.C., in 1953.[68] Throughout the forties and fifties Smith and Winrod stood out as prominent names in America's Christian war against the Jews.

Only some premillennial Dispensationalists, steeped in Christian biblical prophecy, and who relegated Jews and their history to the realm of religious fantasy, saw in the defeat of Hitler a warning to those who dabbled in antisemitism. Writing in the Dispensationalist journal *Bibliotheca Sacra* at the close of the war, Lewis Sperry Chafer cautioned his readers that

> One more nation has gone to confusion having persecuted the Jew. How little this Christ-rejecting world believes in or gives attention to the word of God! . . . it would have been difficult indeed to have made Hitler believe that his cause and his nation would certainly come to grief if they attacked and destroyed the Jew. It is difficult to make modern Gentiles—even many nominal Christians—recognize the order of cause and effect which God unfailingly imposes when the Jew is attacked. . . . The root trouble is that men do not believe that God has an elect nation, a chosen people, a sacred purpose in Israel.[69]

It was not the kind of theologizing that postwar American Jews sought or appreciated. In the wake of the European catastrophe Dispensationalist rhetoric tended only to widen the gap between them and their evangelical neighbors.

16

Toward a New Relationship

1

Thoughts about the Holocaust, an event too barbaric for civilized minds to comprehend, lay dormant in the Protestant world during the decade or so following the Second World War. By the late 1950s, however, a new consciousness about the catastrophe began to surface in the minds of few but significant Protestant religious thinkers.

Adolph Eichmann's capture by Israeli agents in May 1960 and his subsequent trial and execution helped to dramatize issues that had been partially suppressed. Signs of contrition or religious contemplation, however, were infrequent before 1962. Rather, according to one survey of the nation's editorial reaction to the Eichmann trial, "anti-Semitism was generally treated as if it had sprung full blown from the twisted minds of Nazi propagandists."[1] Only in selected cases did Christians raise questions about their collective responsibility. Such an exception was the conservative Protestant periodical *Christianity Today*, when it asked in November 1961: "Could the Nazi persecutions have been perpetrated without a long-standing atmosphere of anti-Jewish attitudes to which the Christian community had subscribed?" That such a question was even raised suggested to an observer from the American Jewish Committee that revelations gleaned from the Eichmann event had "penetrated the consciousness and influenced the perceptions of religious editors to a degree not immediately evident."[2]

The troubling uncertainty to which pious-minded Protestants would increasingly turn in the following years concerned the degree to which Christian teachings could be held responsible for the crimes of Nazism. It was a French Jew, Jules Marx Isaac, who first urged Christians to consider this problem. Isaac, a respected historian who had managed to evade Gestapo arrest, had lost his wife and daughters to the Nazi gas chambers in 1943. The tragedy prompted him when the war was over to inquire about the social and religious reasons that made the Holocaust possible. Isaac's subsequent research led to the publication of three influential books, *Jesus and Israel* (1947), *The Origins of Anti-Semitism* (1962), and *The Teaching of Contempt* (1964). Together, these works pointed unmistakably to the centuries of Christian teachings about Jews and their faith as the principal factors in the production and persistence of antisemitism. In the remaining years of his life Isaac exerted every effort to persuade Christian intellectuals, clergy, and even Pope Pius XII, to revise their Christian liturgical and instructional material. In these endeavors Isaac received the support of the American Jewish Committee, the B'nai B'rith, prominent ministers, and scholars of both faiths.[3]

A more modest effort to achieve a similar end was undertaken in the United States by Bernhard Olson of the Yale Divinity School. A graduate of Drew Theological Seminary, Olson was an ordained minister of the Methodist church. He was employed by the National Conference of Christians and Jews and served in 1971 as the executive officer of the first International Conference on the Holocaust to be held on German soil, an event which he did not live to see.[4] Olson's overriding desire was to persuade Christian educators to remove from their curricular material stereotypical statements about Jews, both biblical and contemporary. In 1960 he wrote an essay criticizing Sunday school portrayals of the Pharisees. "The Pharisees play a role in Judaism comparable to that of the Saints in Christianity," he explained to Christian teachers. "Christians would be offended if the Jews were to vilify the disciples, the apostle Paul and the Christian Fathers."[5]

His pathbreaking work *Faith and Prejudice,* published in 1963, which grew out of his doctoral dissertation, was the first systematic examination of anti-Judaism in Christian teaching material in the United States undertaken by a Christian scholar. Olson confronted Christian teaching's inconsistency in characterizing antisemitism on the one hand as a moral failing and, on the other, as providential retribution for disobedience.[6] Sunday school textbooks of all Protestant groups, with a varying degree of intensity, he wrote, bestowed a measure of collective guilt upon the Jewish people for the Crucifixion. He urged editors of religious texts "to adopt the policy of reminding commentators on the Passion story that the teaching of this story had terrible consequences for the Jews, and that centuries of Jewish oppression, deprivation, and torture should encourage them to treat more humbly and with repentant awe a theme that lends itself to the designs of Satan as well as to those of God."[7]

Olson's work was followed by additional evaluations of Christian textbooks. One study undertaken in the mid-sixties and confined to the West Coast of the United States was conducted by two California sociologists, Charles Y. Glock and Rodney Stark. Its findings and conclusions were far more devastating than Olson's. Both sociologists were stunned by the blatant hostility toward Jews that was disguised as religious teaching. "Perhaps naively, we expected that this religious process had become more or less vestigial," they wrote after concluding their research. "We were entirely unprepared to find these old religious traditions so potent and so widespread in modern society." Although only one of the investigators was Jewish, both "shared equally a sense of shock and dismay that a faith which proclaims the brotherhood of man can be so perverted into a *raison d'être* for bigotry."[8]

Glock and Stark wondered if traditional Christian orthodoxy was "incompatible with Christ's teachings of brotherhood." They discovered that while American Christians directed some contempt toward all religious outsiders, the Jews were recipients of a special hostile attention. To most Christians Jews continued to remain collectively guilty, fated to suffer divine judgment for their responsibility for the Crucifixion of Jesus. "Their tribulations will not cease until they extirpate their guilt by accepting salvation through Christ."[9]

Equally disconcerting was the authors' revelation that Christian ministers, many of whom were engaged in works of goodwill, were not aware that their teachings fostered antisemitism. Glock and Stark called for "a systematic reappraisal of Christian education, *both* as it teaches its history and doctrine *and* in the way it deals with the question of anti-Semitism as such. . . . Until the process by which religion fosters anti-Semitism has been abolished, the Christian conscience must bear the guilt of bigotry."[10]

The impact of such studies was not immediately evident. Jewish groups who undertook their own studies were not elated with the progress in interfaith relations induced by such efforts. Gerald S. Strober, for example, an authority on religious curriculum, working under the joint sponsorship of the American Jewish Committee and the NCCJ, produced a work in 1972 entitled *Portrait of the Elder Brother: Jews and Judaism in Protestant Teaching Materials*. Its objective was to determine if Olson's findings had created an imprint upon church school publications. Strober examined materials of twelve denominations, both conservative and mainstream, and concluded that Olson's findings "had not had the long-term effect which its initial reception seemed to promise"; that "the defects uncovered by Olson nine years ago persist in today's teaching materials."[11]

Despite such discouraging conclusions the movement in American Protestantism to uproot antisemitism in Christian teachings continued. It received encouragement from the work of the Second Vatican Council convened by Pope John XIII in 1962. The Vatican's Declaration on Non-Christian Religions, issued at the close of Vatican II in 1965, although a document weakened by numerous political compromises, had incorporated a measure of the spirit of Jules Isaac's original intentions. For the first time in the history of the Roman Catholic church, the Vatican acknowledged the common patrimony of Christians and Jews, rejected the traditional accusations of Jewish collective guilt for the Crucifixion, and condemned antisemitism. The council's efforts signified a turning point in interfaith associations and served as an example of a first step that all Christians could take in reassessing their relationship with Jews.[12]

Vatican II also generated an interest in interreligious conversations or "dialogue" between Christians and Jews. To be sure, liberal Protestants had for years displayed an interest in such activities, but these now received a universal endorsement. Robert McAfee Brown, a professor of religion at Union Theological Seminary in New York and a Protestant observer at Vatican II, returned from that event an avid proponent of religious dialogue with Jews, because, as he put it,

> *Christians cannot understand who they are apart from Judaism.* Not only do both Catholicism and Protestantism have their historical roots in Judaism, but their theological and liturgical roots as well, and they therefore stand in a different relationship to Judaism than to other world religions. Judaism is not just another world religion. . . . It is that religion *par excellence* which helps to define for them who they are, with which both must come to terms, and apart from which neither can understand itself or the other.[13]

Brown introduced a theme that would be repeated by those Protestants who sought a new relationship with Jews; that is, that Jews and Christians "have an inextricably bound destiny," a need to work together, so that Christians could avoid "the distorted perspective that such attempts have produced in the past when carried out in isolation."[14]

2

Dialogue between Christians and Jews had become an accepted practice in American religious life ever since it had been formalized by the NCCJ during the 1920s. Its purpose at that time was to counteract, through interreligious conversations and educational programs, the bigotry perpetrated by the KKK and other hate groups. The experience, however, reached a much higher level of seriousness during the post-Holocaust era. By that time an increasing number of Protestants and Jews became convinced that if future catastrophes were to be avoided, a greater mutual understanding and empathy had to be cultivated. It was particularly incumbent upon Christians to learn more about their "elder brother," upon whom they had for centuries inflicted misery and humiliation. "We Protestant Americans need our . . . Jewish neighbors even more than they need us," remarked Franklin H. Littell, one of the leading Protestant proponents of dialogue, in 1969. "Above all we need them because living with them can help us to bury forever the temptation to long for the good old days when we thought to have our way by force."[15]

Protestant proponents of dialogue agreed that the contemporary world was too small, too threatening, a place for people of different faiths to remain ignorant about each other. More importantly, as Christians, they came to realize that they could not fully understand themselves without some comprehension of the Jewish experience.[16] To offer their congregants a deeper knowledge of Jewish beliefs and practices, some denominations revised their Sunday school curriculums. In 1963, for example, Belden Menkus, an educational analyst for the Southern Baptist Sunday School Board, invited Rabbi Arthur Gilbert of the NCCJ to coordinate a team of Jewish scholars and educators to write a textbook that would explain Judaism to Baptist teachers. Such accomplished Jewish scholars as Alvin J. Reines, Mordechai Waxman, Ira Eisenstein, Arthur Hertzberg, and others contributed essays on different aspects of Judaism.[17] Almost without precedent, no missionary objective motivated this project, one that was sponsored by the leading evangelical organization in the United States. It exemplified the distance that even some evangelicals were prepared to travel during the 1960s.

More than ever American Protestants wanted to exchange ideas with Jews, to gain knowledge about their religious beliefs. Many knew little about Judaism beyond what they had acquired from biblical readings or imbibed from their Sunday school teachers. The antisemitic outbursts of the 1930s and the Holocaust of the forties were events about which they were becoming increasingly conscious. Northern Baptist students were taught in 1966 that Christians must think about the Holocaust. "The main reason for remembering these crimes is that they show us how inhuman people can become when they regard other people as less than human. The great misfortune is that these events are a part of, and arise out of, a general rejection of Jews simply because they are Jewish."[18]

American Lutheran institutional support for dialogue with Jews was offered in 1971 when the Division of Theological Studies of the Lutheran Council prepared a series of "Guidelines for Conversations Between Lutherans and Jews." Given the past relationship of the German Lutheran church with Nazism, efforts by American Lutherans to converse with Jews assumed a special significance. Composed by a Lutheran, Paul D. Opshal, and a rabbi and member of the American Jewish Committee, Marc H. Tannenbaum, the guidelines represented a belated, but significant advance in interfaith associations. They encouraged Lutherans to initiate conversations with Jews, but warned that "neither polemics nor conversions are the aim of such conversations."[19]

In 1974 the American Lutheran church reaffirmed its renewed tie of friendship with its Jewish neighbors by adopting an official statement that stressed the common biblical and ethical roots of both religious communities. It urged Christians to "become aware of that history in which they have deeply alienated the Jews" and have acquiesced in crimes against them. "Whole generations of Christians have looked with contempt upon this people who were condemned to remain wanderers on the earth on the false charge of Deicide.

Christians ought to acknowledge with repentance and sorrow their part in this tragic history of estrangement." Lutherans were encouraged to ponder the degree of their responsibility in bringing about the Holocaust. They were requested to join with Jews "in an effort to understand the theological and moral significance of what happened during the Holocaust."[20]

Significantly, Lutherans were advised to seek in Christendom's past the seeds that had brought them to the present condition. They were informed that they "bear a special responsibility for this tragic history of persecution, because the Nazi movement found a climate of hatred already in existence." The Lutheran emphasis on the study of postbiblical Jewish history was a new departure in the American Protestant experience. "It is so unfortunate that so few Christians have studied Judaism as it grew and flowered in the centuries since the New Testament era. The first step for Lutherans, therefore, is to devote themselves to completing this long-neglected homework."[21]

Significant also was the Lutheran admission that the "Nazi period fostered a revival of Luther's own medieval hostility toward Jews." Lutherans were advised to recognize that "those who study and admire Luther should acknowledge unequivocally that his anti-Jewish utterances are entitled to no defense."[22] Living in the post-Holocaust era, American Lutherans were justifiably troubled with Luther; not with his theology, but with his writings about and behavior toward the Jewish people. "What are we to do with Luther today?" asked Gerhard D. Forde, an American Lutheran theologian. His counsel was to view Luther's writings "as part of the tragedy of Jewish-Christian relationships, poisoned by centuries of acrimony, for which Christians, no doubt, bear a major share of the blame." Luther, Forde asserted, should be recognized as one who both mirrored and perpetuated the Christian antisemitism of his time.[23]

Similar currents of thought guided the leadership of other denominations. The establishment of the Center for Jewish-Christian Studies and Relations by the New York Episcopal Diocese's General Theological Seminary, in 1986, is one example. Its purpose, to further dialogue with Jews and to combat antisemitism, was becoming by this time an acceptable denominational practice. In the same year, Southern Baptists conducted a three-day Symposium on the New Testament and Judaism, an event sponsored jointly with the Interreligious Affairs Department of the Anti-Defamation League of B'nai B'rith.[24] Such examples offer evidence of an altered mutual pattern of behavior taking place among Protestants and Jews.

3

Jews were aware of the process of reassessment that Christianity in general and Protestantism in particular were undergoing in the wake of the *Shoah*, the destruction of Europe's Jews. For them to participate in religious conversations with Gentiles at this critical juncture, some Jewish observers reasoned, might help to usher in a new and healthier relationship between the two American faiths. It was clear that with or without Jewish participation, a new ecumenical spirit had intruded itself into the American religious scene, one which was bound to affect the future relationship of Christians and Jews, and from which Jews would gain little if they remained aloof.[25]

European-born and educated Abraham Joshua Heschel, one of the most prominent theologians of the post-Holocaust generation, was an avid proponent of dialogue. Heschel, who in his pedagogical efforts worked closely with the philosopher Martin Buber, taught Talmud in Germany and England before emigrating to the United States in 1940. Although an Orthodox rabbi, for many years Heschel served on the faculty of the Conservative Jewish Theological Seminary. His ecumenical outlook became evident in 1965 when Heschel also received an appointment to the Protestant Union Theological Seminary in New York. He was one of the few American Jews who advised the Vatican leadership during its efforts to formulate a statement of policy on the Jews. Heschel identified people's contempt for each other's religious belief as the "agony of History." "We must insist upon loyalty to the unique and holy treasures of our own tradition and at the same time," wrote Heschel in 1965, acknowledge "that in this aeon of religious diversity may be the providence of God." He asked that mankind cultivate a respect for each other's spiritual commitments. The ecumenical spirit, he noted, was "born of the insight that God is greater than religion, that faith is deeper than dogma . . . and that religion involves the total situation of man, his attitudes and deeds, and must therefore never be kept in isolation."[26]

The radical Jewish theologian Richard L. Rubenstein also pleaded for the need to place human beings above dogma, but in the process he went much further than Heschel or other Jewish writers would dare to go. A Conservative rabbi, Rubenstein holds an M.H.L. degree from the Jewish Theological Seminary and a Ph.D. from Harvard. Rubenstein's subsequent books and his efforts to speak to both communities are, by his own admission, more popular among non-Jewish than among Jewish readers. He asserted in 1966 that the greatest obstacle to Jewish-Christian understanding "is that the true dialogue, the genuine meeting of persons, is impossible so long as Jew and Christian are committed to the religio-historic myths of their respective communities." The Jew, Rubenstein declared with unusual daring, must release his hold on the "doctrine of the election of Israel and the Torah as the sole content of God's revelation to mankind"; while the Christian, in turn, must de-emphasize "the decisive character of the Christ event in human history," a myth that "must be at best an error and at worst blasphemy." To hold on to these myths inflexibly, insisted Rubenstein, would obstruct a meaningful dialogue between the two faiths. "Not only do the mythic contents of our religious faiths impede meaningful community; they absolutely preclude it."[27] Yet Rubenstein's unorthodox demands concealed his general agreement with other Jewish thinkers about dialogue, that human beings, not dogmas, should be placed at the center of the interfaith encounters. "If we concentrate less on what our religious inheritances promise and threaten and more on the human existence which we share through the traditions, we will achieve the superlative yet simple knowledge of who we truly are. . . . If we fail to learn the simple lesson that the community of men is possible only through the encounter of persons rather than of myths or abstractions, we will only doom future generations to repeat the horrible deeds of our times."[28]

Irving Greenberg, an Orthodox rabbi and an accomplished historian, theologian, and communal leader, was also a creative participant in the ecumenical movement. Greenberg's central focus has been on the religious and ethical implications of the Holocaust, both for Christians and Jews. As a consequence of the Holocaust, he has argued, neither system of belief can remain the same. He is surprised that "both religions have gone on since 1945 as if nothing had happened to change their central understanding." To Greenberg it was "obvious that it cannot be done, that the Holocaust cannot be ignored." The horrible chapter has raised the disturbing question whether it is possible for those who can "believe after such an event dare talk about God who loves and cares without making a mockery of those who suffered."[29]

The question that gnaws at Greenberg, and with which he confronts his Christian audience, is: What did Christianity contribute to make the Holocaust possible? Since so few Christians spoke out on behalf of the Jews, he wonders if there is something inherent in Christian teaching that "supported or created a positive context for anti-Semitism and even murder." And if that was so, asks Greenberg, is Christianity lost? It is an enigma that modern Christianity must face and to which it must respond. He cautions, however, that whatever the response might be, it must abide by a "fundamental criterion" that "no statement, theological or otherwise, should be made that would not be credible in the presence of burning children."[30] Christianity, asserts Greenberg, has barely survived the Holocaust. "I do not believe that it can survive a second—with any real moral capital at all."[31]

While some Jews participated in dialogue with Christians with the hope that such conversations might reduce the level of antisemitism, others wondered if such a goal was a realistic expectation. In the wake of the Holocaust some Jewish writers questioned whether Jews and Christians possessed any significant theological principles in common. Early in the fifties, Bernard Heller, a professor of Jewish ethics at the Jewish Institute of Religion in New York, even questioned the usefulness of the phrase "Judeo-Christian tradition," an expression which was coming increasingly into vogue following the Second World War. Heller noticed that as a product of nineteenth-century German scholarship, the concept had been totally ineffective in halting the destruction of six million Jewish lives, or the "callous indifference of the Western nations" to the slaughter.[32] Unlike other liberal writers, Jews or Protestants, Heller believed "the claim that Judaism and Christianity shared a fund of common professions and practices" was "an unwarranted assumption." To imply the existence of "a Judeo-Christian tradition" as "an inducement to or justification for goodwill—constitutes poor strategy."[33]

The Conservative Jewish theologian Arthur A. Cohen shared this semantic antipathy for the "Judeo-Christian tradition." "I regard this conception as an ideologizing of a fundamental and irreconcilable disagreement. There is a Jewish-Christian nexus . . . but the reciprocity of their relation arises, not from the assumption of their community, but from the assumption of their differences."[34] Cohen recognized only irreconcilable differences between Judaism and Christianity. "Christian and Jew remained opposed," he wrote in 1970. Both are theological enemies. Reconciliation ought not to be assumed because of contemporary gestures of friendship. Jews and Christians, argued Cohen, must learn to live with their enmity, to rise above their theological differences and concern themselves with human needs instead. He calls for a "Judeo-Christian humanism" to replace the religious, more popular concept.[35] Like Rubenstein, Cohen urges both sides to let go of their sacred myths while conversing: "The Jew need not learn to hear the Christian speak of the Christ nor must the Christian learn to hear the Jew speak of the dominion of Torah in the time of the Messiah; but both must come to hear in each other the sounds of truth. . . . It is the commonality of human suffering that is the commonality of Christian and Jew; and there must come, as a miracle of Grace, a means of expressing that shared experience."[36]

Samuel Sandmel's *We Jews and Jesus*, which appeared in 1965, suggests that this provost of Hebrew Union College and student of Christian texts is also conscious of the limitations of interfaith conversations. Sandmel believes that committed Jews can find little that is inspiring in the teachings of Jesus; even his martyrdom is not a particularly meaningful event for Jews. "So many Jews became martyrs at the hands of later Christians that his martyrdom seems to us perhaps too unexceptionable for special notice. We Jews have so suffered, because Christians in ages past made us suffer, that it is difficult for us to acknowledge that Jesus suffered unusually."[37] He sees little point in comparing the two faiths. "I have no disposition to set the one against the other, and to make meaningless comparisons." He does not regard one faith as superior to the other. "Judaism is mine, and I consider it good and I am at home in it, and I love it, and I want it. That is how I want the Christians to feel about their Christianity."[38]

The prolific rabbinic scholar Jacob Neusner also betrays a degree of disillusionment with dialogue. The experience, he observes, might produce an improved mutual understanding of each other's religious beliefs. It might even allow Jews and Christians to better understand their own beliefs. But it will not necessarily reduce the level of antisemitism. Even though religious identities in American society have lost much of their past meaning, writes Neusner, conflict between Christians and Jews over questions of religious pageantry and religious exercises in the nation's common schools and other public institutions is bound to increase.[39]

Dialogue, some Jews believe, will not ensure against the rise of another Hitler, and its practice will not eradicate Jewish anxieties about their future security. "Post-Holocaust exchanges do not quell the sense of danger, but arouse new anxieties," writes the Holocaust historian Nora Levin.[40] Despite the declaration of Protestant churches and the World Council of Churches that antisemitism is a "sin against God and man," some Jews continue to believe that such declarations amount to little more than opportunities that allow American Protestants to "congratulate themselves on their liberality, and rejoice that they and their churches had always been on the side of the angels." One writer suggests that dialogue had little to do with the decline of antisemitism in the United States during the last quarter of the twentieth century. On the contrary, "Dialogue is itself a symptom, not a cause, of the declining respectability of anti-Jewish attitudes."[41]

Many orthodox Jews have from the very first suspected the value of inter-religious conversations. Rabbi Eliezer Berkowitz, a professor of philosophy at the Hebrew Theological College in Skokie, Illinois, remains unenthusiastic about the outcome of Vatican II. Christian willingness to converse with Jews, believes Berkowitz, stemmed not from a new tolerance and humility, but from Christianity's loss of political and social power. He does not approve of Jewish participation in dialogues with Protestants. On one occasion he declared: "Judaism is Judaism because it rejects Christianity, and Christianity is Christianity because it rejects Judaism. What is usually referred to as the Judeo-Christian tradition exists only in Christian and secularist fantasy. As far as Jews are concerned, Judaism is fully sufficient. There is nothing in Christianity for them."[42]

Traditionalist opposition to interreligious conversations received its most commanding endorsement from Rabbi Joseph H. Soloveitchik, former head of Rabbi Isaac Elchanan Theological Seminary of Yeshiva University. An acknowledged intellectual leader of halachik Judaism, Soloveitchik had since the mid-1960s questioned the value that Jews would derive from interfaith conversations. Jewish religious uniqueness, he insists, precludes a successful dialogue with people of another faith. He disapproves of any Jewish efforts to extend intellectual bridges toward other religious communities. "This otherness stands in the way of complete mutual understanding," wrote Soloveitchik in 1964. In spite of their sociability and cultural interests, Christians and Jews will continue to remain spiritual strangers to each other. "The great encounter between God and man is a wholly personal private affair incomprehensible to the outsider." Besides, argues the influential rabbi, the contemporary generation is not yet ripe for dialogue. "We certainly have not been authorized by our history, sanctified by the martyrdom of millions, to even hint to another faith community that we are mentally ready to revise historical attitudes, to trade favors pertaining to fundamental matters of faith."[43]

While in matters of dialogue Soloveitchik speaks for the majority of American traditionalists, a radical but respectable minority insists otherwise, as evidenced by the utterances of Heschel and Greenberg. One of the most recent of such potent challenges to Berkowitz and Soloveitchik has come from the pen of the traditionalist thinker David Novak, surprisingly, a former student of Soloveitchik, who holds a doctorate from Georgetown University and a rabbinical degree from the Jewish Theological Seminary of America.

Novak recognizes that Orthodoxy's resistance to dialogue with Christians stems from its conviction that Christian attitudes toward Jews have not altered appreciably since the Middle Ages; that all Christian groups view Jews alike, with disdain. Yet, because Novak detects in the pagan values of modern secular society a greater "threat to both Judaism and Christianity," Jews, he believes, are obligated to join with Christians in the task of salvaging the crumbling spiritual foundations of Western civilization.[44]

Consequently, he urges both Jews and Christians to view each other with a greater degree of tolerance, to avoid triumphalism without succumbing to religious relativism or to the "Temptation of Syncretism." "A common threat has created a new common situation," declares Novak. "It is thus inevitable that historically perceptive Jews and Christians should be rediscovering each other." In confrontation with the dominant and threatening secular demands of modernity, Novak believes that interreligious conversations are in accord with the highest demands of halachik principles.[45] It is a provocative thought which many Orthodox Jews will undoubtedly find troublesome.

4

Not all American Protestants were impervious to Jewish anxieties, and a number were moved by Greenberg's call for a religious reassessment. Stunned by the revelations of the Holocaust, a number of theologians began by the mid-sixties to reevaluate the central principles of their religious existence.

Franklin Hamlin Littell, an ordained Methodist minister, is a distinguished representative of that select group. Littell studied at Cornell, the Union Theological Seminary, and for many years served as a professor of religion at Temple University. A writer and a student of the German churches' resistance to Nazism, Littell was also elected president of the Christians Concerned for Israel and is an honorary chairman and founder of the Anne Frank Institute of Philadelphia. An assertive critic of religious and social extremism, Littell has from the early 1960s called upon American Protestants to reexamine their religious commitments in the light of the *Shoah.*

During the 1970s Littell emerged as one of the leading Protestant thinkers preoccupied with the theological implications of the Holocaust. He views the event as a major turning point in the sacred history of Christians and Jews. He has probed for the theological elements in Christian teachings that helped pave the way for the catastrophe. "The truth about the murder of European Jewry by baptized Christians is this," wrote Littell in 1975. "It raises in a most fundamental way the question of the credibility of Christianity. Was Jesus a false messiah?" asks Littell. "No one can be a true messiah whose followers feel compelled to torture and destroy other human persons who think differently."[46]

Littell has identified three theological components of Christian antisemitism. One is the "superseding or displacement myth," the belief that Christianity had displaced Judaism in the eyes of God. A theological principle imbedded deep in Christian teaching, it is a distortion, asserts Littell, developed to suit the founding fathers of Christianity. Second, observes Littell, the deicide myth has added to the Christian contempt for the Jew; while third and equally ominous in its implications is the myth that "the destruction of the Second Temple and the dispersion of the Jews signified God's judgment upon them for their rejection of the Christian Messiah." This devastating concept carried the concomitant implication that Jews were destined to suffer, wither and eventually disappear.[47] Littell also accuses Christendom of "expropriating the Old Testament" and of reading "back into it their own interpretations of the historical process when they did not excise the Jewish component altogether."[48]

He challenges the comforting idea that Nazism was a "pagan," essentially anti-Christian ideology. "The trouble with this line of argument is that it relieves the Christians and their leaders of their guilt from what happened." The German churches did nothing to halt the slaughter of Jews. Littell recalls that Hitler died a Roman Catholic, while Hermann Goering expired a Lutheran. A mass in Hitler's memory is celebrated annually in Madrid. Christians, therefore, cannot come back today and claim no responsibility for what happened. Besides, to relieve the churches of responsibility by categorizing the Nazis as "neopagans" ignores the centuries of teaching that made the Holocaust possible.[49]

To reestablish their credibility, Littell challenges the churches to deal honestly with their past. He calls for a long period of "spiritual wrestling" and "repentance," an end to "cheap grace" and "easy conversions," a reform of preaching and teaching as a preparation for a "new level of Christian awareness" of its culpability in the crime against the Jews.[50] As a start he proposes that churches transform their false teachings about the Jews into truthful and positive affirmations. For example, instead of the proposition that the Jewish people have been displaced by the "New Israel," churches must begin to state that through baptism Christians might also earn a portion of God's promise to Israel. Or in place of the myth that the Jews crucified Christ, Christians must teach that "crucifixion was a Roman, never a Jewish, penalty."[51]

Like other post-Holocaust Protestant writers, Littell urges Christians to turn to the Jews, rather than to each other, in order to learn about the crimes of Christendom. More than ever Christians must recognize the need for their dependance upon Jews for guidance out of the darkness. He suggests that they pursue the study of the history of the Jewish people, for their own fate is inexorably intertwined with that of the Jews. In one of his most powerful utterances, Littell writes that "When the Body of Christ is discovered at Auschwitz, it will be raised from among the victims, not hidden among Catholics and Protestants."[52]

Littell opposes any attempt by Christians to witness to Jews. He doubts whether such activity is authorized in the teachings of the New Testament. More to the point, he believes that the tragedy of the Holocaust has rendered all missionary activity among Jews irrelevant, if not immoral, since the entire enterprise has been based on misconceptions and negative judgments about Judaism. A more fruitful service for Christians is to work for the survival, rather than the extinction, of the Jewish people.[53]

Littell warns against the liberal Christian hostility toward Jewish particularity. He recalls from his studies of German religion that the liberal Christian expression of love for humanity rarely encompassed the Jewish people. Christian liberal intellectuals and academics of the Third Reich were among the first to fall in step with the Nazi racial program. No German university became a center of resistance against Hitler. "The death camps were designed by professors and built by Ph.D's." Writing in 1971, Littell observed that the problem with liberal antisemitism continues to plague the United States, where Christendom continues to bask in the balmy universalism of the nineteenth century.[54]

5

Few Protestant theologians have been more persuasive than Paul M. Van Buren in his attempt to draw American Christians closer to Jewish fundamentals. A graduate of Harvard, the Episcopal Theological School, and the University of Basel, Van Buren is an ordained minister of the Episcopal church and, like Littell, a professor of theology at Temple University. He is convinced that American Protestantism dare not proceed with business as usual without reevaluating its beliefs in the light of the Holocaust.[55] But the issue that emerges most prominently from his writings concerns the theological relationship with the Jewish people that Christians must learn to accept.

He admits, as do many other thoughtful Christians, that both Christianity and Judaism are intertwined, that despite Christianity's traditional anti-Judaism, Christians know that they were born out of and cannot, therefore, define themselves apart from Israel. Yet, like some contemporary Jewish writers, Van Buren challenges the accuracy of the term "Judeo-Christian tradition." Rather, his reading of Christian history tells him that what has in fact evolved "was a pagan-Christian tradition," a form of Christianity torn from its Jewish moorings. "When we speak of Israel, we speak of different roots, which for centuries we have denied and in our own century have tried to wipe out." Christianity, he argues, had moved in a "fundamentally wrong" direction. In the process it had developed a spiritual "sickness which Judaism was quick to detect and point out, but which arrogance, conceit and self-interest prevented Christians from hearing." The culminating fruit "of our pagan-Christian tradition was the Holocaust."[56]

Some representatives of early Christianity blundered, writes Van Buren, when they began to imagine that the New Testament represented a guide to a totally new religion, unconnected with its Jewish heritage. A spirit of paganism influenced Christianity during its formative years. Christians, Van Buren demands, must challenge this distorted tradition. "Whatever we may say about the roots and rise of that tradition, we today—after 1945—can no longer continue it."[57]

Even so, despite their common roots, explains Van Buren, in what might be considered his central thesis, Christians and Jews have each been assigned different avenues to the One God. As Gentiles, Christians must worship the God of Israel through Jesus Christ, unlike Jews, who may call upon and who know God the Father directly. "We are Gentiles, preponderantly, who worship the God of Israel. It is one thing for the Jews to call upon God as Father and to know him immediately and always as their God. That is their right and their duty because of their election. . . . For Gentiles to call upon this God is another thing."[58] The ultimate responsibility of Gentiles, says Van Buren, is to focus upon Jesus as Son, "since it was and is because of Him that we too dare to claim that we are on our way to adoption as sons and daughters of the same one God."

Van Buren points to the very survival of the Jewish people, despite the countless persecutions that they have suffered at the hands of Christians, as a "sign of God's faithfulness." The Christian church must understand that God has not broken his covenant with the Jewish people. Indeed, if that were the case, as some pious Christians propose, it would be a most terrifying prospect for Christianity; if that were so, what hope then would there be for anyone?[59]

To be sure, there are moments in Van Buren's writing that leave Jews uncomfortable. His tendency to theologize about Jews and their history, to view them as "a people with a special role in history, living lights of humanity," although such words might have pleased some late nineteenth-century Reformers, represents a form of thinking that does not necessarily diminish hostility toward them.[60] Van Buren's desire for Christians to share vicariously in the catastrophe of the Holocaust is understandable for one engaged in a reevaluation of traditional Protestant thought. Still, his attempt to cast the horrors of the Holocaust in theological terms diminishes the degree and reality of Jewish suffering. Van Buren's ultimate flight of insensitivity is expressed in his hope that the Jewish people might eventually recognize that their desire for redemption is also shared by the Christian world. "For all they know," writes Van Buren, their "Messiah may turn out to be Jesus of Nazareth." This veiled expectation, articulated at the close of a work filled with much good sense and lofty intentions, takes one by surprise. It is a thought that smacks of the very triumphalism which Van Buren urges his coreligionists to avoid.[61]

6

More boldly than most Protestant theologians, A. Roy Eckardt has pushed forward the theological frontiers of the post-Holocaust generation. Inspired by his mentor Reinhold Niebuhr, Eckardt, a Methodist clergyman, was among the first scholars to probe the Christian roots of the European catastrophe.[62] From his post at Lehigh University, where he served for many years as professor and chairman of the Department of Religion, Eckardt has conducted a relentless attack on the Christian responsibility for antisemitism. "Opposition to Jews is the one constant of Christian history," its one unifying theme throughout the centuries. The Christian world, he believes, is responsible for the invention of antisemitism. No other prejudice, racial or ethnic animosity can be compared to it. What is more, recourse to historical explanations alone or to the theories of the social sciences will explain neither its character nor its persistence.[63]

For Eckardt, the attack upon the Jewish people mirrors the ambivalence with which Christians view their own faith. Envied for their chosenness, hated for their alleged rejection and murder of the Son of God, the Jews emerged as the only group through which the Christian is able to "get back at" Christ for the challenge he makes upon the Christian's life. Unable to divest himself of the Christian burden, the Christian strikes out at God's chosen people, the Jews, who are accessible and vulnerable.[64]

Neither does Eckardt find the rhetoric of the New Testament blameless. Indeed, he is among the first Christian theologians to trace the origin of antisemitism to the "Word of God." "To shut my eyes to the antisemitic proclivities of the Christian Scripture is indefensible," he wrote in 1971. Within this context, the false and evil charge of Deicide, flung at the Jewish people for centuries and repeated even today by leading representatives of Christendom, is understandably high on his list of christological myths marked for elimination. The charge of Deicide, according to Eckardt, cannot be viewed merely as a historic event, for its power is such that it continues to haunt Jewish-Christian relationships.[65]

For this reason Eckardt is deeply disappointed at the Second Vatican Council's Declaration of 1965, which purportedly absolved the Jewish people of the charge of Deicide. He finds the document weakly worded; it even repeats the charge that some Jews were guilty of the Crucifixion. Its puny efforts came too late to have genuine meaning, lacking "the slightest mark of Christian contrition." "Could there be a more damning judgment upon the Church of our century than this one—that not until after the day of Auschwitz did Christians see fit to fabricate a correction of the record?"[66]

Like Niebuhr whom he admired, but with less hesitation, Eckardt challenged the Christian denigration of Jewish Law. Juxtaposing *Torah* and Christian love, according to Eckardt, can only result in the strengthening of the foundation of Christian antisemitism. Similarly, his assault upon the oft-repeated declaration that the "New Israel" had displaced the "Old" adds force to Littell's challenge and to what is usually seen in traditional theological texts. Eckardt views the theology of displacement as an "affront to the Ruler of the Universe."[67]

It is understandable why Eckardt's repudiation of the supersessionist-triumphalist christology of the Crucifixion and Resurrection leads him to an emphatic rejection of Christian missionary activity among Jews. Jews need no Christian guidance along the road to salvation, he declares. What is more, he sees Christian conversionism as a denial of God, since it denies "the unbroken covenant of God and Israel." "Were the Church to seek to convert Jews away from Judaism, it would be attacking not simply the Jewish community but the foundation of Christianity." Most importantly, Eckardt believes that the end of antisemitism will begin only when Christians refrain from their efforts to convert Jews. In this, the post-Holocaust age, Eckardt equates any attempt to absorb Jews into Christianity with a "spiritual Final Solution."[68]

Like other sensitive Protestants of recent years, Eckardt's imagination has been moved by a search for meaning in the *Shoah*. Since its purpose was to "eradicate every Jew from the world," no historical event can be compared to it. Jews have been persecuted before, but in this case the very "*being* of Jewishness" was slated for abolition; Jewish existence was deemed a capital crime. The persecution of no other people, according to Eckardt, could be placed on the same level with the Holocaust.[69]

Because of this event, he wonders and on occasion despairs of the possibility of a genuine relationship between Christians and Jews. He admits sadly that the Nazi gas chambers represented the logical outcome of centuries of Christian teaching about Jews, and for that reason he believes that the Final Solution has also altered forever the central meaning of the Christian faith. He views the Holocaust as a "greater trauma for Christians than for Jews," for it raises questions about the moral credibility of Christianity. In the aftermath of the Holocaust, the moral question that is posed concerns Christian survival. In a sense, Eckardt notes ironically, "Christian children may be made to follow in the trail of the Jewish children, though confronted not by physical extinction but by eventual spiritual death."[70]

In one of his most daring assertions, Eckardt declares: "After Auschwitz, the Crucifixion cannot be accepted as the determinative symbol of redemptive suffering." It cannot be seen as the ultimate and "absolute horror upon which the Christian faith can and should, dialectically, build its hope." In the face of burning Jewish children "the death of Jesus upon the Cross fades into comparative moral triviality."[71]

Christians, Eckardt believes, must henceforth accept the Final Solution as a central event in their own lives, an event which could not have occurred without their complicity. "Many of the Nazi executions of Jews," Eckardt repeatedly reminds his readers, "were carried out by believing Christians." Neither should the *Shoah* be reduced to "an aberration," "a nightmare," or a hideous historical mutation, he warns. On the contrary, it should be seen as the culmination of Christian history.[72]

So that this singular act of inhumanity, described by Eckardt as one of "transcending uniqueness," be permanently implanted upon the Christian memory, Eckardt marks the year 1941 as the dividing line between "two epochs," "B.S." being "the age before the *Shoah*" and "A.S." "the age of the *Shoah* and its aftermath." The division, Eckardt explains, will serve also to separate humanity into those "who take the *Shoah*-event with absolute seriousness" and "those who do not." Without a genuine expression of repentance Eckardt sees no future for Jewish-Christian relations.[73]

Eckardt is not oblivious to the risk involved in reminding Christians of their complicity. He admits that it may evoke resentment, give sadistic pleasure to sick minds, and even serve to perpetuate antisemitism. "In gazing down the abyss, may we not open the abyss within ourselves?" Yet the risk, he is convinced, is worth taking, for he sees much greater danger in silence and ignorance about the most tragic event in the history of Western civilization. And it is the latter that concerns him most; for few have as yet contemplated the meaning of the Holocaust. Most Christians, Eckardt laments, continue to live as if there had never been a Final Solution. Antisemites even deny that the event had occurred. In its own way, such a denial, by robbing the victims of their tragedy, underscores further the transcendent singularity of the Final Solution.[74]

Tension between the two faiths will continue, Eckardt believes, until Christianity acknowledges the self-sufficiency of the Jewish system of belief, that Christianity is not for the Jews, and that the two faiths, each in its own inimitable way, are separate and complete. Indeed, the Jewish people deserve praise for their centuries of resistance and stubborn refusal to succumb to the pressures of Christianity. "Jewish non-acceptance of Jesus," Eckardt declares, "remains the most sublime and heroic instance of Israel's faithfulness to the Covenant with God." Christians must know that for Jews Christianity "is in essence false."[75]

Christianity's inability to sever its ties with the Jewish faith, out of which it was born and with which it feels bound, has made it difficult for it to accept Jews "simply as people, ordinary people." Since this Christian perspective will continue to create uneasiness among Jews, Eckardt wonders if a permanent parting of the ways may not be the best solution. Like Jews, Christians must also learn to accept their autonomy and divorce their identity and eschatological thinking from that of the living Jews. "Loved ones part from one another and go their different ways," he writes, "though they need not thereby cease their loving or their caring."[76] This admission must have been difficult for Eckardt to make. Certainly his willingness to rethink some of the most sacred assumptions of his own belief places him today in the forefront of the Christian crusade against antisemitism.

17

Jewish Sovereignty and
the Protestant Right

1

Few issues gauge better the character and quality of Protestant-Jewish relations during the post-Holocaust era than does the Protestant attitude toward Jewish national aspirations. Evangelical premillennialists, as has been noted, driven by eschatological impulses, looked forward to a Jewish return to their ancestral home. By the middle of the nineteenth century Christian Zionism contained a peculiar intensity matched only, but for different reasons, by a handful of Zionists. For this reason the increasing support that American Jews extended toward the building of a Jewish homeland in Palestine in the late nineteenth and early twentieth centuries received a sympathetic hearing in Protestant evangelical circles. Indeed, for many American Christians the establishment of the British Mandate over Palestine was seen as the culminating phase of the 2,000-year dispersion of the Jewish people.

When the British government tried to mollify Palestinian Arabs in 1939 by issuing a White Paper that imposed a severe restriction on Jewish immigration into Palestine, a number of American Protestants joined with Jews to protest the British move. To counter British designs, American Jews formed an American Zionist Emergency Council (AZEC), which from the very first sought the cooperation of non-Jews. It appealed to labor unions, churches, ministers' associations, and Rotary, Lion, Elk, and Kiwanis clubs. Its members circulated petitions, sent letters and telegrams to congressional and administrative officials; and they tried to extract pro-Zionist resolutions from state legislative bodies and municipal governments.[1]

Because of AZEC's efforts two Christian organizations emerged that cooperated with the Zionist cause, the American Palestine Committee (APC), founded in 1932, and the Christian Council for Palestine (CCP), organized ten years later because of the efforts of such clergymen as Henry A. Atkinson and Reinhold Niebuhr. By 1946, both groups merged to form the American Christian Palestine Committee (ACPC), which in 1947 counted 15,000 members. According to Carl Hermann Voss, first executive director of the ACPC, these organizations, financed largely by American Jews, were actively involved in mobilizing public and government opinion in support of increased access of Jewish wartime survivors to Palestine.[2]

Voss recalls that Henry Atkinson, an early chairman of the group and an activist in ecumenical affairs, believed firmly that "the destiny of the Jews is a matter of immediate concern to the Christian conscience, the amelioration of their lot a duty that rests upon all who profess Christian principles." Atkinson recognized the bitter truth, that no country, including his own, had been willing to open its doors to the persecuted Jews of wartime Europe. Therefore, he stated in 1943, "we must look to Palestine, and we believe this little country can be the haven of refuge for the millions of homeless Jews in Axis-occupied countries."

The Christian Council was vocal in its denunciation of the British White Paper and in its support for a Jewish national homeland in Palestine. It issued publications, "convoked regional conferences, organized discussion groups and seminars on Palestine, and supplied lecturers to colleges, churches and clubs." Its representatives lobbied members of Congress on issues pertaining to a Jewish homeland. As the subject of Jewish statehood emerged in 1947, both Atkinson and Niebuhr appeared before legislative committees on Zionism's behalf.[3]

The effectiveness of such Christian organizations should not be measured by their relatively small membership. Their importance lay rather in their initiation of an organized structure for American Christian Zionism, a group through which Jews could find ready access to the Christian world. They provided a channel for public information and influence upon labor, the media, academic and political circles, groups that helped shape American opinion about Jewish national needs. Although one should not overestimate the importance of Christian support for political Zionism, its numbers were too few, its funding was too meager; still, as one historian admits, American Zionists could not have exerted the political leverage that they did without the sympathetic acquiescence of Christian America.[4]

2

The idea of Jewish nationalism and the birth of the state of Israel were endorsed by a number of the leading American theological voices, many of whom were representatives of orthodox and evangelical Protestantism. Among the foremost was that of Reinhold Niebuhr, America's most prominent Protestant thinker and a founding member of the Christian Council on Palestine.

As Niebuhr watched the unfolding catastrophe enveloping Europe's Jews, he concluded that a nationalistic solution was the only feasible response to their plight. By the mid-1930s he had already become a conspicuous Christian defender of Jewish national aspirations. A confirmed advocate of a pluralistic social model, Niebuhr was quick to empathize with Jewish collective yearnings. Ethnic and religious homogeneity were unappealing concepts to Niebuhr. He found little that was attractive about America's assimilationist and melting-pot ideals.[5] As news of mass killings of Jews spread, Niebuhr's interest in Zionism intensified. Owing to its record of antisemitism, he placed the responsibility for the survival of Europe's Jews on the entire Christian world. "It is a problem which Hitler did not create but only aggravated," he wrote. "The very quality of our civilization is involved in the solution of the Jewish national problem."[6]

He challenged the popular belief that the Jewish people constituted a religious rather than a national entity and, consequently, were not entitled to a separate national existence. He was also disturbed by those American Jews who refused to accept the ethnic foundations of their life, who succumbed "to the illusion that they are a purely cultural or religious community." Such notions, he feared, would interfere with the advance of the Zionist movement.[7] He believed that the impulse for collective survival was as legitimate as was the desire for individual freedom. He challenged those who would argue for the latter but ignore the former. "A type of liberalism which fights for and with the Jews on the first battle line but leaves them to fight alone on the second," he wrote, "is informed by an unrealistic universalism."[8]

Niebuhr recognized the danger that a free and open society held for Jewish survival. Assimilation, he remarked in 1944, was "a less painful form of death but it is death nevertheless."[9] Although the tragic experiences of the Second World War gave the Zionist solution a pragmatic urgency, Niebuhr did not discount the movement's religio-historical claims. These, he recognized, were rooted in an ancient and legitimate legacy, in a unique religious covenant experience.[10] The Jewish people, he believed, required a homeland where they could proceed with their creative cultural and religious evolution; a place, as he remarked, where they could be themselves, "neither 'understood' nor misunderstood, neither appreciated or condemned, but where they can be what they are."[11] This is not to suggest that Niebuhr was free of all ambivalent feelings about the new state of Israel. He confessed a fear that Israel's religious nationalists would endanger the state's democratic institutions. In 1957 he wrote that if the Orthodox had their way "they would fasten upon this essentially secular community political standards directly derived from the book of Deuteronomy." However, such anxieties were fleeting and did not diminish his enthusiastic support for the Zionist experiment.[12]

Ever conscious of the new state's precarious existence in the midst of a hostile Arab world, Niebuhr also did not ignore the tribulations of the Palestinian Arabs. For years he wondered how the collective desires of the two peoples could be resolved. Periodically he unfolded plans for economic and technical assistance, hoping that by introducing modernity into the Arab Middle East that tensions between Jews and their neighbors would abate. He was fully conscious of the "depth of the Arab spirit of vengeance" toward the Jewish state, the festering hostility that the presence of thousands of Palestinian refugees produced, and the Arab suspicion of Israel's democratic institutions and technological efficiency. Yet, as a Christian Realist, he recognized also that there might not exist a perfectly "just" solution to the perplexities of the region.[13]

In matters pertaining to Israel's security, Niebuhr's voice was always predictable. The increasing hostility of Egypt, for example, buttressed by a flow of Soviet arms, prompted Niebuhr to warn in 1956 that "the very life of the new nation of Israel is at stake." He urged the United States to overcome its reluctance to supply Israel with weapons. The Western world, too, he argued, owed a measure of security to the Jewish state.[14] Indeed, the lack of understanding displayed by his own government toward Israel, when it refused to evacuate the Sinai Desert in 1956, disturbed him, as did the anti-Israel posture of the United Nations. He defended Israel's right to hold on to its conquest until it was offered clear guarantees by the United Nations and the major powers for the security of its borders.[15]

A decade later, although gravely ill, Niebuhr again would not be stilled when the Arab world, following the lead of Egypt's president Gamal Abdel Nasser, threatened Israel with annihilation. "No simile better fits this war," Niebuhr editorialized in June 1967 after the Jewish state struck back successfully, "than the legend of David and Goliath." From Niebuhr's standpoint Israel's preemptive attack was fully justified. "Obviously a nation that knows that it is in danger of strangulation will use its fists." The attitude was in keeping with Niebuhr's Christian Realism. Clearly pacifism was as inappropriate to him in 1967 as it was in 1940.[16]

3

Reinhold Niebuhr represented a faint but significant trend in modern Protestant orthodoxy for the support of the Jewish state. Among this group were also Franklin H. Littell and A. Roy Eckardt, both of whom, as we have seen, were at the forefront of the movement to reassess Christian theology in the light of the Holocaust. It was their belief, however, that such theological reevaluation would bear few fruit without concomitant Christian cooperation in Jewish national needs. From a theological standpoint both traveled further than did Niebuhr in their championship of the state of Israel.

The extent of this journey can be seen in Littell's assertion that the Jewish state possesses a unique religious meaning not only for Jews, but also for Christians. Like other neo-orthodox writers, Littell links the two events of

Holocaust and Israel's rebirth as examples of the death and resurrection of the Jewish people. Israel, Littell insists, is as much a miracle for the Christian world as it is for the Jewish. "The Holocaust and the restoration of Israel," he wrote in 1973, "are basic events in Christian history—of the same order as the Exodus, Sinai, the fall of Rome."[17]

Littell explains to those Christians who question the biblical authority upon which the Jewish right to self-definition is based that Zionism has a far better scriptural foundation than does Christendom. Jewish nationhood and statehood comprise the only kind of ethnic identity to which God has given his explicit approval. He tells those who would question Israel's legitimacy that "the new code word for Antisemitism is *Anti-Zionism,*" and that "No one can be an enemy of Zionism and be a friend of the Jewish people today."[18] Yet, unlike many American evangelical Christians, Littell's support for Israel does not stem from an attachment to Christian prophecy, but from a conviction that Christian atonement for their responsibility for Jewish suffering could be experienced through the support of Jewish national needs.

In accordance with this belief, Littell insists that Christians must do more than profess a mere sympathy for the Jewish state. For the sake of Christianity's revitalization, its adherents must also develop a heightened sense of awareness of the events that Jews confront daily in Israel.[19] Because the safety of the Jewish state has deep religious implications for Littell, he finds it difficult to separate international events from their theological implications. He was disappointed at the Second Vatican Council's capitulation to Arab demands to dilute its statement on the Jews. Against the background of the Holocaust and the military threat that Israel continues to face daily, the Vatican statement, which for the first time absolved Jews collectively of the crime of Deicide, made no moral sense to Littell. "It is not the Jews, but the so-called Christians who need absolution. No crime in human history can equal the guilt which lies upon Christendom."[20]

A firm believer in putting his theology to work, Littell launched in the fall of 1970 a program designed "to call the attention of pastors and laymen in America's churches to the importance of Israel." His efforts resulted in the founding of an organization called Christians Concerned for Israel, which proceeded to arrange seminars, study groups, lectures, and the distribution of pamphlets and books about Israel to various Christian groups. Littell also served as the president of the National Christian Leadership Conference for Israel (NCLCI), an ecumenical, pro-Israel group.[21]

Littell rallied national support for Israel during the Lebanese War of 1982, a conflict in which Israel's invasion of Lebanon in retaliation for Palestine Liberation Organization incursions into northern Israel was widely criticized in liberal Christian circles. The NCLCI ran full-page advertisements in major American newspapers entitled "Christians in Solidarity With Israel." Pronouncing that "we believe it is the basic right and duty of every government to insure the safety and security of its citizens," Littell and his group moved to the defense of the Jewish state at a time when that nation's efforts to protect its citizens were greeted with universal condemnation. Neither did Littell shy away from political action as he and his supporters organized yet another group, the National Christian Congress. It was designed to pressure American legislators and senators to refrain from approving government sales of sophisticated lethal weapons to Israel's Arab enemies. It was action in keeping with Littell's belief that Christian sympathy alone was not enough.[22]

His wide contacts with American Protestants outside of the fundamentalist movement had convinced Littell that the state of Israel commands substantial support within the American Christian community, even though, as he admitted in 1981, this was not always reflected in the pronouncements of the national media and bureaucracy of the National Council of Churches. Littell believes, however, that among the "people out in the congregations," the state of Israel and its security continues to attract a commitment, "at least as numerous and at least as prestigious as those who are hostile" to it.[23]

4

Like his mentor Niebuhr, A. Roy Eckardt has been for years a staunch supporter of the Jewish state; and he agrees with Littell that Christian support for Israel is widespread in the United States, although its partisans sit "in back of the church."[24] More so than most Protestant theologians Eckardt has probed for meaning in the emergence of Israel, and he has pondered its impact upon the Christian world. He also sees the two events—Holocaust and national rebirth—altering forever the relationship between Christians and Jews. Jewish statehood, he believes, has put a final end to "the dreadful epoch of Jewish martyrdom."[25]

Eckardt has little sympathy for those Christians perplexed by the theological meaning of the birth of the Jewish state, who believe that the Jewish return to their ancestral home is a dreadful miscalculation, a "violation of Christian eschatology." On the contrary, Eckardt sees the birth of Israel as a repudiation of the "Christian fantasy" that Jews are doomed to perpetual dispersion and rootlessness. Christian support for Israel's survival, he believes, as does Littell, constitutes the only meaningful gesture of atonement for Christianity's past mistreatment of the Jewish people.[26]

Eckardt has repeatedly challenged the Arab denial of Israel's right to a sovereign existence. "To contend that Jews have a right to exist as an ethnic or a religious community . . . but not as a sovereign nation . . . is an example of antisemitism," he wrote in 1970, for it denies the Jewish people a basic human need accorded to all other collective groups.[27] The Arab world's yearning for Israel's demise, its repeated efforts to destroy the Jewish state, Eckardt views as politicide, another form of genocide. He is, therefore, skeptical about the future relationship of Israel and her Arab neighbors. He knows that in the Arab mind, peace with Israel is equated with the abolition of Israel. Israel's aspiration for survival is matched by Arab dreams of its extinction. "No reconciliation or compromise is possible," he notes, "between antagonists one of whom rejects the reality of the other." Eckardt sees hatred of the Jewish state as another form of antisemitism. *"It is impossible to separate Arab anti-Israelism and anti-Zionism from antisemitism."* What is more, Arab hatred of the Jewish state has much in common with Nazism, from which the Arabs have borrowed heavily. Only hatred of Israel has been able to unite the Arab world, as it has for centuries united Christendom. Islam, with little discouragement from the West, has inherited Christianity's animosity toward Israel and the Jewish people.[28]

Neither does Eckardt absolve the Western world, including the United States. Western deceitfulness manifests itself by a "general schizophrenia which judges Israel at one moment by superhuman standards . . . and at the next moment by subhuman standards." In the United Nations Israel is condemned repeatedly for defending itself, while her Arab terrorist aggressors escape even mild rebuke.[29]

Even more regrettable, according to Eckardt, is that in regard to Israel, American church organizations and their leaders have adopted a similar double standard. He points to Henry P. Van Deusan, former president of the Union Theological Seminary, to the American Friends Service Committee, a Quaker organization, to the World Council of Churches, and to the editors of the widely read *Christian Century*, as examples of Christian individuals and groups ever ready to "lecture Israel" on the slightest pretext, but who are quick to tolerate and forgive the most barbaric acts of Arab terror. Why is it, he asks, that no other nation but Israel "is told to practice universal sainthood?" Is it possible, he wonders, that the church conceals a suppressed desire, "a secret wish for the demise of Israel?"[30] It appears, Eckardt observes, that "whenever Israel is assailed, certain . . . macabre elements in the Christian soul are stirred to sympathy with the assailants."[31] He is left to conclude that in the Christian mind, the state of Israel—repeatedly reproached for its militancy, aggressiveness, inflexibility, vengefulness, and irreligiosity—has replaced the mythical Jew as a target for Christian abuse.[32] Clearly the Christian world has drawn few lessons from the Holocaust.

Christian attempts to read theological meaning into the founding and history of Israel, Eckardt views also as reprehensible, a sinister strain of antisemitism, because it is disguised. He agrees with Niebuhr that the "theologization of politics is a guarantor of immorality," for it imposes unnatural demands upon Jews and invests their misfortunes with biblical meaning. He warns Christians against the temptation to instruct Israelis "as if they were biblical prophets."[33]

For this reason Eckardt finds the Dispensationalist theology of Christian Zionism disturbing. Despite the guise of friendship that this evangelical wing of Protestantism assumes toward the Jewish state, its adherents see little value in its emergence except as it might serve as a preparation for the Second Coming. Christian Zionists invest Israel with a divine importance, theologize its political existence and in the process rob its citizens of their humanity and their dignity.[34] "In the theater of nation-states, no demands can be legitimately made of Israel that are not made of Egypt, the United States, India, Nigeria, Jordan, et al.," he writes. Nevertheless, "this is not at all to deny the constitutive link between the will and purpose of God and the Jewish State." Eckardt parts roads with Dispensationalists, who he believes erroneously call themselves Christian Zionists, since their concern is not for the fulfillment of Judaism, but for the exploitation of Judaism to achieve their own ends. A valid Christian Zionism can only be an acknowledgment that the birth of Israel "is a special event within the spiritual life," and for the well-being "of the Jewish people *and the Jewish people alone.*"[35]

This is not to say that Christianity's liberal Left has not also erred in its views about Jewish nationalism. Unlike the evangelicals who picture Israel as a "political church," the liberal Left views Judaism exclusively in religious rather than in cultural and national terms. Consequently, it sees no need for a Jewish state at all. In its own way, according to Eckardt, liberal Protestantism denies the Jewish people a fundamental necessity, one which Niebuhr and Littell have also demanded, the need to pursue a normal collective and political existence.[36]

5

However, American premillennial Dispensationalist thought cannot be discounted, especially since much of American Protestantism's vision of Israel has been shaped by its growing influence. Its resurgence in American life after a temporary decline in the years preceding World War II has been one of the remarkable characteristics of recent American culture. The emergence of the Soviet threat, America's fear of the spread of communism during the 1950s, fueled a call for Christian renewal. The political conservatism of the decade opened a new era of respectability for the Protestant Right, as it did for organized religion in general. A growing number of political officeholders identified themselves openly with evangelical Protestantism. Presidents Dwight Eisenhower and Richard Nixon flaunted their association with the Reverend Billy Graham, a leading activist behind America's Christian awakening.[37]

Although the new evangelical crusade moderated somewhat in the face of the Vietnam War and the Watergate scandal, its retreat was temporary. With the election of Jimmy Carter to the presidency in 1976, an individual who proclaimed himself a "born-again" Christian had moved into the White House. And with Ronald Reagan's election in 1980 and George Bush's in 1988, the Christian Right was assured of further support from the nation's highest office. By the mid-1980s premillennialism commanded the allegiance of more Americans than ever before.[38] A 1982 Gallop Poll estimated that thirty-five percent of all Americans claimed to be "born-again" Christians. Other surveys have numbered American evangelical Christians at almost 40 million.[39]

The evangelical view of Zionism and the state of Israel was conditioned by the eschatology of premillennial Dispensationalism. The progress of the Zionist experiment suggested to evangelicals that God's plan was unfolding as prophesied, that the rapture of the church was near and the tribulation was close at hand. What guided their concern about these events was not necessarily compassion for Jewish suffering under Hitler, or the desperate Jewish need for a homeland, but for the prophetic meaning that contemporary events conveyed. Yet none of this should diminish the perception of their support to the Zionist movement and the state of Israel, or the impact that such an eschatology imposed upon America's attitude toward Israel.[40]

Since the 1970s, some evangelical Protestants have been quick to rise to Israel's defense. Even during the less popular war which Israel waged in Lebanon against the PLO in 1982, evangelicals displayed their solidarity with the Jewish state. While the Israeli Army advanced into southern Lebanon, and while its actions were censured by liberal Christians and Jews, evangelical ministers, joined in an organization which they called TAV (the last letter of the Hebrew alphabet), arranged a series of conferences in California and elsewhere to show their support for Israel's "Peace of Galilee" campaign.[41] Douglas R. Shearer, founder and president of TAV, a businessman and lay preacher, explained that his group's support for Israel stemmed from "an uncompromising adherence to the scriptural passage which promised that land to the Jews."[42]

If Jewish leaders found such pronouncements awkward, they were at least reassured by the activities that accompanied them, coming as they did from a segment of Christianity that ordinarily filled them with uncertainty. Rabbi Marc H. Tannenbaum, Interreligious Affairs Director of the American Jewish Committee, was pleased at the prospect of developing closer ties with the Christian Right. He recognized that American evangelists were the "largest and fastest growing block of pro-Israeli, pro-Jewish sentiment in this country."[43]

6

By 1980 Jerry Falwell, pastor of the 18,000 member Thomas Road Baptist Church in Lynchburg, Virginia, a congregation that he formed in 1956, emerged as the leading voice of the Religious Right. He also founded Moral

Majority, Inc., an evangelical political pressure group, and Liberty University, a Christian institution of higher learning, over which Falwell presides and from where his television program, "The Old Gospel Hour," is aired nationally.[44]

Although they share many of his ideas, Falwell has not been received with enthusiasm by Billy Graham and other mainline evangelical conservatives. Neither do orthodox theologians, such as Eckardt and Littell, find inspiration in his fundamentalist message. Nevertheless, Falwell's influence in Dispensationalist circles has been unusual, as has been his frank insistence of the genuineness of his affection for Jews and their national experience.[45]

Born in Lynchburg, Virginia, in 1933, Falwell grew up during the Great Depression and the Second World War, in a family whose roots can be traced to Virginia's pioneers. Falwell's early comprehension of Judaism stemmed almost exclusively from his Bible readings and the rumors that he absorbed from local gossip. He admits that his early understanding of Jews was "very provincial." Raised in a Southern "red-neck" home, Falwell was exposed frequently to a negative attitude toward Jews, one which changed, he recalls, after his Christian conversion in 1952.[46]

Falwell, a biblical literalist who graduated from Baptist Bible College in Springfield, Missouri, in 1956, adheres firmly to the doctrine of "biblical inerrancy." He is convinced that it is a Christian duty to share the gospel of Jesus with every individual, including Jews; and he has offered his leadership to the movement to include prayer and the subject of "creationism" in the public school curriculum. To elevate the general tone of America's morals, Falwell has struggled to eliminate pornography from the nation's media and to declare abortions illegal.[47] He holds strong international views as well. Falwell and his followers are adamant about the necessity for building America's military might, are opposed to the limitation of nuclear development, and urge American support for any country opposed to the Soviet Union or its doctrines.[48]

Falwell has repeatedly professed his friendship for the Jewish people and his abhorrence of antisemitism. As a fundamentalist he accepts the "chosenness" of the Jewish people and their destiny to play a special role in God's overall plan. Unlike Eckardt and Littell, Falwell does not accept the idea that antisemitism is rooted in Christian teachings, although he acknowledges that Jews have been slaughtered in the name of Christianity. Falwell resents "all antisemitic groups which hide behind Christianity" and urges all Christian ministers to expose them. Antisemitism, according to Falwell, is the very antithesis of Christianity. In 1981 he pronounced his belief that "anti-Semitism was produced by Satan himself as an antithesis to the God of heaven who selected and ordained the Jewish people as His own chosen family."[49]

As a Dispensationalist, Falwell believes that "God has outlined a vast and glorious future for Israel"; that the Jewish nation is destined to "play a key role in the future events of this world." Consequently, he rejects the supersessionist theology inherited by other Christians. "God has a separate, but mutually compatible, plan and purpose for both Israel and the Church."[50] Falwell understands that Jews who are true to their faith could never accept the Christian Savior as their Messiah, just as Christians committed to theirs could not restrain themselves from preaching the message of Christ to all people. Still, he welcomes a dialogue with Jews. "We must be willing to sit down as citizens of the universe whose futures are clearly interwoven and interdependent."

Falwell's attitude toward Jews and Judaism has persuaded a few Jewish leaders to reevaluate their attitude toward him. Joshua O. Haberman, rabbi emeritus of the Liberal Washington Hebrew Congregation, remarked in 1986 that "for six million American Jews, a decent, amicable relationship with the largest and fastest growing religious community in America is a matter of survival."[51] Haberman rejects the belief prevalent among liberal Jews that Jerry Falwell and other neofundamentalist leaders are preparing to Christianize the public schools, eradicate the principle of separation of church and state, and reject the pluralistic character of American society. Haberman believes that Jerry Falwell does not represent an aberration in American life, but expresses widely held convictions that are not threatening to American democratic institutions.

More than anything else, it is Falwell's support for the state of Israel that has convinced some Jews to view the famous evangelist in a different light. Falwell not only scrutinizes events in Israel from a biblical and Dispensationalist perspective, but takes an active interest in the progress of its people, its security, and its friendship with the United States. "As a Zionist and as one who in the Christian community is probably the most outspoken supporter of Israel and the Jewish people the world over," declared Falwell, "I would say I have become a radical on this issue."[52]

Falwell has been consistent in his support for Israel, especially during those times when his more liberal colleagues were openly critical of the Jewish state. Falwell condemns the American media for lying in wait, ever ready to direct attention to Israel's defects, to publicly denounce it. "There is no question that the media displays a double standard in reporting of Israel," declared the fundamentalist preacher. "I can think of few nations who receive a more biased treatment from the media than Israel."[53] Falwell has lobbied for the sale of American armaments to Israel and against their sale to her Arab enemies. He has condemned Pope John Paul for meeting with the PLO's leader, Yasser Arafat, an act which Falwell says will only "encourage the forces of evil and darkness"; and he considers "unbelievable" the Vatican's refusal to acknowledge the legitimacy of the Jewish state. Falwell has urged the American government to move its embassy from Tel Aviv to Jerusalem, the official capital of the

Jewish state.[54] His pro-Israel record has induced a number of Jewish leaders to view neofundamentalism more benignly.

7

Orthodox and evangelical enthusiasm for the state of Israel has not been matched by the more liberal denominations. Here, talk about the biblical meaning of Jewish national resurrection has been not only rare but disputed. The historian Hertzel Fishman has documented the indifference, even resentment, that greeted the birth of the Jewish state in the pages of the *Christian Century*, America's leading liberal nondenominational weekly magazine.[55] Liberal Protestants not only objected to the establishment of a Jewish sovereign nation, but exerted efforts to prevent its consummation. The American Council of Judaism, the unrepresentative Jewish anti-Zionist organization, could always count on the support of liberal Protestantism in its obstructionist tactics. In matters pertaining to Israel, liberals found it convenient to view the American Council as the authentic voice of American Jewry. To dissuade the American government from offering its support to the UN Partition Resolution of 1947, liberal Protestants formed their own pro-Arab lobby, the Committee for Justice and Peace in the Holy Land. Sitting on its executive committee were some of America's leading liberal Protestant figures—Henry Sloan Coffin, Daniel Bliss, Harry Emerson Fosdick, and others.[56]

High on the list of anti-Zionist Protestant pro-Arab groups was perched the American Friends of the Middle East (AFME), an organization formed shortly after Israel was founded. The New York journalist Dorothy Thompson, daughter of a Methodist minister, served as its first president, with prominent Protestant clergy on its national council. Its executive vice president, Garland Evans Hopkins, was an associate editor of the *Christian Century*.

Dorothy Thompson, who had been for many years an outspoken supporter of the Zionist cause, made an abrupt alteration in her views during the late 1940s when she began to berate the Jewish people and their homeland. Her widely read articles and column in the New York *Herald Tribune* accused American Zionists of a dual loyalty. Her disillusionment with the Jewish cause was stimulated, it seems, by the aggressive tactics employed on the eve of the birth of the Jewish state by such Zionist fringe groups as the Irgun and Stern. Her vocal outbursts of resentment at the desperate Jewish efforts to achieve sovereignty at the close of the Second World War created a rift between her and her former supporters.[57] Unlike Reinhold Niebuhr, her contemporary, Thompson could not accept the justification and the reality of the Zionist struggle.

The reaction of the Unitarian minister and social activist John Haynes Holmes was not all that different. An early supporter of the Zionist idea, Holmes could not reconcile his Christian universalism with the birth of a

Jewish sovereign enclave. Holmes remained comfortable so long as Zionists continued to talk of a Jewish "commonwealth," but political solutions for the Jewish people made him uncomfortable. As a pacifist, he could not acknowledge the legitimacy of the use of military force even for the attainment of legitimate national goals.[58]

Israel was portrayed by Protestant anti-Zionists as aggressive and intolerant in its treatment of Arab refugees. In 1951 the Near East Christian Council, a group dominated by Near Eastern Protestant missionaries and supported by the World Council of Churches, convened in Beirut for the purpose of discussing the plight of the Palestinian Arabs. Its resolutions pictured the Arab refugees as victims of a catastrophe engineered by the Zionist state; and they imposed upon Israel the entire obligation to resolve the crisis.[59] They made no mention about Arab obligations in this matter, or of the hundreds of thousands of Jewish refugees persecuted by and expelled from Arab lands.

It was difficult for many American Protestant liberals to accept the necessity for a Jewish national solution. The popular pastor Harry Emerson Fosdick, who had been impressed with the historical wealth of the Holy Land and who had admired the devotion and courage of the early Jewish pioneers, was not as appreciative of the political transformation that had taken place in Palestine. "I would regard it as an injustice to the Arabs to put them under Jewish rule without their consent," wrote Fosdick shortly before Israel's creation.[60] The dedication of American-Jewish Zionists also made Fosdick uneasy. In 1960 he wrote that "We resent the Zionist endeavor to make the State of Israel the center of patriotism for American Jews. The Jewish people here are American like all the rest of us, and Judaism is not a nationalistic cult, but is one of the great universal faiths."[61] Like other Christian liberals Fosdick resented what he perceived as America's special treatment of Israel, "as though Israel were America's baby." He also suggested that American Zionists might be guilty of a dual loyalty.[62]

Fosdick joined Henry Sloan Coffin, president of Union Theological Seminary in New York, and William E. Hocking, an emeritus professor of philosophy at Harvard, in anti-Zionist polemics and activities. Coffin, an officer of the International Missionary Council and editor of the widely read *Christianity and Crisis*, warned American Jews that their support of Israel could jeopardize their standing as American citizens, and would encourage public hostility toward them.[63] Similarly, Hocking, a prominent spokesman for liberal Protestantism, like Dorothy Thompson, had traveled the road from pro- to anti-Zionism. A champion of missionary activity in the Near East, he emerged by the 1940s as the outstanding anti-Zionist intellectual in the United States.

Hocking had opposed the creation of a Jewish state. In 1944, while a remnant of Europe's Jews was seeking refuge in Palestine, and while their American brethren were beseeching Great Britain to lift its immigration barriers to Palestine, Hocking accused Judaism of becoming "too much the religion of 'return.'"[64] Hocking was in full sympathy with the work of the Jewish anti-Zionist American Council for Judaism. Following the birth of Israel he declared that the Jews were impostors in an Arab world. He was critical of America's economic support of the Jewish state and warned government officials that their favored treatment of Israel would alienate the Arab world. He accused American Zionists of creating a climate of contempt toward Arab character and culture.[65]

Protestant Dispensationalist support for Israel offered an additional endorsement to liberal suspicions of the Jewish national experience. Typical is the writing of Grace Halsell, a Washington, D.C., journalist who had served as a speech writer for Pres. Lyndon Johnson. Halsell is disturbed by the alleged alliance forged between Zionists and the Christian Right. Her explanation for the unholy alliance points to the Israeli desire to receive a nod of approval for its conquest of Arab lands; the conviction of both parties that their alliance would result in mutual advantages—"more arms, bigger armies, more bombs," and the ability to achieve their "goals through military power." "Leaders in both camps favor unlimited military buildup of nuclear weapons and other armaments," writes Halsell. "Christian Right leaders are nationalistic, militaristic, each with a dogma that demands the highest priority in their lives—a dogma centered around Israel and a cult of land."[66]

Halsell's suspicion of American evangelists and their Dispensationalist theology colors her vision of Israel and its search for security. Her focus on Israeli society is directed not at its achievements for Jewish liberation, but at the activities of "Gush terrorists" and the explosive rhetoric of Rabbi Meir Kahane and "his messianic vision." She dreads the imagined sinister alliance that she believes has been forged between Zionists and American evangelicals, a mixture that she contends has resulted in the introduction of more weapons into the Middle East than into any other area of the world. It "represents the most dangerous powder keg for nuclear confrontation."[67]

8

Actually, Halsell's anxieties notwithstanding, most American Jews lived uncomfortably with the Christian Right, or with such related groups as the Mormon church, Jehovah's Witnesses, and Seventh-day Adventists. For justifiable reasons Jews suspect the motives that support Christian interest in the Jewish state. When late in 1984 the Mormon church unveiled plans to erect an extension of Brigham Young University in Jerusalem, Israeli and American Jews saw the new campus as a potential focal point for missionary activity. Assurances by Mormon leaders that proselytizing was not among the underlying purposes of the Jerusalem structure did not satisfy interested Jews. One Anglo-Jewish newspaper noted that "part of the seven-story educational complex is the inclusion of a 'Visitors Center,' which like other Mormon visitors centers around the world are beachheads for launching massive missionary activities."[68] Commenting on Mormon intentions, Jacob Neusner remarked,

> Nothing they do is selfless. Everything they do has the single goal of converting everyone they can. Pure and simple. The proposed BYU Center will provide access, not only to Israeli Jewry, but also (and especially) to large numbers of foreign, including American Jewish youth who study in Jerusalem. . . . Until the Mormon Church . . . recognizes the legitimacy of Judaism for Israel, the Jewish people, they can want nothing other than to convert as many of us as they can get their hands on.[69]

Liberal American Jews have good reason to suspect the genuineness of the Dispensationalist caress of the Jewish state. The Dispensationalist belief that the great upheaval that will follow Christ's return will leave millions of Jews slaughtered with the exception of those who have accepted Jesus Christ as their savior repels Jews, as it does Halsell. Likewise, Jews find annoying the evangelical tendency to view every outbreak of violence, not in human, but in biblical, prophetic terms. And they become uneasy when they and their beliefs are subjected to Christian theologization. They object to the role assigned to Israel in a script written by Dispensationalists. For Jews, Israel is not a symbol in a Christian drama. "We shall, I am afraid, never truly understand each other if the church persists in making its calculations with a mythical Jew and a spiritualized concept of the land," writes Jakob J. Petuchowski.[70] There is a ring of truth in Jack R. Fischel's remark that fundamentalists are the friends of Jews, but only for the wrong reasons.[71]

Equally disconcerting to American Jewish observers are the inconsistencies that they detect between evangelical words and actions. Falwell's Moral Majority has backed congressional and senatorial candidates such as Sen. Jesse Helms of South Carolina, whose voting record until the late 1980s has been anti-Israel. Helms and other senators and legislators of the Christian Right have in numerous cases resisted grants-in-aid to Israel and did little during the administration of Pres. Ronald Reagan to block the sale of sophisticated weapons to Arab countries. President Reagan's visit to the Bitburg cemetery in West Germany in 1985, where former SS Nazi officers were interred, was endorsed by many members of the Christian Right. Although the president's journey to the Nazi graves was viewed by millions of people as morally repugnant, Reagan refused to cancel his visit despite the eloquent pleas of the Jewish writer Elie Wiesel and other Jewish and Christian religious leaders. His persistence in this matter underscored the superficiality of American conservative concern for the most deeply felt Jewish issues. For political and Christian expediency, Jerry Falwell and his Moral Majority helped to defeat some of the staunchest political friends of Israel, liberals such as Sen. Frank Church of

Idaho, merely because of their opposition to school prayers, antiabortion laws, or the inclusion of the "science" of creationism in the public school curriculums.[72]

The neofundamentalist outburst against American Jews generated by the showing of the film *The Last Temptation of Christ*, released by Universal Pictures in the summer of 1988, underscores further the tenuous thread that unites evangelicals and Jews. Because both the chairman of the board and president of MCA, the entertainment conglomerate that owns Universal Pictures, happened to be Jewish, Jerry Falwell, Pat Robertson, and other representatives of the Protestant Right warned that the release of the film could unleash a wave of anti-Jewish enmity throughout the United States. That such an irresponsible suggestion (which shortly after was "clarified" and repudiated) could be openly invoked, even though the author of the book upon which the film was based and the director of the film were non-Jews, raised questions about the genuineness of evangelical professions of friendship with Jews.[73]

Nevertheless, the incident of *The Last Temptation,* or others which will inevitably follow, has not and will not discourage a persistent minority of Jews and Christians from conversation and religious cooperation, although such events, as Gershon Greenberg observes, should make both groups "aware of the dangers of collaborating in deception."[74] Only time will tell whether the recent bursts of philo-semitism of orthodox and evangelical Protestants are a product of recent events, a reaction to the *Shoah,* the birth of the state of Israel and the cold war, that is, a mood reflective of its own time and place, or one of greater resiliency and durability.

18

Disparate Encounters

Until the mid-1960s a remarkable consistency underlay the relationship of Protestants and Jews; but any generalization about this association must recognize the variety of fronts upon which the two historic faiths have met. American Jews, themselves divided ideologically, have learned to face a variety of Protestantisms. This book identifies ten such encounters.

First, from the very beginning of American history Jews have confronted a Protestantism divided into an unprecedented multitude of denominational and theological communities. Protestantism's divisiveness promoted a religious milieu in which Jewish conspicuousness as a non-Christian minority was minimized. This condition granted Jews a measure of security despite their numerical inferiority. Notwithstanding the religious dedication of the early Protestant settlers and their determination to transfer their denominational orthodoxy unchanged to the transatlantic world, frontier conditions molded an environment for religious voluntarism and tolerance.

During the eighteenth century theological disagreements were superimposed upon denominational differences, creating additional cleavages of various shades of Right and Left within American Protestantism. The religious condition produced by these dissensions tended to minimize further the anomaly of Judaism in a Christian environment. Jewish survival in early America was achieved, therefore, not because of the intrinsic goodness of American Christianity, or as a result of a carefully reasoned theory of toleration, but through a fortuitous set of circumstances.

Divisiveness also legitimized the notion of ecclesiastical anarchy, a concept which the handful of American Jews put to good use during the nineteenth century. Protestant practice served as a model upon which many Jews selectively patterned their own religious decorum, and to some degree even their thinking. Like Protestants, Jews encamped themselves in a number of ecclesiastical battalions—Reform, Conservative, and various shades of Orthodoxy, to which they added by the third decade of the twentieth century Reconstructionism, a movement that redefined Judaism as a civilization.[1] Like nominal

Protestants, there were also those Jews who eschewed all religious commitments, who for a variety of reasons declined to claim any religious affiliation. In short, Judaism underwent the kind of splintering that American Protestant voluntarism inspired.

Second, Jews and Protestants shared a biblical front; a dedication to the Word of God. Like Calvin and his early followers, Jews, too, were a law-centered people; indeed, their commitment inspired the behavior of early Protestants.[2] For American Christians, as for Jews, biblical attachment transcended denominational and ideological divisions and served as a unifying bond. More important, the centrality of the Bible, be it in the age of Cotton Mather or Bill Moody, bequeathed a special place for the historical Jew in the mind of Protestant America.

Early Americans imagined themselves to be God's Chosen People, inheritors of Israel's covenant. The revolutionary generation became preoccupied with biblical analogies, frequently comparing its own tribulations and victories with those of the ancient Hebrews. It looked to the polity of ancient Israel for an inspiring model upon which to pattern its own society. To be sure, American bibliocentricism did not necessarily sharpen Protestant insight into the Jewish conditions of its own time. Although it provided a special place for the historic Jews in the Protestant imagination, that place was not always a flattering one.

Third, Protestant millennial thought also reserved a special corner for Jews, ancient and contemporary, in the Christian conscience. Throughout American history many Protestants adhered to an ancient Christian conviction that a special role had been reserved by God for the Jewish people, one which would unfold during the final hours of history. Such thinking, which had invaded the Protestant imagination during the early days of America's religious experience, grew to become a central concern of many pious Americans. By the second half of the nineteenth century it came to dominate the thinking of premillennial Dispensationalists, the most rapidly growing transdenominational Protestant group in the United States. Their belief that God's covenant with Israel had not been abrogated or displaced differed sharply from traditional Christian theology.

A fourth observation is that a logical outgrowth of millennarian thought, one of particular significance for the future relationship of Jews and Protestants, concerns the restorationist views held by premillennial Protestants. A desire to witness a return of the Jews to Zion was present at the very beginning of America's Christian history. Later in the nineteenth century, anticipating a Jewish restoration, a few believers established Christian settlements in Palestine. Many premillennialists believed that the world was about to end, an event which would be accompanied by the return of Christ to earth, the rapture of the church, the tribulation of sinners, and the restoration of the

Jews. Such thinking accounts for the sympathy toward the early Zionist movement and the founding of the state of Israel displayed by evangelical Protestants. To the premillennial Dispensationalist mind the presence of a Jewish
state stands as concrete evidence that God's plan is unfolding. That the
evangelical attitude toward the Jewish state has been driven by its unique
eschatology, rather than by a genuine concern for the national needs of the
Jewish people, does not completely detract from its importance in shaping
Protestant attitudes toward Israel.

Fifth, evangelical Protestantism, which dominated a significant portion of
eighteenth- and nineteenth-century American Christian thought, did not
always provide a reassuring environment for American Jews. The early Christian certainty that the Protestant Reformation would be consummated in
America was hardly a consolation for the few Jews who resided there, as was the
prevailing belief that the first settlers had inherited the covenant from sinful
Israel. The early Calvinist belief that because of their transgressions Jews had
lost their hallowed relationship with God hardly differed from traditional
christological notions that American settlers had left behind in Europe. Neither did early American biblical typology, employed frequently by the nation's
pious well into the first half of the nineteenth century, which displaced Jewish
history with a defunct past of value only to Christian readers, prove conducive
to any meaningful interfaith associations.

Even premillennial Dispensationalists, who rejected the usual doctrines of
supersessionism, tended to view Jews not as real people, but principally as
objects with which to enhance their own salvation. Their negative view of the
world around them, which they believed was on the verge of imminent destruction because of the sinful nature of its inhabitants, was an alien sentiment for
Jews. Premillennial eschatology, which looked forward with anticipation to the
end of history, was an incomprehensible doctrine for Jews. Premillennial theology, which anticipates a great upheaval following Christ's return to earth, one
which would leave millions of Jews who did not receive Christ slaughtered,
repelled Jews.

Most disappointing to Jews was that the voices of evangelical Protestants
offered little support to Jews during the dark days of Nazism. While Dispensationalists were forbidden to participate in acts of antisemitism, which they
considered the work of Satan, neither did their theology equip them with
appropriate tools to impede its progress. Indeed, they viewed German anti-
Jewish measures, including the Final Solution, as part of God's mysterious
purpose that lay beyond the pale of human understanding. Dispensationalists
found it difficult to think about Jews as individuals. They preferred to see them
as a collectivity, whose destiny was linked to the fulfillment of Christian
salvation.

My sixth point is that until the middle of the twentieth century, Protestant efforts to witness to Jews, despite their limited success, were unrelenting. Such exertions crossed denominational as well as ideological lines, engrossing the efforts of postmillennialists, premillennialists, and amillennialists.

During the first half of the nineteenth century proselytizing efforts became well organized, well financed, and supported by prominent American evangelists. Jews soon faced an array of Protestant evangelists eager to offer them immediate salvation. Christian outreach assumed a frantic urgency in the late nineteenth century, a time when millions of eastern European Jews arrived on American shores. Huddled in the nation's larger cities, they were seen by American Protestant leaders as religiously deprived, a threat to the nation's moral values. Liberal Protestants, organized in the Federal Council of Churches and lodged in institutional settlement houses, were as eager to bring the Jews to Christ as were their more orthodox counterparts.

Even news of Germany's systematic slaughter of Europe's Jews did not weaken evangelical resolve to draw Jews away from their ancestral heritage. On the contrary, news of Nazi barbarism made American missionaries all the more insistent that their efforts to divest Jews of their traditional beliefs constituted the grandest gesture of Christian love, the ultimate act of Christian compassion. From the perspective of America's Jews, who were forced to devise a variety of rebuttals and defenses in their confrontation with missionaries, this was not Protestantism's finest hour. Christian witness to Jews constituted the major obstacle against the improvement of Jewish-Christian relations.

Seventh, and an equally consistent trait of the conservative wing of American Protestantism, was its desire to Christianize America. Throughout American history many Protestants were blunt in their insistence that the United States was and should remain a Christian nation.[3] While many honored the principle of separation of church and state as an idea worth preserving, they made every effort to evade it in practice. They were convinced that only through the inculcation of Protestant values would the survival of American democratic institutions be assured.

When these socioreligious sentiments were translated into legislation, such as Sunday-Sabbath laws and the Christianization of national holidays, measures which were frequently upheld by state courts as constitutional, American Jews felt threatened. Attempts by Protestant theocrats to Christianize the public schools through Bible readings and sectarian instruction, some of it patently hostile to Judaism, further isolated American Jews. The Protestant crusade, awakened and energized by a vast number of Jewish immigrants, was intensified during the closing years of the nineteenth century, reaching its pinnacle during the 1920s. Not surprisingly, Protestants were found at the forefront of the immigration restriction movement.

My eighth point is that only a thin line separated theocrats from preachers in their hatred toward Jews. By the opening of the twentieth century antisemites were ensconced on the extreme Right of American Protestantism. During the 1920s and thirties, domestic and international events converged to make Christian antisemitism respectable. Unwittingly, the fundamentalist crusade inspired extremist movements such as the Ku Klux Klan, an organization which envisioned itself as the custodian of Protestant values. Klansmen and clergy supported each other in their common endeavor to strengthen evangelical Protestantism.

Throughout the 1930s, when American Jews were desperately seeking Christian support on behalf of their European coreligionists, hundreds of antisemitic organizations, inspired by German Nazism, many claiming Protestant affiliation, flourished in the United States. With few exceptions, in respect to the treatment of Jews, mainline Protestant leaders failed to offer their congregants moral direction during these difficult times. As the Nazi noose tightened around the fate of Europe's Jews, American Jews found themselves alone, surrounded by an indifferent Protestant world.

Christian antisemitism became a deeply imbedded virus, difficult to extricate from the soul of at least an element of Christendom. It continues its malevolent work even in our own day. By the end of the twentieth century, blatantly antisemitic organizations, most of them, to be sure, hovering on the extreme fringe of the Protestant world, masquerading as defenders of Protestant America, flourished in the United States with relative impunity. Besides a variety of Ku Klux Klan organizations, which by 1988 claimed a combined membership of about 5,000, a host of other groups have sprung to life in recent years.[4]

One, the Lord's Covenant Church, was founded by Shelden Emry in Phoenix, Arizona. Emry, who for years before his death in 1985 managed the "America's Promise" radio program, was fond of promoting such contrivances as the Jewish threat to Christianity and the hoax of the Holocaust.[5] Conspicuous among contemporary hate groups are those associated with the "Identity Church" movement, whose ideological roots stem from the Anglo-Israelism beliefs of the nineteenth century. Anglo-Israelism holds that the true descendants of the Lost Ten Tribes, that is the Chosen People, are white Anglo-Saxons. They have concluded that Jesus was not a Jew, but an ancestor of white northern Europeans. Jews, they charge, are descendants of Satan and should be exterminated. As premillennialists, many Identity followers believe that Jesus' return is at hand, an event which will be signaled by a cataclysm, a race war, in which "only members of the Identity Movement will survive to build a 'New Israel' in America."[6]

One of the most notorious of these groups is the Aryan Nations, an Idaho-based, paramilitary Identity group, centered around Rev. Richard Butler's Church of Jesus Christ Christian. Butler, an admirer of Hitler, anticipates the establishment of a white racist state in the United States.[7] A similar ideology is supported by the Christian-Patriots Defense League, an antisemitic group founded in 1977. Its message warns of the "inescapable collapse of the present structure," one which reflects "the Pharisaical anti-Christ system," and is directed at America's Jewish population. It also predicts that America's collapse will be accompanied by a cataclysmic racial conflict for which it urges all white Christian Americans to prepare.[8] American Jews, although aware of the un-representative Christian character of these groups, cannot ignore their Christian symbolism and ominous rhetoric.

The ninth area of Protestant-Jewish confrontation occurs on the front of Protestant liberalism. Like their orthodox counterparts, not all liberals agree about matters of doctrine and practice; but for the past century and a half they have shared a common ethos that has set them apart from their more conservative coreligionists.

In a certain sense American Jews have been more comfortable in the presence of Protestant liberals than with other Christian groups. Liberalism's pose of tolerance of religious differences, its insistence upon and defense of such principles as freedom of conscience and the separation of church and state, and its general display of social consciousness seemed more in accord with Jewish sensibilities. Its postmillennial optimism was also more compatible with Jewish thought.

Yet imbedded in Protestant liberalism were some serious limitations that inhibited the progress of interfaith harmony. As an outgrowth of eighteenth-century rationalism, Protestant liberalism, although it rejected Calvinism's rigid biblicism, had from the very first viewed Judaism as an antiquated system of belief, inferior to the elevated moral standards of the founder of Christianity. This outlook was as true of Thomas Jefferson as it was of Ralph Waldo Emerson or H. Richard Niebuhr.

Throughout the nineteenth century liberals accused Jews of being enslaved to the letter of the Mosaic law, obsessed with ceremonial and ritualistic trivialities. If they did not charge the Jews with the crime of Deicide, they did accuse them of "Pharisaic" behavior. If they did not stress the need to bring Jews into the community of Christ, they leaned in the opposite direction by their desire to cleanse Christian life of the narrow parochialism of the Jewish faith. Like their more conservative brethren, liberal Protestants believed that Christianity had superseded Judaism, if not by the appearance of the Christian Messiah, then through an evolutionary process of religious maturity. To the liberal Protestant mind the religion of Israel had become an outmoded relic of the past, which refused to die.

Neither did liberal leaders display much enthusiasm for Jewish nationalism, preferring to view Judaism in religious, rather than in cultural or national terms. Jewish self-determination remained an uncomfortable idea for liberals, which they included as further evidence of Jewish obsessive particularism.

My tenth and final point is that by the mid-1960s, when thoughtful Christians first began to probe for some comprehension of the Final Solution, a selected but important group of American Protestant theologians, a number of them neo-orthodox in their orientation, began to reevaluate the direction of their own teachings in respect to Judaism and the Jewish people. During the past two decades, therefore, American Jews have for the first time confronted a group of Protestants determined to alter their traditional outlook and behavior toward them.

The central problem with which these Protestant thinkers grappled was the degree of culpability for the crimes of Nazism that should be assigned to traditional Christian teachings. In the light of their findings, a few, such as Franklin H. Littell and A. Roy Eckardt, charged that Nazism was not a reversion to pagan values, but was an outgrowth of centuries of Christians' preaching falsehoods about the Jews. The Holocaust, they concluded, had, therefore, altered forever the relationship of Christians and Jews. In an unprecedented challenge to Christian triumphalism, some acknowledged that Judaism is a self-sufficient religious system that does not require Christian guidance.

High on the list of such Protestant reevaluations is an insistence that Christians grant unconditional support to the beleaguered state of Israel, an obligation undertaken not for reasons of eschatology, but as a recognition of Judaism's particularity. A secure Israel, they argue, stands as proof that God has not forsaken the Jewish people. Christian support also serves as a meaningful sign of atonement for Christianity's sins against the Jews. They see the denial of Jewish national needs, or withdrawal of support from the Jewish state, as a new and sinister strain of antisemitism.

Although such radical views are relatively rare in American Protestantism, they nevertheless represent a new front, a revolutionary departure in Protestantism's attitude toward the Jews. To what extent the results of such religious reassessments will succeed in impressing themselves upon the multifaceted community of American Protestantism remains to be seen. Recognizing the divided outlook that has characterized American Protestantism from the very beginning of the nation's history, it is doubtful that such recent theological reevaluations will receive widespread denominational endorsement. In any case, American Protestantism will continue, as it has in the past, to speak to American Jews with a multitude of voices.

Notes

Abbreviations

AJA   *American Jewish Archives*
AJHQ   *American Jewish Historical Quarterly*
AJH   *American Jewish History*
JSS   *Jewish Social Studies*
PAJHS *Publications of American Jewish Historical Society*

1. From the Old World to the New

1. Haim Hillel Ben-Sasson, ed., *A History of the Jewish People* (Cambridge, Mass.: Harvard Univ. Press, 1976), pp. 639–44, 654–57.

2. Salo Wittmayer Baron, *A Social and Religious History of the Jews* (New York: Columbia Univ. Press; Philadelphia: The Jewish Publication Society of America, 1969), 13:214–15.

3. George L. Mosse, *The Reformation*, 3d ed. (New York: Holt, Rinehart and Winston, 1963), p. 27; Owen Chadwick, *The Reformation* (Harmondsworth, England: Penguin Books, 1964), pp. 11–17, 27–29.

4. Robert H. Ayers, *Judaism and Christianity: Origins, Developments, and Recent Trends* (Lanham, Md.: Univ. Press of America, 1983), p. 249; Mosse, *The Reformation*, p. 27; Chadwick, *The Reformation*, pp. 54–55, 74–75.

5. Mosse, *The Reformation*, pp. 59–61.

6. Ibid., pp. 61–62; Ayers, *Judaism and Christianity*, pp. 268–70, 273–77, 279.

7. Mosse, *The Reformation*, p. 71.

8. Chadwick, *The Reformation*, pp. 85–86.

9. Mosse, *The Reformation*, pp. 74–80; Ayers, *Judaism and Christianity*, p. 264.

10. Baron, *Social and Religious History*, 13:198.

11. Ernst Troeltsh, quoted in Baron, *Social and Religious History*, 13:206.

12. Martin Luther, quoted in Baron, *Social and Religious History*, 13:227, 229; Ben-Sasson, *History of the Jewish People*, pp. 648–53.

13. Baron, *Social and Religious History*, 13:280–83, 285–87, 289–91.

14. Chadwick, *The Reformation*, pp. 168–79.

15. J. Van Den Berg, "Eschatological Expectations Concerning the Conversion of the Jews in the Netherlands During the Seventeenth Century," in *Puritans, the Millen-*

nium and the Future of Israel: Puritan Eschatology, 1600–1660, ed. Peter Toon (Cambridge: James Clarke, 1970), pp. 137–39.

16. Mosse, *The Reformation,* pp. 81–93, 95–101; Chadwick, *The Reformation,* pp. 117–25.

17. Barbara W. Tuchman, *Bible and Sword: England and Palestine from the Bronze Age to Balfour* (New York: New York Univ. Press, 1956), p. 52.

18. Peter Toon, "English Puritans, Millennialism and Jewish Restoration," in *Puritans, the Millennium and the Future of Israel,* ed. Toon, pp. 16–18.

19. Franz Kobler, *The Vision Was There: A History of the British Movement for the Restoration of the Jews to Palestine* (London: Lincolns-Prager, 1956), pp. 26, 36–37.

20. Peter Toon, "The Question of Jewish Immigration," in *Puritans, the Millennium and the Future of Israel,* ed. Toon, pp. 116–17.

21. Toon, "Jewish Immigration," pp. 119–21, 125.

22. Jacob Rader Marcus, *The Colonial American Jew, 1492–1776* (Detroit: Wayne State Univ. Press, 1970), 1:69–74, 76–77, 79, 81; Charles McLean Andrews, *The Colonial Period of American History* (New Haven: Yale Univ. Press, 1964), 3:242–43.

23. Abram Vossen Goodman, *American Overture: Jewish Rights in Colonial Times* (Philadelphia: The Jewish Publication Society of America, 1947), pp. 9–10.

24. Quoted in William Warren Sweet, *Religion in Colonial America* (New York: Cooper Square Publishers, 1965), p. 200; see also H. Shelton Smith, Robert T. Handy, and Lefferts A. Loetscher, *American Christianity: An Historical Interpretation with Representative Documents* (New York: Charles Scribner's Sons, 1960–63), 1:59–61.

25. Sanford H. Cobb, *The Rise of Religious Liberty in America* (New York: Macmillan, 1902), p. 302; Andrews, *Colonial Period,* 3:86.

26. Reprinted in Morris U. Schappes, ed. *A Documentary History of the Jews in the United States, 1654–1875* (New York: Schocken Books, 1971), p. 2.

27. Ibid, p. 4.

28. Marcus, *Colonial American Jew,* 1:223–26, 244–45.

29. Goodman, *American Overture,* p. 99; Cobb, *Rise of Religious Liberty,* p. 326; Marcus, *Colonial American Jew,* 1:399–401.

30. Quoted in Smith, Handy, and Loetscher, *American Christianity,* 1:43; Leon Huhner, "The Jews of Virginia from the Earliest Times to the Close of the Eighteenth Century," *PAJHS* 20 (1911): 85.

31. Cobb, *Rise of Religious Liberty,* pp. 168–70, 362–63; "An Act Concerning Religion in the Maryland Colony," in John F. Wilson and Donald L. Drakeman, eds., *Church and State in American History* (Boston: Beacon Press, 1987), pp. 14–15.

32. Isaac M. Fein, *The Making of an American Jewish Community: The History of Baltimore Jewry from 1773 to 1920* (Philadelphia: The Jewish Publication Society of America, 1971), p. 6; "An Act Concerning Religion," pp. 14–18.

33. Fein, *An American Jewish Community,* pp. 7–8; Marcus, *Colonial American Jew,* 1:448–50; Jacob H. Hollander, "Some Unpublished Material Relating to Dr. Jacob Lumbrozo of Maryland," *PAJHS* 1 (1893): 33–34.

34. "The Fundamental Constitutions of Carolina," in Wilson and Drakeman, eds., *Church and State in American History,* pp. 18–19; Charles Reznikoff, *The Jews of Charleston: A History of an American Jewish Community* (Philadelphia: The Jewish Publication Society of America, 1950), pp. 13–14.

35. Goodman, *American Overture*, p. 154–55; Reznikoff, *Jews of Charleston*, pp. 4, 8, 21; Marcus, *Colonial American Jew*, 1:345.

36. Albert M. Friedenberg, "The Jews of New Jersey from the Earliest Times to 1850," *PAJHS* 17 (1909): 15; Edwin Wolf II and Maxwell Whiteman, *The History of the Jews of Philadelphia from Colonial Times to the Age of Jackson* (Philadelphia: The Jewish Publication Society of America, 1957), p. 13.

37. William Penn, quoted in Cobb, *Rise of Religious Liberty*, pp. 441–42, 444–45.

38. Goodman, *American Overture*, pp. 121–22; "William Penn's Preface to the Original Edition of George Fox's Journal, 1694," in John L. Nickalls, ed., *The Journal of George Fox*, rev. ed. (Cambridge: Cambridge Univ. Press, 1952), p. xvii.

39. Nickalls, *The Journal of George Fox*, pp. 36, 40, 63, 203, 333.

40. Bliss Forbush, *Elias Hicks: Quaker Liberal* (New York: Columbia Univ. Press, 1956), p. 78; Frederick B. Tolles, *James Logan and the Culture of Provincial America* (Boston: Little, Brown, 1957), p. 6; Edwin Wolf II, *James Logan, 1674–1751: Bookman Extraordinary* (Philadelphia: The Library Company of Philadelphia, 1971), pp. 1, 10.

41. Goodman, *American Overture*, pp. 124–25.

42. Marcus, *Early American Jewry*, 2:278; Cobb, *Rise of Religious Liberty*, p. 419; Leon Huhner, "The Jews of Georgia in Colonial Times," *PAJHS* 10 (1902): 66–69.

43. Letter from the trustees of Georgia to James Oglethorpe, quoted in Goodman, *American Overture*, p. 178.

44. Huhner, "Jews of Georgia," pp. 71–72, 79.

45. John McKay Sheftall, "The Sheftalls of Savannah: Colonial Leaders and Founding Fathers of Georgia Judaism," in *Jews of the South*, ed. Samuel Proctor and Louis Schmier (Macon, Ga.: Macon Univ. Press, 1984), p. 68; quotations from Goodman, *American Overture*, p. 191, and Huhner, "Jews of Georgia," p. 76.

46. Huhner, "Jews of Georgia," 76–77, 82–86, 92–93.

47. Sidney E. Mead, "From Coercion to Persuasion: Another Look at the Rise of Religious Liberty and the Emergence of Denominationalism," *Church History* 25 (December 1956): 319.

48. Ibid.

49. Smith, Handy, and Loetscher, *American Christianity*, 1:23, 143; Marcus, *Colonial American Jew*, 1:509–11, 514–15.

2. New England Puritans and the Biblical Jews

1. Perry Miller, *Orthodoxy in Massachusetts, 1630–1650*, (1933; reprint, New York: Harper and Row, 1970), pp. 9, 15–17, 24, 41.

2. Ibid., pp. 55–58; Austin Warren, *The New England Conscience* (Ann Arbor: Univ. of Michigan Press, 1966), pp. 33, 53.

3. Miller, *Orthodoxy in Massachusetts*, pp. 64–65, 72, 150, 160–63.

4. Harry S. Stout, "Word and Order in Colonial New England," in *The Bible in America: Essays in Cultural History*, ed. Nathan O. Hatch and Mark A. Noll (New York: Oxford Univ. Press, 1982), pp. 19, 29; David S. Lovejoy, *Religious Enthusiasm in the New World: Heresy to Revolution* (Cambridge, Mass.: Harvard Univ. Press, 1985), pp. 101–2.

5. See Robert H. Pfeiffer, "The Teaching of Hebrew in Colonial America," *The Jewish Quarterly Review* 65 (1955): 364.

6. Moshe Davis, ed., *With Eyes Toward Zion: Scholars Colloquium on American–Holy Land Studies* (New York: Arno Press, 1977), p. 8.

7. William Bradford, quoted in Jesper Rosenmeier, "'With My Owne Eyes': William Bradford's *Of Plymouth Plantation,*" in *The American Puritan Imagination: Essays in Revaluation,* ed. Sacvan Bercovitch (London: Cambridge Univ. Press, 1974), p. 78.

8. Isidore S. Meyer, *The Hebrew Exercises of Governor William Bradford* (Plymouth, Mass.: Pilgrim Society, 1973), pp. 9–11, 14, 19.

9. David de Sola Pool, "Hebrew Learning among Puritans of New England prior to 1700," *PAJHS* 20 (1911): 38–43, 48, 51; see also Pfeiffer, "The Teaching of Hebrew in Colonial America," pp. 363–64.

10. Warren, *The New England Conscience,* pp. 66, 68, 70, 72; Pool, "Hebrew Learning among the Puritans," pp. 37, 39; Dan A. Oren, *Joining the Club: A History of Jews and Yale* (New Haven: Yale Univ. Press, 1985), pp. 305–9.

11. Pool, "Hebrew Learning among the Puritans," pp. 74, 78–83.

12. Increase Mather, quoted in Lee M. Friedman, "Judah Monis, First Instructor in Hebrew at Harvard Univ.," *PAJHS* 22 (1914): 2; see also Samuel Eliot Morison, *Three Centuries of Harvard, 1636–1936* (Cambridge, Mass.: Harvard Univ. Press, 1937), p. 57.

13. Morison, *Three Centuries of Harvard,* p. 57; Friedman, "Judah Monis," pp. 2–5.

14. John Cotton quoted in Friedman, "Judah Monis," p. 14.

15. Quoted in ibid., p. 19.

16. Conrad Cherry, *God's New Israel: Religious Interpretations of American Destiny* (Englewood Cliffs, N.J.: Prentice-Hall, 1971), pp. 26–27.

17. Ibid., p. 27; Sacvan Bercovitch, *The American Jeremiad* (Madison: Univ. of Wisconsin Press, 1978), pp. 3, 5–7; Thomas Shepard, Jr., "Eye Slave," in *The Puritans in America: A Narrative Anthology,* ed. Alan Heimert and Andrew Delbanco (Cambridge, Mass.: Harvard Univ. Press, 1985), pp. 247–60.

18. In this connection, see H. Richard Niebuhr, "The Idea of the Covenant and American Democracy," in *Puritanism and the American Experience,* ed. Michael McGiffert (Reading, Mass.: Addison-Wesley, 1969), pp. 220, 223.

19. Peter Bulkley, "The Gospel-Covenant," in *The Puritans in America,* ed. Heimert and Delbanco, p. 120.

20. Perry Miller, *The New England Mind: From Colony to Province* (Cambridge, Mass.: Harvard Univ. Press, 1953), p. 85.

21. Ibid., pp. 86, 475.

22. Alan Heimert and Andrew Delbanco, "Introduction," in *The Puritans in America,* ed. Heimert and Delbanco, pp. 11–12; Bercovitch, *American Jeremiad,* pp. 14, 79.

23. John F. Berens, *Providence and Patriotism in Early America, 1640–1815* (Charlottesville: Univ. Press of Virginia, 1978), pp. 16–17; Rosenmeier, "'With My Owne Eyes,'" pp. 80–81; John Cotton, "God's Promise to His Plantations," in *The Puritans in America,* ed. Heimert and Delbanco, pp. 75, 77.

24. Peter Toon, ed., *Puritans, the Millennium and the Future of Israel: Puritan Eschatology, 1600–1660* (Cambridge: James Clarke, 1970), p. 6.

25. Ruth H. Bloch, *Visionary Republic: Millennial Themes in American Thought, 1756–1800* (Cambridge: Cambridge Univ. Press, 1985), p. xi; B. S. Capp, "Extreme Millenarianism," in *Puritans, the Millennium and the Future of Israel,* ed. Toon, pp. 66, 71–74, 180.

26. Bloch, *Visionary Republic,* pp. 6–8.

27. Increase Mather, "The Mystery of Israel's Salvation," in *The Puritans in America*, ed. Heimert and Delbanco, pp. 239–40, 242, 246.

28. Samuel Sewall, "Diary," in *The Puritans in America*, ed. Heimert and Delbanco, pp. 177–78; Pool, "Hebrew Learning among the Puritans," pp. 52–55.

29. Kenneth Silverman, *The Life and Times of Cotton Mather* (New York: Harper and Row, 1984), pp. 3–4, 175, 193–94, 197–99.

30. Cotton Mather, quoted in Isidore S. Meyer, "A Fount of American Democracy," *The Menorah Journal* 27 (October-December 1939): 253.

31. Cotton Mather, quoted in Lee M. Friedman, *Pilgrims in a New Land* (Philadelphia: The Jewish Publication Society of America, 1948), pp. 16–17.

32. Silverman, *Cotton Mather*, pp. 303–4, 410–11; Cotton Mather, quoted in Pool, "Hebrew Learning among the Puritans," p. 73.

33. Silverman, *Cotton Mather*, pp. 236–37, 303–4; Cotton Mather, "Reserved Memorials," in *The Puritans in America*, ed. Heimert and Delbanco, p. 326, Mather's emphasis.

34. Cotton Mather, quoted in Lee M. Friedman, "Cotton Mather and the Jews," *PAJHS* 26 (1918): 201–2; Charles L. Chaney, *The Birth of Missions in America* (South Pasadena, Calif.: William Carey Library, 1976), p. 53. For Cotton Mather's revised views about Jewish conversion, see Mel Scult, *Millennial Expectations and Jewish Liberties* (Leiden: E. J. Brill, 1978), pp. 49–51.

35. Mather, quoted in Friedman, "Cotton Mather and the Jews," p. 207.

36. Martin E. Marty, *Pilgrims in Their Own Land: 500 Years of Religion in America* (New York: Penguin Books, 1985), p. 76; H. Shelton Smith, Robert T. Handy, and Lefferts A. Loetscher, *American Christianity: An Historical Interpretation with Representative Documents* (New York: Charles Scribner's Sons, 1960–63), 1:144.

37. Roger Williams, "Queries of Highest Considerations," in *Church and State in American History*, ed. John F. Wilson and Donald L. Drakeman (Boston: Beacon Press, 1987), p. 9.

38. Warren, *The New England Conscience*, p. 55, 58; Smith, Handy, and Loetscher, *American Christianity*, 1:145.

39. Roger Williams, "The Bloody Tenent of Persecution," in *The Complete Writings of Roger Williams* (New York: Russell and Russell, 1963), 1:75; Roger Williams, "The Bloody Tenent Yet More Bloody," in ibid., 4:173.

40. Roger Williams, quoted in William Lee Miller, *The First Liberty: Religion and the American Republic* (New York: Alfred A. Knopf, 1986), pp. 193–94.

41. Roger Williams, "Mr. Cotton's Letter Lately Printed, Examined and Answered," in *The Complete Writings of Roger Williams*, 1:356; Roger Williams, "The Bloody Tenent of Persecution, for Cause of Conscience," in ibid., 3:128.

42. Warren, *The New England Conscience*, p. 56; see also Roger Williams, "The Bloody Tenent of Persecution," in *The Puritans in America*, ed. Heimert and Delbanco, p. 199.

43. Ezra Stiles, *Extracts from the Itineraries and Other Miscellanies of Ezra Stiles, D.D., LL.D., 1755–1794*, ed. Franklin Bowditch Dexter (New Haven: Yale Univ. Press, 1916), 1:52; see also Friedman, *Pilgrims in a New Land*, pp. 35, 53.

44. Abram Vossen Goodman, *American Overture: Jewish Rights in Colonial Times* (Philadelphia: The Jewish Publication Society of America, 1947), p. 58.

3. Revivalism and Rationalism

1. H. Shelton Smith, Robert T. Handy, and Lefferts A. Loetscher, *American Christianity: An Historical Interpretation With Representative Documents* (New York: Charles Scribner's Sons, 1960–63), 1:310–11. Jon Butler challenges the standard accounts of the Great Awakening; see his "Enthusiasm Described and Decreed: The Great Awakening as Interpretive Fiction," *The Journal of American History* 69 (September 1982): 305–25.

2. Smith, Handy, and Loetscher, *American Christianity*, 1:311–12.

3. Martin E. Marty, *Pilgrims in Their Own Land: 500 Years of Religion in America* (New York: Penguin Books, 1985), p. 109.

4. Sidney E. Mead, "From Coercion to Persuasion: Another Look at the Rise of Religious Liberty and the Emergence of Denominationalism," *Church History* 25 (December 1956): 331; Ruth H. Bloch, *Visionary Republic: Millennial Themes in American Thought, 1756–1800* (Cambridge: Cambridge Univ. Press, 1985), p. 13; John F. Berens, *Providence and Patriotism in Early America, 1640–1815* (Charlottesville: Univ. Press of Virginia, 1978), pp. 29, 32, 315.

5. Mead, "From Coercion to Persuasion," p. 332; Butler, "Enthusiasm Described," pp. 316, 324; William Lee Miller, *The First Liberty: Religion and the American Republic* (New York: Alfred A. Knopf, 1986), p. 214.

6. Edwin S. Gustad, "Institutional Effects of the Great Awakening," in *Church and State in American History*, ed. John F. Wilson and Donald L. Drakeman, 2d ed. (Boston: Beacon Press, 1987), p. 50.

7. Jacob Rader Marcus, *The Colonial American Jew, 1492–1776* (Detroit: Wayne State Univ. Press, 1970), 2:961–62.

8. Smith, Handy, and Loetscher, *American Christianity*, 1:323–24.

9. Quoted in Jacob Rader Marcus, *Early American Jewry* (Philadelphia: The Jewish Publication Society of America, 1953), 2:53, 55.

10. Bloch, *Visionary Republic*, pp. 16–18; Marty, *Pilgrims in Their Own Land*, pp. 111–14.

11. C. C. Goen, "Jonathan Edwards: A New Departure in Eschatology," *Church History* 28 (March 1959):26; Stephen J. Stein, "Editor's Introduction," in Jonathan Edwards, *Apocalyptic Writings* (New Haven: Yale Univ. Press, 1977), pp. 10–11.

12. Jonathan Edwards, *The Great Awakening*, ed. C. C. Goen (New Haven: Yale Univ. Press, 1972), p. 365.

13. Jonathan Edwards, *Original Sin* (New Haven: Yale Univ. Press, 1970), p. 272; Edwards, *Apocalyptic Writings*, pp. 219–20.

14. Jonathan Edwards, "Unbelievers Contemn the Glory and Excellency of Christ," in *Works of President Edwards*, Research and Source Work Series, no. 271 (New York: Burt Franklin, 1968), 7:406; Edwards, *Original Sin*, p. 293.

15. Edwards, *Original Sin*, pp. 286, 337.

16. Jonathan Edwards, "The Perpetuity and Change of the Sabbath," in *Works of President Edwards*, 7:500–501.

17. Ibid., 7:516–18.

18. Edwards, *Apocalyptic Writings*, pp. 292–96.

19. Ibid., pp. 134–35.

20. John Wesley, *The Works of John Wesley* (1872; reprint, Grand Rapids, Mich.: Zondervan Publishing, 1958–59), 5:2–3 (hereafter cited as *Works*).

21. Wesley, *Works*, 2:354, 453, 14:147–60; John Wesley, "Thoughts Upon Baron Montesquieu's 'Spirit of Laws,' (1781)," in *Works*, 13:415–16.

22. John Wesley, "For the Jews," in *The Works of John Wesley*, ed. Franz Hildebrandt and Oliver A. Beckerlegge (Oxford: Clarendon Press, 1983), 7:615.

23. Wesley, *Works*, 1:20–21, 158, 329; see also John Wesley, "The New Birth," in *Works*, 6:69.

24. John Wesley, "Upon Our Lord's Sermon on the Mount," in *Works*, 5:248, 319, 321, 329–30.

25. John Wesley, "The Righteousness of Faith," *Works*, 5:71–72; Wesley, "Sermon on the Mount," 5:310–11.

26. Wesley, "Thoughts Upon Baron Montesquieu's 'Spirit of Laws,'" 13:192.

27. John Wesley, "Of Reason and Religion," in *Works*, 8:192.

28. Wesley, "For the Jews," 7:617.

29. Smith, Handy, and Loetscher, *American Christianity*, 1:377, 379, 382.

30. Biographical information is from Edmund S. Morgan, *The Gentle Puritan: A Life of Ezra Stiles, 1727–1795* (New Haven: Yale Univ. Press, 1962), pp. 90–91, 109–13, 117, 292, 376; Ezra Stiles, *Extracts from the Itineraries and Other Miscellanies of Ezra Stiles, D.D., LL.D., 1755–1794*, ed. Franklin Bowditch Dexter (New Haven: Yale Univ. Press, 1916), p. 1; Ezra Stiles, *The Literary Diary of Ezra Stiles*, ed. Franklin Bowditch Dexter (New York: Charles Scribner's Sons, 1901), 1:524–25.

31. Morgan, *The Gentle Puritan*, pp. 22–23, 77, 96, 114.

32. Ibid., pp. 166, 169, 179.

33. Ibid., pp. 72, 447–49.

34. Morris Aaron Gutstein, *The Story of the Jews of Newport* (New York: Bloch Publishing, 1936), pp. 115–16.

35. Stiles, *Diary of Ezra Stiles*, 1:6; see also Morris Jastrow, "References to Jews in the Diary of Ezra Stiles," *PAJHS* 10 (1902): 9.

36. Stiles, *Diary of Ezra Stiles*, 1:36, 97–98, 256.

37. Ibid., p. 382.

38. Alexander Guttman, "Ezra Stiles, Newport Jewry, and a Question of Jewish Law," *AJA* 34 (April 1982): 99–102.

39. Ezra Stiles, quoted in Arthur A. Chiel, "The Rabbis and Ezra Stiles," *AJHQ* 61 (June 1972): 294–95.

40. Stiles, *Diary of Ezra Stiles*, 1:392, 443, 594; Chiel, "The Rabbis and Ezra Stiles," p. 303; Rachel Wischnitzer, "Ezra Stiles and the Portrait of Menasseh Ben Israel," *AJHQ* 51 (December 1961): 190–94.

41. Arthur A. Chiel, "Ezra Stiles—The Education of an 'Hebrician,'" *AJHQ* 60 (March 1971): 236–38.

42. Stiles, *Diary of Ezra Stiles*, 1:82, 329.

43. Morgan, *The Gentle Puritan*, pp. 378, 398, 400.

44. Stiles, *Diary of Ezra Stiles*, 1:17, 19, 39, 508–9; Jastrow, "Jews in the Diary of Ezra Stiles," p. 16; W. Wilner, "Ezra Stiles and the Jews," *PAJHS* 8 (1900): 122; Arthur A. Chiel, "Ezra Stiles and the Jews: A Study in Ambivalence," in *A Bicentennial Festschrift For Jacob Rader Marcus*, ed. Bertram Wallace Korn (Waltham, Mass.: American Jewish Historical Society; New York: KTAV Publishing House, 1976), p. 64.

45. Stiles, *Diary of Ezra Stiles,* 3:24.
46. Jastrow, "Jews in the Diary of Ezra Stiles," p. 35.

4. Revolutionaries and the Jewish Past

1. John F. Berens, *Providence and Patriotism in Early America, 1640–1815* (Charlottesville: Univ. Press of Virginia, 1978), pp. 81, 110–11; Conrad Cherry, *God's New Israel: Religious Interpretations of American Destiny* (Englewood Cliffs, N.J.: Prentice-Hall, 1971), pp. 61–62, 65.

2. Ruth H. Bloch, *Visionary Republic: Millennial Themes in American Thought, 1756–1800* (Cambridge: Cambridge Univ. Press, 1985), pp. xiii–xiv.

3. Mark A. Noll, "The Image of the United States as a Biblical Nation, 1776–1865," in *The Bible in America: Essays in Cultural History,* ed. Nathan O. Hatch and Mark A. Noll (New York: Oxford Univ. Press, 1982), pp. 41–45; Nathan O. Hatch, *The Sacred Cause of Liberty* (New Haven: Yale Univ. Press, 1977), pp. 16, 96, 109, 167.

4. Benjamin Franklin, quoted in Edwin Wolf II and Maxwell Whiteman, *The History of the Jews of Philadelphia from Colonial Times to the Age of Jackson* (Philadelphia: The Jewish Publication Society of America, 1957), p. 23.

5. Robert P. Hay, "George Washington: American Moses," *American Quarterly* 21 (Winter 1967):782–86, 788.

6. Samuel Langdon, "The Republic of the Israelites: An Example to the American States," reprinted in Cherry, *God's New Israel,* pp. 94–95.

7. Hatch, *Sacred Cause,* pp. 159–60.

8. Hay, "George Washington," p. 788; Langdon, "The Republic of the Israelites," p. 96.

9. Anson Phelps Stokes and Leo Pfeffer, *Church and State in the United States* (New York: Harper and Row, 1964), pp. 64–69.

10. Ibid., pp. 72–75; William Lee Miller, *The First Liberty: Religion and the American Republic* (New York: Alfred A. Knopf, 1986), p. 37.

11. Stokes and Pfeffer, *Church and State,* p. 79; quotation from Charles Reznikoff, *The Jews of Charleston: A History of an American Jewish Community* (Philadelphia: The Jewish Publication Society of America, 1950), p. 59.

12. Wolf and Whiteman, *History of the Jews of Philadelphia,* p. 81.

13. Ibid., p. 82; Morris U. Schappes, ed., *A Documentary History of the Jews in the United States, 1654–1875* (New York: Schocken Books, 1971), pp. 63–66; see also Sanford H. Cobb, *The Rise of Religious Liberty in America* (New York: Macmillan, 1902), pp. 499, 502, 504, 507–9.

14. "The Northwest Ordinance–1787," in *Jews and the Founding of the Republic,* ed. Jonathan D. Sarna, Benny Kraut, and Samuel K. Joseph (New York: Markus Wiener, 1985), p. 98.

15. Stokes and Pfeffer, *Church and State,* p. 90; Cobb, *Rise of Religious Liberty,* pp. 524–27; Miller, *The First Liberty,* pp. 107–9, quotation on p. 111.

16. Herbert Friedenwald, "A Letter of Jonas Phillips to the Federal Convention," *PAJHS* 2 (1894): 107.

17. Norman Cousins, ed., *"In God We Trust": The Religious Beliefs and Ideas of the American Founding Fathers* (New York: Harper and Brothers, 1958), pp. 114–15; George Harmon Knoles, "The Religious Ideas of Thomas Jefferson," *The Mississippi Valley Historical Review* 30 (September 1943): 188.

18. Knoles, "Religious Ideas of Thomas Jefferson," pp. 188–89; Robert M. Healey, *Jefferson on Religion in Public Education* (New Haven: Yale Univ. Press, 1962), pp. 26, 36, 58, 100–101, 104–5.

19. Healey, *Religion in Public Education*, p. 194; quotation from H. Shelton Smith, Robert T. Handy, and Lefferts A. Loetscher, *American Christianity: An Historical Interpretation with Representative Documents* (New York: Charles Scribner's Sons, 1960–63), 1:514.

20. Knoles, "Religious Ideas of Thomas Jefferson," pp. 90–91, 202; Healey, *Religion in Public Education*, p. 225; Daniel Boorstin, *The Lost World of Thomas Jefferson* (Boston: Beacon Press, 1948), p. 156.

21. J. Lesslie Hale, "The Religious Opinions of Thomas Jefferson," *Sewanee Review* 31 (1915): 164–76.

22. "Jefferson's Act for Establishing Religious Freedom," in *Church and State in American History*, ed. John F. Wilson and Donald L. Drakeman (Boston: Beacon Press, 1987), p. 74.

23. Thomas Jefferson, "Occasional Letters Regarding Religion and Government," in *Church and State in American History*, ed. Wilson and Drakeman, p. 79.

24. Knoles, "Religious Ideas of Thomas Jefferson," p. 197.

25. William Short to Thomas Jefferson, December 25, 1789, and January 28, 1790, in *The Papers of Thomas Jefferson*, ed. Julian P. Boyd (Princeton: Princeton Univ. Press, 1950), 1:44, 131.

26. Joseph Marx to Thomas Jefferson, July 3, 1820, and Thomas Jefferson to Joseph Marx, July 8, 1820, in Max J. Kohler, "Unpublished Correspondence Between Thomas Jefferson and Some American Jews," *PAJHS* 20 (1911): 11–12.

27. Thomas Jefferson to Jacob De La Motta, September 1, 1820, in Kohler, "Unpublished Correspondence," p. 21.

28. Thomas Jefferson, quoted in Robert M. Healey, "Jefferson on Judaism and the Jews: 'Divided We Stand, United, We Fall!'" *AJH* 73 (June 1984): 361.

29. In this connection, see Arthur Hertzberg, *The French Enlightenment and the Jews* (New York: Columbia Univ. Press; Philadelphia: The Jewish Publication Society of America, 1968), pp. 268–313.

30. Ibid., pp. 362–63; Thomas Jefferson, *Writings* (New York: Library Classics of the United States, 1984), p. 39.

31. Jefferson quotations from Cousins, *In God We Trust*, p. 148, and Healey, "Jefferson on Judaism," p. 365; see also, "The Principles of Jesus," in *The Complete Jefferson*, ed. Saul K. Padover (New York: Tudor Publishing, 1943), pp. 950–51.

32. Jefferson, quoted in Healey, "Jefferson on Judaism," pp. 371, 373; see also Thomas Jefferson, "Syllabus of an Estimate of the Merit of the Doctrines of Jesus, Compared With Those of Others," in *The Complete Jefferson*, ed. Padover, pp. 948–50.

33. Jefferson, quoted in Healey, "Jefferson on Judaism," p. 115.

34. Howard Ioan Fielding, "John Adams: Puritan, Deist, Humanist," *Journal of Religion* 20 (January 1940): 38; "Adams' Autobiography," in Cousins, *In God We Trust*, pp. 77–78.

35. Lyman H. Butterfield, ed., *Diary and Autobiography of John Adams* (Cambridge, Mass.: Harvard Univ. Press, Belknap Press, 1962), 2:44; Adams quotation from "Letters to F. A. Van Der Kemp, 1809–1816," in Cousins, *In God We Trust*, p. 104.

36. Fielding, "John Adams," pp. 41–42.

37. Ibid., pp. 44–46; Paul K. Conkin, _Puritans and Pragmatists: Eight Eminent American Thinkers_ (New York: Dodd, Mead, 1968), p. 113.

38. Conkin, _Puritans and Pragmatists_, pp. 114, 118, 121.

39. Isidore S. Meyer, "John Adams Writes a Letter," _PAJHS_ 37 (October 1947): 189.

40. Lewis Abraham, "Correspondence Between Washington and Jewish Citizens," _PAJHS_ 3 (1895): 96.

41. John Adams, quoted in Louis Ruchames, "Mordecai Manuel Noah and Early American Zionism," _AJHQ_ 64 (March 1975): 209.

42. Meyer, "John Adams Writes a Letter," p. 200.

43. Benjamin Franklin, "Autobiography," in Cousins, _In God We Trust_, pp. 25–26.

44. See, for example, John J. Zubly to Benjamin Franklin, July 9, 1771, in _The Papers of Benjamin Franklin_, ed. William B. Wilcox (New Haven: Yale Univ. Press, 1959–84), 19:170–72; William Marshall to Benjamin Franklin, October 30, 1772, in ibid., pp. 354–55.

45. Benjamin Franklin, "Toleration in Old and New England," in Benjamin Franklin, _Writings_, ed. J. A. Lemay (New York: The Library of America, 1987), pp. 673–74.

46. Max Greunswald, "Benjamin Franklin's 'Parable on Brotherly Love,' " _PAJHS_ 37 (1947): 147, 152; see also Benjamin Franklin, "A Comparison of the Conduct of the Ancient Jews and the Anti-Federalists in the United States of America," in Franklin, _Writings_, ed. Lemay, pp. 1144–48.

47. Benjamin Franklin, quoted in Wolf and Whiteman, _History of the Jews of Philadelphia_, p. 23.

5. Liberating American Christianity

1. For Jewish population figures, see Ira Rosenwaike, _On the Edge of Greatness: A Portrait of American Jewry in the Early National Period_ (Cincinnati: American Jewish Archives, 1985), pp. 17, 105.

2. Will Herberg, _Protestant-Catholic-Jew: An Essay in American Religious Sociology_ (1955; Garden City, N.Y.: Doubleday, Anchor Books, 1960), p. 85.

3. Winthrop S. Hudson, _American Protestantism_ (Chicago: Univ. of Chicago Press, 1961), pp. 97–98.

4. Charles Chester Cole, Jr., _The Social Ideas of the Northern Evangelists, 1826–1860_ (New York: Columbia Univ. Press, 1954), p. 13.

5. Alexis de Tocqueville, _Democracy in America_ (New York: Vintage Books, 1954), 1:314.

6. Ibid., 1:315–17, 2:28.

7. Herberg, _Protestant-Catholic-Jew_, p. 86; William Lee Miller, _The First Liberty: Religion and the American Republic_ (New York: Alfred A. Knopf, 1986), pp. 249, 262–84.

8. See Perry Miller, "Introduction," in Philip Schaff, _America: A Sketch of its Political, Social, and Religious Character_, ed. Perry Miller (1855; Cambridge, Mass.: Harvard Univ. Press, Belknap Press, 1961), p. xxxiv.

9. "Jews Set the Christians an Example—1784," _AJA_ 27 (November 1975): 228; "The Gentiles of Philadelphia Help the Synagogue—1788," _AJA_ 27 (November 1975): 244.

10. Benjamin Rush to Mrs. Rush, June 27, 1787, in _Letters of Benjamin Rush_, ed. L. H. Butterfield (Princeton: Princeton Univ. Press, 1951), 1:429.

11. Jacob Rader Marcus, "The Handsome Young Priest in the Black Gown," *Hebrew Union College Annual* 40–41 (1969–70): 428, 430.

12. Arthur W. Brown, *William Ellery Channing* (New York: Twayne Publishers, 1961), pp. 72–73; William Henry Channing, *The Life of William Ellery Channing, D.D.* (Boston: American Unitarian Association, 1880), p. 577.

13. Andrew Delbanco, *William Ellery Channing: An Essay on the Liberal Spirit in America* (Cambridge, Mass.: Harvard Univ. Press, 1981), p. 5; Jack Mendelsohn, *Channing, the Reluctant Radical* (Boston: Little, Brown, 1971), p. 274.

14. Delbanco, *William Ellery Channing*, p. 78.

15. William E. Channing, "Unitarian Christianity," in Smith, Handy, and Loetscher, *American Christianity*, 1:495–96.

16. Smith, Handy, and Loetscher, *American Christianity*, 1:493.

17. Sidney E. Ahlstrom and Jonathan S. Carey, eds., *American Reformation of Unitarian Christianity* (Middletown, Conn.: Wesleyan Univ. Press, 1985), p. 301.

18. James Walker, "The Day of Judgment," quoted in *American Reformation*, ed. Ahlstrom and Carey, p. 310.

19. Merle Curti, *The Growth of American Thought* (New York: Harper and Brothers, 1943), p. 304.

20. Paul K. Conkin, *Puritans and Pragmatists: Eight Eminent American Thinkers* (New York: Dodd, Mead, 1968), pp. 151–59.

21. William R. Hutchison, *The Transcendentalist Ministers* (New Haven: Yale Univ. Press, 1959), pp. 66–67; Ralph Waldo Emerson, "Speech at the Second Annual Meeting of the Free Religious Association, at Tremont Temple, Friday, May 28, 1869," in *The Complete Works of Ralph Waldo Emerson*, ed. Edward Waldo Emerson (Cambridge, Mass.: Riverside Press, 1904), 2:491; see also Robert Andrew Everett, "Judaism in Nineteenth-Century American Transcendentalist and Liberal Protestant Thought," *Journal of Ecumenical Studies* 20 (Summer 1983): 397, 399–400.

22. Ralph Waldo Emerson to Emma Lazarus, April 14, November 19, 1868, in *Letters to Emma Lazarus*, ed. Ralph L. Rusk (New York: Columbia Univ. Press, 1939), pp. 4, 9.

23. See, for example, Lidian and Ellen Emerson to Emma Lazarus, September 14, 1876, *Letters to Emma Lazarus*, ed. Rusk, p. 17; Henry Wadsworth Longfellow Dana, "Emma Lazarus and the New England Poets," *The Menorah Journal* 39 (Spring 1951): 32–34.

24. Felix Adler, quoted in Horace L. Friess, *Felix Adler and Ethical Culture* (New York: Columbia Univ. Press, 1981), pp. 41–42.

25. Ralph Waldo Emerson, *The Journals and Miscellaneous Notebooks of Ralph Waldo Emerson* (Cambridge, Mass.: Harvard Univ. Press, Belknap Press, 1964), 7:22.

26. Ralph Waldo Emerson to William Emerson, June 29, 1831, and October 21, 1833, *The Letters of Ralph Waldo Emerson*, ed. Ralph L. Rusk (New York: Columbia Univ. Press, 1939), 1:327, 397; Emerson, *Journals and Miscellaneous Notebooks*, 10:181.

27. Ralph Waldo Emerson, *Young Emerson Speaks*, ed. Arthur Cushman McGiffert, Jr. (Boston: Houghton Mifflin; Cambridge, Mass.: Riverside Press, 1938), pp. 22, 55, 193.

28. Robert J. Lowenberg, *An American Idol: Emerson and the "Jewish Idea"* (Lanham, Md.: Univ. Press of America, 1984), pp. 39, 79–81.

29. Emerson, *Journals and Miscellaneous Notebooks*, 7:321.

30. Lowenberg, *An American Idol*, pp. 85, 89–90, 97, 99.

31. Theodore Parker to E. J. Young, May 4, 1854, in *Life and Correspondence of Theodore Parker*, ed. John Weiss (New York: D. Appleton, 1864), 1:377.

32. Theodore Parker to A. A. Livermore, September 26, 1859, in *Life and Correspondence*, ed. Weiss, p. 361.

33. Theodore Parker, *The Transient and Permanent in Christianity*, ed. George Willis Cooke (Boston: American Unitarian Association, 1903), pp. 352–53.

34. Theodore Parker to S. J. May, November, 12, 1846, and Theodore Parker to 'A Friend,' February 6, 1852, in *Life and Correspondence*, ed. Weiss, 1:355, 401.

35. Ibid., 2:22, 215.

36. Ibid., 2:214.

37. Parker, *Transient and Permanent*, p. 45.

38. Ibid., 52–53; see also Theodore Parker, *Views of Religion* (Boston: American Unitarian Association, 1890).

39. Parker, *Transient and Permanent*, p. 60.

40. Ibid., pp. 16–17.

41. Ibid., p. 60.

42. Ibid., pp. 217, 239, 242, 248–49, 275–76.

43. Ibid., pp. 265, 268–69.

44. Ibid., pp. 368–69.

6. Christianizing Antebellum Society

1. Charles C. Cole, *The Social Ideas of the Northern Evangelists, 1826–1860* (New York: Columbia Univ. Press, 1954), p. 71; Bernard A. Weisberger, *They Gathered at the River: The Story of the Great Revivalists and Their Impact upon Religion in America* (1958; Chicago: Quadrangle Books, 1966), pp. 3–7, 13.

2. H. Shelton Smith, Robert T. Handy, and Lefferts A. Loetscher, *American Christianity: An Historical Interpretation with Representative Documents* (New York: Charles Scribner's Sons, 1960–63), 1:524–26; Charles I. Foster, "Characteristics of the Evangelical United Front," in *Church and State in American History*, ed. John F. Wilson and Donald L. Drakeman (Boston: Beacon Press, 1987), pp. 117–20.

3. Washington Gladden, *Recollections* (Boston: Houghton Mifflin, 1909), pp. 58–61.

4. Weisberger, *They Gathered at the River*, pp. 26–27.

5. Ibid., pp. 43–44, 78–79.

6. "Chronology of the Life of Charles Grandison Finney," in Charles Grandison Finney, *Lectures on Revivals of Religion*, ed. William McLoughlin (1835; Cambridge, Mass.: Harvard Univ. Press, Belknap Press, 1960), pp. liii–liv; Edward Pessen, *Jacksonian America: Society, Personality, and Politics* (Homewood, Ill.: Dorsey Press, 1969), pp. 77–79; Keith J. Hardman, *Charles Grandison Finney, 1792–1875: Revivalist and Reformer* (Syracuse: Syracuse Univ. Press, 1987), p. xiii.

7. Pessen, *Jacksonian Democracy*, pp. 77–78.

8. William G. McGloughlin, Jr., *Modern Revivalism: Charles Grandison Finney to Billy Graham* (New York: Ronald Press, 1959), pp. 105–6; Hardman, *Charles Grandison Finney*, p. 152.

9. Finney, *Lectures*, pp. 150–51, Finney's emphasis.

10. Ibid., p. 251.

11. Timothy Dwight quotations from Oliver Wendell Elsbree, *The Rise of the Missionary Spirit in America, 1790–1815* (Williamsport, Penn.: Williamsport Printing and Binding, 1928), pp. 122–25; see also Ruth H. Bloch, *Visionary Republic: Millennial Themes in American Thought, 1756–1800* (Cambridge: Cambridge Univ. Press, 1985), pp. 154–56.

12. Elsbree, *Missionary Spirit*, pp. 129, 130–35, 139.

13. Robert T. Handy, "The Protestant Quest for a Christian America, 1830–1930," *Church History* 22 (March 1953): 10.

14. John R. Bodo, *The Protestant Clergy and Public Issues, 1812–1848* (Princeton: Princeton Univ. Press, 1954), p. 21.

15. James H. Moorhead, "Between Progress and Apocalypse: A Reassessment of Millennialism in American Religious Thought, 1800–1880," *The Journal of American History* 71 (December 1984): 524–26, 529, 531; Horace Bushnell, *Nature and Supernatural* (New York: Scribner, Armstrong, 1873), p. 419; Sacvan Bercovitch, *The American Jeremiad* (Madison: Univ. of Wisconsin Press, 1978); p. 176.

16. Mark A. Noll, "The Image of the United States as a Biblical Nation. 1776–1865," in *The Bible in America: Essays in Cultural History*, ed. Nathan O. Hatch and Mark A. Noll (New York: Oxford Univ. Press, 1982), pp. 39, 44–45; George M. Marsden, "Everyone One's Own Interpreter? The Bible, Science, and Authority in Mid-Nineteenth-Century America," in ibid., p. 79.

17. Philip Schaff, *America: A Sketch of Its Political, Social and Religious Character*, ed. Perry Miller (1855; Cambridge, Mass.: Harvard Univ. Press, Belknap Press, 1961), pp. 10, 20, 35, 74–77.

18. Lyman Beecher, *Autobiography, Correspondence, Etc. of Lyman Beecher, D.D.*, ed. Charles Beecher (New York: Harper and Brothers, 1865), 2:249; Lyman Beecher, *Plea for the West*, 2d ed. (Cincinnati: Truman and Smith; New York: Leavitt, Lord, 1835), pp. 60–61.

19. Joseph Story, quoted in Morton Borden, *Jews, Turks, and Infidels* (Chapel Hill: Univ. of North Carolina Press, 1984), p. 101.

20. Joseph Story, *Commentaries on the Constitution of the United States*, vol. 3, quoted in *Church and State in American History*, ed. Wilson and Drakeman, pp. 92–93.

21. Ezra Stiles Ely, "The Duty of Christian Freemen to Elect Christian Rulers," in *Church and State in American History*, ed. Wilson and Drakeman, pp. 97–99.

22. Anson Phelps Stokes and Leo Pfeffer, *Church and State in the United States*, rev. ed. (New York: Harper and Row, 1964), pp. 565–66; Borden, *Jews, Turks, and Infidels*, pp. 60–61.

23. Schaff, *America*, p. 20; see also, Handy, "Protestant Quest for a Christian America," p. 11; Philip Jordon, *The Evangelical Alliance for the United States of America, 1847–1900: Ecumenism, Identity and the Religion of the Republic*, Studies in American Religion, vol. 7 (New York: Edwin Mellen Press, 1982), pp. 109–12.

24. William Lee Miller, *The First Liberty: Religion and the American Republic* (New York: Alfred A. Knopf, 1986), p. 260; Stokes and Pfeffer, *Church and State*, pp. 493, 496; Borden, *Jews, Turks, and Infidels*, p. 106.

25. Stokes and Pfeffer, *Church and State*, pp. 493, 496; Borden, *Jews, Turks, and Infidels*, p. 106.

26. "The Commonwealth vs. Abraham Wolf, Pennsylvania, 1817," in *The Jews of the United States, 1790–1840: A Documentary History*, ed. Joseph L. Blau and Salo W. Baron (New York: Columbia Univ. Press; New York: The Jewish Publication Society of America, 1963), 1:24–25.

27. "Town Council of Columbia vs. Duke and Marks, 1833," in *The Jews of the United States*, ed. Blau and Baron, p. 256; see also Albert M. Friedenberg, "The Jews and the American Sunday Laws," *PAJHS* 11 (1903): 102.

28. James G. Berrett, quoted in Abraham Simon, "Notes of Jewish Interest in the District of Columbia," *PAJHS* 26 (1918): 218.

29. Bordon, *Jews, Turks, and Infidels*, pp. 122–25.

30. Bodo, *Protestant Clergy and Public Issues*, p. 37.

31. George Washington, quoted in Rose S. Klein, "Washington's Thanksgiving Proclamation," *AJA* 20 (November 1968): 159.

32. Quoted in Klein, "Washington's Thanksgiving Proclamation," p. 160.

33. Quoted in Naomi W. Cohen, *Encounter With Emancipation: The German Jews in the United States, 1830–1914* (Philadelphia: The Jewish Publication Society of America, 1984), p. 74.

34. Morris U. Schappes, ed., *A Documentary History of the Jews in the United States, 1654–1875* (New York: Schocken Books, 1971), pp. 237–38.

35. Ibid., pp. 240–42; Max J. Kohler, "Phases in the History of Religious Liberty in America with Particular Reference to the Jews," *PAJHS* 13 (1905): 19.

36. Carl F. Kaestle, *The Evolution of an Urban School System: New York City, 1750–1850* (Cambridge, Mass.: Harvard Univ. Press, 1973), pp. 113, 188; Schaff, *America*, p. 58.

37. Stanley K. Schultz, *The Culture Factory: Boston Public Schools, 1789–1860* (New York: Oxford Univ. Press, 1973), pp. 60–68.

38. Timothy Smith, "Protestant Schooling and American Nationality, 1800–1850," *The Journal of American History* 53 (March 1967): 680, 687.

39. Ruth Miller Elson, *Guardians of Tradition: American Schoolbooks of the Nineteenth Century* (Lincoln: Univ. of Nebraska Press, 1964), pp. 46, 55–56, 81–85.

40. Ibid., pp. 85, 87.

41. Ibid., pp. 85, 97.

42. Hyman B. Grinstein, *The Rise of the Jewish Community of New York, 1654–1860* (Philadelphia: The Jewish Publication Society of America, 1947), pp. 234–39; see also, "The Value of Jewish Day Schools," in *Jewish Education in the United States: A Documentary History*, ed. Lloyd P. Gartner, Classics in Education Series, no. 41 (New York: Teachers College Press, 1969), pp. 63–66.

43. Louis Marshall, quoted in Lloyd P. Gartner, "Temples of Liberty Unpolluted: American Jews and Public Schools, 1840–1875," in *A Bicentennial Festschrift For Jacob Rader Marcus*, ed. Bertram Wallace Korn (Waltham, Mass.: American Jewish Historical Society; New York: KTAV Publishing House, 1976), pp. 175–76.

44. D. Zvi Sobel, "Jews and Christians Evangelization: The Anglo-American Approach," *AJHQ* 58 (December 1968): 246–47, 249.

45. Elias Boudinot to J.S.C.F. Frey, November 26, 1819, in *The Jews of the United States*, ed. Blau and Baron, 3:718; "Will of Elias Boudinot, 1821," in ibid., 3:724–25; see also "Directors Report, 1823," in ibid., 3: 737; "Directors Report, 1824," in ibid.,

3:738–42; Lorman Ratner, "Conversion of the Jews and Pre-Civil War Reform," *American Quarterly* 13 (Spring 1961): 45.

46. David Max Eichhorn, *Evangelizing the American Jew* (Middle Village, N.Y.: Jonathan David Publishers, 1978), pp. 50–51.

47. D. Zvi Sobel, "Protestant Evangelists and the Formation of a Jewish Racial Mystique: The Missionary Discovery of Sociology," *Journal for the Scientific Study of Religion* 5 (Fall 1966): 344–48.

48. W. C. Brownlee, ed., *The History of the Jews from the Babylonian Captivity to the Present Time* (Boston: M. A. Berk, 1847), p. 417. For biographical information, see *Dictionary of American Biography* (New York: Charles Scribner's Sons, 1929), 3:176–77.

49. Brownlee, *History of the Jews*, p. 418.

50. George L. Berlin, *Defending the Faith: Nineteenth-Century American Jewish Writings on Christianity and Jesus* (Albany: State Univ. of New York Press, 1989), pp. 99–101.

51. B. B. Edwards, quoted in *The Jews of the United States*, ed. Blau and Baron, 2:419–24.

52. "Hannah Adams," *Notable American Women, 1607–1950*, ed. Edward T. James (Cambridge, Mass.: Harvard Univ. Press, Belknap Press, 1971), 1:10; Anita Libman Lebeson, "Hannah Adams and the Jews," *Historia Judaica* 8 (October 1946): 119, 122, 133; George L. Berlin, "Joseph S.C.F. Frey: The Jews and Early Nineteenth Century Millenarianism," *Journal of the Early Republic* 1 (Spring 1981): 31.

53. Lebeson, "Hannah Adams and the Jews," p. 130.

54. Eichhorn, *Evangelizing the American Jews*, pp. 102, 112, 114, 118–20, 128, 138; Rudolph Glanz, *Jew and Mormon: Historic Group Relations and Religious Outlook* (New York: Waldon Press, 1963), pp. 86–88.

7. Fashioning an American Judaism

1. Jonathan D. Sarna, "American Christian Opposition to Missions to the Jews," *Journal of Ecumenical Studies* 23 (Spring 1986): 226; Gaylord P. Albaugh, "Anti-Missionary Movement in the United States," *An Encyclopedia of Religion*, ed. Vergilius Ferm (New York: The Philosophical Library, 1945), pp. 27–28.

2. George L. Berlin, "Joseph S.C.F. Frey. the Jews, and Early Nineteenth Century Millenarianism," *Journal of the Early Republic* 1 (Spring 1981): 47; Sarna, "American Christian Opposition," pp. 228–29, 233.

3. Hyman B. Grinstein, *The Rise of the Jewish Community of New York, 1654–1860* (Philadelphia: The Jewish Publication Society of America, 1947), p. 156.

4. Grinstein, *Jewish Community of New York*, pp. 383–84; Isaac M. Fein, *The Making of an American Jewish Community: The History of Baltimore Jewry from 1773 to 1920* (Philadelphia: The Jewish Publication Society of America, 1971), p. 57. For a Jewish response to missionaries in Baltimore, see, for example, *A New Year's Gift to the Maryland Ladies' Society for Promoting Christianity among the Jews by the Right Reverend Rabbi, Hebrew Republican Citizen-Soldier* (Baltimore, 1843).

5. [An Israelite], *Israel Vindicated; Being a Refutation of the Calumnies Propagated Respecting the Jewish Nation: In Which the Objects and Views of the American Society for Ameliorating the Condition of the Jews Are Investigated* (New York: Abraham Collins, 1820).

6. Ibid., pp. 4, 17, 31–32, 45–47, 76, 109–10.

7. Ibid., pp. 4, 17, 31–32, 45–47, 76, 96, 109–10; see also Jonathan D. Sarna, "The Freethinkers, the Jews, and the Missionaries: George Houston and the Mystery of *Israel Vindicated*," *AJS Review* 5 (1980): 101–3.

8. George L. Berlin, "Solomon Jackson's *The Jew*: An Early American Jewish Response to the Missionaries," *AJA* 71 (September 1981): 11, 13–14.

9. Ibid., p. 14.

10. Solomon Henry Jackson, *The Jew*, February 1823.

11. In this connection, see Berlin, "Solomon Jackson's *The Jew*," pp. 27–28; Sarna, "American Christian Opposition," pp. 236–38.

12. Jonathan D. Sarna, *Jacksonian Jew: The Two Worlds of Mordecai Noah* (New York: Holms and Meier, 1981), pp. 3, 159–60; see, for example, Mordecai M. Noah, *Discourse on the Restoration of the Jews* (New York: Harper and Brothers, 1845), pp. 20–24.

13. Selig Adler and Thomas E. Connolly, *From Ararat to Suburbia: The History of the Jewish Community of Buffalo* (Philadelphia: The Jewish Publication Society of America, 1960), pp. 6–7; Mordecai M. Noah to J. Q. Adams, July 24, 1820, in *The Jews of the United States, 1790–1840: A Documentary History*, ed. Joseph L. Blau and Salo W. Baron (New York: Columbia Univ. Press; Philadelphia: The Jewish Publication Society of America, 1963), 3:887; Sarna, *Jacksonian Jew*, p. 65.

14. "Noah's Proclamation to the Jews, 1825," in *The Jews of the United States*, ed. Blau and Baron, 3:895–96; Adler and Connolly, *From Ararat to Suburbia*, p. 7.

15. S. Joshua Kohn, "Mordecai Manuel Noah's Ararat Project and the Missionaries," *AJHQ* 55 (December 1965): 162–96; J. Josuah Kohn, "New Light on Mordecai Manuel Noah's Ararat Project," *AJHQ* 59 (December 1969): 210–14.

16. Noah, *Discourse*, p. 54.

17. Ibid., p. 28.

18. For biographical information, I have relied upon Maxwell Whiteman, "The Legacy of Isaac Leeser," in *Jewish Life in Philadelphia, 1830–1940*, ed. Murray Friedman (Philadelphia: Ishi Publications, 1983), pp. 26–27; Maxine S. Seller, "Isaac Leeser: A Jewish-Christian Dialogue in Antebellum Philadelphia," *Pennsylvania History* 35 (July 1968): 231.

19. Seller, "A Jewish-Christian Dialogue," pp. 233, 236–38; Isaac Leeser, *Claims of the Jews to an Equality of Rights* (Philadelphia, 1845); Isaac Leeser, *The Occident*, April 1943.

20. Naomi W. Cohen, "Pioneers of American Jewish Defense," *AJA* 29 (November 1977): 120–22; Seller, "A Jewish-Christian Dialogue," p. 239; Leeser, *Claims of the Jews*, p. 82.

21. "Anti-Jewish Sentiment in California, 1855," *AJA* 12 (April 1960): 19.

22. Lloyd P. Gartner, "Temples of Liberty Unpolluted: American Jews and Public Schools, 1840–1875," in *A Bicentennial Festschrift For Jacob Rader Marcus*, ed. Bertram W. Korn (Waltham, Mass.: American Jewish Historical Society; New York: KTAV Publishing House, 1976), p. 167; Isaac Leeser, "The American Society for Meliorating the Condition of the Jews, and its Organ, The Jewish Chronicle," *The Occident* (April 1943): 43–47; Leeser, *Claims of the Jews*, pp. 32–35, 37; Cohen, "Pioneers of American Jewish Defense," pp. 123–24.

23. George L. Berlin, *Defending the Faith: Nineteenth Century American Jewish*

Writings on Christianity and Jesus (Albany: State Univ. of New York Press, 1989), pp. 33, 36, 44.

24. Jonathan D. Sarna, "The American Jewish Response to Nineteenth-Century Christian Mission," *Journal of American History* 68 (June 1981): 41.

25. James Gottheim Heller, *Isaac M. Wise: His Life, Work and Thought* (Cincinnati: The Union of American Hebrew Congregations, 1965), pp. 256–57, 267.

26. Ibid., pp. 268–69; Cohen, "Pioneers of American Jewish Defense," pp. 144, 146–47.

27. Walter Jacob, *Christianity Through Jewish Eyes: The Quest for Common Ground* (Cincinnati: Hebrew Union College Press, 1974) pp. 67–69; Heller, *Isaac M. Wise,* pp. 624, 629.

28. Isaac M. Wise, quoted in Jacob, *Christianity Through Jewish Eyes,* pp. 70.

29. Ibid., pp. 74, 76, 79–80.

30. Isaac M. Wise, quoted in Heller, *Isaac M. Wise,* p. 639.

31. Isaac M. Wise, *Reminiscences* (Cincinnati: L. Wise and Co., 1901), pp. 16, 75, 217–18.

32. Wise, quoted in Heller, *Isaac M. Wise,* pp. 620–21.

33. Ibid., pp. 652–54.

34. Wise, *Reminiscences,* p. 23.

35. Israel J. Benjamin, *Three Years in America, 1859–1862* (Philadelphia: The Jewish Publication Society of America, 1956), 1:85.

36. Quoted in Fein, *The Making of an American Jewish Community;* pp. 56–57.

37. Sarna, *Jacksonian Jew,* pp. 140–42.

38. Wise, *Reminiscences,* p. 303; see also Benjamin, *Three Years in America,* 1:109.

39. Abraham J. Peck, "The Other 'Peculiar Institution': Jews and Judaism in the Nineteenth Century South," *Modern Judaism* 7 (February 1987): 103, 105–6; Bertram Wallace Korn, *Eventful Years and Experiences: Studies in Nineteenth Century American Jewish History* (Cincinnati: The American Jewish Archives, 1954), pp. 16–17.

40. Wise, *Reminiscences,* p. 79.

41. Edward Wagenknecht, *Daughters of the Covenant: Portraits of Six Jewish Women* (Amherst: Univ. of Massachusetts Press, 1983), pp. 49–51.

42. Sarna, *Jacksonian Jew,* p. 131.

43. Jacob Rader Marcus, "The Handsome Young Priest in the Black Gown," *Hebrew Union College Annual* 40–41 (1969–70): 419.

44. Leon A. Jick, *The Americanization of the Synagogue, 1820–1870* (Hanover, N.H.: Univ. Press of New England, 1976), 70–71, 74; Grinstein, *Jewish Community of New York,* pp. 84, 86; Daniel J. Elazar, "The Development of the American Synagogue," *Modern Judaism* 4 (October 1984): 266–68; Mark Slobin, *Chosen Voices: The Story of the American Cantorate* (Urbana: Univ. of Illinois Press, 1989), pp. 146, and 30–50 passim.

45. Jacob Rader Marcus, *Early American Jewry* (Philadelphia: The Jewish Publication Society of America, 1953), 2:487–88; Adler and Connolly, *From Ararat to Suburbia,* p. 41; Jonathan D. Sarna, "The Impact of the American Revolution on American Jews," *Modern Judaism* 1 (September 1981): 156; see, for example, *Rules and Regulations of the Congregation Mikveh Israel* (Philadelphia, 1813).

46. Lance J. Sussman, "Isaac Leeser and the Protestantization of American Judaism," *AJA* 38 (April 1986): 6–7, 11; Whiteman, "Legacy of Isaac Leeser," pp. 29–30.

47. For these suggestions I am indebted to Lance J. Sussman, "Another Look at Isaac Leeser and the First Jewish Translation of the Bible in the United States," *Modern Judaism* 5 (May 1985): 159–62; and Sussman, "Protestantization of American Judaism," p. 15.

48. Sussman, "Another Look at Isaac Leeser," pp. 179, 181.

49. Lloyd P. Gartner, *Jewish Education in the United States: A Documentary History* (New York: Teachers College Press, 1969), p. 9; Carl F. Kaestle, *The Evolution of an Urban School System: New York City, 1750–1850* (Cambridge, Mass.: Harvard Univ. Press, 1973), pp. 120–21, 124–25; Joseph R. Rosenbloom, "Rebecca Gratz and the Jewish Sunday School Movement in Philadelphia," *PAJHS* 48 (September 1958): 71; Julia Richman, "The Jewish Sunday School Movement in the United States," *The Jewish Quarterly Review* 12 (July 1900): 565.

50. Isaac Leeser, *Memorial of the Sunday School for Religious Instruction of Israelites in Philadelphia* (Philadelphia, 1840), p. 5; Naomi W. Cohen, *Encounter With Emancipation: The German Jews in the United States, 1830–1914* (Philadelphia: The Jewish Publication Society of America, 1984), p. 72.

51. Leeser, *Memorial*, p. 6; Sussman, "Another Look at Isaac Leeser," p. 164.

52. Leeser, *Memorial*, p. 7; quotation from Richman, "The Jewish Sunday School Movement," p. 570; see also Rosenbloom, "Rebecca Gratz," pp. 71–72, 77.

53. Jacob Katz, *Tradition and Crisis: Jewish Society at the End of the Middle Ages* (New York: Schocken Books, 1961), pp. 252–55, 279.

54. Nathan Glazer, *American Judaism*, 2d ed. (Chicago: Univ. of Chicago Press, 1972), pp. 25, 27; Joseph L. Blau, *Judaism in America: From Curiosity to Third Faith*, Chicago History of American Religion Series (Chicago: Univ. of Chicago Press, 1976), p. 35.

55. Lucy S. Dawidowicz, *On Equal Terms: Jews in America, 1881–1981* (New York: Holt, Rinehart and Winston, 1982), pp. 31–33.

56. David Philipson, *The Reform Movement in Judaism* (New York: Macmillan, 1907), p. 467; see also Lou H. Silberman, "American Impact: Judaism in the United States in the Early Nineteenth Century," in *Tradition and Change in Jewish Experience*, ed. A. Leland Jamison (Syracuse: Syracuse Univ. Press, 1978), pp. 74–76, 89–90, 102–3.

57. Thomas Jefferson to Isaac Harby, January 6, 1826, in *The Jews in the United States*, ed. Blau and Baron, 3:704; Edward Rutledge to Isaac Harby, March 17, 1827, in ibid., 3:705.

58. Quoted in *The Jews in the United States*, ed. Blau and Baron, 3:706.

59. Malcolm H. Stern, "Reforming of Reform Judaism—Past, Present, and Future," *AJHQ* 63 (December 1973): 113; Philipson, *The Reform Movement*, pp. 469–71.

60. W. Gunther Plaut, "The Ambiguity of Reform," in *Festschrift for Jacob Rader Marcus*, ed. Korn, p. 430.

61. Isaac M. Wise, "Our Country's Place in History," in *God's New Israel: Religious Interpretations of American Destiny*, ed. Conrad Cherry (Englewood Cliffs, N.J.: Prentice-Hall, 1971), pp. 226, 228.

62. Philipson, *Reform Movement*, p. 475, 479, 483; David Philipson, *Max Lilienthal, American Rabbi: Life and Writings* (New York: Bloch Publishing, 1915), pp. 62, 106.

63. Crawford H. Toy, *The History of the Religion of Israel* (Boston: Unitarian Sunday-School Society, 1891), p. 5.

64. Wise, *Reminiscences*, p. 57; Grinstein, *Jewish Community of New York*, pp. 369–70.

8. Zionward

1. For a good discussion of the early American mystical view of Palestine, see Samuel H. Levine, "Palestine in the Literature of the United States to 1867," in *Early History of Zionism in America*, ed. Isidore S. Meyer (1958; reprint, New York: Arno Press, 1977), pp. 23–25, 2.

2. Moshe Davis, ed., *With Eyes Toward Zion: Scholars Colloquium on American–Holy Land Studies* (New York: Arno Press, 1977), p. 3.

3. Ibid., pp. 6, 246–52.

4. For an example of an early children's schoolbook, see Charles A. Goodrich, *A Geography of the Chief Places Mentioned in the Bible, and the Principal Events Connected with Them, Adapted to Parental, Sabbath-School and Bible-Class Instruction* (New York: Robert Carter and Brothers, 1856), esp. pp. 179–85.

5. See Robert T. Handy, "Introduction," in *The Holy Land in American Protestant Life, 1800–1948: A Documentary History*, ed. Robert T. Handy (New York: Arno Press, 1981), p. xiv.

6. Ibid., pp. 7–9, 16–17.

7. Ibid., p. 25.

8. Ibid., pp. 37, 39–40.

9. See, for example, the series of essays by Jacob Abbott entitled "Memoirs of the Holy Land," in *Harper's New Monthly Magazine* 5 (August, September, October, November, 1852); David H. Finnie, *Pioneers East: The Early American Experience in the Middle East* (Cambridge, Mass.: Harvard Univ. Press, 1967), pp. 262–68.

10. Finnie, *Pioneers East*, p. 269.

11. Handy, *The Holy Land*, p. 108; Franklin Walker, *Irreverent Pilgrims: Melville, Browne, and Mark Twain in the Holy Land* (Seattle: Univ. of Washington Press, 1974), p. 213.

12. Louise Abbie Mayo, "Herman Melville, the Jew and Judaism," *AJA* 28 (November 1976): 172–73; Herman Melville, *Journal of a Visit to Europe and the Levant, October 11, 1856–May 6, 1857*, ed. Howard C. Horsford (Princeton: Princeton Univ. Press, 1955), pp. 137, 155–59.

13. Melville, *Journal*, p. 154; see also Walker, *Irreverent Pilgrims*, pp. 124, 132.

14. Melville, *Journal*, pp. 98–99.

15. Mark Twain, *The Innocents Abroad, or the New Pilgrims' Progress* (New York: Harper and Brothers, 1911), p. 129.

16. Ibid., pp. 386–87; Walker, *Irreverent Pilgrims*, pp. 175, 179.

17. Mark Twain, quoted in Walker, *Irreverent Pilgrims*, p. 218.

18. Ibid.

19. Robert T. Handy, "Sources for Understanding American Christian Attitudes Toward the Holy Land, 1800–1950," in *With Eyes Toward Zion*, ed. Davis, p. 38.

20. Finnie, *Pioneers East*, pp. 114, 117–19; Handy, *The Holy Land*, p. 75.

21. Handy, *The Holy Land*, p. 75; Finnie, *Pioneers East*, pp. 121.

22. Finnie, *Pioneers East*, pp. 123–24, 134; Handy, "Sources for Understanding American Christian Attitudes," p. 39.

23. W. C. Brownlee, ed., *The History of the Jews from the Babylonian Captivity to the Present Time* (Boston: M. A. Berk, 1847), p. 355.

24. Ibid., pp. 356–57.

25. Ibid., p. 359.

26. Handy, *The Holy Land*, pp. 83, 87.

27. Melville, *Journal up the Straits, October 11, 1856–May 5, 1857* (New York: Cooper Square Publishers, 1971), pp. 94–95.

28. Ibid., p. 97.

29. A. E. Thompson, *A Century of Jewish Missions* (Chicago: Fleming H. Revell Company, 1902), pp. 177–79, 182, 186, 189.

30. Davis, *With Eyes Toward Zion*, p. 186.

31. Ibid., p. 185.

32. Bertha Spafford Vester, *Our Jerusalem: An American Family in the Holy City, 1881–1949* (Garden City, N.Y.: Doubleday, 1950), pp. 9, 28–29, 32–36, 41, 44, 51–53.

33. Handy, *The Holy Land*, pp. 164, 166; Vester, *Our Jerusalem*, pp. 56–59, 62–63.

34. Vester, *Our Jerusalem*, pp. 100–101, 114.

35. Handy, *The Holy Land*, p. 168.

36. Abraham J. Karp, "The Zionism of Warder Cresson," in *Early History of Zionism in America*, ed. Isidore S. Meyer (New York: Arno Press, 1977), p. 1; Frank Fox, "Quaker, Shaker, Rabbi: Warder Cresson, the Story of a Philadelphia Mystic," *The Pennsylvania Magazine of History and Biography* 95 (April 1971): 148, 150–55.

37. Fox, "Quaker, Shaker, Rabbi," pp. 156–60.

38. Warder Cresson, *The Key of David* (1852; reprint, New York: Arno Press, 1977), p. 2.

39. Karp, "The Zionism of Warder Cresson," p. 6.

40. Cresson, *Key of David*, p. 121.

41. Karp, "The Zionism of Warder Cresson," p. 7; Fox, "Quaker, Shaker, Rabbi," pp. 171–73; Cresson, *Key of David*, pp. 205–6.

42. Cresson, *Key of David*, p. 206, Cresson's emphasis.

43. Ibid., pp. 107–10.

44. Ibid., pp. 141–43, 224, 221.

45. Karp, "The Zionism of Warder Cresson," pp. 8–9; Fox, "Quaker, Shaker, Rabbi," pp. 184–85, 187–89; *The Jewish Encyclopedia*, 1912, s.v. "Cresson, Warder," by Herbert Friedenwald.

46. "Testimony of the Prophet Joseph Smith," *The Book of Mormon: An Account Written by the Hand of Mormon upon Plates Taken from the Plates of Nephi* (Salt Lake City: The Church of Jesus Christ of Latter-day Saints, 1986), n. p.; see also John Henry Evans, *Joseph Smith, an American Prophet* (New York: Macmillan, 1936), p. 221.

47. Stanley P. Hirshson, *The Lion of the Lord: A Biography of Brigham Young* (New York: Alfred A. Knopf, 1969), p. 139.

48. For the story of Joseph Smith, see Keith Huntress, ed., *Murder of an American Prophet* (San Francisco: Chandler Publishing, 1960).

49. Eldin Ricks, "Zionism and the Mormon Church," *Herzl Year Book* 5 (1963): 148.

50. Rudolph Glanz, *Jew and Mormon: Historic Group Relations and Religious Outlook* (New York: Waldon Press, 1963), pp. 108–13, 321–29.

51. Susa Young Gates, *The Life Story of Brigham Young* (New York: Macmillan, 1930), p. 149; *The Book of Mormon*, 1 Nephi 1:2; Glanz, *Jew and Mormon*, pp. 218–20, 284–85; James B. Allen and Glen M. Leonard, *The Story of the Latter-day Saints* (Salt Lake City: Deseret Book Company, 1976), p. 340.

52. Joseph Smith, quoted in Glanz, *Jew and Mormon*, p. 142.

53. Glanz, *Jew and Mormon*, pp. 138–41; Evans, *Joseph Smith*, p. 232.

54. *The Book of Mormon* 1 Nephi 10:2–4, 3 Nephi 29:8.

55. Joseph Smith, quoted in Ricks, "Zionism and the Mormon Church," p. 54; see also Joseph Smith, *History of the Church of Jesus Christ of Latter-day Saints. Period 1* (Salt Lake City: Deseret Book Company, 1960), 4:167–76.

56. Hirshson, *The Lion of the Lord*, p. 237.

57. Wilford Woodruff, quoted in Ricks, "Zionism and the Mormon Church," pp. 162; see also Gates, *Brigham Young*, p. 149.

58. Quotations in Glanz, *Jew and Mormon*, 20–21, 42–47, 103.

59. For the term *restorationism*, I am indebted to Lawrence J. Epstein's excellent study, *Zion's Call: Christian Contributions to the Origins and Development of Israel* (Lanham, Md.: Univ. Press of America, 1984), p. 1; see also the pathbreaking work of Yona Malachy, *American Fundamentalism and Israel: The Relation of Fundamentalist Churches to Zionism and the State of Israel* (Jerusalem: Hebrew Univ. of Jerusalem, 1978), pp. 4–6.

60. Timothy P. Weber, *Living in the Shadow of the Second Coming: American Premillennialism, 1875–1925* (New York: Oxford Univ. Press, 1979), pp. 10–11.

61. Jonathan Edwards, *Apocalyptic Writings*, ed. Stephen J. Stein (New Haven: Yale Univ. Press, 1977), pp. 19, 28, 134–35.

62. John Wesley, "For the Jews," in *The Works of John Wesley*, ed. Franz Hildebrandt and Oliver Beckerlegge (Oxford: Clarendon Press, 1983), 7:616.

63. Ezra Stiles, *The Literary Diary of Ezra Stiles*, ed. Franklin Bowditch Dexter (New York: Charles Scribner's Sons, 1901), 2:465–66.

64. Joseph P. Shulim, "Napoleon as the Jewish Messiah: Some Contemporary Conceptions in Virginia," *Jewish Social Studies* 7 (July 1945): 275–80.

65. Ethan Smith, *View of the Hebrews* (Poultney, Vt.: Smith and Shute Publishers, 1823), pp. iv, 49.

66. Quoted in Isaac M. Fein, "*Niles' Weekly Register* on the Jews," *PAJHS* 50 (September 1960): 11–12.

67. Mordecai M. Noah, *Discourse on the Restoration of the Jews* (New York: Harper and Brothers, 1845), p. 28.

68. Ibid., pp. 40–41.

69. Louis Ruchames, "Mordecai Manuel Noah and Early American Zionism," *AJHQ* 64 (March 1975): 223.

70. Malachy, *American Fundamentalism and Israel*, pp. 21–29.

71. Weber, *Living in the Shadow*, pp. 11, 182.

72. Ernest R. Sandeen, "Toward a Historical Interpretation of the Origins of Fundamentalism," *Church History* 36 (March 1967): 67–68; *Encyclopedia Judaica*, 1971, s.v. "Christian Zionism," by Yonah Malachy.

73. Sandeen, "Toward a Historical Interpretation," pp. 70–71.

74. W. B. Nicholson, "The Gathering of Israel," in *Premillennial Essays of the Prophetic Conference Held in the Church of the Holy Trinity, New York City,* ed. Nathaniel West (Chicago: Fleming H. Revell Company, 1879), p. 222.

75. Ibid., pp. 232, 234, 240.

76. Charles K. Imbrie, "The Regeneration," in *Premillennial Essays of the Prophetic Conference,* pp. 126, 137.

77. Nathaniel West, "Prophecy and Israel," in *Prophetic Studies of the International Prophetic Conference, Chicago, November, 1886* (Chicago: Fleming H. Revell Company, 1886), p. 122.

78. Ibid., pp. 126, 128–29.

79. David Rausch, *Zionism Within Early American Fundamentalism, 1878–1914* (Lewiston, N.Y.: Edwin Mellen Press, 1979), p. 107.

80. Ibid., pp. 262–64.

81. Quotations from Marvin Feinstein, "The Blackstone Memorial," *Midstream* 7 (June 1968): 77–78.

82. Ibid., pp. 79–89.

9. At Ease in the Gilded Age

1. William James, *The Variety of Religious Experiences* (New York: Longmans, Green, and Co., 1902), pp. 476–77.

2. John Higham, *Send These To Me: Jews and Other Immigrants in Urban America* (New York: Atheneum, 1975), pp. 198–200.

3. H. Richard Niebuhr, *The Social Sources of Denominationalism* (Cleveland: World Publishing Company, 1957); Sidney E. Mead, "Denominationalism: The Shape of Protestantism in America," *Church History* 23 (December 1954); Will Herberg, *Protestant-Catholic-Jew: An Essay in American Religious Sociology* (Garden City, N.Y.: Doubleday, Anchor Books, 1960), p. 37; Andrew M. Greeley and Peter H. Rossi, *The Denominational Society: A Sociological Approach to Religion in America* (Glenview, Ill.: Scott, Foresman and Co., 1972), p. 1.

4. Joseph L. Blau, *Judaism in America: From Curiosity to the Third Faith,* Chicago History of American Religion Series, (Chicago: Univ. of Chicago Press, 1976), p. 16.

5. Nathan Glaser, *American Judaism,* 2d ed. (Chicago: Univ. of Chicago Press, 1972), pp. 41–47; "Authentic Report of the Proceedings of the Rabbinical Conference Held in Pittsburgh, November 16, 17, 18, 1885," in *The Changing World of Reform Judaism: The Pittsburgh Platform in Retrospect,* ed. Walter Jacob (Pittsburgh: Rodef Shalom Congregation, 1985), pp. 108–9.

6. Corrine Azen Krause, "The Historical Setting of the Pittsburgh Platform," in *The Changing World of Reform Judaism,* ed. Jacob, pp. 5, 13–14.

7. "Authentic Report of the Proceedings of the Rabbinical Conference," p. 92.

8. Ibid., p. 92.

9. Ibid., pp. 106, 112.

10. Blau, *Judaism in America,* pp. 60–61; Henry S. Morais, "Sabato Morais: A Memoir," in *Proceedings of the Sixth Biennial Convention of the Jewish Theological Seminary Association, Held in the City of Philadelphia . . . March 20, 1898* (New York: Press of Philip Cowen, 1898); Robert Gordis, *Judaism in a Christian World* (New York: McGraw-Hill, 1966), p. 27; quotations from Naomi M. Cohen, *Encounter With Emancipation:*

The German Jews in the United States, 1830–1914 (Philadelphia: The Jewish Publication Society of America, 1984), p. 181.

11. Pamela S. Nadell, *Conservative Judaism in America: A Biographical Dictionary and Sourcebook* (New York: Greenwood Press, 1988), pp. 264–65; Howard Singer, "The Judaism Born in America," *Commentary* 82 (December 1986): 41; Blau, *Judaism in America*, p. 62.

12. Marc Lee Raphael, ed., *Jews and Judaism in the United States: A Documentary History* (New York: Behrman House, 1983), pp. 46, 217–18, 220.

13. Blau, *Judaism in America*, pp. 47, 49.

14. Gordis, *Judaism in a Christian World*, p. 27.

15. Jeffrey S. Gurock, "From Exception to Role Model: Bernard Drachman and the Evolution of Jewish Religious Life in America, 1880–1920," *AJH* 76 (June 1986): 468–69; Feingold, *Zion in America: The Jewish Experience from Colonial Times to the Present* (New York: Hippocrene Books, 1974), pp. 191–92.

16. Leonard Dinnerstein, "The Funeral of Rabbi Jacob Joseph," in *Anti-Semitism in American History*, ed., David A. Gerber (Urbana: Univ. of Illinois Press, 1986), p. 279.

17. Aaron Rothkoff, "The American Sojourn of Ridbaz: Religious Problems Within the Immigrant Community," *AJHQ* 57 (June 1968): 557–60, 571.

18. Gurock, "From Exception to Role Model," pp. 457–68, 482, 484.

19. For population figures, see James G. Heller, *Isaac M. Wise: His Life, Work and Thought* (Cincinnati: The Union of American Hebrew Congregations, 1965), p. 461.

20. Felix Adler, quoted in Benny Kraut, *From Reform Judaism to Ethical Culture: The Religious Evolution of Felix Adler* (Cincinnati: Hebrew Union College Press, 1979), p. 31.

21. Stuart E. Rosenberg, *The Jewish Community in Rochester, 1843–1925* (New York: Columbia Univ. Press, 1954), p. 91; Steven Hertzberg, *Strangers Within the Gate City: The Jews of Atlanta, 1845–1915* (Philadelphia: The Jewish Publication Society of America, 1978), pp. 67–70.

22. George L. Berlin, *Defending the Faith: Nineteenth Century American Jewish Writings on Christianity and Jesus* (Albany: State Univ. of New York Press, 1989), pp. 70–73, 189–90.

23. Felix Adler, quoted in Horace L. Friess, *Felix Adler and Ethical Culture* (New York: Columbia Univ. Press, 1981), p. 68; Kraut, *From Reform Judaism to Ethical Culture*, pp. 71–75, 77, 207.

24. Kraut, *From Reform Judaism to Ethical Culture*, p. 134.

25. Kerry M. Olitzky, "The Sunday-Sabbath Movement in American Reform Judaism: Strategy or Evolution?" *AJA* 34 (April 1982): 75–77; Kraut, *From Reform Judaism to Ethical Culture*, pp. 114, 126–27; David Philipson, *The Reform Movement in Judaism* (New York: Macmillan, 1907), pp. 503–4.

26. Kraut, *From Reform Judaism to Ethical Culture*, p. 117; Olitzky, "Sunday-Sabbath Movement," p. 80.

27. Emil G. Hirsch, "The Philosophy of the Reform Movement in American Judaism," *Central Conference of American Rabbis Yearbook* 5 (1895): 110.

28. Quoted in Stuart E. Rosenberg, "The *Jewish Tidings* and the Sunday Service Question," *PAJHS* 42 (June 1953): 373.

29. Cyrus Adler quoted in ibid., p. 382.

30. Olitzky, "The Sunday-Sabbath Movement," pp. 84–85.

31. I am indebted to Tony Fels's insightful essay, "Religious Assimilation: Jews and Freemasonry in Gilded-Age San Francisco," *AJH* 74 (June 1985): 369–403.

32. Jeanne Abrams, "Remembering the Maine: The Jewish Attitude Toward the Spanish-American War as Reflected in *The American Hebrew,*" *AJH* 76 (June 1987): 441, 447, 451–52; Martin E. Marty, *Modern American Religion* (Chicago: Univ. of Chicago Press, 1986), vol. 1: *The Irony of It All, 1893–1919*, pp. 307–9.

33. "Address by Ex-President Grover Cleveland," *PAJHS* 14 (1906): 11–12; "Letter from President Roosevelt," *PAJHS* 14 (1906): 19.

34. Gordis, *Judaism in a Christian World*, p. 13.

35. Arnold M. Eisen, *The Chosen People in America: A Study in Jewish Religious Ideology* (Bloomington: Indiana Univ. Press, 1983), p. 3.

36. Ibid., p. 7.

37. Ibid., p. 51.

38. Isaac M. Wise, quoted in Heller, *Isaac M. Wise*, p. 586.

39. Esther L. Panitz, "The Polarity of American Jewish Attitudes toward Immigration (1870–1891)," *AJHQ* 52 (December 1963): 108–12, 114–17; Yehezkel Wyszkowski, "*The American Hebrew*: An Exercise in Ambivalence," *AJH* 76 (March 1987): 344–45.

40. Panitz, "Polarity of American Jewish Attitudes," pp. 340, 346–47.

41. "Authentic Report of the Proceedings of the Rabbinical Conference," p. 108.

42. Melvin Weinman, "The Attitude of Isaac Mayer Wise Toward Zionism and Palestine," *AJA* 3 (January 1951): 4–7; Heller, *Isaac M. Wise*, p. 697.

43. Michael A. Meyer, "American Reform Judaism and Zionism: Early Efforts at Ideological Rapprochement," *Studies in Zionism* 7 (Spring 1983): 54.

44. David Philipson, *My Life as an American Jew: An Autobiography* (Cincinnati: John G. Kidd and Son, 1941), pp. 70, 72, 124.

45. Marc Lee Raphael, "Rabbi Jacob Voorsanger of San Francisco on Jews and Judaism: The Implications of the Pittsburgh Platform," *AJHQ* 63 (December 1973): 200, 202–3.

46. Quoted in Richard Libowitz, "Some Reactions to *Der Judenstaat* among English-speaking Jews in the United States," in *Jewish Civilization: Essays and Studies,* ed. Ronald A. Brauner (Philadelphia: Reconstructionist Rabbinical College, 1979), 1:129; see also Philipson, *My Life as an American Jew,* pp. 136–37; Heller, *Isaac M. Wise,* pp. 603–4; Weiman, "Attitude of Isaac Mayer Wise Toward Zionism," pp. 9–11.

47. Quotations from Libowitz, "Some Reactions to *Der Judenstaat,*" pp. 129–30.

48. Emma Lazarus, "The Jewish Problem," *The Century Magazine* 25 (February 1883): 610; see also Henry Wadsworth Longfellow Dana, "Emma Lazarus and the New England Poets," *The Menorah Journal* 39 (Spring 1951): 38–40.

49. Meyer, "American Reform Judaism and Zionism," p. 5; Melvin I. Urofsky, *American Zionism from Herzl to the Holocaust* (Garden City, N.Y.: Anchor Books, 1976), p. 89.

50. Stephen Wise, *Challenging Years: The Autobiography of Stephen Wise* (New York: G. P. Putnam's Sons, 1949), p. 54; Meyer, "American Reform Judaism and Zionism," pp. 55–56.

51. Emma Lazarus, quoted in David R. Mesher, "Emma Lazarus: Zionism, American Style," *Journal of American Jewish Literature* 2 (1982): 203.

52. Kaufman Kohler, quoted in Meyer, "American Reform Judaism and Zionism," p. 64.

53. Philipson, *My Life As American Jew*, pp. 138–39; Urofsky, *American Zionism*, pp. 87, 90–91, 156.

10. Liberal Crusade

1. H. Shelton Smith, Robert T. Handy, and Lefferts A. Loetscher, *American Christianity: An Historical Interpretation with Representative Documents* (New York: Charles Scribner's Sons, 1960–63), 2:255–56.

2. Crawford H. Toy, *The History of the Religion of Israel* (Boston: Unitarian Sunday-School Society, 1891), pp. 147–48; see also James Freeman Clarke, *Ten Great Religions, Part 2: A Comparison of All Religions* (Boston: Houghton Mifflin, 1883), pp. 359–60.

3. Benny Kraut, "Judaism Triumphant: Isaac Mayer Wise on Unitarianism and Liberal Christianity," *AJS Review* 78 (1982–83): 195.

4. Octavius Brooks Frothingham, *Recollections and Impressions, 1822–1890* (New York: G. P. Putnam's Sons, 1891), pp. 65, 119, 120.

5. Ibid., pp. 121–22, 141, 317; Kraut, "Judaism Triumphant," p. 196.

6. Octavius Brooks Frothingham, *The Religion of Humanity* (New York: David G. Francis, 1873), p. 313, 317; Frothingham, *Recollections*, pp. 278; see also William R. Hutchison, *The Modernist Impulse in American Protestantism* (Cambridge, Mass.: Harvard Univ. Press, 1976), p. 37.

7. Frothingham, *Religion of Humanity*, pp. 330, 334–35.

8. Charles W. Eliot, *The Religion of the Future: A Lecture Delivered at the Close of the Eleventh Session of the Harvard Summer School of Theology, July 22, 1909* (New York: Frederick A. Stokes Co., 1909), pp. 16–17.

9. Charles W. Eliot, "Address by President Eliot of Harvard University," *PAJHS* 14 (1906): 70, 83.

10. Gustav Gottheil, "The Position of the Jews in America," *The North American Review* 127 (July-August 1878): 86.

11. Ibid., pp. 89, 96.

12. David Philipson, *Max Lilienthal, American Rabbi: Life and Writings* (New York: Bloch Publishing, 1915), p. 96; see also Moncure Daniel Conway, *Autobiography: Memories and Experiences of Moncure Daniel Conway* (New York: Negro Univ. Press, 1904), 2: 418.

13. Max Lilienthal, quoted in Philipson, *Max Lilienthal*, pp. 97–98.

14. David Philipson, *My Life as an American Jew: An Autobiography* (Cincinnati: John G. Kidd and Son, 1941), p. 215.

15. Ibid., pp. 86–87, 212, 257.

16. Kraut, "Judaism Triumphant," p. 198.

17. Stuart E. Rosenberg, *The Jewish Community in Rochester, 1843–1925* (New York: Columbia Univ. Press, 1954), pp. 86, 191; Bernard G. Rudolph, *From a Minyan to a Community: A History of the Jews of Syracuse* (Syracuse: Syracuse Univ. Press, 1970), p. 256; Morris A. Gutstein, *A Priceless Heritage: The Epic Growth of Nineteenth Century Chicago Jewry* (New York: Bloch Publishing, 1953), p. 313.

18. John Haynes Holmes, *I Speak for Myself: The Autobiography of John Haynes*

Holmes (New York: Harper and Brothers, 1959), pp. 265–66; Carl Hermann Voss, *Rabbi and Minister: The Friendship of Stephen S. Wise and John Haynes Holmes* (Cleveland: World Publishing Company, 1964), pp. 17–20, 130–33; Stephen Wise, *Challenging Years: The Autobiography of Stephen Wise* (New York: G. P. Putnam's Sons, 1949), pp. 126–27; Melvin I. Urofsky, *A Voice That Spoke for Justice: The Life and Times of Stephen S. Wise* (Albany: State Univ. of New York Press, 1982), pp. 83–86.

19. Holmes, *I Speak for Myself*, p. 108; Wise, *Challenging Years*, p. 286.

20. Charles Sprague Smith, *Working with the People* (New York: A. Wessels Company, 1904), pp. 62–63, 65–66, 68, 71–73; Egal Feldman, "American Ecumenism: Chicago's World's Parliament of Religions of 1893," *A Journal of Church and State* 9 (Spring 1967): 198.

21. "Relations With Christian Colleagues," in Richard Gottheil, *The Life of Gustav Gottheil: Memoir of a Priest in Israel* (Williamsport, Penn.: Baynard Press, 1936), n. p.; "A Modern Religious Controversy," *The Outlook* 90 (December 24, 1910): 890.

22. Walter R. Houghton, ed., *Neely's History of the Parliament of Religions and Religious Congresses at the World's Columbian Exposition* (Chicago: 1893), pp. 15–18, 23, 971–72; Rossiter Johnson, *A History of the World's Columbian Exposition Held in Chicago in 1893* (New York: D. Appleton and Company, 1897), 4:222; Paul A. Carter, *The Spiritual Crisis of the Gilded Age* (DeKalb, Ill.: Northern Illinois Univ. Press, 1971), p. 210; Martin E. Marty, *Modern American Religion*, vol. 1, *The Irony of It All, 1893–1919* (Chicago: Univ. of Chicago Press, 1986), 1:20.

23. "The Parliament of Religions," *Current Literature* 14 (October 1893): 293.

24. John Henry Barrows, "The World's First Parliament of Religions," *The Homiletic Review* 25 (May 1893): 394–95.

25. John Henry Barrows, *The World's Parliament of Religions* (Chicago: Parliament Publishing Company, 1893), 1:15.

26. Ibid., p. 15; Houghton, *Neely's History of the Parliament*, p. 13.

27. "Address of President Charles Carroll Bonney of 'The World's Congress Auxiliary,'" in *Neely's History of the Parliament*, ed. Houghton, 1:71–72; Feldman, "American Ecumenism," p. 184.

28. Quotations from Ronald Bishop, "Religious Confrontation, A Case Study: The 1893 Parliament of Religions," *Numen: International Review for the History of Religions* 16 (April 1969): 71; Feldman, "American Ecumenism," pp. 184–85.

29. Barrows, *World's Parliament of Religions*, 1:4–5.

30. Union of American Hebrew Congregations, *Judaism at the World's Parliament of Religions* (Cincinnati: Robert Clarke and Co., 1894), pp. xxi–xxii.

31. Gutstein, *A Priceless Heritage*, pp. 315–16; Cyrus Adler, *I Have Considered the Days* (Philadelphia: The Jewish Publication Society of America, 1941), p. 178.

32. Rebecca Trachtenberg Alpert, "Jewish Participation at the World's Parliament of Religions, 1893," in *Jewish Civilization: Essays and Studies*, ed. Ronald A. Brauner (Philadelphia: Reconstructionist Rabbinical College, 1979), 1:111–12.

33. Kaufman Kohler, "Synagogue and Church in their Mutual Relations, Particularly in Reference to the Ethical Teachings," in Union of American Hebrew Congregations, *Judaism at the World's Parliament*, p. 114.

34. Alexander Kohut, "What the Hebrew Scriptures Have Wrought for Mankind," in Union of American Hebrew Congregations, *Judaism at the World's Parliament*, pp. 46–48.

35. Josephine Lazarus, "The Outlook of Judaism," in Union of American Hebrew Congregations, *Judaism at the World's Parliament*, pp. 300–303.

36. Quotations from Bishop, "Religious Confrontation," p. 69.

37. Joseph Silverman, "Popular Errors About the Jews," in Union of American Hebrew Congregations, *Judaism at the World's Parliament*, p. 286.

38. Alexander Kohut, quoted in Alpert, "Jewish Participation," p. 113.

39. Quotations from James G. Heller, *Isaac M. Wise: His Life, Work and Thought* (Cincinnati: The Union of American Hebrew Congregations, 1965), p. 468; Philipson, *My Life as an American Jew*, p. 90; see also David Einhorn Hirsch, *Rabbi Emil G. Hirsch, the Reform Advocate* (Chicago: Whitehall Company, 1968), p. 28.

40. Feldman, "American Ecumenism," p. 193.

41. Minot J. Savage, ed., *The World's Congress of Religions* (Boston: Arena Publishing, 1893), pp. 4–5.

42. F. Max Muller, "The Real Significance of the Parliament of Religions," *The Arena* 2 (December 1894): 1–3, 12–13.

43. J. F. Chafee, "Comparative Religion," *Methodist Review* 70 (May 1896): 410; George S. Goodspeed, ed. *The World's First Parliament of Religions* (Chicago: Hill and Schumann, 1895), p. 45.

44. Henry Churchill King, *The Moral and Religious Challenge of Our Time* (New York: Macmillan, 1911), p. 146; Washington Gladden, *The Church and Modern Life* (Boston: Houghton Mifflin, 1908), p. 30; Lyman Abbott, "Lessons From the Parliament of Religion," *Christian Thought* 11 (August 1893–July 1894): 220–23.

45. Lyman Abbott, "The Growth of Religious Tolerance in the United States," *The Forum* 23 (July 1897): 654–55.

46. Quotations from Naomi Cohen, "The Challenge of Darwinism and Biblical Criticism to American Judaism," *Modern Judaism* 4 (May 1984): 147.

47. Julia Ward Howe, "Shall the Frontier of Christendom Be Maintained?" *The Forum* 12 (November 1896): 322–23.

48. Edward Bellamy, *Equality.* 11th ed. (1897; New York: D. Appleton and Company, 1910), pp. 503–4.

49. Morris Jastrow. "The First International Congress for the History of Religions," *International Journal of Ethics* 10 (July 1900): 503–4.

50. Walter Rauschenbusch, *A Theology for the Social Gospel* (New York: Macmillan, 1918), p. 48.

51. Ronald C. White, Jr., and C. Howard Hopkins, eds., *The Social Gospel: Religion and Reform in Changing America* (Philadelphia: Temple Univ. Press, 1976), pp. xiii–xix, 3–6; W. A. Visser 'T Hooft, *The Background of the Social Gospel in America* (Haarlem, The Netherlands: H. D. Tjeenk Willink and Zoon, 1928), p. 26.

52. Charles S. Macfarland, *Christian Unity in the Making: The First Twenty-Five Years of the Federal Council of the Churches of Christ in America, 1905–1930* (New York: The Federal Council of Churches of Christ in America, 1948), pp. 42–46; quotations from John A. Hutchison, *We Are Not Divided: A Critical and Historical Study of the Federal Council of the Churches of Christ in America* (New York: Round Table Press, 1941), pp. 42, 46–47.

53. Ferenc Morton Szasz, *The Divided Mind of Protestant America, 1800–1930* (Birmingham: Univ. of Alabama Press, 1982), pp. 42–44; quotations from Hooft, *Background of the Social Gospel*, p. 46.

54. For biographical information I have relied upon Dores Robinson Sharpe, *Walter Rauschenbusch* (New York: Macmillan, 1942).

55. Rauschenbusch, *Theology for the Social Gospel*, pp. 57, 60; see also Walter Rauschenbusch, *Christianity and the Social Crisis* (New York: Macmillan, 1914), p. 65.

56. Washington Gladden, *Recollections* (Boston: Houghton Mifflin, 1909), pp. 58–59.

57. Washington Gladden, *Social Salvation* (Boston: Houghton Mifflin, 1902), pp. 14–15.

58. Ibid., pp. 26, 30; see also John Haynes Holmes, *The Revolutionary Function of the Modern Church* (New York: G. P. Putnam's Sons, Knickerbocker Press, 1912), pp. 152, 253.

59. Charles Reynolds Brown, *The Social Message of the Modern Pulpit* (New York: Charles Scribner's Sons, 1911), pp. 70–71, 77–78, 203–5.

60. Rauschenbusch, *Christianity and the Social Crisis*, p. 13.

61. Ibid., pp. 11–12, 21.

62. Ibid., p. 12.

63. Lyman Abbott, *The Life and Literature of the Ancient Hebrews* (Boston: Houghton Mifflin, 1901), pp. 48–49.

64. Lyman Abbott, *The Spirit of Democracy* (Boston: Houghton Mifflin, 1910), p. 4.

65. Brown, *The Social Message*, pp. viii, 81, 204–5; see also W. N. Sloan, *Social Regeneration: The Work of Christianity* (Philadelphia: Westminster Press, 1902), pp. 82–83.

66. Felix Adler, *An Ethical Philosophy of Life* (New York: D. Appleton and Co., 1918), pp. 21–22, 118; Benny Kraut, *From Reform Judaism to Ethical Culture: The Religious Evolution of Felix Adler* (Cincinnati: Hebrew Union College Press, 1979), pp. 70–71; Henry Neumann, *Spokesmen for Ethical Religion* (Boston: Beacon Press, 1951), pp. 17–23.

67. Frothingham, *Recollections*, p. 267.

68. Lyman Abbott, *The Theology of an Evolutionist* (1897; reprint, New York: Outlook Co., 1925), p. 12; Holmes, *Revolutionary Function of the Modern Church*, pp. 58–59, 66, 71–72; Gladden, *Social Salvation*, p. 12.

69. Rauschenbusch, *Theology for the Social Gospel*, pp. 6–11.

70. K[aufman] Kohler, *Jewish Theology: Systematically and Historically Considered* (Cincinnati: Riverdale Press, 1943), pp. 17, 311–14, 318–19, 477–48.

71. Emil G. Hirsch, "Elements of Universal Religion," in Barrows, *World's Parliament of Religions*, 5:1306.

72. Melvin I. Urofsky, *A Voice That Spoke for Justice: The Life and Times of Stephen S. Wise* (Albany: State Univ. of New York Press, 1982), pp. 91, 99–110; Voss, *Rabbi and Minister*, pp. 97–99, 121–24.

73. Solomon Schechter, *Aspects of Rabbinic Theology* (1909; New York: Schocken Books, 1961), pp. 18–19, 76, 79, 90–92.

74. Ibid., pp. 107–9.

75. Egal Feldman, "The Social Gospel and the Jews," *American Jewish Historical Quarterly* 58 (March 1969): 316–22.

11. Anti-Judaism and the New Theology

1. Crawford H. Toy, *Judaism and Christianity* (Boston: Little, Brown, 1892), p. 349.

2. James Freeman Clarke, *Ten Great Religions: An Essay in Comparative Theology* (1871; Boston: Houghton Mifflin, 1899), pp. 19–20.

3. Walter Rauschenbusch, *Christianity and the Social Crisis* (New York: Macmillan, 1914), p. 61.

4. Walter Rauschenbusch, *A Theology for the Social Gospel* (New York: Macmillan, 1918), pp. 213–16.

5. Octavius B. Frothingham, *The Religion of Humanity* (New York: David G. Francis, 1873), pp. 24–25, 69–76; Octavius B. Frothingham, *Recollections and Impressions, 1822–1890* (New York: G. P. Putnam's Sons, 1891), p. 280.

6. Minot Savage, quoted in Benny Kraut, "Judaism Triumphant: Isaac Meyer Wise on Unitarianism and Liberal Christianity," *AJS Review* 78 (1982–83): 211.

7. Lyman Abbott, "Was Jesus Christ a Jew?" *The Outlook* 74 (June 6, 1903): 312.

8. Lyman Abbott, *The Life and Literature of the Ancient Hebrews* (Boston: Houghton Mifflin, 1901), p. 388.

9. For biographical information see, "Charles David Williams," *Dictionary of American Biography*, ed. Dumas Malone (New York: Charles Scribner's Sons, 1936), 20:251–52; Charles D. Williams, *A Valid Christianity for To-Day* (New York: Macmillan, 1909), pp. 22–23.

10. Toy, *Judaism and Christianity*, p. 242.

11. Ibid., pp. 243–44

12. Rauschenbusch, *Christianity and the Social Crisis*, pp. 73, 86; Rauschenbusch, *Theology for the Social Gospel*, pp. 215–16.

13. Charles S. Macfarland, *Jesus and the Prophets* (New York: G. P. Putnam's Sons, Knickerbocker Press, 1905), p. 213.

14. Williams, *A Valid Christianity*, pp. 57, 59–60.

15. John Haynes Holmes, *The Revolutionary Function of the Modern Church* (New York: G. P. Putnam's Sons, Knickerbocker Press, 1912), pp. 188–89, 196.

16. Rauschenbusch, *Theology for the Social Gospel*, p. 249.

17. Williams, *A Valid Christianity*, pp. 22–24.

18. Ibid., pp. 55–56.

19. Robert Andrew Everett, "Judaism in Nineteenth-Century American Transcendentalist and Liberal Protestant Thought," *Journal of Ecumenical Studies* 20 (Summer 1983): 413.

20. Lyman Abbott, "The Debt of Modern Civilization to Judaism," *The Outlook* 98 (August 5, 1911): 777.

21. Rauschenbusch, *Christianity and the Social Gospel*, p. 113; Toy, *Judaism and Christianity*, p. 139; Crawford H. Toy, *The History of the Religion of Israel* (Boston: Unitarian Sunday-School Society, 1891), p. 8.

22. Aaron Ignatius Abell, *The Urban Impact on American Protestantism, 1865–1900* (Cambridge, Mass.: Harvard Univ. Press, 1943), p. 243.

23. Shailer Mathews, *The Social Gospel* (Philadelphia: Griffith and Knowland Press, 1910), pp. 41–42, 117–18.

24. "Prejudice Against the Jews: Its Nature, Its Causes and Remedies. A Consensus of Opinion by Non-Jews," *The American Hebrew* 42 (April 4, 1890): 165.

25. Ibid., p. 165.

26. Ibid., pp. 167, 171–72.

27. Ibid., pp. 171–73.

28. Ibid., pp. 172–73.

29. David James Burrell, "How a More Kindly Relation Between Jews and Christians May Be Furthered," *The American Citizen* 1 (December 1912): 282; "Editorial," ibid., 2 (February 1913): 38; "Editorial," ibid., 2 (June 1913): 280–81; see also "The Problem of the Jew," ibid., 3 (December 1913): 381.

30. For biographical information see Gregory Weinstein, *The Ardent Eighties and After: Reminiscences of a Busy Life* (New York: International Press, 1947), pp. 91–94; Stanton Coit, *The Soul of America* (New York: Macmillan, 1914), pp. 59–60.

31. Ibid., p. 62.

32. Ibid., p. 64.

33. Ibid., p. 66.

34. Richard Hofstadter, *Social Darwinism in American Thought* (1944; Boston: Beacon Press, 1955), pp. 9–16, 24–25; Charles Howard Hopkins, *The Rise of the Social Gospel in American Protestantism* (New Haven: Yale Univ. Press, 1940), p. 130.

35. Lyman Abbott, *The Theology of an Evolutionist* (1897; New York: Outlook Company, 1925), p. 19.

36. H. Shelton Smith, Robert T. Handy, and Lefferts A. Loetscher, *American Christianity: An Historical Interpretation with Representative Documents* (New York: Charles Scribner's Sons, 1960–63), 2:302, 304.

37. Ferenc Morton Szasz, *The Divided Mind of Protestant America, 1800–1930* (Birmingham: Univ. of Alabama Press, 1982), p. 40.

38. David Einhorn Hirsch, *Rabbi Emil G. Hirsch, the Reform Advocate* (Chicago: Whitehall Co., 1968), p. 71; Emil G. Hirsch, "The Philosophy of the Reform Movement in American Judaism," *Central Conference of American Rabbis Yearbook* 5 (1895): 95, 103.

39. Claude G. Montefiore, "Some Notes on the Effect of Biblical Criticism upon the Jewish Religion," *The Jewish Quarterly Review* 4 (January 1892): 296.

40. Abbott, *Life and Literature of the Ancient Hebrews*, p. 163; Naomi W. Cohen, "The Challenges of Darwinism and Biblical Criticism to American Judaism," *Modern Judaism* 4 (May 1984): 132–33, 139, 141.

41. Jonathan D. Sarna and Nahum M. Sarna, "Jewish Bible Scholarship and Translations in the United States," in *The Bible and Bibles in America*, ed. Ernest S. Frerichs (Atlanta: Scholars Press, 1988), p. 84.

42. Montefiore, "Biblical Criticism," p. 293.

43. Isaac M. Wise, quoted in James G. Heller, *Isaac M. Wise: His Life, Work and Thought* (Cincinnati: The Union of American Hebrew Congregations, 1965), p. 531.

12. Defending the Evangelical Tradition, 1880–1915

1. Timothy P. Weber, *Living in the Shadow of the Second Coming: American Premillennialism, 1875–1925* (New York: Oxford Univ. Press, 1979), pp. 36–37.

2. Bernard A. Weisberger, *They Gathered at the River: The Story of the Great Revivalists and Their Impact Upon Religion in America* (1958; Chicago: Quadrangle Books,

1966), pp. 160–68; Paul A. Carter, *The Spiritual Crisis of the Gilded Age* (DeKalb, Ill.: Northern Illinois Univ. Press, 1971), p. 213.

3. Carter, *Spiritual Crisis of the Gilded Age*, pp. 17–20, 22–23.

4. Ibid., pp. 32–33; 35–36.

5. Ibid., pp. 105, 127.

6. William G. McGoughlin, Jr., *Modern Revivalism: Charles Grandison Finney to Billy Graham* (New York: Ronald Press, 1959), pp. 257–58.

7. For biographical information I have relied upon James F. Findley, Jr., *Dwight L. Moody: American Evangelist, 1837–1899* (Chicago: Univ. of Chicago Press, 1969).

8. Dwight L. Moody, quoted in David Rausch, *Zionism Within Early American Fundamentalism, 1878–1914* (Lewiston, N.Y.: Edwin Mellen Press, 1979), p. 155.

9. Rausch, *Zionism Within Early American Fundamentalism*, p. 193.

10. For these figures I am indebted to Morton Rosenstock, *Louis Marshall, Defender of Jewish Rights* (Detroit: Wayne State Univ. Press, 1965), pp. 11–12, 15.

11. See, for example, Richard Wheatley, "The Jews in New York," *The Century Magazine* 63 (January 1892): 323–42, 512–32; the best study of American xenophobia is still John Higham's *Strangers in the Land: Patterns of American Nativism, 1860–1925* (New Brunswick: Rutgers Univ. Press, 1955).

12. Henry Adams to Charles Miles Gaskell, July 31, 1896, *Letters of Henry Adams, 1892–1918*, ed. Worthington Chauncey Ford (Boston: Houghton Mifflin, 1938), p. 111; Arnold A. Rogow, ed., *The Jew in a Gentile World* (New York: Macmillan, 1961), pp. 292–93.

13. See Michael N. Dobkowski, *The Tarnished Dream: The Basis of American Anti-Semitism* (Westport, Conn.: Greenwood Press, 1979).

14. Madison C. Peters, *Justice to the Jew* (New York: McLure Co., 1908), p. 237; for biographical information, see "Madison Clinton Peters," *Dictionary of American Biography* (New York: Charles Scribner's Sons, 1934), 1:507–8.

15. Peters, *Justice to the Jew*, pp. 238–41.

16. See Higham, *Strangers in the Land*; Barbara Miller Solomon, *Ancestors and Immigrants* (Cambridge, Mass.: Harvard Univ. Press, 1956).

17. Julius Weinberg, "Edward A. Ross," *The McGraw-Hill Encyclopedia of World Biography* (New York: McGraw-Hill, 1973), 9:282–83; Edward Alsworth Ross, *The Old World in the New: The Significance of Past and Present Immigration to the American People* (New York: Century Co., 1914), pp. 143–44.

18. Ross, *Old World in the New*, pp. 152–54.

19. In this connection see E. Digby Baltzell, *The Protestant Establishment: Aristocracy and Caste in America* (New York: Random House, 1964), pp. 96–98, 105–8.

20. Josiah Strong, *Our Country: Its Possible Future and Its Present Crisis* (New York: Baker and Taylor, 1885), pp. 30, 42, 128–29; Josiah Strong, *Our World: The New World Life* (Garden City, N.Y.: Doubleday, Page, 1914), pp. 169, 174–75, 264–67, 282.

21. Strong, *Our Country*, p. 160.

22. Daniel Dorchester, "The City as a Peril," in *National Perils and Opportunities: General Christian Conference Held in Washington, D.C., December 7, 8, 9, 1887* (New York: Baker and Taylor, 1887), pp. 19–20.

23. Ibid., p. 22.

24. Simon J. McPherson, "The City as a Peril," in *National Perils and Opportunities,* pp. 38, 34.

25. Dorchester, "The City as a Peril," p. 28.

26. H. H. Boyesen, "Immigration," in *National Perils and Opportunities,* p. 55.

27. J. F. Hurst, "Estrangement of the Masses from the Church," in *National Perils and Opportunities,* p. 105.

28. Howard B. Gross, *Aliens or Americans?* (New York: Eaton and Mains, 1906), p. 240.

29. Ozora S. Davis, "The Church and the Immigrant," in *Federal Council of the Churches of Christ in America: Report of the First Meeting,* ed. Elias B. Sanford (New York: Revell Press, 1909), p. 255.

30. Gross, *Aliens or Americans?* pp. 270–71, 297.

31. David Max Eichhorn, *Evangelizing the American Jew* (Middle Village, N. Y.: Jonathan David Publishers, 1978), pp. 141, 147–48, 151, 165–66.

32. A. E. Thompson, *A Century of Jewish Missions* (Chicago: Fleming H. Revell Company, 1902), pp. 77–78.

33. Arno Clemens Gaebelein, *Half a Century: The Autobiography of a Servant* (New York: Publication Office "Our Hope," 1930), p. 21.

34. Ibid., p. 52.

35. Jeffrey S. Gurock, "Jacob A. Riis: Christian Friend or Missionary Foe? Two Jewish Views," *AJH* 71 (September 1981): 41.

36. James M. King, "The Christian Resources of Our Country," *National Perils and Opportunities,* p. 261.

37. Ibid., p. 265.

38. Philip Schaff, *Church and State in the United States* (1888; New York: Arno Press, 1972), pp. 53, 55.

39. David J. Brewer, *The United States: A Christian Nation* (Philadelphia: John C. Winston Company, 1905), p. 12.

40. King, "Christian Resources," pp. 266–67.

41. Schaff, *Church and State,* p. 75.

42. Joseph R. Brandon, "Opposition to Religious Exercises in the Public Schools," in *Jewish Education in the United States: A Documentary History,* ed. Lloyd P. Gartner, Classics in Education Series, no. 41 (New York: Teachers College Press, 1969), p. 92; Nina Morais, "Jewish Ostracism in America," *The North American Review* 133 (September 1881): 270.

43. Morais, "Jewish Ostracism," p. 269.

13. Liberalism and the Genesis of Political Zionism

1. Yonathan Shapiro, *Leadership of the American Zionist Organization* (Urbana: Univ. of Illinois Press, 1971), pp. 24–25.

2. Richard Gottheil, "The Aims of Zionism," in *The Zionist Idea: A Historical Analysis and Reader,* ed. Arthur Hertzberg (Cleveland: World Publishing Company, and Philadelphia: The Jewish Publication Society of America, 1964), p. 499.

3. Shapiro, *Leadership of the American Zionist Movement,* pp. 37, 39–44, 47.

4. E. Digby Baltzell, *The Protestant Establishment: Aristocracy and Caste in America* (New York: Random House, 1964), pp. 187–94; Shapiro, *Leadership of the American*

Zionist Organization, pp. 62–64, 69; Allon Gal, "Brandeis, Judaism, and Zionism," in *Brandeis and America,* ed. Nelson L. Dawson (Lexington: Univ. Press of Kentucky, 1989), pp. 65–98.

5. Melvin I. Urofsky, *American Zionism from Herzl to the Holocaust* (Garden City, N.Y.: Anchor Books, 1976), pp. 113–18.

6. Louis D. Brandeis, quoted in Urofsky, *American Zionism,* pp. 117–18, Brandeis's emphasis; see also Louis D. Brandeis, "The Jewish Problem and How to Solve It," in *The Zionist Idea,* ed. Hertzberg, pp. 519–20.

7. Shapiro, *Leadership of the American Zionist Organization,* p. 71.

8. Robert T. Handy, ed., *The Holy Land in American Protestant Life, 1800–1948: A Documentary History* (New York: Arno Press, 1981), pp. 48–50.

9. Ibid., p. 71.

10. A. A. Berle, *The World Significance of a Jewish State* (New York: Mitchell Kennerley, 1918), pp. 7, 12.

11. Ibid., pp. 15–16, 24, 27–28, 30.

12. Ibid., pp. 35–36, 39.

13. Ibid., pp. 46–47.

14. John Haynes Holmes, *Palestine To-Day and To-Morrow: A Gentile's Survey of Zionism* (1929; reprint, New York: Arno Press, 1977), pp. 87–88; see also John Haynes Holmes, *I Speak For Myself* (New York: Harper and Brothers, 1959), pp. 130–34; Carl Hermann Voss, *Rabbi and Minister: The Friendship of Stephen S. Wise and John Haynes Holmes* (Cleveland: World Publishing Company, 1964), pp. 55–56.

15. Holmes, *Palestine To-Day and To-Morrow,* p. 89.

16. Ibid., p. 90.

17. Ibid., p. 94.

18. Ibid., pp. 113, 120–21.

19. Ibid., p. 132.

20. Voss, *Rabbi and Minister,* p. 256.

21. For an excellent discussion of Dispensationalist views of Zionism, see David A. Rausch, "Protofundamentalism's Attitudes Toward Zionism, 1878–1918," *Jewish Social Studies* 43 (Spring 1981): 137–52; see also David A. Rausch, *Zionism Within Early American Fundamentalism, 1878–1914* (Lewiston, N.Y.: Edwin Mellen Press, 1979), pp. 223–24.

22. A. E. Thompson, *A Century of Jewish Missions* (Chicago: Fleming H. Revell Company, 1902), p. 57.

23. Handy, *The Holy Land,* pp. 201–2.

24. Arno C. Gaebelein, quoted in David A. Rausch, "Arno C. Gaebelein (1861–1945): Fundamentalist Protestant Zionist," *AJH* 68 (September 1978): 45; see also Yona Malachy, *American Fundamentalism and Israel* (Jerusalem: Hebrew Univ. of Jerusalem, 1978), p. 133.

25. Handy, *The Holy Land,* p. 181.

26. William E. Blackstone, "May the United States Intercede for the Jews?" in *Christian Protagonists for Jewish Restoration* (New York: Arno Press, 1977), pp. 15–23.

27. "Memorial Presented to President Harrison, March 5th, 1891," in *Christian Protagonists for Jewish Restoration,* pp. 1–14.

28. Malachy, *American Fundamentalism and Israel,* p. 139; Timothy P. Weber, *Living*

in the Shadow of the Second Coming: American Premillennialism, 1875–1925 (New York: Oxford Univ. Press, 1979), p. 140.

29. Weber, *Living in the Shadow*, pp. 129–30, 136; see also, Eldin Ricks, "Zionism and the Mormon Church," *Herzl Year Book* 5 (1963): 163–66, 168.

30. Thompson, *Century of Jewish Missions*, p. 57.

31. Malachy, *American Fundamentalism and Israel*, pp. 141–42.

32. Stuart E. Knee, "The King-Crane Commission of 1919: The Articulation of Political Anti-Zionism," *AJA* 29 (April 1977): 24–33; quotations from Urofsky, *American Zionism*, p. 217.

33. John Dewey, "The Principle of Nationality," *The Menorah Journal* 3 (1917): 208.

34. Quotations from Morton Rosenstock, *Louis Marshall, Defender of Jewish Rights* (Detroit: Wayne State Univ. Press, 1965), pp. 43–44; see also Herbert Parzen, "The Lodge-Fish Resolution," *AJHQ* 60 (September 1970): 77.

35. Thorstein Veblen, *Essays in Our Changing Order*, ed. Leon Ardzrooni (New York: Viking Press, 1934), pp. 225–26.

36. Ibid., pp. 230–31.

37. Philip Marshall Brown, "Zionism and Anti-Semitism," *The North American Review* 210 (November 1919): 657–58; for biographical information see *Who Was Who in America* (Chicago: Marquis Who's Who, 1968), 4:126.

38. Brown, "Zionism and Anti-Semitism," p. 661.

39. Holmes, *Palestine To-Day and To-Morrow*, p. 167.

40. Ibid., p. 257.

41. Ibid., p. 270.

42. Robert Moats Miller, *Harry Emerson Fosdick: Preacher, Pastor, Prophet* (New York: Oxford Univ. Press, 1985), pp. 10, 73, 80–81, 412–15.

43. Harry Emerson Fosdick, *A Pilgrimage to Palestine* (Chautauqua, N.Y.: Chautauqua Press, 1928), p. 272.

44. Miller, *Harry Emerson Fosdick*, pp. 184–87.

45. Fosdick, *Pilgrimage to Palestine*, pp. 278, 281–85.

46. Ibid., p. 286.

47. Ibid., p. 293.

48. David Polish, "The Changing and the Constant," *AJA* 35 (November 1981): 273–74.

49. Louis Marshall to David Philipson, September 5, 1918, in *Louis Marshall, Champion of Liberty: Selected Papers and Addresses*, ed. Charles Reznikoff (Philadelphia: The Jewish Publication Society of America, 1957), 2:720.

50. Louis Marshall to Simon Wolf, March 4, 1919, in *Louis Marshall*, ed. Reznikoff, 2: 723.

51. David Philipson, *My Life as an American Jew* (Cincinnati: John C. Kidd and Son, 1941), pp. 305; see also Parzen, "The Lodge-Fish Resolution," 76–77.

14. The Triumphant Twenties

1. For an excellent discussion of this topic see John Higham, *Strangers in the Land: Patterns of American Nativism, 1860–1925* (New Brunswick: Rutgers Univ. Press, 1955), pp. 247–49.

2. John Higham, *Send These to Me: Jews and Other Immigrants in Urban America* (New York: Atheneum, 1975), p. 187; Morton Rosenstock, *Louis Marshall, Defender of Jewish Rights* (Detroit: Wayne State Univ. Press, 1965), pp. 99, 281.

3. Rosenstock, *Louis Marshall*, pp. 111–14; E. Digby Baltzell, *The Protestant Establishment: Aristocracy and Caste in America* (New York: Random House, 1964), p. 204; see also Higham, *Strangers in the Land*, p. 179.

4. Higham, *Strangers in the Land*, pp. 322–24.

5. Quotation from Rosenstock, *Louis Marshall*, p. 217; see also Higham, *Strangers in the Land*, pp. 171–72.

6. For a biographical sketch of Burton J. Hendrick, see *Dictionary of American Biography* (New York: Charles Scribner's Sons, 1974), Supplement 4, 1946–50, pp. 367–68.

7. Burton J. Hendrick, *The Jews of America* (Garden City, N.Y.: Doubleday, Page, 1923), pp. 96–98, 104, 140–41.

8. Ibid., p. 171.

9. Kenneth L. Roberts, *Why Europe Leaves Home* (1922; New York: Arno Books, 1977), p. 15; for biographical information about Roberts, see *Dictionary of American Biography* (New York: Charles Scribner's Sons, 1980), Supplement 6, 1956–60), pp. 545–46.

10. Roberts, *Why Europe Leaves Home*, pp. 48–49, 52.

11. Cyrus Adler, *I Have Considered the Days* (Philadelphia: The Jewish Publication Society of America, 1941), p. 329; Higham, *Strangers in the Land*, p. 280.

12. Louis Marshall to George Haven Putnam, October 28, 1920, in *Louis Marshall, Champion of Liberty: Selected Papers and Addresses*, ed. Charles Reznikoff (Philadelphia: The Jewish Publication Society of America, 1957), 1: 338.

13. Louis Marshall to George Haven Putnam, October 13, 1920, in *Louis Marshall*, ed. Reznikoff, 1: 338–39.

14. For a review of the *Dearborn Independent's* anti-Jewish rhetoric, see Rosenstock, *Louis Marshall*, 1: 282–84; see also Higham, *Strangers in the Land*, pp. 282–84.

15. Rosenstock, *Louis Marshall*, 1: 146–47.

16. Louis Marshall to Henry Ford, June 3, 1920, in *Louis Marshall*, ed. Reznikoff, 1: 329.

17. Statement by Henry Ford to Louis Marshall, in *Louis Marshall*, ed. Reznikoff, 1: 378–79; Rosenstock, *Louis Marshall*, pp. 188, 190.

18. David Philipson, *My Life as an American Jew: An Autobiography* (Cincinnati: John G. Kidd and Son, 1941), p. 330.

19. Ernest R. Sandeen, "Toward a Historical Interpretation of the Origins of Fundamentalism," *Church History* 36 (March 1967): 77, 83.

20. See for example the essays by Henry H. Beach, "Decadence of Evolution," and George Frederick Wright, "The Passing of Evolution," in *The Fundamentals: A Testimony to the Truth*, ed. R. A. Torrey et al. (1917; reprint, Grand Rapids, Mich.: Baker Book House, 1970), 1:59–71, 72–87.

21. Robert H. Ayers, *Judaism and Christianity: Origins, Developments and Recent Trends* (Lanham, Md.: Univ. Press of America, 1983), pp. 412–13; Ferenc Morton

Szasz, *The Divided Mind of Protestant America, 1800–1930* (Birmingham: Univ. of Alabama Press, 1982), pp. 92–95, 137.

22. William R. Hutchison, *The Modernist Impulse in American Protestantism* (Cambridge, Mass.: Harvard Univ. Press, 1976), p. 258.

23. Canon Dyson Hague, "The History of the Higher Criticism," in *The Fundamentals*, ed. Torrey et al., 2:9–12; Arno C. Gaebelein, "Fulfilled Prophecy, A Potent Argument for the Bible," in ibid., 2:12–143.

24. See, for example, C. I. Scofield, "The Grace of God," in *The Fundamentals*, ed. Torrey et al., 3:98–109; James M. Gray, "The Inspiration of the Bible—Definition, Extent and Proof," in ibid., 2:9–43; Daniel Hoffman Martin, "Why Save the Lord's Day," in ibid., 4:199–211; David Rausch, *Zionism Within Early American Fundamentalism, 1878–1914* (Lewiston, N.Y.: Edwin Mellen Press, 1979), pp. 289–91, 233.

25. Hutchison, *The Modernist Impulse*, pp. 274–75.

26. H. Richard Niebuhr, *The Social Sources of Denominationalism* (1929; reprint, Cleveland: World Publishing Company, 1957), p. 7.

27. Ibid., p. 11.

28. Ibid., p. 280.

29. Shailer Mathews, *New Faith for Old: An Autobiography* (New York: Macmillan, 1936), pp. 183–87.

30. Ibid., pp. 188–89.

31. Higham, *Strangers in the Land*, pp. 290–96; Everett R. Clinchy, *All in the Name of God* (New York: John Day Company, 1934), pp. 99–100, 103; David M. Chalmers, *Hooded Americanism: The First Century of the Ku Klux Klan, 1865–1965* (Garden City, N.Y.: Doubleday, 1965), pp. 110, 245.

32. John Moffatt Mecklin, *The Ku Klux Klan: A Study of the American Mind* (New York: Russell and Russell, 1963), pp. 20, 110; Clinchy, *All in the Name of God*, pp. 102, 106.

33. Edward Y. Clarke, quoted in Rosenstock, *Louis Marshall*, p. 203.

34. Quoted in Clinchy, *All in the Name of God*, p. 105.

35. Wyn Craig Wade, *The Fiery Cross: The Ku Klux Klan in America* (New York: Simon and Schuster, 1987), pp. 169–72, 175, 178; Chalmers, *Hooded Americanism*, pp. 245–49.

36. Wade, *The Fiery Cross*, pp. 169–73, 175–78; Chalmers, *Hooded Americanism*, pp. 245–49.

37. Wade, *The Fiery Cross*, p. 185.

38. Robert Moats Miller, "A Note on the Relationship Between the Protestant Churches and the Revived Ku Klux Klan," *Journal of Southern History* 22 (August 1956): 356–58, 364–65.

39. Clinchy, *All in the Name of God*, pp. 105–106.

40. Quoted in John A. Hutchison, *We Are Not Divided: A Critical and Historical Study of the Federal Council of the Churches of Christ in America* (New York: Round Table Press, 1941), p. 42–44.

41. Ibid., p. 138; Lance J. Sussman, "'Toward Better Understanding': The Rise of the Interfaith Movement in America and the Role of Rabbi Isaac Landman," *AJA* 34 (April 1982): 45.

42. Benny Kraut, "Towards the Establishment of the National Conference of Christians and Jews: The Tenuous Road to Religious Goodwill in the 1920s," *AJH* 77 (March 1988): 394–96.

43. Ibid., pp. 404–9; Clinchy, *All in the Name of God*, pp. 118–22; Sussman, "Better Understanding," pp. 40–42, 47.

44. Clinchy, *All in the Name of God*, pp. 1, 118–22; Kraut, "National Conference of Christians and Jews," pp. 404–9; quotation from Philipson, *My Life as an American Jew*, p. 417.

45. Clinchy, *All in the Name of God*, pp. 121, 172–73,

46. Ibid., pp. 143, 145, 179.

47. George F. Moore, quoted in Samuel Sandmel, *We Jews and Jesus* (New York: Oxford Univ. Press, 1965), pp. 115–16.

48. George Foot Moore, "Christian Writers on Judaism," *Harvard Theological Review* 14 (July 1921): 197.

49. Ibid., pp. 198, 213–14, 221, 230.

50. Ibid., pp. 239–40.

51. George Foot Moore, "Intermediaries in Jewish Theology, Memra, Shekina, Matatron," *Harvard Theological Review* 15 (July 1922): 41.

52. Although acknowledging its seminal importance, Jacob Neusner also offers a provocative critique of this work; see his "'Judaism' After Moore: A Programmatic Statement," *Journal of Jewish Studies* 31 (1980): 141–56.

53. George Foot Moore, *Judaism in the First Centuries of the Christian Era* (1930; reprint, New York: Schocken Books, 1971), 1: ii–viii, 3, 39.

54. Ibid., pp. 110–11.

55. Ibid., pp. 128–29.

56. Ibid., pp. 263, 479, 483.

57. Ibid., p. 60.

58. Sandmel, *We Jews and Jesus*, pp. 100–101.

15. Hear No Evil, See No Evil

1. H. Shelton Smith, Robert T. Handy, and Lefferts A. Loetscher, *American Christianity: An Historical Interpretation With Representative Documents* (New York: Charles Scribner's Sons, 1960–63), 2:424; William E. Nawyn, *American Protestantism's Response to Germany's Jews and Refugees, 1933–1941* (Ann Arbor: UMI Research Press, 1982), p. 32.

2. See below for Reinhold Niebuhr's theology of neo-orthodoxy; see also Robert H. Ayers, *Judaism and Christianity: Origins, Developments and Recent Trends* (Lanham, Md.: Univ. Press of America, 1983), pp. 422–41.

3. Nawyn, *Protestantism's Response*, pp. 29–31; Smith, Handy, and Loetscher, *American Christianity*, 2:422.

4. Smith, Handy, and Loetscher, *American Christianity*, p. 26.

5. Henry Feingold, *Zion in America* (New York: Hippocrene Books, 1974), p. 274; Lucy S. Dawidowicz, *On Equal Terms: Jews in America, 1881–1981* (New York: Holt, Rinehart and Winston, 1982), p. 106.

6. Dawidowicz, *On Equal Terms*, pp. 66–68.

7. "Report of the Secretary of the Anti-Defamation League, 1935," in *Jews and Judaism in the United States: A Documentary History*, ed. Marc Lee Raphael (New York: Behrman House, 1983), p. 140; Naomi W. Cohen, *Not Free to Desist: The American Jewish Committee, 1906–1966* (Philadelphia: The Jewish Publication Society of America, 1972), pp. 200–202, 205–7.

8. For a biographical sketch of Basil Mathews, see *Who Was Who in America* (Chicago: A. N. Marquis Company, 1966), 3:562.

9. Basil Mathews, *The Jew and the World Ferment* (New York: Friendship Press, 1935), p. 80.

10. William Ernest Hocking, *Living Religions and a World Faith* (New York: Macmillan, 1940), pp. 262–69.

11. Raymond Kennedy, "The Position and Future of the Jews in America," in *Jews in a Gentile World: The Problem of Anti-Semitism*, ed. Isacque Graeber and Steuart Henderson Britt (New York: Macmillan, 1942), pp. 427–28.

12. Jessie Bernard, "Biculturality: A Study in Social Schizophrenia," in *Jews in a Gentile World*, ed. Graeber and Britt, p. 293.

13. J. O. Hertzler, "The Sociology of Anti-Semitism Through History," in *Jews in a Gentile World*, ed. Graeber and Britt, pp. 67–68.

14. Ibid., pp. 70–74.

15. Ibid., pp. 98–99.

16. Ellis Freeman, "The Motivation of Jew-Gentile Relationships," in *Jews in a Gentile World*, ed. Graeber and Britt, pp. 173–74.

17. J. F. Brown, "The Origin of the Anti-Semitic Attitude," in *Jews in a Gentile World*, ed. Graeber and Britt, pp. 134, 142, 146.

18. Richard Breitman and Alan M. Kraut, *American Refugee Policy and European Jewry, 1933–1945* (Bloomington: Indiana Univ. Press, 1987), p. 3.

19. Henry L. Feingold, *The Politics of Rescue: The Roosevelt Administration and the Holocaust, 1938–1945* (New Brunswick: Rutgers Univ. Press, 1970), pp. 17–18, 21; David S. Wyman, *The Abandonment of the Jews: America and the Holocaust, 1941–1945* (New York: Pantheon Books, 1984), pp. 312–13.

20. Edward S. Shapiro, "The Approach of War: Congressional Isolationism and Anti-Semitism, 1939–1941," *AJH* 74 (September 1984): 64–65; Deborah E. Lipstadt, *Beyond Belief: The American Press and the Coming of the Holocaust, 1933–1945* (New York: Free Press, 1986), pp. 92, 97, 108–11.

21. Lipstadt, *Beyond Belief*, pp. 121, 125, 128.

22. Breitman and Kraut, *American Refugee Policy*, pp. 226, 229.

23. Nawyn, *Protestantism's Response*, p. 183.

24. Ibid., pp. 86–87.

25. Ibid., pp. 185–86, 191, 193–95.

26. John C. Mager, "Nazis, Jews, and the War: What the *Lutheran Witness* Said, 1934–1945," *American Lutheran* 47 (November 1964): 11.

27. Nawyn, *Protestantism's Response*, pp. 95–97, 103–5.

28. Leo P. Ribuffo, *The Old Christian Right: The Protestant Far Right from the Great Depression to the Cold War* (Philadelphia: Temple Univ. Press, 1983), pp. 80–90, 110–11, 117.

29. Ibid., pp. 128–35, 146–47, 154–57, 167–73.

30. Conrad Hoffmann, Jr., "Hitler and the Jews—A Christian View," *Missionary Review of the World* 58 (July 1935): 332; Conrad Hoffmann, Jr., "Jewry in Distress! What of It?" *Missionary Review of the World* 61 (June 1938): 262.

31. Robert W. Ross, *So It Was True: The American Protestant Press and the Nazi Persecution of the Jews* (Minneapolis: Univ. of Minnesota Press, 1980), p. 101; William R. Glass, "Fundamentalism's Prophetic Vision of the Jews: The 1930s," *Jewish Social Studies* 47 (Winter 1985): 63–67, 70–71.

32. Glass, "Fundamentalism's Prophetic Vision," p. 68.

33. Ross, *So It Was True*, p. 133; Nawyn, *Protestantism's Response*, pp. 156–58.

34. Stephen Wise, *Challenging Years: The Autobiography of Stephen Wise* (New York: G. P. Putnam's Sons, 1949), p. 295.

35. John Haynes Holmes, *Through Gentile Eyes: A Plea for Tolerance and Good Will* (New York: Jewish Opinion Publishing Corporation, 1938), pp. 65, 67.

36. Ibid., pp. 70–73.

37. Ibid., p. 74.

38. Robert Moats Miller, *Harry Emerson Fosdick: Preacher, Pastor, Prophet* (New York: Oxford Univ. Press, 1985), pp. 195–96, 491, 507–9, 516–17; Moshe R. Gottlieb, *American Anti-Nazi Resistance, 1933–1941* (New York: KTAV Publishing House, Inc., 1982), pp. 347–48.

39. For Niebuhr's early disillusionment with liberal Christianity, see his *Moral Man and Immoral Society: A Study of Ethics and Politics* (New York: Charles Scribner's Sons, 1932), p. 79; Reinhold Niebuhr, "Ten Years That Shook My World," *Christian Century* 56 (April 26, 1939): 542–46; Egal Feldman, "Reinhold Niebuhr and the Jews," *Jewish Social Studies* 46 (Summer–Fall 1984): 293.

40. Milton Steinberg, "The Outlook of Reinhold Niebuhr—A Description and Appraisal," *The Reconstructionist* 11 (December 14, 1945), 11; Levi Olan, "Reinhold Niebuhr and the Hebraic Spirit: A Critical Inquiry," *Judaism* 5 (Spring 1956): 122.

41. Emil L. Fackenheim, "Judaism, Christianity and Reinhold Niebuhr: A Reply to Levi Olan," *Judaism* (Fall 1956): 319; Abraham J. Heschel, "A Hebrew Evaluation of Reinhold Niebuhr," in *Reinhold Niebuhr: His Religious, Social, and Political Thought*, ed. Charles W. Kegley and Robert W. Bretall (New York: Macmillan, 1956), pp. 392–93.

42. Niebuhr, *Moral Man*, pp. xi, 75, 256; Reinhold Niebuhr, "Moralists in Politics," *The Christian Century* 49 (July 6, 1932): 857.

43. Reinhold Niebuhr, *An Interpretation of Christian Ethics* (New York: Harper and Brothers, 1935), p. 156; Reinhold Niebuhr, "Christian Radicalism," *Radical Religion* 5 (Winter 1936): 8.

44. Feldman, "Reinhold Niebuhr and the Jews," p. 294.

45. Reinhold Niebuhr, "Christian Pledge to Boycott Nazi Germans," *Radical Religion* 4 (Spring 1939): 13.

46. Reinhold Niebuhr, "Religion and the New Germany," *The Christian Century* 50 (June 28, 1933): 844–45; Reinhold Niebuhr, "The Churches in Germany," *The American Scholar* 3 (Summer 1934): 348.

47. Reinhold Niebuhr, *Leaves from the Notebook of a Tamed Cynic* (New York: Richard R. Smith, 1930), p. 96; Reinhold Niebuhr, "Pacifism and the Use of Force," in *Love and Justice: Selections from the Shorter Writings of Reinhold Niebuhr*, ed. D. B. Robertson (Philadelphia: Westminster Press, 1959), pp. 249–50; Reinhold Niebuhr,

"Why I Leave the F.O.R.," *The Christian Century* 51 (January 3, 1934): 18–19; for Fosdick's pacifism, see Miller, *Harry Emerson Fosdick*, pp. 330–31, 491, 506–9, 516–17.

48. Reinhold Niebuhr, "Pacifism Against the Wall," in *Love and Justice*, ed. Robertson, pp. 260–61; Reinhold Niebuhr, *Beyond Tragedy: Essays on the Christian Interpretation of History* (1937; New York: Charles Scribner's Sons, 1948), p. 181; Reinhold Niebuhr, "Must Democracy Use Force?" *The Nation* 148 (January 28, 1939): 117–18; Reinhold Niebuhr, *Christianity and Power Politics*, (1940; New York: Archon Books, 1969), pp. 16–17, 28, 33–34.

49. Reinhold Niebuhr, "An End to Illusion," *The Nation* 150 (June 29, 1940): 779; Reinhold Niebuhr, "The Christian Faith and the World Crisis," *Christianity and Crisis* 1 (June 16, 1940): 2–3, 5.

50. Wyman, *Abandonment of the Jews*, p. 61; Lipstadt, *Beyond Belief*, pp. 154–58, 164–65.

51. Lipstadt, *Beyond Belief*, pp. 240–41, 250–51.

52. In this connection see Lucy S. Dawidowicz, *The War Against the Jews* (New York: Holt, Rinehart and Winston; Philadelphia: The Jewish Publication Society of America, 1975).

53. Feingold, *Politics of Rescue*, pp. 304–5; Wyman, *Abandonment of the Jews*, pp. 321–23, 326–27.

54. Ross, *So It Was True*, pp. 169–71.

55. Quotation from Hertzel Fishman, *American Protestantism and a Jewish State* (Detroit: Wayne State Univ. Press, 1973), p. 54; Ross, *So It Was True*, pp. 174–75.

56. Quoted in Ross, *So It Was True*, p. 199; see also Lipstadt, *Beyond Belief*, pp. 185, 233.

57. Peter W. Ludlow, "The International Protestant Community in the Second World War," *Journal of Ecclesiastical History* 29 (July 1978): 314, 357.

58. Breitman and Kraut, *American Refugee Policy*, pp. 244, 247–49; Wyman, *Abandonment of the Jews*, pp. 62, 339; Feingold, *Politics of Rescue*, p. 307; Robert Michael, "America and the Holocaust," *Midstream* 21 (February 1985): 15–16.

59. Leonard Dinnerstein, *America and the Survivors of the Holocaust* (New York: Columbia Univ. Press, 1982), pp. 13, 46–49.

60. Ibid., pp. 137–38, 174, 181, 263.

61. Ibid., pp. 197, 217, 263–65.

62. Quoted in Ross, *So It Was True*, p. 236.

63. David M. Chalmers, *Hooded Americanism: The First Century of the Ku Klux Klan, 1865–1965* (Garden City, N.Y.: Doubleday, 1965), pp. 345–46, 351–52; Ralph Lord Roy, *Apostles of Discord: A Study of Organized Bigotry and Disruption on the Fringes of Protestantism* (Boston: Beacon Press, 1953), pp. 26–33.

64. Roy, *Apostles of Discord*, pp. 39–41.

65. Ibid., p. 46–47.

66. Ibid., pp. 53–56.

67. Leo P. Ribuffo, *The Old Christian Right: The Protestant Far Right from the Great Depression to the Cold War* (Philadelphia: Temple Univ. Press, 1983), p. 234.

68. Roy, *Apostles of Discord*, pp. 59, 63, 65, 72.

69. Lewis Sperry Chafer, "The Jew: A World Issue," *Bibliotheca Sacra* 102 (April 1945): 129–30.

16. Toward a New Relationship

1. American Jewish Committee, *The Eichmann Case in the American Press* (New York: Institute of Human Relations Press, 1962), pp. 45, 67, 84.

2. Ibid., p. 86.

3. Louis Auster, "Jules Marx Isaac: An Unsung Hero," *Midstream* 30 (February 1984): 30–31.

4. Franklin H. Littell, "Bernhard E. Olson (1910–1975)," *Journal of Ecumenical Studies* 12 (Fall 1975, special issue), pp. 582–83.

5. Bernhard E. Olson, "Christian Education and the Image of the Pharisees," *Religious Education* (November-December 1960): 410.

6. Bernhard E. Olson, *Faith and Prejudice: Intergroup Problems in Protestant Curricula* (New Haven: Yale Univ. Press, 1963), pp. 94, 99, 265, 267.

7. Ibid., p. 149.

8. Charles Y. Glock and Rodney Stark, *Christian Beliefs and Anti-Semitism* (New York: Harper Torchbooks, 1966), p. 207.

9. Ibid., p. 208.

10. Ibid., p. 212.

11. Gerald S. Strober, *Portrait of the Elder Brother: Jews and Judaism in Protestant Teaching Materials* (New York: The American Jewish Committee, National Conference of Christians and Jews, 1972), p. 12.

12. Robert McAfee Brown, *The Ecumenical Revolution: An Interpretation of the Catholic-Protestant Dialogue* (Garden City, N.Y.: Doubleday, 1967), pp. 262–64; George A. Lindbeck, "The Jews, Renewal and Ecumenism, *Journal of Ecumenical Studies* 2 (Fall 1965): 471–73.

13. Brown, *The Ecumenical Revolution*, p. 248, Brown's emphasis.

14. Ibid., p. 249.

15. Franklin H. Littell, *The Church and the Body Politic* (New York: Seabury Press, 1969), p. 70.

16. Leonard Swidler, "Jews and Christians in Dialogue," *Journal of Ecumenical Studies* 12 (Fall 1975, special issue): 581–82.

17. Belden Menkus, *Meet the American Jew* (Nashville, Tenn.: Broadman Press, 1963).

18. LaVonne Althouse, *When Jew and Christian Meet* (New York: Friendship Press, 1966), p. 13.

19. Paul D. Opshal and Marc H. Tannenbaum, "Some Observations and Guidelines for Conversations Between Lutherans and Jews," in *Speaking of God Today: Jews and Lutherans in Conversations*, eds. Paul Opshal and Marc H. Tannenbaum (Philadelphia: Fortress Press, 1974), pp. 163–64.

20. "The American Lutheran Church and the Jewish Community," in *Luther, Lutherans and the Jewish People* (New York: American Lutheran Church, 1977), p. 24 (pamphlet).

21. Ibid., pp. 25–27.

22. Gerhard D. Forde, "Luther and the Jews: A Review and Some Preliminary Reflections," in *Luther, Lutherans and the Jewish People*, pp. 6–20.

23. Ibid., pp. 11–14; see also "Luther, Lutheranism and the Jews," *Christian Jewish Relations* 16 (September 1983): 18–21.

24. "Documentation and Reflection: A Jewish-Christian Dialogue," *Anglican Theological Review* 56 (October 1974): 441–62; "Ecumenical Events," *Journal of Ecumenical Studies* 16 (Fall 1979): 826–27; "Ecumenical Events," *Journal of Ecumenical Studies* 17 (Summer 1980): 569–70, 760–62; "Ecumenical Events," *Journal of Ecumenical Studies* 22 (Fall 1985, special issue): 638; "Ecumenical Events," *Journal of Ecumenical Studies* 23 (Spring 1986): 342–43; *The Jewish Week*, May 20, 1988.

25. Walter Jacob, *Christianity Through Jewish Eyes: The Quest for Common Ground* (Cincinnati: Hebrew Union College Press, 1974), pp. 7, 14, 228.

26. Abraham Joshua Heschel, *The Insecurity of Freedom* (Philadelphia: The Jewish Publication Society of America, 1966), p. 181; see also, Abraham Joshua Heschel, "No Religion Is an Island," in *Disputations and Dialogue: Readings in the Jewish-Christian Encounter*, Frank E. Talmage (New York: KTAV Publishing House, and Anti-Defamation League of B'nai B'rith), pp. 343–59; for biographical information see Pamela S. Nadell, *Conservative Judaism in America: A Biographical Dictionary and Sourcebook* (New York: Greenwood Press, 1988), pp. 138–41.

27. Richard L. Rubenstein, *After Auschwitz: Radical Theology and Contemporary Judaism* (Indianapolis: Bobbs-Merrill, 1966), p. 75; biographical information is found in *Contemporary Authors* 17, new rev. ser. (Detroit: Gale Research, 1986), pp. 391–96.

28. Rubenstein, *After Auschwitz*, p. 80.

29. Irving Greenberg, "Judaism and Christianity after the Holocaust," *Journal of Ecumenical Studies* 12 (Fall 1975, special issue), 521–22, 525.

30. Ibid., pp. 527, 529

31. Ibid., p. 544.

32. Bernard Heller, "The Judeo-Christian Tradition Concept: Aid or Deterrent to Goodwill?" *Judaism* 2 (August 1953): 138.

33. Ibid., pp. 136–37.

34. Arthur A. Cohen, *The Myth of the Judeo-Christian Tradition* (New York: Schocken Books, 1971), pp. 51–52.

35. Ibid., pp. 211, 215–17, 221–22.

36. Ibid., p. 222.

37. Samuel Sandmel, *We Jews and Jesus* (New York: Oxford Univ. Press, 1965), p. 110.

38. Ibid., p. 151.

39. Jacob Neusner, *American Judaism: Adventure in Modernity* (Englewood Cliffs, N.J.: Prentice-Hall, 1972), p. 68.

40. Michael Goldberg, "Bonnhoeffer and the Limits of Jewish-Christian Dialogue," *Books and Religion* 14 (March 1986): 3–4; Nora Levin, "A Jewish View of Dialogue," *Christian Jewish Relations* 17 (June 1984): 37.

41. Howard Singer, "The Rise and Fall of Interfaith Dialogue," *Commentary* 83 (May 1987): 52–53, 55.

42. Eliezer Berkowitz, quoted in Brown, *The Ecumenical Revolution*, p. 252.

43. Joseph B. Soloveitchik, "Confrontations," *Tradition: A Journal of Orthodox Jewish Thought* 6 (Summer 1964): 15, 24–25.

44. David Novak, "A Jewish Defense of Dialogue," *This World* 24 (Spring 1989): 20, 25, 34–35, 36.

45. Ibid., pp. 35–36.

46. Franklin H. Littell, *The Crucifixion of the Jews* (New York: Harper and Row, 1975), p. 17.

47. Franklin H. Littell, "Recent Jewish History: Lessons for Christians," *Gratz College Annual of Jewish Studies* 1 (1972): 114.

48. Littell, *Crucifixion of the Jews*, pp. 28, 32, 110.

49. Ibid., pp. 47–49.

50. Ibid., pp. 112, 114.

51. Franklin H. Littell, "Christendom, Holocaust and Israel: The Importance for Christians of Recent Major Events in Jewish History," *Journal of Ecumenical Studies* 10 (Summer 1973): 483–87.

52. Franklin H. Littell, "Have Jews and Christians a Common Future?" *Journal of Church and State* 13 (Spring 1971): 314–15; Littell, *Crucifixion of the Jews*, p. 131.

53. Littell, *Crucifixion of the Jews*, pp. 88–89; Franklin H. Littell, "Why a Christian Authority Opposes Missionaries," *The Jewish Week*, April 8, 1983, p. 17.

54. Littell, "Recent Jewish History," p. 108; Franklin H. Littell, "*Kirchenkampf and Holocaust:* The German Church Struggle and Nazi Anti-Semitism in Retrospect," *Journal of Church and State* 13 (Spring 1971): 214, 216, 219.

55. Paul M. Van Buren, *The Burden of Freedom: Americans and the God of Israel* (New York: Seabury Press, 1976), pp. 4–7.

56. Ibid., pp. 65–66.

57. Paul M. Van Buren, *Discerning the Way: A Theology of the Jewish Christian Reality* (New York: Seabury Press, 1980), pp. 48, 134; Paul M. Van Buren, "The Jewish People in Christian Theology: Present and Future," in *The Jewish People in Christian Preaching,* ed. Darrell J. Fasching, Symposium Series, vol. 10 (New York: Edwin Mellen Press, 1984), p. 19; Paul M. Van Buren, "Affirmation of the Jewish People: A Condition of Theological Coherence," *Journal of the American Academy of Religion* 45 (Supplement, September 1977): 1082.

58. Van Buren, *Discerning the Way*, p. 69.

59. Van Buren, "Affirmation of the Jewish People," p. 1088.

60. Van Buren, *Burden of Freedom*, p. 80.

61. See, for example, Van Buren, "The Jewish People in Christian Theology," p. 33.

62. Egal Feldman, "American Protestant Theologians on the Frontiers of Jewish-Christian Relations," in *Anti-Semitism in American History,* ed. David A. Gerber (Urbana: Univ. of Illinois Press, 1986), p. 373, 383n.

63. A. Roy Eckardt, *Your People, My People: The Meeting of Jews and Christians* (New York: New York Times Book Company, 1974), p. 79; A. Roy Eckardt, "Can There Be a Jewish-Christian Relationship?" *The Journal of Bible and Religion* 33 (April 1965): 122.

64. A Roy Eckardt, *Christianity and the Children of Israel* (New York: King's Crown Press, 1948), pp. 43–45, 50–56; A. Roy Eckardt, "Theological Approaches to Anti-Semitism," *Jewish Social Studies* 33 (October 1971): 275–77, 283; Eckardt, *Your People, My People*, p. 80.

65. Eckardt, "Theological Approaches to Anti-Semitism," p. 282; Eckardt, *Your People, My People*, p. 38; Eckardt, *Christianity and the Children of Israel*, pp. 1–2; A. Roy Eckardt, *Elder and Younger Brothers: The Encounter of Jews and Christians* (New York: Charles Scribner's Sons, 1967), pp. 116–19.

66. Eckardt, "Can There be a Jewish-Christian Relationship?" pp. 123–24; Eckardt, *Your People, My People,* pp. 42–45.

67. A. Roy Eckardt, "Jurgen Moltmann, the Jewish People, and the Holocaust," *Journal of the American Academy of Religion* 44 (December 1976): 681; Eckardt, "Can There Be a Jewish-Christian Relationship?" p. 127; A. Roy Eckardt and Alice L. Eckardt, *Long Night's Journey into Day: Life and Faith after the Holocaust* (Detroit: Wayne State Univ. Press, 1982), p. 128.

68. A. Roy Eckardt, "Contemporary Christian Theology and a Protestant Witness for the Shoah," *Shoah: A Review of Holocaust Studies and Commemorations* 2 (Spring 1980): 11; Eckardt, *Jews and Christians,* p. 73; Eckardt, *Elder and Younger Brother,* pp. 141, 152–53; A. Roy Eckardt, "Christian Responses to the *Endlösung,*" *Religion in Life* 48 (Spring 1978): 39.

69. A. Roy Eckardt, *Jews and Christians: The Contemporary Meeting* (Bloomington: Indiana Univ. Press, 1986), p. 30.

70. Feldman, "American Protestant Theologians," p. 174; Eckardt, *Jews and Christians,* p. 65.

71. A. Roy Eckardt, "The Recantation of the Covenant?" in *Confronting the Holocaust: The Impact of Elie Wiesel,* ed., Alvin H. Rosenfeld and Irving Greenberg (Bloomington: Indiana Univ. Press, 1978), pp. 102–4; Eckardt, *Long Night's Journey,* pp. 99–104.

72. Eckardt, "Christian Responses to the *Endlösung,*" pp. 34–35; A. Roy Eckardt, "Christians and Jews: Along a Theological Frontier," *Encounter* 40 (Spring 1979): 92; Eckardt, *Long Night's Journey,* pp. 17, 23.

73. Eckardt, "Christians and Jews," p. 95; Eckardt, "Contemporary Christian Theology," pp. 12–13.

74. Eckardt, *Long Night's Journey,* pp. 28–39; Eckardt, "Christian Responses to the *Endlösung,*" pp. 34, 41.

75. Eckardt, *Christianity and the Children of Israel,* p. 46; Eckardt, *Elder and Younger Brothers,* pp. 105, 160, 242; Eckardt, "Christians and Jews," p. 96.

76. Eckardt, *Long Night's Journey,* p. 122.

17. Jewish Sovereignty and the Protestant Right

1. Doreen Bierbrier, "The American Zionist Emergency Council: An Analysis of a Pressure Group," *AJHQ* 60 (September 1970): 91.

2. Carl Hermann Voss, "The American Christian Palestine Committee," in *Essays in American Zionism, 1917–1948: The Herzl Year Book,* ed. Melvin I. Urofsky (1975; New York: Herzl Press, 1978), 8:242–45; Yona Malachy, "Christian Zionism," *Encyclopedia Judaica* (Jerusalem: Keter Publishing House, 1971), 16:1155.

3. Harry A. Atkinson, "'The Jewish Problem' is a Christian Problem," in *The Holy Land in American Protestant Life, 1800–1948,* ed. Robert T. Handy (New York: Arno Press, 1981), 228.

4. Voss, "American Christian Palestine Committee," pp. 259–60; Bierbrier, "American Zionist Emergency Council," pp. 104–5.

5. Egal Feldman, "Reinhold Niebuhr and the Jews," *Jewish Social Studies* 46 (Summer–Fall 1984): 293; Reinhold Niebuhr, "Jews after the War, pt. 1," *The Nation* 154, (February 21, 1942): 214.

6. Niebuhr, "Jews after the War," p. 214.

7. Ibid., p. 215.

8. Ibid., p. 216; Reinhold Niebuhr, "Jews after the War, pt. 2," *The Nation* 154 (February 28, 1942): 253.

9. Reinhold Niebuhr, "Toward a Program for Jews, pt. 1," "Survival and Religion," *Contemporary Jewish Record* 7 (June 1944): 241.

10. Reinhold Niebuhr, *The Structure of Nations and Empires* (New York: Charles Scribner's Sons, 1959), pp. 161–62; see also Reinhold Niebuhr, *Discerning the Signs of the Times* (New York: Charles Scribner's Sons, 1946), pp. 75–76; Reinhold Niebuhr, "Christians and the State of Israel," *Christianity and Crisis* 14 (Summer 1949): 3–4.

11. Niebuhr, "Jews after the War, pt. 1," p. 216; "Jews after the War, pt. 2," p. 253.

12. Reinhold Niebuhr, "Our Stake in the State of Israel," *The New Republic* 136 (February 4, 1957): 10; Feldman, "Reinhold Niebuhr and the Jews," p. 301n.40.

13. Feldman, "Reinhold Niebuhr and the Jews," p. 297; Reinhold Niebuhr, "Mideast Impasse: Is There a Way Out?" *The New Leader* 39 (June 4, 1956): 10.

14. Reinhold Niebuhr, "Editorial Notes," *Christianity and Crisis* 16 (April 2, 1956): 34; Reinhold Niebuhr, "New Hope for Peace in the Middle East," *Christianity and Crisis* 16 (May 28, 1956): 65–66.

15. Reinhold Niebuhr, "The U.N. Is Not a World Government," *The Reporter* 16 (March 7, 1957): 32; Reinhold Niebuhr, "The Moral World of Foster Dulles," *The New Republic* 139 (December 1, 1958): 6.

16. Reinhold Niebuhr, "David and Goliath," *Christianity and Crisis* 27 (June 26, 1967): 141; see also A. Roy Eckardt, *Your People, My People: The Meeting of Jews and Christians* (New York: New York Times Book Company, 1974), p. 206.

17. Franklin H. Littell, "Christendom, Holocaust and Israel: The Importance for Christians of Recent Major Events in Jewish History," *Journal of Ecumenical Studies* 10 (Summer 1973): 496–97.

18. Franklin H. Littell, *The Crucifixion of the Jews* (New York: Harper and Row, 1975), pp. 94–95, 97, Littell's emphasis.

19. Franklin H. Littell, "Politics, Theology and the Jews," *Journal of Ecumenical Studies* 2 (Fall 1965): 476.

20. Ibid., p. 477.

21. Franklin H. Littell, "Recent Jewish History: Lessons for Christians," *Gratz College Annual of Jewish Studies* 1 (1972): 111–12; Franklin H. Littell, "Christian Congress for Israel," *Near East Report* 25 (November 20, 1981): 213.

22. Grace Halsell, *Prophecy and Politics: Militant Evangelists on the Road to Nuclear War* (Westport, Conn.: Lawrence Hill and Company, 1986), p. 179.

23. Littell, "Christian Congress for Israel," p. 213.

24. A. Roy Eckardt, *Jews and Christians: The Contemporary Meeting* (Bloomington: Indiana Univ. Press, 1986), p. 79.

25. A. Roy Eckardt, "Eretz Israel: A Christian Affirmation," *Midstream* 14 (March 1968): 12; A. Roy Eckardt, "Toward an Authentic Jewish-Christian Relationship," *Journal of Church and State* 13 (Spring 1971): 271.

26. A. Roy Eckardt and Alice L. Eckardt, "Silence in the Churches," *Midstream* 13 (October 1967): 28; Eckardt, "Eretz Israel," p. 11; A. Roy Eckardt and Alice Eckardt, *Encounter with Israel: A Challenge to Conscience* (New York: Association Press, 1970), p.

261; A. Roy Eckardt, "The Fantasy of Reconciliation in the Middle East," *The Christian Century* 88 (October 13, 1971): 1202; see also A. Roy Eckardt, "Is There a Way out of the Christian Crime? The Philosophical Question of the Holocaust," *Holocaust and Genocide Studies* 1 (1986): 126.

27. Eckardt, *Encounter with Israel,* p. 231.

28. Ibid., pp. 200–202, 219–22, Eckardt's emphasis; A. Roy Eckardt, "The Fantasy of Reconciliation," p. 1199; A. Roy Eckardt, "The Devil and Yom Kippur," *Midstream* 20 (August-September 1974): 69.

29. Eckardt, "Eretz Israel," p. 10, Eckardt, *Encounter with Israel,* pp. 184, 205.

30. A. Roy Eckardt, quoted in Feldman, "American Protestant Theologians on the Frontiers of Jewish-Christian Relations," in *Anti-Semitism in American History,* ed. David A. Gerber (Urbana: Univ. of Illinois Press, 1986), p. 177.

31. Eckardt, "Silence in the Churches," pp. 28, 32; A. Roy Eckardt, "The Protestant View of Israel," *Encyclopedia Judaica Year Book, 1974* (Jerusalem: Keter Publishing House, 1974), p. 162; Eckardt, "The Devil and Yom Kippur," pp. 67–68, 71, 73–74.

32. A. Roy Eckardt, "Christian Perspectives on Israel," *Midstream* 18 (October 1972): 40–41; A. Roy Eckardt, "The Nemesis of Christian Antisemitism," *Journal of Church and State* 13 (Spring 1971): 239.

33. Eckardt, "Nemesis of Christian Antisemitism," p. 237; A. Roy Eckardt and Alice Eckardt, *Long Night's Journey into Day: Life and Faith after the Holocaust* (Detroit: Wayne State Univ. Press, 1982), p. 106; Eckardt, "Christian Perspectives on Israel," pp. 44–45.

34. A. Roy Eckardt and Alice Eckardt, "The Achievements and Trials of Interfaith," *Judaism* 27 (Summer 1978): 320; see also A. Roy Eckardt, "Toward a Secular Theology of Israel," *Religion in Life* 68 (Winter 1979): 462, 466.

35. Eckardt, *Jews and Christians,* pp. 79–80, Eckardt's emphasis.

36. Eckardt, "Toward a Secular Theology of Israel," p. 467.

37. Joel A. Carpenter, "From Fundamentalism to the New Evangelical Right," in *Evangelicalism and Modern America,* ed. George Marsden (Grand Rapids, Mich.: William B. Eerdmans, 1984), pp. 3–8, 15; Richard V. Pierard, "The New Religious Right in American Politics," in ibid., pp. 163–65.

38. Peggy L. Shriver, *The Bible Vote: Religion and the New Right* (New York: Pilgrim Press, 1981), pp. 34–35; Robert Booth Fowler, *A New Engagement: Evangelical Political Thought, 1966–1970* (Grand Rapids, Mich.: William B. Eerdmans, 1982), pp. 2–4, 7–13; Timothy P. Weber, *Living in the Shadow of the Second Coming: American Premillennialism, 1875–1925* (New York: Oxford Univ. Press, 1979), pp. 177–80.

39. R. Laurence Moore, *Religious Outsiders and the Making of Americans* (New York: Oxford Univ. Press, 1986), pp. 157–68.

40. John F. Walvoord, "The Fulfillment of the Abrahamic Covenant," *Bibliotheca Sacra* 102 (January 1945): 27, 32–34; William R. Glass, "Fundamentalism's Prophetic Vision of the Jews: The 1930s," *Jewish Social Studies* 47 (Winter 1985): 65.

41. *New York Times,* February 6, 1983, p. 8.

42. "Fundamentalists and Jews: an Exchange," *Midstream* 29 (November 1983): 49.

43. *New York Times,* February 6, 1983, p. 19.

44. Gabriel Fackre, *The Religious Right and Christian Faith* (Grand Rapids, Mich.:

William B. Eerdmans, 1982), pp. 1–2; Merrill Simon, *Jerry Falwell and the Jews* (Middle Village, N.Y.: Jonathan David Publishers, 1984), pp. xii–xiii.

45. Fowler, *A New Engagement*, p. 245.

46. Jerry Falwell, *Strength for the Journey: An Autobiography* (New York: Simon and Schuster, 1987), pp. 7, 35, 66–67, 80–82; Simon, *Jerry Falwell*, pp. 4–6.

47. Falwell, *Strength for the Journey*, pp. 137, 150–51, 159–60, 190–95, 370–71; John Neuhaus, "What the Fundamentalists Want," *Commentary* 79 (May 1985): 46.

48. Fackre, *The Religious Right*, pp. 11, 25–26, 36–37.

49. Falwell, *Strength for the Journey*, pp. 375–76; Lawrence J. Epstein, *Zion's Call: Christian Contributions to the Origins and Development of Israel* (Lanham, Md.: Univ. Press of America, 1984), p. 131; Simon, *Jerry Falwell*, pp. 9, 13, 18, 25–26.

50. Simon, *Jerry Falwell*, p. 37.

51. Joshua O. Haberman, "Falwell Reconsidered," *Reform Judaism* 15 (Fall 1986): 8–9.

52. Simon, *Jerry Falwell*, pp. 56, 63.

53. Ibid., pp. 87–88.

54. Ibid., pp. 77–80; Arthur Kutcher, "The Battle for Jerusalem's Character," *Reform Judaism* 14 (Spring 1986): 2.

55. Hertzel Fishman, *American Protestantism and a Jewish State* (Detroit: Wayne State Univ. Press, 1973), pp. 30–38; 61–63; Philip Scharper, "Israel the Modern State and Contemporary Christian Points of View," *Lutheran Quarterly* 20 (1968): 255–57.

56. Fishman, *Protestantism and a Jewish State*, p. 84; Robert T. Handy, ed., *The Holy Land in American Protestant Life, 1800–1948: A Documentary History* (New York: Arno Press, 1981), pp. 230–37; see also Kermit Roosevelt, "The Partition of Palestine: A Lesson in Pressure Politics," *The Middle East Journal* 2 (January 1948): 1–16.

57. Carl Hermann Voss and David A. Rausch, "American Christians and Israel, 1948–1988," *American Jewish Archives* 40 (April 1988): 48–49.

58. Ibid., pp. 51–52.

59. Fishman, *Protestantism and a Jewish State*, pp. 129, 136–39.

60. Harry Emerson Fosdick, *The Living of These Days: An Autobiography* (New York: Harper and Brothers, 1956), p. 186.

61. Harry E. Fosdick, quoted in Robert Moats Miller, *Harry Emerson Fosdick: Preacher, Pastor, Prophet* (New York: Oxford Univ. Press, 1985), p. 90.

62. Ibid., p. 191.

63. Fishman, *Protestantism and a Jewish State*, p. 141.

64. William Ernest Hocking, "Faith and World Order," in *The Church and the New World Mind: The Drake Lectures for 1944* (Freeport, N.Y.: Books for Libraries Press, 1944), p. 39.

65. Voss and Rausch, "American Christians and Israel," pp. 56–58.

66. Halsell, *Prophecy and Politics*, pp. 3, 147, 159, 252–54.

67. Ibid., p. 111.

68. Bryce J. Christensen, "Mormons and Jews," *Midstream* 32 (January 1986): 8; *The Jewish Week*, January 11, 1985, April 4, 1986.

69. Jacob Neusner, quoted in Moshe Dann, "The Mormon Church, Israel, and the Arabs," *Midstream* 33 (May 1987): 11.

70. Jakob J. Petuchowski, "A Jewish Response to 'Israel as a Theological Problem in the Christian Church,'" *Journal of Ecumenical Studies* 6 (Summer 1969): 348, 352.

71. Jack R. Fischel, "The Fundamentalists' Perception of Jews," *Midstream* 28 (December 1982): 30–31.

72. Sol Stern, "The Falwell Fallacy: The Limits of Fundamentalist Support for Israel," *Reform Judaism* (Winter 1984): 6.

73. *The Jewish Week*, July 29, August 12, 1988; Steven G. Kellman, "'The Last Temptation of Christ': Blaming the Jews," *Midstream* 34 (December 1988): 33.

74. Gershon Greenberg, "Fundamentalists, Israel and Theological Openness," *Christian Jewish Relations* 19 (September 1986): 32.

18. Disparate Encounters

1. Mordecai M. Kaplan, *Judaism as a Civilization: Towards a Reconstruction of American-Jewish Life* (Philadelphia: The Jewish Publication Society of America, 1981), pp. 173–85.

2. Milton R. Konvitz, *Judaism and the American Idea* (Ithaca, N.Y.: Cornell Univ. Press, 1978), pp. 53, 123, 139.

3. The persistence of Protestant theocrats in pressing for this principle is evidenced by a resolution passed by the Arizona Republican party at its annual state convention in January 1988. It declared the United States to be a Christian nation and called for a "government based on Scripture" and "our Lord Jesus Christ" (*Jewish Week*, February 10, 1989, p. 4).

4. *Extremism on the Right: A Handbook* (New York: Anti-Defamation League of B'nai B'rith, 1988), p. 26.

5. Ibid., p. 38.

6. Ibid., p. 21; Ronald H. Bayor, "Klans, Coughlinites and Aryan Nations: Patterns of American Anti-Semitism in the Twentieth Century," *AJH* 76 (December 1986): 192.

7. *Extremism on the Right*, p. 6.

8. Ibid., pp. 10–11.

Selected Bibliography

The following list represents the sources that I have found most helpful in writing this book. For additional listings the reader should consult the notes.

Articles

Abbott, Lyman. "The Debt of Modern Civilization to Judaism." *The Outlook* 98 (August 5, 1911): 774–77.

———. "The Growth of Religious Tolerance in the United States." *The Forum* 23 (July 1897): 653–60.

———. "Lessons from the Parliament of Religion." *Christian Thought* 11 (August 1893–July 1894): 220–23.

Abrams, Jeanne. "Remembering the Maine: The Jewish Attitude Toward the Spanish-American War as Reflected in *The American Hebrew.*" *American Jewish History* 76 (June 1987): 439–55.

"Address by Ex-President Grover Cleveland." *Publications of American Jewish Historical Society* 14 (1906): 11–17.

"Address by President Eliot of Harvard University." *Publications of American Jewish Historical Society* 14 (1906): 78–83.

Alpert, Rebeca Trachtenberg. "Jewish Participation at the World's Parliament of Religions, 1893." In *Jewish Civilization: Essays and Studies*, edited by Ronald A. Brauner, vol. 1, pp. 111–21. Philadelphia: Reconstructionist Rabbinical College, 1979.

"The American Lutheran Church and the Jewish Community." In *Luther, Lutherans and the Jewish People*, pp. 24–30. New York: American Lutheran Church, 1977.

"Anti-Jewish Sentiment in California, 1855." *American Jewish Archives* 12 (April 1960): 15–33.

Armerding, Carl Edwin. "The Meaning of Israel in Evangelical Thought." In *Evangelicals and Jews in Conversation on Scripture, Theology and History*, edited by Marc H. Tannenbaum, Marvin R. Wilson, and A. James Rudin, pp. 119–140. Grand Rapids, Mich.: Baker Book House, 1978.

Auster, Louis. "Jules Marx Isaac: An Unsung Hero." *Midstream* 30 (February 1984): 30–32.

"Authentic Report of the Proceedings of the Rabbinical Conference Held at Pittsburgh, November 16, 17, 18, 1885." In *The Changing World of Reform Judaism: The Pittsburgh*

Platform in Retrospect, edited by Walter Jacob, pp. 91–123. Pittsburgh: Rodef Shalom Congregation, 1985.

Barrows, John Henry. "Results of the Parliament of Religions." *The Forum* 18 (September 1894): 54–67.

———. "The World's First Parliament of Religions." *The Homiletic Review* 25 (May 1893): 387–95.

Bayor, Ronald H. "Klans, Coughlinites and Aryan Nations: Patterns of American Anti-Semitism in the Twentieth Century." *American Jewish History* 76 (December 1986): 181–96.

Berg, J. Van Den. "Eschatological Expectations Concerning the Conversion of the Jews in the Netherlands During the Seventeenth Century." In *Puritans, The Millennium and the Future of Israel: Puritan Eschatology 1600–1660,* edited by Peter Toon, pp. 137–53. Cambridge: James Clarke and Co., 1970.

Berlin, George L. "Solomon Jackson's *The Jew:* An Early American Jewish Response to the Missionaries." *American Jewish Archives* 71 (September 1981): 10–28.

Bernard, Jessie. "Biculturality: A Study in Social Schizophrenia." In *Jews in a Gentile World,* edited by Isacque Araelson and Stewart Henderson Britt, pp. 264–93. New York: Macmillan, 1942.

Bierbrier, Doreen. "The American Zionist Emergency Council: An Analysis of a Pressure Group." *American Jewish Historical Quarterly* 60 (September 1970): 82–105.

Bishop, Ronald. "Religious Confrontation, A Case Study: The 1893 Parliament of Religions." *Numen: International Review for the History of Religions* 16 (April 1969): 63–76.

Blackstone, William E. "May the United States Intercede for the Jews?" in *Christian Protagonists for Jewish Restoration,* pp. 15–23. New York: Arno Press, 1977.

Boller, Paul F., Jr. "George Washington and Religious Liberty." *William and Mary Quarterly* 17 (1960): 486–506.

Boyesen, H. H. "Immigration." In *National Perils and Opportunities: General Christian Conference Held in Washington, D.C., December 7, 8, 9, 1887,* pp. 52–74. New York: Baker and Taylor, 1887.

Brecker, Frank W. "Woodrow Wilson and the Origins of the Arab-Israeli Conflict." *American Jewish Archives* 39 (April 1987): 23–47.

Brown, Philip Marshall. "Zionism and Anti-Semitism." *The North American Review* 210 (November 1919): 656–62.

Brown, Robert McAfee. "The Holocaust: The Crisis of Indifference." *Conservative Judaism* 31 (Fall–Winter 1976–77): 17–20.

Burrell, David James. "How a More Kindly Relation Between Jews and Christians May Be Furthered." *The American Citizen* 1 (December 1912): 281–83, 285.

Butler, Jon. "Enthusiasm Described and Decreed: The Great Awakening as Interpretive Fiction." *The Journal of American History* 69 (September 1982): 305–25.

Chafer, Lewis Sperry. "The Jew: A World Issue." *Bibliotheca Sacra* 102 (April 1945): 129–30.

Chiel, Arthur A. "Ezra Stiles—The Education of an 'Hebrician.'" *American Jewish Historical Quarterly* 60 (March 1971): 235–41.

———. "Ezra Stiles and the Jews: A Study in Ambivalence." In *A Bicentennial Festschrift for Jacob Rader Marcus,* edited by Bertram W. Korn, pp. 63–76. Waltham,

Mass.: American Jewish Historical Society; New York: KTAV Publishing House, 1976.

————. "Ezra Stiles' Rabbi Tobiah." *American Jewish Historical Quarterly* 59 (December 1969): 228–29.

————. "The Rabbis and Ezra Stiles." *American Jewish Historical Quarterly* 61 (June 1972): 294–312.

Christensen, Bryce J. "Mormons and Jews." *Midstream* 32 (January 1986): 8–11.

Clifford, Clark M. "Factors Influencing President Truman's Decision to Support Partition and Recognize the State of Israel." In *The Palestine Question in American History,* by Clark M. Clifford et al., pp. 24–45. New York: Arno Press, 1978.

Cohen, Naomi W. "The Challenges of Darwinism and Biblical Criticism to American Judaism." *Modern Judaism* 4 (May 1984): 121–57.

————. "Pioneers of American Jewish Defense." *American Jewish Archives* 29 (November 1977): 116–50.

Crane, Elaine F. "Uneasy Coexistence: Religious Tensions in Eighteenth Century Newport." *Newport History* 53 (Summer 1980): 101–11.

Dana, Henry Wadsworth Longfellow. "Emma Lazarus and the New England Poets." *The Menorah Journal* 39 (Spring 1951): 32–42.

Dann, Moshe. "The Mormon Church, Israel, and the Arab." *Midstream* 33 (May 1987): 10–11.

Davis, Moshe. "The Holy Land Idea in American Spiritual History." In *With Eyes Toward Zion,* edited by Moshe Davis, pp. 3–33. New York: Arno Press, 1977.

Dorchester, Daniel. "The City as a Peril." In *National Perils and Opportunities: General Christian Conference Held in Washington, D.C., December 7, 8, 9, 1887,* pp. 19–37. New York: Baker and Taylor, 1887.

Eckardt, A. Roy. "Anti-Israelism, Anti-Semitism and the Quakers." *Christianity and Crisis* 31 (September 20, 1971): 180–86.

————. "Can There Be a Jewish Christian Relationship?" *The Journal of Bible and Religion* 33 (April 1965): 122–30.

————. "Christian Perspectives on Israel." *Midstream* 18 (October 1972): 40–50.

————. "Christians and Jews: Along a Theological Frontier." *Encounter* 40 (Spring 1979): 89–127.

————. "Contemporary Christian Theology and a Protestant Witness for the Shoah." *Shoah: A Review of Holocaust Studies and Commemorations* 2 (Spring 1980): 10–13.

————. "The Devil and Yom Kippur." *Midstream* 20 (August-September 1974): 67–75.

————. "Eretz Israel: A Christian Affirmation." *Midstream* 14 (March 1968): 9–12.

————. "The Fantasy of Reconciliation in the Middle East." *The Christian Century* 88 (October 13, 1971): 1198–202.

————. "Jurgen Moltmann, the Jewish People, and the Holocaust." *Journal of the American Academy of Religion* 44 (December 1976): 675–91.

————. "The Mystery of the Jews' Rejection of Christ." *Theology Today* 18 (April 1961): 51–59.

————. "The Nemesis of Christian Antisemitism." *Journal of Church and State* 13 (Spring 1971): 227–44.

————. "The Protestant View of Israel." *Encyclopedia Judaica Year Book,* 1974, pp. 158–66. Jerusalem: Keter Publishing House, 1974.

————. "The Recantation of the Covenant?" In *Confronting the Holocaust: The Impact of Elie Wiesel,* edited by Alvin H. Rosenfeld and Irving Greenberg, pp. 159–68. Bloomington: Indiana Univ. Press, 1978.

————. "Theological Approaches to Anti-Semitism," *Jewish Social Studies* 33 (October 1971): 272–84.

————. "Toward an Authentic Jewish-Christian Relationship." *Journal of Church and State* 13 (Spring 1971): 271–83.

————. "Toward a Secular Theology of Israel." *Religion in Life* 48 (Winter 1979): 462–73.

Eckardt, A. Roy, and Alice L. Eckardt. "The Achievements and Trials of Interfaith." *Judaism* 27 (Summer 1978): 318–23.

————. "Again, Silence in the Churches." *The Christian Century* 84 (August 2, 1987): 992–95.

————. "Silence in the Churches." *Midstream* 13 (October 1967): 27–32.

Eckardt, Alice L. "The Holocaust: Christian and Jewish Responses." *Journal of the American Academy of Religion* 42 (1974): 453–59.

————. "Yom Ha-Shoah Commandments: A Christian Declaration." *Midstream* 27 (April 1981): 37–41.

Eitches, Edward. "Maryland's 'Jew Bill.'" *American Jewish Historical Quarterly* 60 (March 1971): 258–78.

Elazar, Daniel J. "The Development of the American Synagogue." *Modern Judaism* 4 (October 1984): 266–68.

Everett, Robert Andrew. "Judaism in Nineteenth-Century American Transcendentalist and Liberal Protestant Thought." *Journal of Ecumenical Studies* 20 (Summer 1983): 396–413.

Fackenheim, Emil L. "Judaism, Christianity, and Reinhold Niebuhr: A Reply to Levi Olan." *Judaism* 5 (Fall 1956): 316–24.

Fein, Isaac M. *"Niles' Weekly Register* on the Jews." *Publications of the American Jewish Historical Society* 50 (September 1960): 3–22.

Feinstein, Marvin. "The Blackstone Memorial." *Midstream* 7 (June 1968): 76–89.

Feldman, Egal. "American Ecumenism: Chicago's World's Parliament of Religions of 1893." A *Journal of Church and State* 9 (Spring 1967): 180–99.

————. "American Protestant Theologians on the Frontiers of Jewish-Christian Relations." In *Anti-Semitism in American History,* edited by David A. Gerber, pp. 363–85. Urbana: Univ. of Illinois Press, 1986.

————. "Reinhold Niebuhr and the Jews." *Jewish Social Studies* 46 (Summer–Fall 1984): 293.

————. "The Social Gospel and the Jews." *American Jewish Historical Quarterly* 58 (March 1969): 308–22.

Fels, Tony. "Religious Assimilation: Jews and Freemasonry in Gilded-Age San Francisco." *American Jewish History* 74 (June 1985): 369–403.

Fielding, Howard Ioan. "John Adams: Puritan, Deist, Humanist." *Journal of Religion* 20 (January 1940): 33–46.

Fingerhut, Eugene R. "Were the Massachusetts Puritans Hebraic?" *New England Quarterly* 40 (December 1967): 521–31.

Fischel, Jack R. "The Fundamentalists' Perception of Jews." *Midstream* 28 (December 1982): 30–31.

Forde, Gerhard D. "Luther and the Jews: A Review and Some Preliminary Reflections." In *Luther, Lutherans and the Jewish People*, pp. 6–20. New York: American Lutheran Church, 1977.

Fox, Frank. "Quaker, Shaker, Rabbi: Warder Cresson, the Story of a Philadelphia Mystic." *The Pennsylvania Magazine of History and Biography* 95 (April 1971): 147–94.

Freeman, Ellis. "The Motivation of Jew-Gentile Relationships." In *Jews in a Gentile World*, edited by Isacque Graeber and Steuart Henderson Britt, pp. 149–78. New York: Macmillan, 1982.

Friedenberg, Albert M. "The Jews and the American Sunday Laws." *Publications of the American Jewish Historical Society* 11 (1903): 101–15.

Friedenwald, Herbert. "A Letter of Jonas Phillips to the Federal Convention." *Publications of the American Jewish Historical Society* 2 (1894): 107–10.

Friedman, Lee M. "Cotton Mather and the Jews." *Publications of the American Jewish Historical Society* 26 (1918): 201–10.

———. "Judah Monis, First Instructor in Hebrew at Harvard University." *Publication of the American Jewish Historical Society* 22 (1914): 1–24.

Gal, Allon. "Brandeis, Judaism, and Zionism." In *Brandeis and America*, edited by Nelson L. Dawson, pp. 65–98. Lexington: Univ. Press of Kentucky, 1989.

Gartner, Lloyd P. "Temples of Liberty Unpolluted: American Jews and Public Schools, 1840–1875." In *A Bicentennial Festschrift for Jacob Rader Marcus*, edited by Bertram W. Korn, pp. 157–89. Waltham, Mass.: American Jewish Historical Society; New York: KTAV Publishing House, 1976.

Glass, William R. "Fundamentalism's Prophetic Vision of the Jews: The 1930s." *Jewish Social Studies* 47 (Winter 1985): 63–76.

Goen, C. C. "Jonathan Edwards: A New Departure in Eschatology." *Church History* 28 (March 1959): 25–40.

Goldblatt, Charles Israel. "The Impact of the Balfour Declaration in America." *American Jewish Historical Quarterly* 57 (June 1968): 455–515.

Gottheil, Gustav. "The Position of the Jews in America." *The North American Review* 127 (July-August 1878): 81–96.

Greenberg, Gershon. "Fundamentalists, Israel and Theological Openness." *Christian Jewish Relations* 19 (September 1986): 27–33.

Greenberg, Irving. "Judaism and Christianity after the Holocaust." *Journal of Ecumenical Studies* 12 (Fall 1975, special issue): 521–51.

Griesman, B. Eugene. "Philo-Semitism and Protestant Fundamentalism: The Unlikely Zionists." *Phylon* 37 (Fall 1976): 197–211.

Gruenewald, Max. "Benjamin Franklin's 'Parable on Brotherly Love.'" *Publications of the American Jewish Historical Society* 37 (1947): 147–52.

Gurock, Jeffrey S. "From Exception to Role Model: Bernard Drachman and the Evolution of the Jewish Religious Life in America, 1880–1920." *American Jewish History* 76 (June 1986): 468–69.

————. "Jacob A. Riis: Christian Friend or Missionary Foe? Two Jewish Views." *American Jewish History* 71 (September 1981): 20–47.

Guttman, Alexander. "Ezra Stiles, Newport Jewry, and a Question of Jewish Law." *American Jewish Archives* 34 (April 1982): 98–102.

Haberman, Joshua O. "Falwell Reconsidered." *Reform Judaism* 15 (Fall 1986): 8–9.

Haberman, Joshua O., et al. "Fundamentalism and Jews." *Midstream* 29 (November 1983): 45–50.

Handy, Robert T. "The Protestant Quest for a Christian America, 1830–1930." *Church History* 22 (March 1953): 8–20.

————. "Sources for Understanding American Christian Attitudes Toward the Holy Land, 1800–1950." In *With Eyes Toward Zion*, edited by Moshe Davis, pp. 34–56. New York: Arno Press, 1977.

Hatch, Nathan O. "Sola Scriptura and Novus Ordo Seclorum." In *The Bible in America*, edited by Nathan O. Hatch and Mark A. Noll, pp. 59–78. New York: Oxford Univ. Press, 1982.

Hay, Robert P. "George Washington: American Moses." *American Quarterly* 21 (Winter 1967): 780–91.

Healey, Robert M. "Jefferson on Judaism and the Jews: 'Divided We Stand, United, We Fall!'" *American Jewish History* 73 (June 1984): 359–74.

Heller, Bernard. "The Judeo-Christian Tradition Concept: Aid or Deterrent to Goodwill?" *Judaism* 2 (August 1953): 133–39.

Heschel, Abraham J. "A Hebrew Evaluation of Reinhold Niebuhr." In *Reinhold Niebuhr: His Religious, Social, and Political Thought*, edited by Charles W. Kegley and Robert W. Bretall, pp. 391–410. New York: Macmillan, 1956.

Hirsch, Emil G. "Elements of Universal Religion." In *The World's Parliament of Religions*, edited by John H. Barrows, pp. 1306–7. Chicago: Parliament Publishing Co., 1893.

————. "The Philosophy of the Reform Movement in American Judaism." *Central Conference of American Rabbis Yearbook* 5 (1895): 90–112.

Hocking, William Ernest. "Faith and World Order." In *The Church and the New World Mind: The Drake Lectures for 1944*, pp. 13–42. Freeport, N.Y.: Books for Libraries Press, 1944.

Hoffmann, Conrad, Jr. "Hitler and the Jews—A Christian View." *Missionary Review of the World* 58 (July 1935): 327–32.

————. "Jewry in Distress! What of It?" *Missionary Review of the World* 61 (June 1938): 261–62.

Hollander, J. H. "Some Unpublished Material Relating to Dr. Jacob Lumbrozo of Maryland." *Publications of the American Jewish Historical Society* 1 (1893): 25–39.

Howe, Julia Ward. "Shall the Frontier of Christendom Be Maintained?" *The Forum* 22 (November 1896): 321–26.

Huhner, Leon. "The Jews of Georgia in Colonial Times." *Publications of the American Jewish Historical Society* 10 (1902): 65–95.

————. "The Jews of New England (Other than Rhode Island) Prior to 1800." *Publications of the American Jewish Historical Society* 11 (1903): 75–99.

————. "The Jews of Virginia from the Earliest Times to the Close of the Eighteenth Century." *Publications of the American Jewish Historical Society* 20 (1911): 85–105.

Hunnicutt, Benjamin Kline. "The Jewish Sabbath Movement in the Early Twentieth Century." *American Jewish History* 69 (December 1979): 196–225.

Jacob, Walter. "Isaac Mayer Wise's Views on Christianity." *Judaism* 15 (Fall 1966): 437–49.

Jastrow, Morris. "The First International Congress for the History of Religions." *International Journal of Ethics* 10 (July 1900): 503–4.

———. "References to Jews in the Diary of Ezra Stiles." *Publications of the American Jewish Historical Society* 10 (1902): 5–36.

Karp, Abraham J. "The Zionism of Warder Cresson." In *Early History of Zionism in America*, edited by Isidore S. Meyer, pp. 1–20. New York: Arno Press, 1977.

Kellman, Steven G. " 'The Last Temptation of Christ': Blaming the Jews." *Midstream* 34 (December 1988): 33.

Klein, Rose S. "Washington's Thanksgiving Proclamation." *American Jewish Archives* 20 (November 1968): 156–62.

Knee, Stuart E. "The King-Crane Commission of 1919: The Articulation of Political Anti-Zionism." *American Jewish Archives* 29 (April 1977): 22–52.

Knoles, George Harmon. "The Religious Ideas of Thomas Jefferson." *The Mississippi Valley Historical Review* 30 (September 1943): 187–204.

Kohler, Max J. "Unpublished Correspondence Between Thomas Jefferson and Some American Jews." *Publications of the American Jewish Historical Society* 20 (1911): 11–30.

Kohn, S. Joshua. "Mordecai Manuel Noah's Ararat Project and the Missionaries." *American Jewish Historical Quarterly* 55 (December 1965): 162–96.

———. "New Light on Mordecai Manuel Noah's Ararat Project." *American Jewish Historical Quarterly* 59 (December 1969): 210–14.

Krause, Corinne Azen. "The Historical Setting of the Pittsburgh Platform." In *The Changing World of Reform Judaism: The Pittsburgh Platform in Retrospect*, edited by Walter Jacob, pp. 5–16. Pittsburgh: Rodef Shalom Congregation, 1925.

Kraut, Benny. "The Ambivalent Relations of American Reform Judaism with Unitarianism in the Last Third of the Nineteenth Century." *Journal of Ecumenical Studies* 23 (Winter 1986): 58–68.

———. "Judaism Triumphant: Isaac Mayer Wise on Unitarianism and Liberal Christianity." *AJS Review* 78 (1982–83): 179–230.

———. "Towards the Establishment of the National Conference of Christians and Jews: The Tenuous Road to Religious Goodwill in the 1920s." *American Jewish History* 77 (March 1988): 388–412.

———. "Unitarianism on the Reform Jewish Mind." In *Proceedings of the Eighth World Congress of Jewish Studies, Jerusalem, August 16–21, 1981*, pp. 91–98. Jerusalem: World Union of Jewish Studies, 1982.

Langdon, Samuel. "The Republic of the Israelites: An Example to the American States." In *God's New Israel*, by Conrad Cherry, pp. 93–105. Englewood Cliffs, N.J.: Prentice-Hall, 1971.

Lazarus, Emma. "The Jewish Problem." *The Century Magazine* 25 (February 1883): 602–11.

Lebeson, Anita Libman. "Hannah Adams and the Jews." *Historia Judaica* 8 (October 1946): 113–34.

Lebow, Richard Ned. "Woodrow Wilson and the Balfour Declaration." *Journal of Modern History* 40 (December 1968): 501–23.

"Letter from President Roosevelt." *Publications of the American Jewish Historical Society* 14 (1906): 18–20.

Levin, Nora. "A Jewish View of Dialogue." *Christian Jewish Relations* 17 (June 1984): 35–42.

Levine, Samuel H. "Palestine in the Literature of the United States to 1867." In *Early History of Zionism*, edited by Isidore S. Meyer, pp. 21–38. New York: Arno Press, 1977.

Libowitz, Richard. "Some Reactions to *Der Judenstaat* among English-speaking Jews in the United States." In *Jewish Civilization: Essays and Studies*, edited by Ronald A. Brauner, vol. 1, pp. 123–40. Philadelphia: Reconstructionist Rabbinical College, 1979.

Lindbeck, George A. "The Jews, Renewal and Ecumenism." *Journal of Ecumenical Studies* 2 (Fall 1965): 471–73.

Littell, Franklin H. "Bernhard E. Olson (1910–1975)." *Journal of Ecumenical Studies* 12 (Fall 1975, special issue): 582–83.

———. "Christendom, Holocaust and Israel: The Importance for Christians of Recent Major Events in Jewish History." *Journal of Ecumenical Studies* 10 (Summer 1973): 483–97.

———. "Christian Congress for Israel." *Near East Report* 25 (November 20, 1981): 213.

———. "Have Jews and Christians a Common Future?" *Journal of Church and State* 13 (Spring 1971): 303–15.

———. "*Kirchenkampf* and Holocaust: The German Church Struggle and Nazi Anti-Semitism in Retrospect." *Journal of Church and State* 13 (Spring 1971): 210–26.

———. "Politics, Theology and the Jews." *Journal of Ecumenical Studies* 2 (Fall 1965): 476.

———. "Recent Jewish History: Lessons for Christians." *Gratz College Annual of Jewish Studies* 1 (1972): 107–19.

———. "Uprooting Antisemitism: A Call to Christians." *Journal of Church and State* 17 (1975): 15–24.

———. "Why a Christian Authority Opposes Missionaries." *The Jewish Week*, April 8, 1983, p. 17.

Ludlow, Peter W. "The International Protestant Community in the Second World War." *Journal of Ecclesiastical History* 29 (July 1978): 311–62.

"Luther, Lutheranism and the Jews." *Christian Jewish Relations* 16 (September 1983): 17–22.

McAllister, David. "The Origin and Progress of the Movement for the Religious Amendment of the Constitution of the United States." In *Proceedings of the Fifth National Reform Convention to Aid in Maintaining the Christian Features of the American Government and Securing a Religious Amendment to the Constitution of the United States Held in Pittsburgh, Feb. 4, 5, 1874*, pp. 1–19. Philadelphia: Christian Statesman Association, 1874.

McPherson, Simon J. "The City as a Peril." In *National Perils and Opportunities. General*

Christian Conference Held in Washington, D.C., December 7, 8, 9, 1887, pp. 38–47. New York: Baker and Taylor, 1887.

Mager, John C. "Nazis, Jews, and the War: What the *Lutheran Witness* Said, 1934–1945." *American Lutheran* 47 (November 1964): 10–13.

Marcus, Jacob Rader. "The Handsome Young Priest in the Black Gown." *Hebrew Union College Annual* 40–41 (1969–70): 409–67.

Marsden, George M. "Everyone's Own Interpreter? The Bible, Science, and Authority in Mid-Nineteenth-Century America." In *The Bible in America: Essays in Cultural History,* edited by Nathan O. Hatch and Mark A. Noll, pp. 79–100. New York: Oxford Univ. Press, 1982.

Mayo, Louise Abbie. "Herman Melville, the Jew and Judaism." *American Jewish Archives* 28 (November 1976): 172–79.

Mead, Sidney E. "Denominationalism: The Shape of Protestantism in America." *Church History* 23 (December 1954): 291–320.

———. "From Coercion to Persuasion: Another Look at the Rise of Religious Liberty and the Emergence of Denominationalism." *Church History* 25 (December 1956): 317–37.

"Memorial of the Sunday School for Religious Instruction of Israelites in Philadelphia." In *Second Annual Examination of the Sunday School for Religious Instruction of Israelites in Philadelphia,* pp. 5–8. Philadelphia, 1840.

Mesher, David R. "Emma Lazarus: Zionism, American Style." *Journal of American Jewish Literature* 2 (1982): 198–203.

Meyer, Isidore S. "John Adams Writes a Letter." *Publications of American Jewish Historical Society* 37 (October 1947): 189.

Meyer, Michael A. "American Reform Judaism and Zionism: Early Efforts at Ideological Rapprochement." *Studies in Zionism* 7 (Spring 1983): 54.

Miller, Robert Moats. "A Note on the Relationship Between the Protestant Churches and the Revived Ku Klux Klan." *Journal of Southern History* 22 (August 1956): 355–68.

Montefiore, Claude G. "Some Notes on the Effect of Biblical Criticism upon the Jewish Religion." *The Jewish Quarterly Review* 4 (January 1892): 293–306.

Moore, George Foot. "Christian Writer on Judaism." *Harvard Theological Review* 14 (July 1921): 197–254.

———. "Intermediaries in Jewish Theology, Memra, Shekina, Matatron." *Harvard Theological Review* 15 (July 1922): 41–85.

Moorhead, James H. "Between Progress and Apocalypse: A Reassessment of Millennialism in American Religious Thought, 1800–1880." *The Journal of American History* 71 (December 1984): 524–42.

Morais, Henry S. "Sabato Morais: A Memoir." In *Proceedings of the Sixth Biennial Convention of the Jewish Theological Seminary Association, Held in the City of Philadelphia . . . March 20, 1898,* pp. 63–93. New York: Press of Philip Cowen, 1898.

Morais, Nina. "Jewish Ostracism in America." *The North American Review* 133 (September 1881): 265–75.

Morris, Maxwell H. "Roger Williams and the Jews." *American Jewish Archives* 3 (January 1951): 24–27.

Morris, Richard B. "The Role of the Jews in the American Revolution." In *Jews and the Founding of the Republic*, edited by Jonathan D. Sarna et al., pp. 15–29. New York: Markus Wiener Publishing, 1985.

Muller, F. Max. "The Real Significance of the Parliament of Religions." *The Arena* 2 (December 1894): 1–14.

Nicholson, W. R. "The Gathering of Israel." In *Premillennial Essays of the Prophetic Conference Held in the Church of the Holy Trinity, New York City*, edited by Nathaniel West, pp. 222–40. Chicago: Fleming H. Revell Company, 1879.

Neuhaus, John. "What the Fundamentalists Want." *Commentary* 79 (May 1985): 46.

Niebuhr, H. Richard. "The Idea of the Covenant and American Democracy." In *Puritanism and the American Experience*, edited by Michael McGiffert, pp. 219–25. Reading, Mass.: Addison-Wesley, 1969.

Niebuhr, Reinhold. "The Blindness of Liberalism." *Radical Religion* 2 (Autumn 1936): 4–5.

———. "The Catholic Heresy." *The Christian Century* 54 (December 8, 1937): 1524–25.

———. "Christian Pledge to Boycott Nazi Germany." *Radical Religion* 4 (Spring 1939): 12–13.

———. "Christians and the State of Israel." *Christianity and Crisis* 14 (Summer 1949): 3–5.

———. "The Churches in Germany." *The American Scholar* 3 (Summer 1934): 344–51.

———. "The Confession of a Tired Radical." *The Christian Century* 45 (August 30, 1928): 1046–47.

———. "The Crisis in the Suez Canal." *Christianity and Crisis* 16 (September 17, 1956): 113–14.

———. "A Critique of Pacifism." *The Atlantic Monthly* 139 (May 1927): 637–41.

———. "David and Goliath." *Christianity and Crisis* 27 (June 26, 1967): 141–42.

———. "An End to Illusion." *The Nation* 150 (June 29, 1940): 778–79.

———. "Germany Must be Told." *The Christian Century* 50 (August 9, 1933): 1014–15.

———. "Jews after the War." 2 Parts. *The Nation* 154 (February 21, 1942; February 28, 1942): 214–16, 253–55.

———. "Leaves from the Notebook of a War-Bound American." *The Christian Century* 56 (December 27, 1939): 1607–8.

———. "Let Liberal Churches Stop Fooling Themselves!" *The Christian Century* 48 (March 25, 1931): 402–4.

———. "Mideast Impasse: Is There a Way Out?" *The New Leader* 39 (June 4, 1956): 9–10.

———. "Mission and Opportunity: Religion in a Pluralistic Culture." In *Social Responsibility in an Age of Revolution*, edited by Louis Finkelstein, pp. 177–211. New York: The Jewish Theological Seminary of America, 1971.

———. "Must Democracy Use Force?" *The Nation* 148 (January 28, 1939): 117–19.

———. "A New View of Palestine." *The Spectator* 177 (August 16, 1946): 162–63.

———. "Our Stake in the State of Israel." *The New Republic* 136 (February 4, 1957): 9–12.

————. "Pacifism and America First." *Christianity and Crisis* 1 (June 16, 1941): 2–5.

————. "Pacifism and the Use of Force." In *Love and Justice: Selections from the Shorter Writings of Reinhold Niebuhr,* edited by D. B. Robertson, pp. 247–53. Philadelphia: Westminster Press, 1959.

————. "Palestine: British-American Dilemma." *The Nation* 163 (August 31, 1946): 238–39.

————. "The Plight of the Jews." *Radical Religion* 3 (Fall 1938): 8–9.

————. "Religion and the New Germany." *The Christian Century* 50 (June 28, 1933): 843–45.

————. "The Significance of Suez." *Christianity and Crisis* 16 (October 1956): 123.

————. "Ten Years That Shook My World." *The Christian Century* 56 (April 26, 1939): 542–46.

————. "Toward a Program for Jews." *Contemporary Jewish Record* 7 (June 1944): 239–46.

————. "The U.N. Is Not a World Government." *The Reporter* 16 (March 7, 1957): 30–32.

————. "The Unsolved Religious Problem in Christian-Jewish Relations." *Christianity and Crisis* 26 (December 12, 1966): 279–83.

————. "Why I Am Not a Christian." *The Christian Century* 44 (December 15, 1927): 1482–83.

————. "Why I Leave the F.O.R." *The Christian Century* 51 (January 3, 1934): 17–19.

Noll, Mark A. "The Image of the United States as a Biblical Nation, 1776–1865." *The Bible in America: Essays in Cultural History,* edited by Nathan O. Hatch and Mark A. Noll, pp. 39–58. New York: Oxford Univ. Press, 1982.

Norden, Margaret K. "American Editorial Response to the Rise of Adolph Hitler: A Preliminary Consideration." *American Jewish Historical Quarterly* 59 (March 1970): 290–301.

Olan, Levi. "Reinhold Niebuhr and the Hebraic Spirit: A Critical Inquiry." *Judaism* 5 (Spring 1956): 108–22.

Olitzky, Kerry M. "The Sunday-Sabbath Movement in American Reform Judaism: Strategy or Evolution?" *American Jewish Archives* 34 (April 1982): 75–88.

————. "Sundays at Chicago Sinai Congregation: Paradigm for a Movement." *American Jewish History* 74 (June 1985): 356–68.

Olson, Bernhard E. "Christian Education and the Image of the Pharisees." *Religious Education* (November-December 1960): 410–17.

Owen, Dennis E., and Barry Mesch. "Protestants, Jews and the Law." *The Christian Century* 101 (June 6–13): 601–4.

Panitz, Esther. "The Polarity of American Jewish Attitudes Towards Immigration (1870–1891)." *American Jewish Historical Quarterly* 52 (December 1963): 99–130.

Parzen, Herbert. "The Lodge-Fish Resolution." *American Jewish Historical Quarterly* 60 (September 1970): 71–81.

Peck, Abraham J. "That Other 'Peculiar Institution': Jews and Judaism in the Nineteenth Century South." *Modern Judaism* 7 (February 1987): 99–114.

Petuchowski, Jakob J. "A Jewish Response to 'Israel as a Theological Problem in the Christian Church.'" *Journal of Ecumenical Studies* 6 (Summer 1969): 348–53.

Pfeiffer, Robert H. "The Teaching of Hebrew in Colonial America." *The Jewish Quarterly Review* 65 (1955): 363–64.

Plesur, Milton. "The American Press and Jewish Restoration During the Nineteenth Century." In *Early History of Zionism in America,* edited by Isidore S. Meyer, pp. 55–76. New York: Arno Press, 1977.

Podesta, Anthony. "The Rising Tide of the Religious Right." *Reform Judaism* 14 (Summer 1986): 18–19.

Polish, David. "The Changing and the Constant." *American Jewish Archives* 35 (November 1981): 263–341.

Pool, David de Sola. "Hebrew Learning among Puritans of New England prior to 1700." *Publications of the American Jewish Historical Society* 20 (1911): 31–83.

"Prejudice Against the Jews: Its Nature, Its Causes and Remedies. A Consensus of Opinion by Non-Jews." *The American Hebrew* 42 (April 4, 1890): 165ff.

Raphael, Marc Lee. "Rabbi Jacob Voorsanger of San Francisco on Jews and Judaism: The Implications of the Pittsburgh Platform." *American Jewish Historical Quarterly* 63 (December 1973): 180–203.

Rausch, David A. "Arno C. Gaebelein (1861–1945): Fundamentalist Protestant Zionist." *American Jewish History* 68 (September 1978): 43–56.

———. "Protofundamentalism's Attitudes Toward Zionism, 1878–1918." *Jewish Social Studies* 43 (Spring 1981): 137–52.

Richman, Julia. "The Jewish Sunday School Movement in the United States." *The Jewish Quarterly Review* 12 (July 1900): 563–601.

Ricks, Eldin. "Zionism and the Mormon Church." In *Herzl Year Book* 5 (1963): 147–74.

Roosevelt, Kermit. "The Partition of Palestine: A Lesson in Pressure Politics." *The Middle East Journal* 2 (January 1948): 1–16.

Rosenberg, Stuart E. "The *Jewish Tidings* and the Sunday Service Question." *Publications of American Jewish Historical Society* 42 (June 1953): 371–85.

Rosenbloom, Joseph R. "Rebecca Gratz and the Jewish Sunday School Movement in Philadelphia." *Publications of American Jewish Historical Society* 48 (September 1958): 71.

Rosenmeier, Jesper. " 'With My Owne Eyes': William Bradford's *Of Plymouth Plantation.*" In *The American Puritan Imagination: Essays in Reevaluation,* edited by Sacvan Bercovitch, pp. 77–106. London: Cambridge Univ. Press, 1974.

Rothkoff, Aaron. "The American Sojourns of Ridbaz: Religious Problems Within the Immigrant Community." *American Jewish Historical Quarterly* 57 (June 1968): 557–72.

Ruchames, Louis. "Mordecai Manuel Noah and Early American Zionism." *American Jewish Historical Quarterly* 64 (March 1975): 195–223.

Sandeen, Ernest R. "Toward a Historical Interpretation of the Origins of Fundamentalism." *Church History* 36 (March 1967): 66–83.

Sarna, Jonathan D. "American Christian Opposition to the Missions to the Jews." *Journal of Ecumenical Studies* 23 (Spring 1986): 226.

———. "The American Jewish Response to Nineteenth-Century Christian Mission." *Journal of American History* 68 (June 1981): 35–51.

———. "The Freethinkers, the Jews, and the Missionaries: George Houston and the Mystery of *Israel Vindicated.*" *AJS Review* 5 (1980): 101–14.

———. "The Impact of the American Revolution on American Jews." *Modern Judaism* 1 (September 1981): 149–60.

Scharper, Philip. "Israel the Modern State and Contemporary Christian Points of View." *Lutheran Quarterly* 20 (1968): 255–57.

Seller, Maxim S. "Isaac Leeser: A Jewish-Christian Dialogue in Antebellum Philadelphia." *Pennsylvania History* 35 (July 1968): 231–42.

Shapiro, Edward S. "The Approach of War: Congressional Isolationism and Anti-Semitism, 1939–1941." *American Jewish History* 74 (September 1984): 45–65.

Simon, Abraham. "Notes of Jewish Interest in the District of Columbia." *Publications of the American Jewish Historical Society* 26 (1918): 211–18.

Singer, Howard. "The Rise and Fall of Interfaith Dialogue." *Commentary* 83 (May 1987): 50–55.

Smith, Timothy L. "Protestant Schooling and American Nationality, 1800–1850." *The Journal of American History* 53 (March 1967): 679–95.

Sobel, D. Zvi. "Protestant Evangelists and the Formation of a Jewish Racial Mystique: The Missionary Discovery of Sociology." *Journal for the Scientific Study of Religion* 5 (Fall 1966): 343–56.

Steinberg, Milton. "The Outlook of Reinhold Niebuhr—A Description and Appraisal." *The Reconstructionist* 11 (December 14, 1945): 10–15.

Stern, Malcolm H. "The 1820s: American Jewry Comes of Age." In *A Bicentennial Festschrift for Jacob Rader Marcus,* edited by Bertram W. Korn, pp. 539–49. Waltham, Mass.: American Jewish Historical Society; New York: KTAV Publishing House, 1976.

———. "Reforming of Reform Judaism—Past, Present, and Future." *American Jewish Historical Quarterly* 63 (December 1973): 113.

Stern, Sol. "The Falwell Fallacy: The Limits of Fundamentalist Support for Israel." *Reform Judaism* (Winter 1984): 5–6.

Street, Nicholas. "The American States Acting over the Part of the Children of Israel in the Wilderness and Thereby Impeding Their Entrance into Canaan's Nest." In *God's New Israel,* edited by Conrad Cherry, pp. 67–81. Englewood Cliffs, N.J.: Prentice-Hall, 1971.

Strum, Harvey. "Louis Marshall and Anti-Semitism at Syracuse University." *American Jewish Archives* 35 (April 1983): 1–11.

Sussman, Lance J. "Another Look at Isaac Leeser and the First Jewish Translation of the Bible in the United States." *Modern Judaism* 5 (May 1985): 159–90.

———. "Isaac Leeser and the Protestantization of American Judaism." *American Jewish Archives* 38 (April 1986): 1–21.

———. "'Toward Better Understanding': The Rise of the Interfaith Movement in America and the Role of Rabbi Isaac Landman." *American Jewish Archives* 34 (April 1982): 35–51.

Swidler, Leonard. "Jews and Christians in Dialogue." *Journal of Ecumenical Studies* 12 (Fall 1975, special issue): 581–82.

Van Buren, Paul M. "Affirmation of the Jewish People: A Condition of Theological Coherence." *Journal of the American Academy of Religion* 45 (Supplement, September 1977): 1075–1100.

Voss, Carl Hermann. "The American Christian Palestine Committee." In *Essays in*

American Zionism, 1917–1948. Herzl Year Book, no. 8, edited by Melvin I. Urofsky, pp. 242–62. New York, Herzl Press, 1975.

Voss, Carl Hermann, and David A. Rausch. "American Christians and Israel, 1948–1988." *American Jewish Archives* 40 (April 1988): 41–81.

Wacker, Grant. "The Holy Spirit and the Spirit of the Age in American Protestantism, 1880–1910." *The Journal of American History* 12 (June 1985): 45–62.

Walvoord, John F. "The Fulfillment of the Abrahamic Covenant." *Bibliotheca Sacra* 102 (January 1945): 27–36.

———. "Israel's Blindness." *Bibliotheca Sacra* 102 (July 1945): 280–90.

———. "Israel's Restoration." *Bibliotheca Sacra* 102 (October 1945): 405–16.

Weber, Paul J. "James Madison and Religious Equality: The Perfect Separation." *The Review of Politics* 44 (April 1982): 163–86.

Weinman, Melvin. "The Attitude of Isaac Mayer Wise Toward Zionism and Palestine." *American Jewish Archives* 3 (January 1951): 3–21.

West, Nathaniel. "Prophecy and Israel." In *Prophetic Studies of the International Prophetic Conference, Chicago, November 1886*, pp. 122–35. Chicago: Fleming H. Revell Company, 1886.

Wheatley, Richard. "The Jews in New York." *The Century Magazine* 63 (January 1892): 323–42, 512–32.

Whiteman, Maxwell. "The Legacy of Isaac Leeser." In *Jewish Life in Philadelphia, 1830–1940*, pp. 26–47. Philadelphia: Ishi Publications, 1983.

Wilner, W. "Ezra Stiles and the Jews." *Publications of the American Jewish Historical Society* 8 (1900): 119–26.

Wischnitzer, Rachel. "Ezra Stiles and the Portrait of Menasseh Ben Israel." *American Jewish Historical Quarterly* 51 (December 1961): 190–94.

Wise, Isaac M. "Our Country's Place in History." In *God's New Israel: Religious Interpretations of American Destiny*, edited by Conrad Cherry, pp. 218–28. Englewood Cliffs, N.J.: Prentice-Hall, 1977.

Wyszkowski, Yehezkel. "*The American Hebrew*: An Exercise in Ambivalence." *American Jewish History* 76 (March 1987): 340–53.

Books

Abbott, Lyman. *The Life and Literature of the Ancient Hebrews*. Boston: Houghton Mifflin, 1901.

———. *The Spirit of Democracy*. Boston: Houghton Mifflin, 1910.

———. *The Theology of an Evolutionist*. 1897. Reprint. New York: Outlook Company, 1925.

Abell, Aaron Ignatius. *The Urban Impact on American Protestantism: 1865–1900*. Cambridge, Mass.: Harvard Univ. Press, 1943.

Adams, Henry. *Letters of Henry Adams, 1892–1918*. 2 vols. Edited by Worthington Chauncey Ford. Boston: Houghton Mifflin, 1938.

Adams, John. *Diary and Autobiography of John Adams*. 4 vols. Edited by L. H. Butterfield. Vol. 2; *Diary 1771–1781*. Cambridge: Harvard Univ. Press, Belknap Press, 1962.

Adler, Cyrus. *I Have Considered the Days*. Philadelphia: The Jewish Publication Society of America, 1941.

Adler, Felix. *An Ethical Philosophy of Life.* New York: D. Appleton and Co., 1918.

Adler, Selig, and Thomas E. Connolly. *From Ararat to Suburbia: The History of the Jewish Community of Buffalo.* Philadelphia: The Jewish Publication Society of America, 1960.

Ahlstrom, Sydney E. *The American Protestant Encounter with World Religions.* The Brewer Lectures on Comparative Religion. Beloit, Wisc.: Beloit College, October 15, 16, and 17, 1962.

Ahlstrom, Sydney E., and Johnathan S. Carey, eds. *An American Reformation of Unitarian Christianity.* Middletown, Conn.: Wesleyan Univ. Press, 1985.

Alexander, Thomas G. *Mormonism in Transition: A History of the Latter-day Saints, 1890–1930.* Urbana: Univ. of Illinois Press, 1986.

Allen, James B., and Glen M. Leonard. *The Story of the Latter-day Saints.* Salt Lake City: Deseret Book Company, 1976.

Althouse, LaVonne. *When Jew and Christian Meet.* New York: Friendship Press, 1966.

American Jewish Committee. *The Eichmann Case in the American Press.* New York: Institute of Human Relations Press, 1962.

Andrews, Charles McLean. *The Colonial Period of American History.* 4 vols. New Haven: Yale Univ. Press, 1964.

————. *Our Earliest Colonial Settlements: Their Diversities of Origin and Later Characteristics.* Ithaca, N.Y.: Cornell Univ. Press, 1933.

Armstrong, Maurice W., Lefferts A. Loetscher, and Charles A. Anderson, eds. *The Presbyterian Enterprise: Sources of American Presbyterian History.* Philadelphia: Westminster Press, 1956.

Ayers, Robert H. *Judaism and Christianity: Origins, Developments and Recent Trends.* Lanham, Md.: Univ. Press of America, 1983.

Bacon, Margaret H. *The Quiet Rebels: The Story of the Quakers in America.* New York: Basic Books, 1969.

Baltzell, E. Digby. *The Protestant Establishment: Aristocracy and Caste in America.* New York: Random House, 1964.

Banki, Judith Hershcopf. *Anti-Israel Influence in American Churches: A Background Report.* New York: Interreligious Affairs Department, The American Jewish Committee Institute of Human Relations, 1979.

Baron, Salo Wittmayer. *A Social and Religious History of the Jews.* 17 vols. New York: Columbia Univ. Press; Philadelphia: The Jewish Publication Society of America, 1969.

Barrows, John Henry, ed. *The World's Parliament of Religions: An Illustrated and Popular Story of the World's First Parliament of Religions, Held in Chicago in Connection with the Columbian Exposition of 1893.* 2 vols. Chicago: Parliament Publishing Company, 1893.

Beecher, Lyman. *Autobiography, Correspondence, Etc., of Lyman Beecher, D.D.* 2 vols. Edited by Charles Beecher. New York: Harper and Brothers, 1864 and 1865.

————. *Plea for the West.* 2nd ed. Cincinnati: Truman and Smith; New York: Leavitt, Lord, 1835.

Bellamy, Edward. *Equality.* 11th ed. 1897; New York: D. Appleton and Company, 1910.

Ben-Sasson, Haim Hillel, ed. *A History of the Jewish People.* Cambridge, Mass.: Harvard Univ. Press, 1976.

Benjamin, Israel J. *Three Years in America: 1859–1862*. 2 vols. Philadelphia: The Jewish Publication Society of America, 1956.

Bercovitch, Sacvan. *The American Jeremiad*. Madison: Univ. of Wisconsin Press, 1978.

———, ed. *The American Puritan Imagination: Essays in Revaluation*. London: Cambridge Univ. Press, 1974.

Berens, John F. *Providence and Patriotism in Early America, 1640–1815*. Charlottesville: Univ. Press of Virginia, 1978.

Berle, A. A. *The World Significance of a Jewish State*. New York: Mitchell Kennerley, 1918.

Berlin, George L. *Defending the Faith: Nineteenth-Century American Jewish Writings on Christianity and Jesus*. Albany: State Univ. of New York Press, 1989.

Black, William Harmon. *If I Were A Jew*. New York: Real Book Co., 1938.

Blau, Joseph L. *Judaism in America: From Curiosity to Third Faith*. Chicago History of American Religion Series. Chicago: Univ. of Chicago Press, 1976.

Blau, Joseph L., and Salo W. Baron, eds. *The Jews of the United States, 1790–1840: A Documentary History*. 3 vols. New York: Columbia Univ. Press; Philadelphia: The Jewish Publication Society of America, 1963.

Bloch, Ruth H. *Visionary Republic: Millennial Themes in American Thought, 1756–1800*. Cambridge: Cambridge Univ. Press, 1985.

Bodo, John R. *The Protestant Clergy and Public Issues, 1812–1848*. Princeton: Princeton Univ. Press, 1954.

Boorstin, Daniel J. *The Lost World of Thomas Jefferson*. Boston: Beacon Press, 1948.

Borden, Morton. *Jews, Turks, and Infidels*. Chapel Hill: Univ. of North Carolina Press, 1984.

Brauner, Ronald A., ed. *Jewish Civilization: Essays and Studies*. Vol. 1. Philadelphia: Reconstructionist Rabbinical College, 1979.

Breitman, Richard, and Alan Kraut. *American Refugee Policy and European Jewry, 1933–1945*. Bloomington: Indiana Univ. Press, 1987.

Brewer, David J. *The United States: A Christian Nation*. Haverford Library Lectures. Philadelphia: John C. Winston Company, 1905.

Brown, Arthur W. *William Ellery Channing*. New York: Twayne Publishers, 1961.

Brown, Charles Brockden. *Arthur Mervyn, or, Memoirs of the Year 1793*. New York: Holt, Rinehart and Winston, 1965.

Brown, Charles Reynolds. *The Social Message of the Modern Pulpit*. New York: Charles Scribner's Sons, 1911.

Brown, Robert McAfee. *The Ecumenical Revolution: An Interpretation of the Catholic-Protestant Dialogue*. Garden City, N.Y.: Doubleday, 1967.

Brownlee, W. C., ed. *The History of the Jews from the Babylonian Captivity to the Present Time*. Boston: M. A. Berk, 1847.

Buckley, Thomas E. *Church and State in Revolutionary Virginia, 1776–1787*. Charlottesville: Univ. Press of Virginia, 1977.

Butterfield, L. H., ed. *Diary and Autobiography of John Adams*. Vol. 2; *Diary 1771–1781*. Cambridge, Mass.: Harvard Univ. Press, Belknap Press, 1962.

———. *Letters of Benjamin Rush*. Vol. 1; *1761–1792*. Princeton, N.J.: Princeton Univ. Press, 1951.

Carter, Paul A. *The Spiritual Crisis of the Gilded Age.* DeKalb, Ill.: Northern Illinois Univ. Press, 1971.

Chadwick, Owen. *The Reformation.* Harmondsworth, England: Penguin Books, 1964.

Chalmers, David M. *Hooded Americanism: The First Century of the Ku Klux Klan, 1865–1965.* Garden City, N.Y.: Doubleday, 1965.

Chaney, Charles L. *The Birth of Missions in America.* South Pasadena, Calif.: William Carey Library, 1976.

Channing, William Henry. *The Life of William Ellery Channing, D.D.* Boston: American Unitarian Association, 1880.

Cherry, Conrad. *God's New Israel: Religious Interpretations of American Destiny.* Englewood Cliffs, N.J.: Prentice-Hall, 1971.

Christian Protagonists for Jewish Restoration. New York: Arno Press, 1977.

Chrystal, William G., ed. *Young Reinhold Niebuhr: His Early Writings, 1911–1931.* St. Louis: Eden Publishing House, 1977.

Chyet, Stanley F. *Lopez of Newport, Colonial American Merchant Prince.* Detroit: Wayne State Univ. Press, 1970.

Clarke, James Freeman. *Ten Great Religions: An Essay in Comparative Theology.* 1871. Boston: Houghton Mifflin, 1899.

———. *Ten Great Religions, Part 2: A Comparison of All Religions.* Boston, Houghton Mifflin, 1883.

Clifford, Clark M., Eugene V. Rostow, and Barbara W. Tuchman. *The Palestine Question in American History.* New York: Arno Press, 1978.

Clinchy, Everett R. *All in the Name of God.* New York: John Day Company, 1934.

Cobb, Sanford H. *The Rise of Religious Liberty in America.* New York: Macmillan, 1902.

Cohen, Arthur A. *The Myth of the Judeo-Christian Tradition.* New York: Schocken Books, 1971.

Cohen, Naomi W. *Encounter with Emancipation: The German Jews in the United States, 1830–1914.* Philadelphia: The Jewish Publication Society of America, 1984.

———. *Not Free to Desist: The American Jewish Committee, 1906–1966.* Philadelphia: The Jewish Publication Society of America, 1972.

Coit, Stanton. *The Soul of America: A Constructive Essay in the Sociology of Religion.* New York: Macmillan, 1914.

Cole, Charles Chester, Jr. *The Social Ideas of the Northern Evangelists, 1826–1860.* New York: Columbia Univ. Press, 1954.

Commager, Henry Steele, ed. *Theodore Parker: An Anthology.* Boston: Beacon Press, 1960.

Conkin, Paul K. *Puritans and Pragmatists: Eight Eminent American Thinkers.* New York: Dodd, Mead, 1968.

Conway, Moncure Daniel. *Autobiography: Memories and Experiences of Moncure Daniel Conway.* Vol. 2. New York: Negro Universities Press, 1904.

Cousins, Norman, ed. *"In God We Trust": The Religious Beliefs and Ideas of the American Founding Fathers.* New York: Harper and Brothers, 1958.

Cresson, Warder. *The Key of David.* 1852. Reprint. New York: Arno Press, 1977.

Curti, Merle. *The Growth of American Thought.* New York: Harper and Brothers, 1943.

Davis, Moshe, ed. *With Eyes Toward Zion: Scholars Colloquium on American–Holy Land Studies.* New York: Arno Press, 1977.

Dawidowicz, Lucy S. *On Equal Terms: Jews in America, 1881–1981.* New York: Holt, Rinehart and Winston, 1982.

————. *The War Against the Jews.* New York: Holt, Rinehart and Winston; Philadelphia: The Jewish Publication Society of America, 1975.

Delbanco, Andrew. *William Ellery Channing: An Essay on the Liberal Spirit in America.* Cambridge, Mass.: Harvard Univ. Press, 1981.

Dewey, John. *A Common Faith.* New Haven: Yale Univ. Press, 1934.

Dinnerstein, Leonard. *America and the Survivors of the Holocaust.* New York: Columbia Univ. Press, 1982. Reprint. 1934.

Dobkowski, Michael N. *The Tarnished Dream: The Basis of American Anti-Semitism.* Westport, Conn.: Greenwood Press, 1979.

Eckardt, A. Roy. *Christianity and the Children of Israel.* New York: King's Crown Press, 1948.

————. *Elder and Younger Brothers: The Encounter of Jews and Christians.* New York: Charles Scribner's Sons, 1967.

————. *Jews and Christians: The Contemporary Meeting.* Bloomington: Indiana Univ. Press, 1986.

————. *Your People, My People: The Meeting of Jews and Christians.* New York: New York Times Book Company, 1974.

Eckardt, A. Roy, and Alice L. Eckardt. *Encounter with Israel: A Challenge to Conscience.* New York: Association Press, 1970.

————. *Long Night's Journey into Day: Life and Faith after the Holocaust.* Detroit: Wayne State Univ. Press, 1982.

Edwards, Jonathan. *Apocalyptic Writings.* Edited by Stephen J. Stein. New Haven: Yale Univ. Press, 1977.

————. *The Great Awakening.* Edited by C. C. Goen. New Haven: Yale Univ. Press, 1972.

————. *Original Sin.* New Haven: Yale Univ. Press, 1970.

————. *The Works of President Edwards.* Research and Source Work Series, no. 271. New York: Burt Franklin, 1968.

Eichhorn, David Max. *Evangelizing the American Jew.* Middle Village, N.Y.: Jonathan David Publishers, 1978.

Eisen, Arnold M. *The Chosen People in America: A Study in Jewish Religious Ideology.* Bloomington: Indiana Univ. Press, 1983.

Eliot, Charles W. *The Religion of the Future: A Lecture Delivered at the Close of the Eleventh Session of the Harvard Summer School of Theology, July 22, 1909.* New York: Frederick A. Stokes Co., 1909.

Elsbree, Oliver Wendell. *The Rise of the Missionary Spirit in America, 1790–1815.* Williamsport, Penn.: Williamsport Printing and Binding, 1928.

Elson, Ruth Miller. *Guardians of Tradition: American Schoolbooks of the Nineteenth Century.* Lincoln: Univ. of Nebraska Press, 1964.

Emerson, Ralph Waldo. *The Complete Works of Ralph Waldo Emerson.* Edited by Edward Waldo Emerson. Cambridge, Mass.: Riverside Press, 1904.

————. *The Journals and Miscellaneous Notebooks of Ralph Waldo Emerson.* 13 vols. Cambridge, Mass.: Harvard Univ. Press, Belknap Press, 1964.

————. *The Letters of Ralph Waldo Emerson.* Edited by Ralph L. Rusk. 6 vols. New York: Columbia Univ. Press, 1939.

————. *Young Emerson Speaks.* Edited by Arthur Cushman McGiffert, Jr. Boston: Houghton Mifflin; Cambridge, Mass.: Riverside Press, 1938.

Epstein, Lawrence J. *Zion's Call: Christian Contributions to the Origins and Development of Israel.* Lanham, Md.: Univ. Press of America, 1984.

Evans, John Henry. *Joseph Smith, an American Prophet.* New York: Macmillan, 1936.

Extremism on the Right: A Handbook. New York: The Anti-Defamation League of B'nai B'rith, 1988.

Fackre, Gabriel. *The Religious Right and Christian Faith.* Grand Rapids, Mich.: William B. Eerdmans, 1982.

Falwell, Jerry. *Strength for the Journey: An Autobiography.* New York: Simon and Schuster, 1987.

Fasching, Darrell J., ed. *The Jewish People in Christian Preaching.* Symposium Series, vol. 10. New York: Edwin Mellen Press, 1984.

Fein, Isaac M. *The Making of an American Jewish Community: The History of Baltimore Jewry from 1773 to 1920.* Philadelphia: The Jewish Publication Society of America, 1971.

Feingold, Henry L. *The Politics of Rescue: The Roosevelt Administration and the Holocaust, 1938–1945.* New Brunswick: Rutgers Univ. Press, 1970.

————. *Zion in America: The Jewish Experience from Colonial Times to the Present.* New York: Hippocrene Books, 1974.

Findley, James F., Jr. *Dwight L. Moody: American Evangelist, 1837–1899.* Chicago: Univ. of Chicago Press, 1969.

Fink, Reuben. *America and Palestine.* New York: American Zionist Emergency Council, 1944.

Finney, Charles Grandison. *Lectures on Revivals of Religion.* 1835. Edited by William G. McLoughlin. Cambridge, Mass.: Harvard Univ. Press, Belknap Press, 1960.

Finnie, David H. *Pioneers East: The Early American Experience in the Middle East.* Cambridge, Mass.: Harvard Univ. Press, 1967.

Fishman, Hertzel. *American Protestantism and a Jewish State.* Detroit: Wayne State Univ. Press, 1973.

Floreen, Harold, Secretary of the Department for the Christian Approach to the Jewish People. *The Lutheran Parish and the Jews: An Analytical Study Based upon Information Furnished Chiefly by Lutheran Parish Pastors.* Chicago: National Lutheran Council, Division of American Missions, 1948.

Forbush, Bliss. *Elias Hicks: Quaker Liberal.* New York: Columbia Univ. Press, 1956.

Fosdick, Harry Emerson. *The Living of These Days: An Autobiography.* New York: Harper and Brothers, 1956.

————. *A Pilgrimage to Palestine.* Chautauqua, N.Y.: Chautauqua Press, 1928.

Fox, George. *The Journal of George Fox.* Rev. ed. Edited by John L. Nickalls. Cambridge: Cambridge Univ. Press, 1952.

Fox, Richard Wightman. *Reinhold Niebuhr: A Biography.* New York: Pantheon Books, 1985.

Franklin, Benjamin. *The Papers of Benjamin Franklin.* 24 vols. Edited by William B. Wilcox. New Haven: Yale Univ. Press, 1959–84.

———. *Writings.* Edited by J. A. Lemay. New York: The Library of America, 1987.

Friedman, Lee M. *Pilgrims in a New Land.* Philadelphia: The Jewish Publication Society of America, 1948.

Friedman, Murray, ed. *Jewish Life in Philadelphia, 1830–1940.* Philadelphia: Ishi Publications, 1983.

Friess, Horace L. *Felix Adler and Ethical Culture.* New York: Columbia Univ. Press, 1981.

Frothingham, Octavius Brooks. *Recollections and Impressions, 1822–1890.* New York: G. P. Putnam's Sons, 1891.

———. *The Religion of Humanity.* New York: David G. Francis, 1873.

Gaebelein, Arno Clemens. *Half a Century: The Autobiography of a Servant.* New York: Publication Office "Our Hope," 1930.

Gartner, Lloyd P., ed. *Jewish Education in the United States: A Documentary History.* Classics in Education Series, no. 41. New York: Teachers College Press, 1969.

Gates, Susa Young. *The Life Story of Brigham Young.* New York: Macmillan, 1930.

Gerber, David A., ed. *Anti-Semitism in American History.* Urbana: Univ. of Illinois Press, 1986.

Gladden, Washington. *The Church and Modern Life.* Boston: Houghton Mifflin, 1908.

———. *Recollections.* Boston: Houghton Mifflin, 1909.

———. *Social Salvation.* Boston: Houghton Mifflin, 1902.

Glanz, Rudolph. *Jew and Mormon: Historic Group Relations and Religious Outlook.* New York: Waldon Press, 1963.

Glazer, Nathan. *American Judaism.* 2d ed. Chicago: Univ. of Chicago Press, 1972.

Glock, Charles Y., and Rodney Stark. *Christian Beliefs and Anti-Semitism.* New York: Harper Torchbooks, 1966.

Goodman, Abram Vossen. *American Overture: Jewish Rights in Colonial Times.* Philadelphia: The Jewish Publication Society of America, 1947.

Goodrich, Charles A. *A Geography of the Chief Places Mentioned in the Bible, and the Principal Events Connected with Them, Adapted to Parental, Sabbath-School and Bible-Class Instruction.* New York: Robert Carter and Brothers, 1856.

Goodspeed, George S., ed. *The World's First Parliament of Religions.* Chicago: Hill and Schumann, 1895.

Gordis, Robert. *Judaism in a Christian World.* New York: McGraw-Hill, 1966.

Gottheil, Richard. *The Life of Gustav Gottheil: Memoir of a Priest in Israel.* Williamsport, Penn.: Baynard Press, 1936.

Graeber, Isacque, and Steuart Henderson Britt. *Jews in a Gentile World: The Problem of Anti-Semitism.* New York: Macmillan, 1942.

Greeley, Andrew M., and Peter H. Rossi. *The Denominational Society: A Sociological Approach to Religion in America.* Glenview, Ill.: Scott, Foresman and Co., 1972.

Grinstein, Hyman B. *The Rise of the Jewish Community of New York, 1654–1860.* Philadelphia: The Jewish Publication Society of America, 1947.

Gross, Howard B. *Aliens or Americans?* New York: Eaton and Mains, 1906.

Gutstein, Morris Aaron. *A Priceless Heritage: The Epic Growth of Nineteenth Century Chicago Jewry.* New York: Bloch Publishing, 1953.

———. *The Story of the Jews of Newport.* New York: Bloch Publishing, 1936.

Halsell, Grace. *Prophecy and Politics: Militant Evangelists on the Road to Nuclear War.* Westport, Conn.: Lawrence Hill and Company, 1986.

Handy, Robert T. *The American Revolution and Religious Freedom.* New York: The Sol Feinstein Lecture for 1979, delivered at The Jewish Theological Seminary of America, 1979.

————, ed. *The Holy Land in American Protestant Life, 1800–1948: A Documentary History.* New York: Arno Press, 1981.

Hardman, Keith J. *Charles Grandison Finney, 1792–1875: Revivalist and Reformer.* Syracuse: Syracuse Univ. Press, 1987.

Hatch, Nathan O. *The Sacred Cause of Liberty.* New Haven: Yale Univ. Press, 1977.

Hatch, Nathan O., and Mark A. Noll, eds. *The Bible in America: Essays in Cultural History.* New York: Oxford Univ. Press, 1982.

Healey, Robert M. *Jefferson on Religion in Public Education.* New Haven: Yale Univ. Press, 1962.

Heimert, Alan, and Andrew Delbanco, eds. *The Puritans in America: A Narrative Anthology.* Cambridge, Mass.: Harvard Univ. Press, 1985.

Heller, James Gottheim. *Isaac M. Wise: His Life, Work and Thought.* Cincinnati: The Union of American Hebrew Congregations, 1965.

Hendrick, Burton J. *The Jews in America.* Garden City, N.Y.: Doubleday, Page, 1923.

Herberg, Will. *Protestant-Catholic-Jew: An Essay in American Religious Sociology.* 1955. Garden City, N.Y.: Doubleday, Anchor Books, 1960.

Hertzberg, Arthur, ed. *The Zionist Idea: A Historical Analysis and Reader.* Cleveland: World Publishing Company; Philadelphia: The Jewish Publication Society of America, 1964.

Hertzberg, Steven. *Strangers Within the Gate City: The Jews of Atlanta, 1845–1915.* Philadelphia: The Jewish Publication Society of America, 1978.

Heschel, Abraham Joshua. *The Insecurity of Freedom.* Philadelphia: The Jewish Publication Society of America, 1966.

Higham, John. *Strangers in the Land: Patterns of American Nativism, 1860–1925.* New Brunswick, N.J.: Rutgers Univ. Press, 1955.

————. *Send These to Me: Jews and Other Immigrants in Urban America.* New York: Atheneum, 1975.

Hocking, William B., and others. *The Church and the New World Mind: The Drake Lectures for 1944.* Essay Index Reprint Series. Freeport, N.Y.: Books for Libraries Press, 1944.

Hocking, William Ernest. *Living Religions and a World Faith.* New York: Macmillan, 1940.

Hofstadter, Richard. *Social Darwinism in American Thought.* 1944. Boston: Beacon Press, 1955.

Holbrook, Clyde A., ed. *Jonathan Edwards: "Original Sin."* New Haven: Yale Univ. Press, 1970.

Holmes, John Haynes. *I Speak for Myself: The Autobiography of John Haynes Holmes.* New York: Harper and Brothers, 1959.

————. *Palestine To-Day and To-Morrow: A Gentile's Survey of Zionism.* 1929. Reprint. New York: Arno Press, 1977.

————. *The Revolutionary Function of the Modern Church.* New York: G. P. Putnam's Sons, Knickerbocker Press, 1912.

————. *Through Gentile Eyes: A Plea for Tolerance and Good Will.* New York: Jewish Opinion Publishing Corporation, 1938.

Hooft, W. A. Visser 'T. *The Background of the Social Gospel in America.* Haarlem, The Netherlands: H. D. Tjeenk Willink and Zoon, 1928.

Hopkins, Charles Howard. *The Rise of the Social Gospel in American Protestantism.* New Haven: Yale Univ. Press, 1940.

Houghton, Walter R., ed. *Neely's History of the Parliament of Religions and Religious Congresses at the World's Columbian Exposition.* 2 vols. Chicago, 1893.

Hudson, Winthrop S. *American Protestantism.* Chicago: Univ. of Chicago Press, 1961.

Huntress, Keith, ed. *Murder of an American Prophet.* San Francisco: Chandler Publishing, 1960.

Hutchison, John A. *We Are Not Divided: A Critical and Historical Study of the Federal Council of the Churches of Christ in America.* New York: Round Table Press, 1941.

Hutchinson, William R. *The Modernist Impulse in American Protestantism.* Cambridge, Mass.: Harvard Univ. Press, 1976.

————. *The Transcendentalist Ministers.* New Haven: Yale Univ. Press, 1959.

[An Israelite.] *Israel Vindicated; Being a Refutation of the Calumnies Propagated Respecting the Jewish Nation: In Which the Objects and Views of the American Society for Ameliorating the Condition of the Jews Are Investigated.* New York: Abraham Collins, 1820.

Jacob, Walter. *Christianity Through Jewish Eyes: The Quest for Common Ground.* Cincinnati: Hebrew Union College Press, 1974.

————, ed. *The Pittsburgh Platform in Retrospect: The Changing World of Reform Judaism.* Pittsburgh: Rodef Shalom Congregation, 1985.

Jacquet, Constant A., Jr. *Yearbook of American and Canadian Churches, 1984.* Nashville, Abingdon Press, 1984.

James, William. *The Varieties of Religious Experience.* New York: Longmans, Green, and Co., 1902.

Jamison, A. Leland, ed. *Tradition and Change in Jewish Experience.* Syracuse: Syracuse Univ. Press, 1978.

Jefferson, Thomas. *The Complete Jefferson.* New York: Tudor Publishing, 1943.

————. *The Papers of Thomas Jefferson.* 21 vols. Edited by Julian P. Boyd. Princeton: Princeton Univ. Press, 1950.

————. *Writings.* New York: Library Classics of the United States, 1984.

The Jew; Being a Defence of Judaism Against All Adversaries, and Particularly Against the Invidious Attacks of Israel's Advocate. Vol. 1. New York, 1821.

Jick, Leon A. *The Americanization of the Synagogue, 1820–1870.* Hanover, N.H.: Univ. Press of New England, 1976.

Johnson, Rossiter. *A History of the World's Columbian Exposition Held in Chicago in 1893.* 4 vols. New York: D. Appleton and Company, 1897.

Jordan, Philip D. *The Evangelical Alliance for the United States of America, 1847–1900: Ecumenism, Identity and the Religion of the Republic.* Studies in American Religion, vol. 7. New York: Edwin Mellen Press, 1982.

Kaestle, Carl F. *The Evolution of an Urban School System: New York City, 1750–1850.* Cambridge, Mass.: Harvard Univ. Press, 1973.

Katz, Jacob. *Tradition and Crisis: Jewish Society at the End of the Middle Ages.* New York: Schocken Books, 1961.

Kegley, Charles W., and Robert W. Bretall, eds. *Reinhold Niebuhr: His Religious, Social, and Political Thought.* The Library of Living Theology, vol. 11. New York: Macmillan, 1956.

King, Henry Churchill. *The Moral and Religious Challenge of Our Times.* New York: Macmillan, 1911.

Kobler, Franz. *The Vision Was There: A History of the British Movement for the Restoration of the Jews to Palestine.* London: Lincolns-Prager, 1956.

Kohler, K[aufman]. *Jewish Theology: Systematically and Historically Considered.* Cincinnati: Riverdale Press, 1943.

Konovitz, Milton R. *Judaism and the American Idea.* Ithaca, N.Y.: Cornell Univ. Press, 1978.

Korn, Bertram Wallace. *Eventful Years and Experiences: Studies in Nineteenth Century American Jewish History.* Cincinnati: The American Jewish Archives, 1954.

————, ed. *A Bicentennial Festschrift for Jacob Rader Marcus.* Waltham, Mass.: American Jewish Historical Society; New York: KTAV Publishing House, 1976.

Kraut, Benny. *From Reform Judaism to Ethical Culture: The Religious Evolution of Felix Adler.* Cincinnati: Hebrew Union College Press, 1979.

Leeser, Isaac. *Claims of the Jews to an Equality of Rights.* Philadelphia, 1845.

————. *Memorial of the Sunday School for Religious Instruction of Israelites in Philadelphia.* Philadelphia, 1840.

Levin, Alexandra Lee. *The Szolds of Lombard Street: A Baltimore Family, 1859–1909.* Philadelphia: The Jewish Publication Society of America, 1960.

Lipstadt, Deborah E. *Beyond Belief: The American Press and the Coming of the Holocaust, 1933–1945.* New York: Free Press, 1986.

Littell, Franklin Hamlin. *The Church and the Body Politic.* New York: Seabury Press, 1969.

————. *The Crucifixion of the Jews.* New York: Harper and Row, 1975.

————. *From State Church to Pluralism: A Protestant Interpretation of Religion in American History.* Garden City, N.Y.: Anchor Books, Doubleday, 1962.

Lowenberg, Robert J. *An American Idol: Emerson and the "Jewish Idea."* Lanham, Md.: Univ. Press of America, 1984.

Luther, Lutherans and the Jewish People. New York: American Lutheran Church, 1977. Pamphlet.

Macfarland, Charles S. *Christian Unity in the Making: The First Twenty-Five Years of the Federal Council of the Churches of Christ in America, 1905–1930.* New York: The Federal Council of the Churches of Christ in America, 1948.

————. *Jesus and the Prophets.* New York: G. P. Putnam's Sons, Knickerbocker Press, 1905.

Madison, James. *The Writings of James Madison.* 9 vols. Edited by Gaillard Hunt. New York: G. P. Putnam's Sons, 1900–10.

Malachy, Yona. *American Fundamentalism and Israel: The Relation of Fundamentalist*

Churches to Zionism and the State of Israel. Jerusalem: Hebrew Univ. of Jerusalem, 1978.

Marcus, Jacob Rader. *The Colonial American Jew, 1492–1776.* 3 vols. Detroit: Wayne State Univ. Press, 1970.

———. *Early American Jewry.* 2 vols. Philadelphia: The Jewish Publication Society of America, 1951, and 1953.

Marsden, George, ed. *Evangelicalism and Modern America.* Grand Rapids, Mich.: William B. Eerdmans, 1984.

Marshall, Louis. *Louis Marshall, Champion of Liberty: Selected Papers and Addresses.* 2 vols. Edited by Charles Reznikoff. Philadelphia: The Jewish Publication Society of America, 1957.

Marty, Martin E. *Modern American Religion.* Vol. 1, *The Irony of It All: 1893–1919.* Chicago: Univ. of Chicago Press, 1986.

———. *Pilgrims in Their Own Land: 500 Years of Religion in America.* New York: Penguin Books, 1985.

———. *Righteous Empire: The Protestant Experience in America.* New York: Harper and Row, 1970.

Mathews, Basil. *The Jew and the World Ferment.* New York: Friendship Press, 1935.

———. *John R. Mott: World Citizen.* New York: Harper and Brothers, 1934.

Mathews, Shailer. *New Faith for Old: An Autobiography.* New York: Macmillan, 1936.

———. *The Social Gospel.* Philadelphia: Griffith and Knowland Press, 1910.

McGiffert, Michael, ed. *Puritanism and the American Experience.* Reading, Mass.: Addison-Wesley, 1969.

McGoughlin, William G., Jr. *Billy Sunday Was His Real Name.* Chicago: Univ. of Chicago Press, 1955.

———. *Modern Revivalism: Charles Grandison Finney to Billy Graham.* New York: Ronald Press, 1959.

Mecklin, John Moffatt. *The Ku Klux Klan: A Study of the American Mind.* New York: Russell and Russell, 1963.

Melville, Herman. *Journal of a Visit to Europe and the Levant, October 11, 1856–May 6, 1857.* Edited by Howard C. Horsford. Princeton: Princeton Univ. Press, 1955.

———. *Journal up the Straits, October 11, 1856–May 5, 1857.* New York: Cooper Square Publishers, 1971.

Mendelsohn, Jack. *Channing, the Reluctant Radical.* Boston: Little, Brown, 1971.

Menkus, Belden. *Meet the American Jew.* Nashville, Tenn., Broadman Press, 1963.

Meyer, Isidore S., ed. *Early History of Zionism in America.* 1958. Reprint. New York: Arno Press, 1977.

———. *The Hebrew Exercises of Governor William Bradford.* Plymouth, Mass.: Pilgrim Society, 1973.

Miller, Perry. *The New England Mind: From Colony to Province.* Cambridge, Mass.: Harvard Univ. Press, 1953.

———. *The New England Mind: The Seventeenth Century.* New York: Macmillan, 1939.

———. *Orthodoxy in Massachusetts, 1630–1650.* 1933. Reprint. New York: Harper and Row, 1970.

Miller, Robert Moats. *Harry Emerson Fosdick: Preacher, Pastor, Prophet.* New York: Oxford Univ. Press, 1985.

Miller, William Lee. *The First Liberty: Religion and the American Republic.* New York: Alfred A. Knopf, 1986.

Moore, George Foot Moore. *Judaism in the First Centuries of the Christian Era: The Age of Tannaim.* 3 vols. 1930. Reprint in 2 vols. New York: Schocken Books, 1971.

Moore, R. Laurence. *Religious Outsiders and the Making of Americans.* New York: Oxford Univ. Press, 1986.

Morgan, Edmund S. *The Gentle Puritan: A Life of Ezra Stiles, 1727–1795.* New Haven: Yale Univ. Press, 1962.

Morison, Samuel Eliot. *The Puritan Pronaos: Studies in the Intellectual Life of New England in the Seventeenth Century.* New York: New York Univ. Press, 1936.

———. *Three Centuries of Harvard, 1636–1936.* Cambridge, Mass.: Harvard Univ. Press, 1937.

Morse, Arthur D. *While Six Million Died; A Chronicle of American Apathy.* New York: Random House, 1968.

Mosse, George L. *The Reformation.* 3d ed. New York: Holt, Rinehart and Winston, 1963.

Nadell, Pamela S. *Conservative Judaism in America: A Biographical Dictionary and Sourcebook.* New York: Greenwood Press, 1988.

National Perils and Opportunities: The Discussions of the General Christian Conference, Held in Washington, D.C., December 7, 8 and 9, 1887, under the Auspices and Directions of the Evangelical Alliance for the United States. New York: Baker and Taylor, 1887.

Nawyn, William E. *American Protestantism's Response to Germany's Jews and Refugees, 1933–1941.* Ann Arbor: UMI Research Press, 1982.

Neumann, Henry. *Spokesmen for Ethical Religion.* Boston: Beacon Press, 1951.

Neusner, Jacob. *American Judaism: Adventure in Modernity.* Englewood Cliffs, N.J.: Prentice-Hall, 1972.

A New Year's Gift to the Md. Ladies' Society for Promoting Christianity among the Jews by the Right Reverend Rabbi, Hebrew Republican Citizen-Soldier. Baltimore, 1843.

Nickalls, John L., ed. *The Journal of George Fox.* Rev. ed. Cambridge: Cambridge Univ. Press, 1952.

Niebuhr, H. Richard. *The Social Sources of Denominationalism.* 1929. Reprint. Cleveland: World Publishing Company, 1957.

Niebuhr, Reinhold. *Beyond Tragedy: Essays on the Christian Interpretation of History.* 1937. New York: Charles Scribner's Sons, 1948.

———. *The Children of Light and the Children of Darkness: A Vindication of Democracy and a Critique of Its Traditional Defense.* 1944. Reprint. New York: Charles Scribner's Sons, 1947.

———. *Christian Realism and Political Problems.* New York: Charles Scribner's Sons, 1953.

———. *Christianity and Power Politics.* 1940. Reprint. New York: Archon Books, 1969.

———. *Discerning the Signs of the Times.* New York: Charles Scribner's Sons, 1946.

———. *Does Civilization Need Religion? A Study in the Social Resources and Limitations of Religion in Modern Life.* New York: Macmillan, 1929.

————. *An Interpretation of Christian Ethics.* New York: Harper and Brothers, 1935.

————. *Justice and Mercy.* New York: Harper and Row, 1974.

————. *Leaves from the Notebook of a Tamed Cynic.* New York: Richard R. Smith, 1930.

————. *Man's Nature and His Communities: Essays on the Dynamics and Enigmas of Man's Personal and Social Existence.* New York: Charles Scribner's Sons, 1965.

————. *Moral Man and Immoral Society: A Study in Ethics and Politics.* New York: Charles Scribner's Sons, 1932.

————. *The Nature and Destiny of Man: A Christian Interpretation.* 1941. Reprint (2 vols. in 1). New York: Charles Scribner's Sons, 1949.

————. *Reflections on the End of an Era.* New York: Charles Scribner's Sons, 1934.

————. *The Structure of Nations and Empires.* New York: Charles Scribner's Sons, 1959.

Noah, Mordecai M. *Discourse on the Restoration of the Jews.* New York: Harper and Brothers, 1845.

Opshal, Paul D., and Marc H. Tannenbaum, eds. *Speaking of God Today: Jews and Lutherans in Conversation.* Philadelphia: Fortress Press, 1974.

Olson, Bernhard E. *Faith and Prejudice: Intergroup Problems in Protestant Curricula.* New Haven: Yale Univ. Press, 1963.

Padover, Saul K., ed. *The Complete Jefferson, Containing His Major Writings, Published and Unpublished, Except His Letters.* New York: Tudor Publishing, 1943.

Parker, Theodore. *The Transient and Permanent in Christianity.* Edited by George Willis Cooke. Boston: American Unitarian Association, 1903.

————. *Views of Religion.* Boston: American Unitarian Association, 1890.

Pentecost, J. Dwight. *Things to Come: A Study in Biblical Eschatology.* Grand Rapids, Mich.: Zondervan Publishing House, 1958.

Pessen, Edward. *Jacksonian America: Society, Personality, and Politics.* Homewood, Ill.: Dorsey Press, 1969.

Peters, Madison C. *Justice to the Jew.* New York: McClure Co., 1908.

Philipson, David. *Max Lilienthal, American Rabbi: Life and Writings.* New York: Bloch Publishing, 1915.

————. *My Life as an American Jew: An Autobiography.* Cincinnati: John G. Kidd and Son, 1941.

————. *The Reform Movement in Judaism.* New York: Macmillan, 1907.

————, ed. *Reminiscences by Isaac M. Wise.* Cincinnati: Leo Wise and Co., 1901.

Premillennial Essays of the Prophetic Conference, Held in the Church of the Holy Trinity, New York City. Edited by Nathaniel West. Chicago: Fleming H. Revell Company, 1879.

Proceedings of the Fifth National Reform Convention, to Aid in Maintaining the Christian Features of the American Government, and Securing a Religious Amendment to the Constitution of the United States, Held in Pittsburgh, February 4, 5, 1874. Philadelphia, 1874.

Proceedings of the Sixth Biennial Convention of the Jewish Theological Seminary Association Held in the City of Philadelphia, Adar 26, 5658, March 20 '98. New York: Press of Philip Cowen, 5658–1898.

Prophetic Studies of the International Prophetic Conference, Chicago, November, 1886. Chicago: Fleming H. Revell Company, 1886.

Proctor, Samuel, and Louis Schmier, eds. *Jews of the South.* Macon, Ga.: Mercer Univ. Press, 1984.

Quinley, Harold E., and Charles Y. Glock. *Anti-Semitism in America.* New Brunswick, N.J.: Transaction Books, 1983.

Raphael, Marc Lee. *Jews and Judaism in a Midwestern Community: Columbus, Ohio, 1840–1975.* Columbus: Ohio Historical Society, 1979.

———, ed. *Jews and Judaism in the United States: A Documentary History.* New York: Behrman House, 1983.

Rausch, David. *Zionism Within Early American Fundamentalism, 1878–1914.* Lewiston, N.Y.: Edwin Mellen Press, 1979.

Rauschenbusch, Walter. *Christianity and the Social Crisis.* New York: Macmillan, 1914.

———. *A Theology for the Social Gospel.* New York: Macmillan, 1918.

Reznikoff, Charles. *The Jews of Charleston: A History of an American Jewish Community.* Philadelphia: The Jewish Publication Society of America, 1950.

Ribuffo, Leo P. *The Old Christian Right: The Protestant Far Right from the Great Depression to the Cold War.* Philadelphia: Temple Univ. Press, 1983.

Rischin, Moses. *The Promised City: New York's Jews, 1870–1914.* Cambridge, Mass.: Harvard Univ. Press, 1962.

Roberts, Kenneth L. *Why Europe Leaves Home.* 1922. Reprint. New York: Arno Books, 1977.

Rogow, Arnold A., ed. *The Jew in a Gentile World.* New York: Macmillan, 1961.

Rosenberg, Stuart E. *The Jewish Community in Rochester, 1843–1925.* New York: Columbia Univ. Press, 1954.

Rosenstock, Morton. *Louis Marshall, Defender of Jewish Rights.* Detroit: Wayne State Univ. Press, 1965.

Rosenwaike, Ira. *On the Edge of Greatness: A Portrait of American Jewry in the Early National Period.* Cincinnati: American Jewish Archives, 1985.

Ross, Edward Alsworth. *The Old World in the New: The Significance of Past and Present Immigration to the American People.* New York: Century Co., 1914.

Ross, Robert W. *So It Was True: The American Protestant Press and the Nazi Persecution of the Jews.* Minneapolis: Univ. of Minnesota Press, 1980.

Roy, Ralph Lord. *Apostles of Discord: A Study of Organized Bigotry and Disruption on the Fringes of Protestantism.* Boston: Beacon Press, 1953.

Rubenstein, Richard L. *After Auschwitz: Radical Theology and Contemporary Judaism.* Indianapolis: Bobbs-Merrill, 1966.

Rudolph, Bernard G. *From a Minyan to a Community: A History of the Jews of Syracuse.* Syracuse: Syracuse Univ. Press, 1970.

Rush, Benjamin. *Letters of Benjamin Rush.* Vol. 1; *1761–1792.* Edited by L. H. Butterfield. Princeton: Princeton Univ. Press, 1951.

Rusk, Ralph L., ed. *Letters to Emma Lazarus.* New York: Columbia Univ. Press, 1939.

Sachar, Howard M. *A History of Israel from the Rise of Zionism to Our Time.* New York: Alfred A. Knopf, 1979.

Sandmel, Samuel. *We Jews and Jesus.* New York: Oxford Univ. Press, 1965.

Sanford, Elias B., ed. *Federal Council of the Churches of Christ in America: Report of the First Meeting.* New York: Revell Press, 1909.

Sarna, Jonathan D. *Jacksonian Jew: The Two Worlds of Mordecai Noah.* New York: Holmes and Meier, 1981.

Sarna, Jonathan D., Benny Kraut, and Samuel K. Joseph, eds. *Jews and the Founding of the Republic.* New York: Markus Wiener, 1985.

Savage, Minot J., ed. *The World's Congress of Religions.* Boston: Arena Publishing, 1893.

Schaff, Philip. *America: A Sketch of Its Political, Social, and Religious Character.* 1855. Edited by Perry Miller. Cambridge, Mass.: Harvard Univ. Press, Belknap Press, 1961.

———. *Church and State in the United States.* 1888. New York: Arno Press, 1972.

Schappes, Morris U., ed. *A Documentary History of the Jews in the United States, 1654–1875.* New York: Schocken Books, 1971.

Schechter, Solomon. *Aspects of Rabbinic Theology.* 1909. Reprint. New York: Schocken Books, 1961.

Schultz, Stanley K. *The Culture Factory: Boston Public Schools: 1789–1860.* New York: Oxford Univ. Press, 1973.

Scott, Nathan A. *Reinhold Niebuhr.* Minneapolis: Univ. of Minnesota Press, 1963.

Seager, Robert, II, ed. *The Papers of Henry Clay.* 8 vols. Lexington: Univ. Press of Kentucky, 1954–84.

Shapiro, Yonathan. *Leadership of the American Zionist Organization.* Urbana: Univ. of Illinois Press, 1971.

Sharpe, Dores Robinson. *Walter Rauschenbusch.* New York: Macmillan, 1942.

Shriver, Peggy L. *The Bible Vote: Religion and the New Right.* New York: Pilgrim Press, 1981.

Silverman, Kenneth. *The Life and Times of Cotton Mather.* New York: Harper and Row, 1984.

Simon, Merrill. *Jerry Falwell and the Jews.* Middle Village, N.Y.: Jonathan David Publishers, 1984.

Slobin, Mark. *Chosen Voices: The Story of the American Cantorate.* Urbana: Univ. of Illinois Press, 1989.

Smith, Charles Sprague. *Working with the People.* New York: A. Wessels Company, 1904.

Smith, Ethan. *View of the Hebrews.* Poultney, Vt.: Smith and Shute Publishers, 1823.

Smith, H. Shelton, Robert T. Handy, and Lefferts A. Loetscher. *American Christianity: An Historical Interpretation with Representative Documents.* 2 vols. New York: Charles Scribner's Sons, 1960–63.

Smith, Joseph. *The Book of Mormon.* Salt Lake City: The Church of Jesus Christ of Latter-day Saints, 1986.

———. *History of the Church of Jesus Christ of Latter-day Saints. Period 1.* Salt Lake City: Deseret Book Company, 1960.

Stiles, Ezra. *Extracts from the Itineraries and Other Miscellanies of Ezra Stiles, D.D., LL.D., 1755–1794.* Edited by Franklin Bowditch Dexter. New Haven: Yale Univ. Press, 1916.

———. *The Literary Diary of Ezra Stiles.* 3 vols. Edited by Franklin Bowditch Dexter. New York: Charles Scribner's Sons, 1901.

Stokes, Anson Phelps, and Leo Pfeffer. *Church and State in the United States.* Revised (single volume) ed. New York: Harper and Row, 1964.

Strober, Gerald S. *American Jews: Community in Crisis.* Garden City, N.Y.: Doubleday, 1974.

————. *Portrait of the Elder Brother: Jews and Judaism in Protestant Teaching Materials.* New York: The American Jewish Committee, National Conference of Christians and Jews, 1972.

Strong, Josiah. *Our Country: Its Possible Future and Its Present Crisis.* New York: Baker and Taylor, 1885.

————. *Our World: The New World Life.* Garden City, N.Y.: Doubleday, Page, 1914.

Sweet, William Warren. *Religion in Colonial America.* New York: Cooper Square Publishers, 1965.

Swichkow, Louis J., and Lloyd P. Gartner. *The History of the Jews of Milwaukee.* Philadelphia: The Jewish Publication Society of America, 1963.

Szasz, Ferenc Morton. *The Divided Mind of Protestant America, 1800–1930.* Birmingham: Univ. of Alabama Press, 1982.

Thompson, A. E. *A Century of Jewish Missions.* Chicago: Fleming H. Revell Company, 1902.

Tocqueville, Alexis de. *Democracy in America.* 2 vols. New York: Vintage Books, 1954.

Tolles, Frederick B. *James Logan and the Culture of Provincial America.* Boston: Little, Brown, 1957.

Toon, Peter, ed. *Puritans, the Millennium and the Future of Israel: Puritan Eschatology, 1600–1660.* Cambridge: James Clarke, 1970.

Torrey, R. A., et al., eds. *The Fundamentals: A Testimony to the Truth.* 4 vols. 1917. Reprint. Grand Rapids, Mich.: Baker Book House, 1970.

Toy, Crawford H. *The History of the Religion of Israel.* Boston: Unitarian Sunday-School Society, 1891.

————. *Judaism and Christianity.* Boston: Little, Brown, 1892.

Tuchman, Barbara W. *Bible and Sword: England and Palestine from the Bronze Age to Balfour.* New York: New York Univ. Press, 1956.

Twain, Mark [Samuel L. Clemens]. *Innocents Abroad, or the New Pilgrims' Progress.* New York: Harper and Brothers, 1911.

Union of American Hebrew Congregations. *Judaism at the World's Parliament of Religions.* Cincinnati: Robert Clarke and Co., 1894.

Urofsky, Melvin I. *American Zionism from Herzl to the Holocaust.* Garden City, N.Y.: Anchor Books, 1976.

————. *A Voice That Spoke for Justice. The Life and Times of Stephen S. Wise.* Albany: State Univ. of New York Press, 1982.

————, ed. *Essays in American Zionism, 1917–1948.* Vol. 8, *The Herzl Year Book.* New York: Herzl Press, 1978.

Van Buren, Paul M. *The Burden of Freedom: Americans and the God of Israel.* New York: Seabury Press, 1976.

————. *Discerning the Way: A Theology of the Jewish Christian Reality.* New York: Seabury Press, 1980.

Veblen, Thorstein. *Essays in our Changing Order.* Edited by Leon Ardzrooni. New York: Viking Press, 1934.

Vester, Bertha Spafford. *Our Jerusalem: An American Family in the Holy City, 1881–1949.* Garden City, N.Y.: Doubleday, 1950.

Vorspan, Max, and Lloyd P. Gartner. *History of the Jews of Los Angeles.* Philadelphia: The Jewish Publication Society of America, 1970.

Voss, Carl Hermann. *Rabbi and Minister: The Friendship of Stephen S. Wise and John Haynes Holmes.* Cleveland: World Publishing Company, 1964.

————, ed. *A Summons unto Men: An Anthology of the Writings of John Haynes Holmes.* New York: Simon and Schuster, 1970.

Wade, Wyn Craig. *The Fiery Cross: The Ku Klux Klan in America.* New York: Simon and Schuster, 1987.

Wagenknecht, Edward. *Daughters of the Covenant: Portraits of Six Jewish Women.* Amherst: Univ. of Massachusetts Press, 1983.

Walker, Franklin. *Irreverent Pilgrims: Melville, Browne, and Mark Twain in the Holy Land.* Seattle: Univ. of Washington Press, 1974.

Warren, Austin. *The New England Conscience.* Ann Arbor: Univ. of Michigan Press, 1966.

Weber, Timothy P. *Living in the Shadow of the Second Coming: American Premillennialism, 1875–1925.* New York: Oxford Univ. Press, 1979.

Weinstein, Gregory. *The Ardent Eighties and After: Reminiscences of a Busy Life.* New York: International Press, 1947.

Weisberger, Bernard A. *They Gathered at the River: The Story of the Great Revivalists and Their Impact upon Religion in America.* 1958. Chicago: Quadrangle Books, 1966.

Wesley, John. *The Works of John Wesley.* 14 vols. 1872. Reprint. Grand Rapids, Mich.: Zondervan Publishing, 1958–59.

————. *The Works of John Wesley.* Edited by Franz Hildebrandt and Oliver A. Beckerlegge. Oxford: Clarendon Press, 1983.

White, Ronald C., Jr., and C. Howard Hopkins, eds. *The Social Gospel: Religion and Reform in Changing America.* Philadelphia: Temple Univ. Press, 1976.

Williams, Charles D. *A Valid Christianity for To-Day.* New York: Macmillan, 1909.

Williams, Roger. *The Complete Writings of Roger Williams.* 7 vols. New York: Russell and Russell, 1963.

Wilson, John F., and Donald L. Drakeman, eds. *Church and State in American History.* 2d ed. Boston: Beacon Press, 1987.

Wise, Isaac M. *Reminiscences.* Cincinnati: L. Wise and Co., 1901.

Wise, Stephen. *Challenging Years: The Autobiography of Stephen Wise.* New York: G. P. Putnam's Sons, 1949.

Wolf, Edwin, II, ed. *James Logan, 1674–1751: Bookman Extraordinary.* Philadelphia: The Library Company of Philadelphia, 1971.

Wolf, Edwin, II, and Maxwell Whiteman. *The History of the Jews of Philadelphia from Colonial Times to the Age of Jackson.* Philadelphia: The Jewish Publication Society of America, 1957.

Wolfskill, George, and John A. Hudson. *All but the People: Franklin D. Roosevelt and His Critics, 1933–39.* New York: Macmillan, 1969.

Wyman, David S. *The Abandonment of the Jews: America and the Holocaust, 1941–1945.* New York: Pantheon Books, 1984.

Index

Note on the Author

Egal Feldman, an authority on Jewish and interreligious American history, is Professor of History and Chairman of the History Department at the University of Wisconsin–Superior, where he also teaches courses on the history of the Jews. In addition to many papers and articles on Christian-Jewish relations in the United States, areas of study with which he has been involved for the past twenty-five years, his previous works include *The Dreyfus Affair and the American Conscience, 1895–1906* (1981), and *Fit for Men: A History of New York's Clothing Trade* (1960).